Enchanted Feminism

Many today feel the need to restore a magical, spiritual ground to human existence. One of the most visible responses to this need has been the rise of contemporary pagan Witchcraft, and one of its most interesting voices, Reclaiming. This community was formed over twenty years ago by feminist Witch Starhawk and friends, to teach others about goddess spirituality and reinvented pagan rituals. It has since succeeded in developing an independent spiritual tradition, fostered partly by the success of Starhawk's *The Spiral Dance* and other books, and now has sister communities throughout North America and Europe.

Enchanted Feminism presents the first in-depth study of this important community and spiritual tradition, from a consistent gender perspective. In a unique interdisciplinary approach, Dr Salomonsen adopts the perspectives of both social anthropology and theology to analyse the beliefs and practices of the Reclaiming Witches. Among many issues, she considers their spiritual search for the 'Real', their renunciation of patriarchal religions and attempts to build a new religious identity, their use of ritual and of feminine symbols for the divine, and their involvement with feminist–anarchist politics. The results of her research provide challenging and insightful reading.

Jone Salomonsen is Senior Research Fellow in Theology and Social Anthropology at the University of Oslo.

Religion and Gender
Series editors: Ursula King and Rita M. Gross

The relationship between religion (religious institutions, rites, symbols, language and thought) and human genderedness represents a fast-expanding area of interest to which no single series of publications has been devoted until now. This series will look at how gender 'differences' are embedded in religious institutions and practices around the world and shape approaches to religious authority and sacred power everywhere. Each title will show how debates about women's and men's identity, about their images, roles, status, power and authority, and about body and sexuality, are deeply influenced by and intertwined with religious teachings, even when these are explicitly rejected.

Enchanted Feminism

Ritual, Gender and Divinity among the
Reclaiming Witches of San Francisco

Jone Salomonsen

London and New York

First published 2002
by Routledge
11 New Fetter Lane, London EC4P 4EE

Simultaneously published in the USA and Canada
by Routledge
29 West 35th Street, New York, NY 10001

Routledge is an imprint of the Taylor & Francis Group

© 2002 Jone Salomonsen

Typeset in Bembo by Exe Valley Dataset Ltd
Printed and bound in Great Britain by St Edmundsbury Press, Bury St Edmunds, Suffolk

British Library Cataloguing in Publication Data
A catalogue record for this book is available from the British Library

Library of Congress Cataloging in Publication Data
Salomonsen, Jone, 1956–
    Enchanted feminism: the Reclaiming witches of San Francisco/Jone Salomonsen.
        p. cm. (Religion and gender)
    Includes bibliographical references.
        1. Reclaiming Collective (San Francisco, Calif.) I. Title. II. Series.

BF1577.C2 S25 2001
299–dc21   2001049062

ISBN 0-415-22392-X (hbk)
ISBN 0-415-22393-8 (pbk)

Contents

List of plates

(between pages 154 and 155)

Series Editors' Preface

Gender research has now become more gender-inclusive rather than just women-centred, a change of great theoretical significance. The Religion and Gender Series is dedicated to publishing books which reflect that change. It will feature innovative, original research which moves away from predominantly western to global perspectives, including comparative and interdisciplinary approaches where appropriate. Firmly grounded in religious studies, books in this series will draw on a wide range of disciplines, including gender studies, philosophy, theology, sociology, history, anthropology, as well as women's and men's studies in religion. By recognizing the limitations of previous, exclusively androcentric approaches to the study of religions, this series will help overcome earlier deficiencies in scholarship about religion and open new intellectual horizons in the field.

Although a relatively new area of enquiry, the materials relevant to the study of religion and gender are as old as humanity. They include the roles, lives, and experiences of women and men, as shaped by diverse gender norms, stereotypes and symbols prevalent in different religious, cultural and historical contexts. Issues of gender – what it means to be male or female, and ultimately what it means to be human – are central to social, philosophical, doctrinal, ethical and practical questions in every religion, and gender symbolism is of great significance in all religious worship, spirituality, and doctrine. The Religion and Gender Series publishes new research on these and all other aspects of gender and religion.

Ursula King
Rita M. Gross

Acknowledgements

Thanks are due to a considerable number of people and institutions who have actively supported my studies of Reclaiming Witchcraft and who have patiently waited for the results from the research period 1984-94 to be published. First, I want to thank the Norwegian Research Council and the University of Oslo for having funded my research and work and the Faculty of Theology, which has been my home base, for having furnished me with an infrastructure in a wide sense until both the PhD dissertation and the book were completed. I am particularly grateful to my supervisors at the University of Oslo, Professor of Social Anthropology Eduardo P. Archetti and Professor of Systematic Theology Svein Aage Christoffersen. In the crucial years they provided inspiring readings and comments, well-founded critique and good support. Second, I want to thank my two women mentors, Professor of Cultural Anthropology at Stanford Carol Delaney and Professor of Feminist Theology at Bristol and Oslo Ursula King, who gave wonderful encouragement and detailed comments in the final round. The Norwegian Research Council made the transition from dissertation manuscript to book possible by generously consenting to pay for highly skilled editorial assistance from the American scholar Kalbryn McLean.

I also want to thank my other colleagues – theologians and anthropologists – for sustaining and spirited discussions, as well as friends, women's circles and family who have offered themselves as supporters, advisors, readers or lay editors in the process: Helle Giset, Sharon Ghamari, Luis Kemnitzer, Irene Kiebert, Moher Downing, Janie Kesselman, Kim Berry, Laurie Trupin, Sabina Magliocco, Sarah M. Pike, Serene Jones, Halvor Moxnes, Trygve Wyller, Inge Lønning, Kjetil Hafstad, Kari E. Børresen, Oddbjørn Leirvik, Marit Melhuus, Signe Howell, Paul Heelas, Kjersti Larsen, Sidsel Roalkvam, Jan K. Simonsen, Nancy Frank, Asbjørn Dyrendal, Inger Vederhus, Signe Fyhn, Inger Lise Olsen, Christian Børs Lind, Linda Salomonsen, Synnøve Ness, Toril Røkenes, Sissel H. Pedersen, Lisbeth Mogensen, Johannes Sørensen and Jannike Willoch.

Warm thanks to my husband Tor, my daughters Andrea and Katinka, my step-sons Kim and Kristian, and to my large and loving family for incredible patience and care and for having kept my spirits up throughout. In particular thanks to my mother, Birgit Salomonsen, who for long periods of time generously assisted Tor in guarding the domestic hearth in my daily absence. Connie M. Alvestad had this role during fieldwork and did a wonderful job.

Finally, I want to thank the Reclaiming community in San Francisco for having included me as "the one who was sent to study them" with so much friendship, love and respect and with an amazing willingness to teach me during all these years. I am in particular indebted to Starhawk, Vibra Willow, M. Macha NightMare, Rose May Dance, Pandora O'Mallory, Cybelle and David Miller, to the women in the coven Gossip, to my room mates at Group W and Flamingo Towers, and to all the Witches and pagans in the Bay Area and beyond who willingly shared information with me and agreed to be interviewed. Thanks also to George Franklin, editor of the *Reclaiming Quarterly*, who patiently helped me to gather photos of community activities from more recent years, and to those who actually gave permission to print them: Ben Read, Bob Thawley, Ewa Litauer and Mer DeDanen. I certainly hope that all will receive something back from this book!

I also want to offer my thanks to scholar and priestess of the Goddess, Carol P. Christ who generously read and commented on the whole manuscript in an early phase, and to Anodea Judith and Wendy Hunter Roberts, priestesses in Church of All Worlds, for inviting me to experience their community rites. Thanks also to my dear friends Carol O'Connell and Turi and Hal Reynolds for love and sustenance throughout and to the late Sedonia Cahill, Raven Moon Shadow, Judy Foster and Geoff Yippie! for their blessed gifts.

Last, but not least, special thanks to Professor Clare B. Fischer at the Graduate Theological Union in Berkeley for great support and affirmation ever since my initial studies in 1984, and to the very same institution for profoundly having aided my research by first accepting me as a student and then as a visiting scholar!

Jone Salomonsen
Oslo, 7 November 2000

Introduction

This book represents an in-depth study of how contemporary Witches in the Reclaiming community of San Francisco attempt to construct new cultural visions and new religious agency and identity by means of nature-oriented goddess worship and magical, ritual performance. In late modernity we are witnessing increased religious pluralism, including swift alteration of old spiritual traditions and the invention of new ones. Despite its missionary, universalist efforts, traditional Christianity has not succeeded in replacing other historical religions, such as Judaism, Islam and Buddhism, nor the indigenous spirituality of third-world peoples. Indeed, non-Christian religions have also spread in the west, primarily in the form of new religious movements. Consequently, there is a growing interest in the alternative knowledge, spirituality and ritual practices represented by religions other than the biblical faiths, including shamanism and long-dead ancient paganism. Furthermore, many third-world Christian congregations are attempting to gain new theological insights about the *givenness of life* through, for example, closer contact with the abandoned pagan religiosity of their ancestors, dead and living. An important aim in this rapidly spreading inclination to reorient oneself toward the past in order to improve or transform the human conditions of the present is to restore a felt loss of a living cosmos and a magical, spiritual ground of being to human existence.

An important contribution to this manifold enterprise is contemporary pagan Witchcraft and one of its most interesting voices, Reclaiming. This community of *feminist* Witches was formed in 1979 by two Jewish women, Starhawk and Diane Baker, who intended to teach others about their newly found goddess and her emancipatory rituals. Twenty years later, Reclaiming has grown into a large movement, with sister communities all over the US, Canada and western Europe. An important factor to Reclaiming's success is the fame and distribution of Starhawk's books to a wide public, in particular her first one, *The Spiral Dance: A Rebirth of the Ancient Religion of the Great Goddess* (1979a).

The name "Reclaiming" refers to a spirituality these feminists feel they have reclaimed from ancient paganism and goddess worship in order to heal experiences of estrangement occasioned by patriarchal biblical religions. In fact, they believe that western culture suffers from severe spiritual and social disease because its founding religions apparently deny significant aspects of the nature of reality: (divine) immanence, (ecological) interdependence and the sexed nature of the elemental birthing power (female Creatrix). From this stance, and with a working model of the universe that includes interconnected realms of matter and spirit, feminist Witches have created a compassionate alternative.

Reclaiming has a mission statement to educate the public, both women and men, in their visionary path work. A good example of how Starhawk communicates this work lies in her rewriting of the "Declaration of Human Rights" into a "Declaration of the Four Sacred Things", attempting hereby a general interpretation for a general public of the pre-Socratic doctrine of the four elements, a doctrine that all Witches endorse:

> In company with cultures of many different times and places we name these things as sacred: air, fire, water, and earth. Whether you see them as the breath, energy, blood and body of the planet, or as the blessed gifts of the Creator, or as symbols of the interconnected systems that sustain life, we know that nothing can live without them.
>
> To call these things sacred is to say that they have a value beyond their usefulness for human ends, that they themselves become the standards by which our acts, our economics, our laws and our purposes must be judged. . . . It is everyone's responsibility to sustain, heal and preserve the soil, the air, the fresh and salt waters, and the energy resources that can support diverse and flourishing life.
>
> All people, all living things, are part of the earth-cycle, and so sacred. No one of us stands higher or lower than any other. Only justice can assure balance; only ecological balance can sustain freedom. Only in freedom can that fifth sacred thing we call spirit flourish in its full diversity.
>
> To honor the sacred is to create conditions in which nourishment, sustenance, habitat, knowledge, freedom and beauty can thrive. To honor the sacred is to make love possible.[1]

When Starhawk invokes the four elements, she tries to reestablish and reinterpret the notion that humans are created beings and, therefore, part of the soil and water, breathing in air and fierily digesting the fruits of the earth, and that this cosmological perspective on human living is necessary for "that fifth sacred thing we call spirit to flourish". Her stated aim is not merely to venerate the natural elements but to free the spirit so that love becomes possible.

As a gesture toward understanding Reclaiming Witchcraft and its contribution to contemporary religious life, this book offers a joint ethnographic and theological study of Starhawk and Reclaiming's spiritual and communal alternatives as these were formed and formulated in the period 1984–94. A major concern when critically describing and analysing their alternatives is to demonstrate how and why the notion of having left the Father's House (Jewish and Christian religions) and returned "home" to the Self (Goddess religion) is a basic theme. It manifests, for example, in their favourite image of the Witch as "healer" of the self and "bender" of the world: she is a modern magician whose work is to liberate patriarchal culture and heal its wounds, at both a social and an individual level, and initiate a "new age". Foundational to her "regenerative magic" is the retrieval of ancient names, figures and myths that are believed to predate patriarchal western religion and, therefore, to represent divine reality and the human self, female and male, more truly and more vividly. Also important is the development of new magical rites, such as rites of calendar, rites of passage, and rites of crisis or celebration. They constitute a social and symbolic field within which new models of agency and religious identity are formed, for both women and men. They are also instrumental in Witches' attempts to induce personal growth in individuals or groups and in their anticipation of much-desired social reforms through symbolic action.

The theological concepts and ritual courses endorsed by Reclaiming Witches both challenge and contribute to academic feminist theology, not least by how they rework space and agency and humans' need for spiritual and personal regeneration. They also have something to say to mainstream theology and society, especially as their modus operandi is both a derivative of and a logical revision of that society. In particular, they reflect how *female* human beings may relate to divinity and community in contemporary society through ways of knowing, modes of thinking and forms of representation other than those usually associated with theological hermeneutics.

Background

Reclaiming is not an isolated social experiment, either in North America or Europe. It rather signals the rapid spread of a new multifaceted religious movement that has not immigrated from Asia or the Middle East but is more genuinely a new western creation: (neo)pagan Witchcraft. This movement was, to a large extent, crafted in post-war Great Britain in the 1940s and 1950s as part of a conservative rejection of modernity, socialism and Christianity (Hutton 2000:360). The motivation, at the time, was not to reform western religiosity in any radical sense but to return to spiritual and aesthetic practices that could conjure up the "good old days" of humankind. This nostalgic return was amply nourished by romantic notions of the nobility, sensuality and wisdom of ancient paganism, as well as by the occult philosophy and ritual magic of the European brotherhoods, such as the Freemasons and Rosicrucians. When this spirituality was finally introduced to the public in 1954, the father of modern Witchcraft, Gerald Gardner, claimed direct historical lineage to a presumably peaceful and natural pre-Christian and premodern "Old Religion" in Europe.

This bold attempt was not solely a product of Gardner's imagination but was substantiated by selective reading of contemporary scholars in folklore, anthropology and mythology adhering to German romanticism, such as Margaret Murray (*The Witch Cult in Western Europe*), Jane Harrison (*Prolegomena to the Study of Greek Religion*), Robert Graves (*The White Goddess*), C.G. Leland (*Aradia: Gospel of the Witches*), James Frazer (*The Golden Bough*), Edward Tylor (*Primitive Culture*), and J.J. Bachofen (*Das Mutterrecht*). For example, Murray contributed the idea that people burned as "witches" by the inquisition were killed because they practised an old fertility cult that could be "traced back to pre-Christian times, and appears to be the ancient religion of Western Europe" (Murray 1921:12). Were there still any survivors of this heritage in modern Europe? This is where Gardner's story begins: he claims to have met a group of Witches in the New Forest in England and been initiated to their supposedly age-old rites and mythology by a Dorothy Clutterbuck in September 1939, a woman he met through the Rosicrucian Theatre (Crowley 1989:20). Their tradition was, however, very fragmentary and in the process of dying out. In order to prevent this, Gardner broke the oath of secrecy that the Witches presumably required of their initiates and published their secrets, first in a fictitious form in the novel *High Magic's Aid* in 1949. After Old Dorothy's death in 1951, and the Witchcraft Act was repealed in Britain, he published the nonfictitious *Witchcraft Today* (1954) and *The Meaning of Witchcraft* (1959).[2]

This British civil servant and hobby-folklorist presented Witchcraft as an esoteric, initiatory religion with a magical system kindred to the Mysteries of Eleusis and Isis. He assured the reader that he had faithfully woven together old fragments and only created new ones when necessary. This was in particular the case with the Witches' "lost rituals", which he himself practised in a so-called Witch's coven. Apparently he was the coven's "high priest". After her initiation in 1953, Doreen Valiente became their "high priestess". She worked with Gardner as co-creator until they split apart in 1959". In order to perform the Witches' rites, Gardner had obviously used his experience and knowledge from being a member both of the *Hermetic Order of the Golden Dawn*, the *Co-Masons* – an offshoot from Freemasonry that admits both women and men – and *Ordo Templis Orientis*, which after 1925 was headed by the notorious Aleister Crowley. When Valiente finally published *The Rebirth of Witchcraft* in 1989, she did not veil that Crowley, until his death in 1947, actually played an important role in "reconstructing" the Witches' rites. In fact, when Valiente explained why she entered into close collaboration with Gardner to further refine the rituals, it was because "the influence of the late Aleister Crowley was so prevalent and obvious within the [Witch]cult" (Valiente 1989:60, 54). She resented this impact, partly because of Crowley's unpleasant personality and reputation as a Black Magician.[3] Gardner admitted to having received help from external sources in order to reconstruct the Witches' rites but never to having *invented* Witchcraft as such, or its contemporary existence.

The existence of a New Forest "Witch's coven" in England, with an assumed lineage back to pre-Renaissance Europe, has, however, never been documented. Furthermore, the academic faith in Murray's thesis regarding the early modern witch trials collapsed in the 1970s when attacked by three historians: Trevor-Roper (1970), Keith Thomas (1971) and Norman Cohn (1975). They criticized Murray's methodology and came up with new evidence to support the opposite thesis: that people tried for witchcraft by the inquisition were not practitioners of a reviving pagan nature religion.[4] Thus, from an academic point of view, Gardner (with Crowley and Valiente) must be regarded as the sole inventor of modern Witchcraft, including its practices.

This is not to say that the Witches' Craft was imagined out of context: The historical roots for Gardner's creative inventions can be ascribed, as already mentioned, to occult societies and theosophical ideas, burgeoning in the late nineteenth and early twentieth centuries, to modern anthropology and to the rise of a new, nondenominational spirituality in the west ("New Age"). But there are no direct, genetic connections between the complex beliefs of ancient paganism and the present, only indirect traces. According to the British historian (and archaeologist) Ronald Hutton, these are: 1) the marks of pagan philosophy in high ritual magic and occult philosophy; 2) the leftover practices of "hedge" witchcraft, or the popular magic of the local wise woman and cunning man; 3) the general love affair of the Christian centuries with the art and literature of the ancient world, including Romanticism; and 4) folk rites and feasts connected to seasonal celebrations, like the May-pole dances or the Summer solstice fires (Hutton 1996:4-13). Hutton has elaborated further on these collateral connections in his most recent book, *The Triumph of the Moon: A History of Modern Pagan Witchcraft* (2000), and has left no doubt that Gardner's historical claims, beyond this pool of sources, are unfounded.

Furthermore, because of the obvious connection between Witchcraft and western esoteric traditions, correlations must also be assumed with the religious heritage Gardner insisted to have rejected: Jewish and Christian religions. A British religious studies scholar, Linda Woodhead (1996), has suggested that the "new spirituality" that today flourishes in contemporary western societies represents a single form of religiosity, and that pagan Witchcraft is merely one of its expressions. This "new spirituality" is deeply rooted in European Protestantism and has arisen *as a response* to an increasing dissatisfaction with Christianity (and Judaism). We find its forerunners among radical Protestant sectarians (including the Quakers, Unitarians and Shakers). Although the self-understanding of Witchcraft is to reject this whole tradition, not to revitalize it, nor to purify it from within, Woodhead argues that the most important context in which to understand pagan Witchcraft is a Christian context: Witchcraft is not a new religion, but a new reformation.[5]

If Woodhead is right, this reformation is characterized by public reevaluation of western mysticism and esoteric symbolism, including its pantheism, animism, and emphasis upon the "feminine divine". At the same time, it is also heavily influenced by eastern religions, shamanic traditions, modern anthropology, emancipatory political movements and the forces of globalization – as well as by the anti-globalization movements that aim at preserving ecological balance, local agency and ethnic authenticity, and to liberate the oppressed.

Witchcraft and feminism in the US

Even though no genetic lineage back to ancient paganism can be established for these modern pagans, and their religious authenticity may be said to be fake, their ideas proved to be so vital and powerful that a new religious movement was instigated. Throughout the 1950s, Gerald Gardner and Doreen Valiente trained many wanna-be Witches in their coven and started to name their newly "found" religion "Wicca". As time passed, new covens formed and new, slightly different, interpretations of Wicca developed.[6] In the early 1960s, Gardnerian Wicca immigrated to the US and was soon to take a radical new turn: it was adopted by a handful of feminists in Los Angeles who were seeking a womanly expression of spirituality. Although occult, conservative and sociologically rather deviant, the Gardnerian Witches seemed to represent religious ideas befitting a new age: they worshipped a goddess as well as a god, ritualized on nights when the moon was full in small, autonomous and perfectly gender-balanced covens, and stripped off their clothes to dance in natural nakedness and ecstasy around the elements of nature: fire and earth. And even more peculiar, when compared to the hegemonic position of the male priesthood in western congregations at the time: Witches not only obeyed a priest, but also a priestess. In fact, she was considered superior to him, as the "Great Goddess" was said to be to the "God", alternately her consort and son.

To religious women, who had responded enthusiastically to the second wave of feminism from 1967 onward and presumably abandoned the patriarchal institutions of church and synagogue, Witchcraft offered itself as an exciting alternative. Its practitioners not only welcomed women as priestesses, they also employed female symbolism to represent the face of God/ess and seemed to organize in an anti-hierarchical manner, almost in conformity with the egalitarian principles of the "consciousness-raising" groups in the women's movement. Although pagan Witchcraft also needed reform to fit with radical feminist perspectives, invented as it was in the conservative, androcentric[7] lineage of European secret societies, it obviously promised empowerment and fulfillment of a kind that was felt to be very different from their previous experiences with Christianity and Judaism. This process of transformation and reinterpretation accelerated when six Los Angeles women in 1971 formed the first feminist Witchcraft coven in the US, called "Susan B. Anthony Coven no. 1", under the guidance of their then lesbian-separatist high priestess, Zuzanna Budapest. Eight years later, in 1979, another branch of feminist Witchcraft was established in San Francisco, "supervised" by Starhawk: the Reclaiming tradition.

Neither Budapest nor Starhawk admits to having inherited the basic structure of her spiritual practices fully fledged from Gerald Gardner. They either refer their knowledge to personal revelations, everyday experiences, common sense or a good library. Or, they insist upon hereditary sources, either by birth or initiation, of their own. In the last decade they have also become more reserved about employing the name "Wicca" since European Witches seem to have reached consensus with the Gardnerians that only they are entitled to this label.[8] The feminists do, however, continue to believe in Murray's (and Gardner's) outdated thesis that Witchcraft is of ancient origins and that "somebody" has been able to reconstruct this new/old spiritual path through personal initiation into leftover practices of pre-Christian goddess worship and magic. The witch burning in early modern Europe is still regarded as the climax of an ongoing war between a patriarchal Church and nonpatriarchal indigenous beliefs, and the witch-hunt itself is made into a model that can explain the brutality of later European colonializations or, more recently, the holocaust of the Jews.[9]

For this reason, feminist women have taken on the negatively loaded name "Witch". They want to remember the immense suffering of victims innocently persecuted and killed by the Inquisition, for being pagans or (Christian) heretics, healers or midwives, or just weird.[10] They also want to honour these people's lives by merging their memory with a certain romantic notion of the female hero: a "natural" person who dares to be "herself" and act against the powerful and mighty, and contrary to accepted norms about what it means to be a "woman", in order to "do good" and "be true". The other reason for being a self-proclaimed Witch is intrinsic to how these feminists define the inner, semantic meaning of the name itself. According to Merriam-Webster's Collegiate Dictionary (1995), the word *witch* is derived from the Old English *wicca*, being related to *wigle*, meaning "divination", and perhaps also to *wih*, meaning "holy". But irrespective of its associated linguistic meanings, Webster defines *witch* as someone "credited with unusual malignant supernatural powers, especially a woman practicing usually black witchcraft, often with the aid of a devil or a familiar". Modern Witches overrule this conventional, sociological definition by tracing the root meaning of *witch* and *wicca* further back historically. They claim that the linguistic origin of *wicca* is the Indo-European *wic, weik* or the Norse *vikja*, meaning "to shape, bend or twist". A witch is, therefore, somebody who is "skilled in the craft of shaping, bending and changing reality" and not somebody involved with supernatural evil doing (Adler 1986:11).

On one hand, then, to reclaim "the witch" – who by most people is *wrongly* associated with evil women of the past who were said to have collaborated with the devil (as defined in Webster) – is regarded as an act of solidarity. This argument for choosing their name is an expression of the feminist, political consciousness of contemporary Witchcraft. On the other hand, the name "witch" is not at all regarded as negatively loaded but as a proper name, really meaning "bender" or "wise person", or someone who is committed to nature worship and the goddess-within, the immanent life force. The name is not polluted but is a pure name for pure religious worship, believed to reach back to the "beginnings" of human culture.[11] As such, it is a name to be proud of, a name that should be capitalized: it refers to a religion and its adherents.[12] This argument for choosing a "true" name is an expression of the *esoteric* side of the same movement.

It should be noted, however, that most feminist Witches – also in Reclaiming – choose to refer to their religion as Wicca as soon as they enter public space. This is so because the word "witch" is still too loaded with negative associations, for example, to black magic or gothic-styled teenagers' fascination with vampires and "dangerous, mysterious things". Most young people on a spiritual quest, including young feminist women, thus seek Wicca, not Witchcraft. As feminist Witchcraft ideas have spread, people have just abandoned the word "witch" as too problematic. In this book, however, I will to a large extent keep the distinction between Witchcraft and Wicca. This way the differences between Reclaiming and Gardnerian Witchcraft will not be blurred.

Social significance and academic research

Since Witchcraft was imported to the US, it has grown tremendously and branched off in a variety of schools and interpretations, both feminist and nonfeminist. It has also sparked a general interest in indigenous European pagan worship beyond Witchcraft, represented by pantheons such as Norse, Celtic and Minoan. These pantheons have been superimposed on the fundamental structure of Gardner's Wicca, resulting in the revival of various "nature religions" of European origin (Adler 1979:10). This differentiation of Wicca into *paganism* means that all Witches are pagans, but not all pagans are Witches.[13] Nonetheless, Witchcraft continues to be the largest and most influential branch within this broader pagan movement, which already in 1978 could count committed members in the tens of thousands. American paganism was then to be rated among the three largest new religious movements in the US, the other two being Black Islam and Christian Science (Melton 1987:47). At the turn of the century, the number of practicing Witches and pagans in North America is probably closer to 200,000 (Berger 1999:9).

Why is it that a movement can be so large but still relatively anonymous to the public? Primarily because the new American paganism is constituted as a large network of small, completely autonomous groups or covens. Although they may offer education and usually have a P.O. box address, they seldom proselytize with any real efforts or keep membership lists. Since they mostly prefer to worship in small circles, either outdoors or in private homes, they rarely own congregational buildings. They enjoy gathering at large festivals in remote places and sometimes cluster within certain affinity-based communities, similar to Reclaiming. But communities are seldom delimited geographically. More likely, they are subcultural networks within a broader cultural context in which the participants live and work. The fairly reliable *Circle Guide* to *Pagan Groups* in 1996 listed a total of 273 pagan communities in 20 American states and in Canada. Forty-seven of these were registered as churches and 71 as annual festivals and large-scale gatherings.[14] Furthermore, 107 different pagan periodicals, newsletters or journals were published in North America within this period. In the San Francisco Bay Area alone *Circle Guide* listed nine communities/groups and eight periodicals. "Reclaiming" is only one of these communities and the *Reclaiming Quarterly* only one of the journals.

The single most important reason for this growth of Witchcraft and paganism, and for the spreading of pagan ideas and practices in the US, is probably Starhawk (Orion 1995:8). Her first book, *The Spiral Dance: A Rebirth of the Ancient Religion of the Great Goddess* from 1979, is a continuing bestseller and regarded the best manual and introductory book to Witchcraft by all its different traditions.[15] By 1989, it had sold 100,000 copies. In 2000, the number passed 300,000 (sales numbers obtained from Harper & Row).[16] Obviously Starhawk has more readers than there are practitioners of the Witches' Craft, markedly among feminist theologians and women in the feminist spirituality movement. To the extent that these women are still affiliated with church and synagogue, (neo)pagan ideas and practices will, once again, be brought back into active dialogue with the institutions of Jewish and Christian religions, contributing to their ongoing reformation in new and challenging directions. For example, Starhawk has been an inspirer both to a post-Christian theologian like Carol P. Christ (*Laughter of Aphrodite*) and to a Catholic feminist like Rosemary R. Ruether (*Woman Church*). Her works have also had an influence on the public in general by adding to the modern notion that religious reform and ritual invention is the privilege of any human being, skilled or not, who is able to imagine, honest to her "spirit within" and willing to do the work.[17]

In recent years, many well-researched and mind-opening studies of paganism, Witchcraft and goddess spirituality have been published. Social scientists have been engaged in mapping paganism more adequately onto the new religious scenery, and in particular to distinguish it from the "New Age" movement (Melton 1991; Miller 1995; York 1995; Hardman 1996; Heelas 1996; Lewis 1996). Anthropologists have conducted fieldwork in selected pagan networks and compiled new knowledge through comparative, thematic surveys (Luhrmann 1989; Orion 1995; Magliocco 1996; Berger 1999, Pike 2000). Historians have tried to depict the history of contemporary paganism and Witchcraft through its sources and references (Kelly 1991; Hutton 2000). Religious studies scholars and theologians have either contributed updated descriptions of the feminist spirituality movement, including its entanglement with goddess worship and Witchcraft, or presented their own endeavours in developing feminist theology or feminist ritualizing that also include discourse on the G/goddess (Ruether 1986, 1992, 1998; Christ 1987, 1997; Eller 1993, 2000; King 1993; Procter-Smith 1993, 1995; Gross 1996; Northup 1997; Raphael 1999). Besides these, there are numerous books out by pagans them-selves, describing and promoting their own spiritual paths (Adler 1986; Crowley 1989; Valiente 1989; Jones and Pennick 1995; Harvey 1996; Roberts

1998). Many of these I will not regard as scholarly contributions, but rather as further "primary texts" for the study of modern pagan religiosity.

Starhawk's books are either referred to or discussed in almost every single title mentioned above. Nevertheless, the authors seem to be unaware of the existence of the Reclaiming community or of Starhawk's profound commitment to this community and spiritual tradition. They rather relate to her texts as if they are produced in majestic isolation, as if she has no social grounds within which she lives and works, or as if she does not represent a particular perspective but can be used as a general referral to "what Witches do" or "what Witches believe". This noncontextual reading of Starhawk's books has resulted in a peculiar situation: when, for example, a conscientious scholar like Luhrmann describes Gardnerian Witches in England, she quotes from Starhawk's texts on and off to substantiate her claims. The same is true with Berger's more recent study of a Gardnerian network in New England, US: she often relies on Starhawk and the Reclaiming tradition when filling in her own field notes from this very different community. Northup, who discusses spiritual patterns in women's ritualizing, misinforms us that Starhawk formed the Covenant of the Goddess (and not Reclaiming) in California. She also claims that women's contemporary ritualizing has a purely horizontal dimension without making exceptions to feminist Witches. Even in Hutton's intriguing historical records Starhawk is basically read as a single feminist interpreter, not as the most important founder of a new social and spiritual community.

This lack of differentiation between feminist and nonfeminist versions of Witchcraft, between Californian, East Coast and British customs, or between visionary texts and social practices, is like quoting from Luther when describing the Catholics. An explanation to this odd situation may be that most academic works on Witchcraft so far have been thematical surveys with a large number of pagan groups, not in-depth studies of *one* community or of *one* textual body. Instead of examining Witchcraft as a contextualized lived experience, involving power dynamics, conflicts and disagreements within each and every one of the traditions, they have chosen instead to synthesize and generalize. Some scholars even seem to assume that they ought to romanticize Witches' egalitarian self-presentation as actual facts and so legitimize magical groups.[18]

But this approach prevents us from gaining a more comprehensive view of Witchcraft and of what the feminist alternative really is all about – for example, as encountered in the Reclaiming community of San Francisco. The motivation for my own inquiry has thus been to move beyond idealized narratives, sweeping generalizations and superficial surveys to present a joint ethnography and theological analysis of a single community (Reclaiming) and a single author (Starhawk). I believe this interdisciplinary approach is much needed, both to gain adequate knowledge about feminist Witches' hermeneutics and visionary practices and to critically argue with prevailing theories about contemporary women's religiosity and ritualizing strategies.

Methodology and conceptual frameworks

The theoretical perspectives discussed in this book have been discovered through "indulging" in the material as a participant observer and finally selected during the process of writing. This inductive strategy is consistent with a hermeneutical approach to reading that moves from text to theory and back to text, assuming that careful reading and listening will eventually disclose from the text its implicit theory about itself: how it "asks" to be read to make sense; its rhetorical devices; what it conceals "between the lines". This originally "exegetical" method resembles the empirical aim in anthropology of interpreting a phenomenon horizontally, in solidarity with the indigenous points of view and conceptual frameworks and not from a priori theoretical assumptions or claimed philosophies. From this epistemological stance it is not primarily interesting to apply external theoretical models, that is, models established on the basis of having read "another text" to explain textual meaning in "our text". It is more interesting to *extract* implicit theory and models and then discuss these "extractions" with adequate, already established, theoretical discourse.[19] Therefore, to the extent I use the theories, concepts and ideas of others, it is only as tools to build a "deep" account of Reclaiming Witchcraft (its women, communities and rituals) and to help analyze the interrelated themes of this book (holy hermeneutics, female agency, human growth and regeneration). I shall not prove a general theory or verify a chosen, first hypothesis; nor do I align my theorizing with only one systematic school of thought. In turn, this approach to theory will, I hope, also contrive to refine it, which is always a goal.

Enchanted Feminism is the result of interdisciplinary research. I have tried to balance my primary training as a theologian with my secondary one as an anthropologist, although theological interests mainly determine choice of subject. My theoretical and methodological approaches to feminist Witchcraft are, however, primarily gathered from the field of anthropology, although I seek to balance anthropological discussions with theological requirements of rigorous contextualization of meanings and events. One unavoidable consequence of this approach is that both theologians and anthropologists may find, when measured with the requirements of each discipline separately, that whatever the book may have gained in detail, composition and originality, it probably lacks in depth. Theologians will, for example, look in vain for updated theological discussions of a general order; anthropologists will miss unmitigated theoretical discussions and a broad, holistic analytical approach. Some theologians are likely to find the emphasis on multidimensional lived experience and detailed ethnography to be not so relevant to their discipline; some anthropologists will find that I indulge too much in textual and exegetical inquiries. A common critique may be that there are too many discussions, too many themes – all in all, problems one generally encounters in interdisciplinary approaches.

But again, my approach was not a fixed idea but was "required" by the material itself. For the theologian it was necessary to learn to listen to "the other" without having to reach consensus or state disagreements, that is, to learn the methods of participant observation and gain the competence required to study living communities, not only texts. For the anthropologist, then coming into being, it was important that she discard reductionist and biased approaches to religion and regard feminist Witchcraft as a genuine and qualified religious (and theological) expression. It is my experience that this *inductive, interdisciplinary* approach has proved fruitful; and I hope, in the end, the reader will confirm that the choices made were appropriate. But first, let me introduce some of the premises set on my quest to learn about feminist Witchcraft.

Although "modern Witchcraft" would not have been a concept without Gerald Gardner, and his ideas still prevail, the particular spiritual path offered in Reclaiming has primarily been developed by women. The men who participated in Reclaiming up to 1994 constituted a minority group and did not yet mark the community's *spiritual* work in any substantial sense, although there were important individual exceptions, for example Raven Moonshadow, Rick Dragonstongue, Jody Logan and David Miller. Most men seem to have found a place here not because they were men, but because they were *feminist men*, or sympathizers of feminism.[20] This gives us a unique opportunity to actually be acquainted with an expression of "religious woman" in contemporary western culture. It also gives us an opportunity to learn how (some) women may construct theology, ritual and community, and express their "womanly" faith, when they feel unrestricted by male power, traditional dogma and institutional demands. But, if feminist Witchcraft is predominantly practised as a woman's religion, is it also possible to distinguish specific features of these women's religiosity, features that can be attributed to gender differences *in general?*

This is a difficult question, not least since Reclaiming is a mixture of woman-identified women and feminist women and men. In addition, it essentializes women as a social group and "genderedness" as an analytical construct and takes us right into the core of the essentialist–constructionist controversy. It implies that there are such things as "women's experiences" and "women's theology" that stand apart and above differences *between* empirical women, differences determined by psychosocial factors like class, race, culture, sexual orientation, personality, beliefs, family background, and so forth. But, as will be documented in this book: the differences and disagreements among Reclaiming women are so obvious that to analytically reduce them to one unified body with "common experiences" and "common thoughts" would not be in accordance with the data.

On the other hand, without some level of generalization, people cannot share identities and visions or act politically for common goals. And, as Lesley A. Northup has pointed out, "carried to its logical extreme, the particularist approach would eventually make it impossible to perform any meaningful analysis of a subject" (1997:4). Furthermore, Reclaiming women (and men) do consciously come together with the intention of extracting commonality from their experiences. After years of discussion, experimentation and consensus processing, they were (in 1997) to produce the "Reclaiming Principles of Unity". These principles describe their mutual values when inviting "all genders, all races, all ages and sexual orientations" as welcome to join. But do these principles express (feminist) *women's* religiosity any more than they express (feminist) *men's*, or is feminism the active denominator here?

Another crucial feature of Reclaiming's version of Witchcraft is constant reflection on questions of sexual difference: what is a woman and who is the goddess; what constitutes sexual difference and who is the god? Since Witches are continuously on personal quests for *the Real*, not only for its meaning, this quest also implies the felt reality of sexual difference. To most Witches this difference is not regarded as essential, but as paradoxical: as both ontological and accidental at the same time, as an awareness of being a historically situated, bodily sexed self. When further defining this "bodily sexed self", they may disagree. But as a rule they will contest, to varying degrees, the culturally coded "feminine" and "masculine" of the west and the hegemonic position of the "heterosexual matrix".[21] Apart from this, they have no coherent gender theory.

In order to conceptually grasp the genderedness of social beings Anglo-American feminist theorists have for the last three decades suggested that we differentiate analytically between "sex" as biological facticity and "gender" as the cultural interpretation of that facticity (cf. Rubin 1975). But this differentiation is highly problematic. First because it presumes that a pre-discursive, natural category can be separated from – and therefore also included within – the frameworks of analytic language (cf. Butler 1990). Second because the distinction itself is dualist and superficial in terms of grasping the idea of the lived body as a situation that is open and undetermined although deeply intertwined with the world and other bodily subjects, that is, with what it encounters (cf. Heinämaa 1997). On the level of *lived experience* I claim that one cannot separate natural from cultural as suggested by the sex/gender social theorists.

Furthermore, my goal in this book is not to present an explanation for gender differences by elaborating on a theory on the socio-cultural production of gender, or say, on the foundations of the gendered field of religion, but to describe how actual, empirical women develop a spiritual alternative to Jewish and Christian religions, how they understand themselves as cultural agents and womanly subjects in the midst of this process, and analyze the meanings of their sexed, bodily experiences when interpreted in the context of ritual action and symbolism. Thus, in accordance with my initial remarks on inductive versus deductive strategies, I shall be content to separate between two different approaches to the subject matter: empirical versus analytic. While gender analysis may be both relevant and helpful on a meta-social level it may turn out to be rather reductionist if we try to conform the lived experiences of empirical human beings with its theoretical horizon.

Consequently, when I use the term "sexual difference" it shall connote a *philosophical* notion that may help any person (including a scholar) to come to terms with the ontology of being situated *as* a woman's and/or *as* a man's body, while "gender" shall connote an *analytic* category and meta-perspective that may help the scholar (but not necessarily any person) understand (and contest) historical and cultural assumptions about what it means to hold the subject position of a "woman" and/or "man." The first perspective does not necessarily rule out the second, or vice versa; they just belong to different levels of discourse (irrespective of whether the subject of enunciation is a scholar or an informant).

Thus, when describing Reclaiming women empirically, it is both relevant and meaningful to ask how they perceive of themselves as "women" and how they attempt to create an alternative to male-oriented western religiosity in terms of a new female symbolic order. Aided by the philosophical language of Luce Irigaray, I will document that such creativity tries to respond to the following problems: the envelopes[22] that situate and hold us (body, ecology, society) and the elementals constituting the sexed body; the nature of sisterhood and women's shared experiences; maternal origins and female genealogies from mother to daughter; the interpretation of human existence by means of goddess symbolism and sexualized cosmologies. Furthermore, all Reclaiming Witches seem, irrespective of gender, to build a religious identity in accordance with mystical experiences of "merger"[23] and "regeneration" and with the imagery of "coming home", both to oneself and to the universe. Their chosen symbols are created in extension of, and through confirming analogies to, ordinary human life and the human body, sexuality and parenting, as well as the earth and the seasonal cycles of the natural world. Advocating a spiritual "transfiguration and regeneration of the ordinary", they show no desire to permanently flee the world, nor to symbolically become "like children", but rather to develop and grow as mature adults. Pious western ideals of world renunciation are interpreted as an escape from initiation into adulthood, since such models of piety do not demand the initiatory pattern of leaving mother and father, cultivating one's sexuality and taking on adult responsibility for family, community and society.[24]

The kind of religiosity represented in Reclaiming shows some of the same features that historian Caroline W. Bynum has documented to be characteristic of medieval Christian women. By analyzing medieval texts she found that women were inclined to use religious symbols that were in continuity with their sense of both social and biological self, being deepenings and appreciations of what "woman" at the time was perceived to be, rather than being based on gender reversals or negations, which were more typical of men (Bynum 1987:289). These differences between empirical women and men were again reinforced by social stratification: male authors were priests, female writers represented laity. Men's authority was derived from their education and ordination; women's religious power derived from inspiration or ecstatic visitation. Thus, the opposition between knowledge received *externally* (priests) versus knowledge received *internally* (mystics) was represented as a dichotomy between the learned and the ignorant, which in medieval Europe coincided with the hierarchical opposition between men and women. The situation today is slightly different. As is the case with Reclaiming, gender similarities are more striking than gender differences, meaning that the basic features of Reclaiming Witches' religious identity summarized above apply as much to men as they do to women within this particular *feminist* community.

If the typical features of the new symbolic order created by Reclaiming women (and men) cannot be attributed to gender differences *in general*, then how are they generated? A more comprehensive analysis of the cultural and sociological conditions for the creativity observed in Reclaiming is beyond the scope of this book. I shall be content to show how concrete people choose, in this case, the hermeneutic primacy of (mystical) "experience" and (magical) "ritual". When Witches confess to a theology of "immanence, inter-connection and community" (Starhawk 1990a:73), their discourse resembles to a large extent a subcultural heritage line in the Christian tradition which in medieval times was primarily associated with women (and heretics). The basic theological premise of this heritage line is the postulation that the divine spirit is a gift of creation, not of baptism. It is poured out irrespective of institution, clergy and authority, and "to have" the spirit does not receive meaning on the basis of the continuum "fall–redemption". This heritage line anchors religious authority in the inner self, not in external institutions. It also turns the redemptive scheme of the reforming fathers upside down and praises the created world and the human person "as she is". As will be documented in this book, Witches do not demand repentance and conversion before a person is sanctified and called "holy", nor is this model fundamental to their rituals. A person is first empowered and given plenty of self-confidence and praise for being exactly who she is. Then she is challenged to change and grow and take responsibility for agency in the world.

But the spatial tension between inner and outer in this Jewish and Christian heritage line takes a new turn with Witches' approach to ritual. Ritual in radical Christian sects has always been classified as external and secondary to the internal, primary religious locus: the faith. *Magical* rites have not even been considered part of Christian religion but attributed to primitivism, superstition and the domain of paganism, and ranked as inferior and prior to pure religious worship and personal devotion (Searle 1992:53). This theological resistance to ritual has marked modern culture fundamentally but is about to change. A liberal protestant theologian like Tom F. Driver argues, for example, that the gifts of ritual are social order, community and the transformative power to change both people and their traditions.

In his affirmation of ritual, Driver relies on anthropologists like Roy A. Rappaport, who is very clear that "ritual is not simply an alternative way to express certain things, but that certain things can be expressed only in ritual . . . certain meanings and effects are intrinsic to the ritual form, which is further to suggest that ritual is without equivalents or even alternatives" (1979:174). Driver also suggests Van Gennep's term "magico-religious" to express the conjunction of religious theory and practice to remind us that religion cannot be religion without performance or *praxis*, meaning a certain way of acting or attempting to act in the world. Religious praxis is also established through a certain way of acting ritually, namely, *magic*. In other words, a ritual not only has meaning, it also "works"; it is also "magical" (Driver 1991:168–9).

What magic *is* more specifically will vary with indigenous definitions. Reclaiming people seem to have appropriated theirs from two British occultists: Aleister Crowley, who argued that "magic is the Science and Art of causing change to occur in conformity with will", and Dion Fortune, who taught that "magic is the art of changing consciousness at will" (Starhawk 1979a:108ff.). Magic, then, as a way of acting ritually, can simply be defined as *religious practice undertaken to consciously effect transformation in people and, eventually, in their environment.* Within this framework, the most intriguing theological challenge is not whether to classify prayer as magic, or the Eucharist as a magical rite, but rather to evaluate the philosophical assumptions in theories intended to explain why magic works and their implied ethical tenets.

This affirmative attitude toward the uniqueness of ritual in human life and the implicit critique of the Protestant ritual avoidance did not originate among theologians. Rather, it was influenced by a new academic perception about ritual in general. With the growth of the counter culture from the mid-1960s and the fame of works by Victor Turner, Clifford Geertz and Roy A. Rappaport, scholars began to distance themselves from the notion of ritual as legitimating the status quo and instead began to think of ritual as having "subversive, creative and culturally critical capacities" (Grimes 1990:21).

Ritologist Ronald L. Grimes[25] does in particular attribute this new critical, cultural creativity to feminists, a fact he thinks is ignored by most scholars:

> For the last twenty years or so feminism has been a consistent source of ritual creativity; it provides an ongoing context for ritual experiment unparalleled in any other sector of North American society. This pheno-menon is regularly and, I think, wrongly ignored by most theorists of ritual.
>
> (1990:119)

One of those he has in mind when linking the growth of ritual creativity and the US feminist communities is Starhawk, the work of whom he returns to several times in his argument and analysis (cf. Grimes 1990:118–20). For the very same reason I have chosen my ethnographic field: I regard feminist Witchcraft, as constructed by Starhawk and Reclaiming Witches, as one of the most interesting and successful manifestations of this new feminist-ritualist consciousness. Furthermore, in terms of its success, it should not be under-estimated that young Jewish women founded Reclaiming, and that ex-Catholics and ex-Protestants came in when ritualizing and teaching had already attained a basic rhythm and outline. Being raised Jewish, ritual avoidance was not part of the founders' religious ancestry. This particular feature is the charter of Protestantism and of those raised in Protestant cultures.

A method of compassion

This book is based on long-term fieldwork after a method developed by social anthropologists: participant observation. The intended goal when using this methodological approach is to be able to interpret the Reclaiming community horizontally, in solidarity with their own points of view, not vertically and from externally applied norms. To learn to understand "the other" but still be cognitively distant and loyal to the normativity of scientific reality constructs, classical anthropology has developed what Peter L. Berger calls "various rituals of detachment". The academic penalty for failure to remain detached from indigenous religiosity is "to go native". One is, however, encouraged to "go native" behaviourally (participant observation), even emotionally (empathy). But "to go native" *cognitively* to such an extent that the fundamental articles of a-theistic belief in the scholar's own normative community are questioned is a sign of no longer being able to do social anthropology (Berger 1970:21).

The inadequacies of this native/nonnative scheme and of the dishonest position of the detached "objective" observer have been exposed and criticized by leading anthropologists (for example, Rosaldo (1980), Crapanzano and Garrison (1977), Lewis (1980), Daniel (1984), Jackson (1989) and Csordas (1994)). Instead they encourage their colleagues to empathetically "take belief seriously" in the actual research process and acknowledge the unavoidability of subjectivity, narrative and emotion when studying other human fellows.

Reclaiming Witches identify as modern mystics. Mysticism can be approached textually. But according to Witches this is not enough. In order to really grasp their beliefs, they insist that the scholar engage in ritual, magic and trance work as well. The problem is that the notion "participant observation" does not specify accurately the kind of participation required. The "genuinely social interaction" (Ellen 1984:17) of this method is often conditioned and its requested "direct observations of relevant events" may easily resemble pretension. Such an attitude obviously belongs to the *outsider*, to one who enters in order to gather data, but whose first obligation is a normative commitment to "not going native".

Yet the main reason it is not enough to conduct fieldwork from such a normatively chosen "outside" position is that, in Witches' rituals, covens and classes, there is no outside where an observer can literally put herself. Regarding the practice of modern mystery religions, you are either in, or you are not there at all. Therefore, in my study of feminist Witches, I had to establish a research position for myself in which I became a co-participant and an apprentice, taking my own experiences seriously, observing the development of my own possible new insights, presumably determined by my willingness to put myself under the discipline of magical training and by my abilities for religious imagination, theologizing and engagement in general. Along with, and parallel to my studies of Reclaiming Witches, I did, in other words, become my own informant.[26]

The obvious demands for involvement and subjective experiencing, required from the ethnographic field, have led to my deliberate choice of the label "method of compassion" to designate this approach. "Compassion" in this context does not refer to a wholesale positive embrace, nor to passionate criticisms and arguing, but to something in between: to honesty. It shall designate an attitude in which belief is taken seriously, both cognitively and emotionally. This means to leave behind the anthropological "method of pretension", which is mainly used in order to gain access, be it to rituals, to secret knowledge or to initiations, and instead take on the attitude that "the subjects of one's research might actually know something . . . that is personally valid for the anthropologist", as suggested by anthropologist Katherine P. Ewing (1994:571). On the other hand, when something is taken seriously cognitively, it may also turn out that they do *not* know something that can be personally valid. A method of compassion is necessarily critical since it cannot be operative without continual assessments and evaluations (cf. Grimes 1990: 137). It also means respect for the integrity of the people studied and for myself. Anthropologists may, for example, be eager to gain access to esoteric traditions and learn the knowledge of the initiates. But, if religious initiation is accepted entirely against one's own beliefs or solely in order to publish secret knowledge, the act is incompatible with the ethics embedded in a method of compassion.

The benefits and challenges of becoming my own informant, of simul-taneously exercising engagement (vivid participation) and holding a general view (distant observation) apply in particular to the study of ritual. Regarding magical rituals, engagement is important to understand, distance is important to observe, remember and record details.[27] Since one of the goals of ritual is to alter the consciousness of *all* the participants through trance work, engagement and distance are counter-productive. To the extent that I have managed to be involved all through the ritual, I will also come out with an altered consciousness. Engagement is more than participation, and something else than pretending. To allow oneself to become engaged is to take the intent of ritual seriously. It is to be willing to let the trance induction take you into trance, to be willing to be emotionally moved as is intended by certain ritual elements and to go with what then happens. Distance, on the other hand, means observation, remembering the lyrics and symbols used in trance induction, remembering the ritual proceedings step by step, seeing what happens to the other participants, noticing the social interaction, the symbolism, the artifacts, the movements. However, this very subjective element marks a limit as to how deeply into a religion of this kind one can go. Another aspect is the uncertainty about where a scholarly project like this will lead because an intrinsic part of becoming a "visiting member" of a mystery religion is to make a contract with oneself to change.

The present study is, however, *not about me* in any postmodernist sense (cf. Clifford and Marcus 1986). I have become my own informant for methodological reasons only, in order to understand "the other" deeply and from the inside. This is also my reason for wanting to experience the full range of Witches' rituals, including the initiation process and its ultimate, secret rite. But, when finally deciding to become initiated into the Reclaiming tradition, which I have been, it was after six years of careful consideration and discussion with myself, my informants and my theological and anthropological supervisors (at the University of Oslo). I met Reclaiming in 1984, I asked for initiation in 1991, and it finally happened in 1994. I could not do it only for curiosity or for empirical insight, which, of course, was tempting all the time; the act had to be consistent with a minimum of my own beliefs and values, not violating my integrity as a theologian.[28]

When I first met Reclaiming, I had little knowledge about what an initiation actually was. I was, nevertheless, sincerely against it, regarding any form of initiation ritual as undemocratic, hierarchical, patriarchal and exclusive, emphasizing human "deeds" instead of divine "grace". To ask for initiation at that point was out of the question, even though it would have been helpful to my studies. Ten years later I had changed my mind, partly from being a close observer and witness to another person's initiation process (described in chapter 8), partly from realizing that the absence of working initiation rituals and its embedded notion of the unfinished state of the human person in modern society probably represents as much loss as progress. Thus, to be the subject of an initiation process would perhaps give me a unique opportunity to experience the practical consequences of very different notions of "grace" and the "human person" than what have gained momentum in Protestant churches in the wake of the reforming fathers. In the controversy between Luther and Erasmus over the freedom of the will, Luther conceptualized "grace" as the promise of new life for a will that is so perverted it first must die, whereas "grace" for Erasmus meant help for the weak. For this humanist and mystic, "grace meant help to move persons beyond their present abilities; in Erasmus' own metaphor, grace is the parental boost that helps the child to its feet and enables it to walk" (Gerrish 1993:21). Although "grace" is not a notion in Witchcraft, the analogy to Erasmus' theology is still valid, for the initiation process is interpreted as an opening of "the envelope" for the crafting work of the spirit, visualized as the goddess of rebirth, growth and regeneration.[29]

Since I have been initiated into Reclaiming Witchcraft primarily for hermeneutical and experiential reasons, I am not entitled to initiate anybody else into this tradition. The apprenticeship is over, and although I have learned a lot, I do not intend to bring about any further magical currents from having been initiated except this book and its various receptions in the reader; for my suggested method of compassion demands that we never forget that we are scholars. By this I mean two things. First, we must abandon the luxury of engaging in only those aspects of the religious tradition we are studying that immediately seem attractive or intelligible to us. We must dive as deeply into the religion as possible and let go of the desire to choose from its well only what may suit our own biases. Second, we as scholars are indeed permitted spiritual and personal development from our work, but we may not end up as scholarly converts and proselytizers. Proselytizing and sound academic analysis are two different genres.

The necessity of studying mysticism from an experiential position "within" is not only part of feminist rhetoric. Frits Staal already argued for it in 1975 in his book *Exploring Mysticism*. Considering the superficial knowledge one gets from studying yoga when not entering the experience of actually learning yoga, Staal suggests that the academic student of yoga learn it from a guru, but without "going native". The way to keep the awareness of a scholar throughout the period of learning is, according to Staal, to remember that we have entered the path of yoga to leave it when our learning is completed. We cannot enter it to stay. After leaving the path, Staal designs the scholar's task to be the development of a language to describe mystical yoga.

I agree that we, as scholars, must enter the path of mysticism in order to develop a descriptive terminology. Nevertheless, Staal's scientific belief in the possibilities of learning to be a mystic by the same mental and emotional equipment one uses to learn to cook seems to be put forward by somebody who has been some kind of an "outsider" throughout the process. He does not consider what compassion and the contract to be willing to change – which are both required conditions to actually be able to enter and learn from a mystical path – will actually do to him and his study. Nor does he contemplate how the admission unto such a path challenges the ideology of observer–observed and highlights the ethical dilemmas and co-responsibilities of any researcher in regard to actual happenings and processes among the people studied. And finally, he does not seem to be willing to reflect hermeneutically on the way in which he partakes in the development, twisting and diffusion of the tradition solely by writing a new text. How, for example, do Witches learn about yoga, or manage to incorporate yoga practices into their modernist mixture of meditative techniques? Maybe they have learned from a guru, maybe from having read Staal and his colleagues.

A majority of Witches are educated at western universities and well read in the basic humanistic disciplines, including religious studies and classical anthropology. In the process of constructing their own religious alternative, they appropriate ethnographic and religious literature with the intention of turning what they learn into normative vehicles for cultural reforms, not in some exotic country, but in their own community. Academic texts are therefore never merely descriptions or representations of "other" forms of life but participate in cultural changes in western societies as well, totally independent of the scholar's perhaps "purely descriptive" intentions.

In my own discipline, which is systematic or constructive theology, it is not regarded as a fundamental methodological problem to move between "outside" and "inside" positions, or to gain personal experiences from the phenomenon studied. Nor is engagement regarded as something that might blur the objectivity of the descriptions. The situation is rather the opposite: first-hand experience *may* open the possibility to deep insight and the best description possible. Questioning the positivist and conflictual ideology of observer–observed is an inherent part of this theological discipline. In fact, the father of modern constructive theology, Friedrich Schleiermacher (1768-1834), has formulated the experiential nature of theology thus: "Anyone who has not experienced will not understand" (cf. Gerrish 1993:32). Hence, the art of competent constructive theology is to evolve and deepen religious (and theological) experience, compassion and understanding in the student, at the same time that she learns the skills of critical analysis and acquires the ability to deconstruct or revise the very same phenomenon that triggers her interest.

Thus, my experience when studying the mystery religion of feminist Witchcraft cannot report on the problems proposed by Frits Staal, namely, the supposed dilemma of moving back and forth between inside and outside and the temptation to go native. To move back and forth between compassion and analysis is not at all the difficult part. But *to stay in*, in touch with "the native's" affirmative compassion, is indeed difficult. To accept those symbols as sacred that to my taste were vulgar, to play with pagan names as if they were real names for divine reality, to let go of criticism and be open to the ecstasy of ritual, to meditate on certain symbols "until they revealed their esoteric knowledge", and to grant exception to the belief that this really was *im*possible – when taken altogether – this is what has been difficult, challenging and rewarding.

No academic discipline has developed adequate methodology for the study of modern mystery religions because such a task requires a thorough interdisciplinary approach. In my case, anthropology has contributed the basic qualitative tools: fieldwork, participant observation and the skills of active listening to "the other", including that which we do not like to hear. Theology has contributed the training of being in two mindsets simultaneously, which means to be able to engage in the phenomenon studied as well as to be critical and analytic.

As merely a sociologist or anthropologist I would never have been admitted to Reclaiming's inner circles. But as a theologian and feminist I was regarded as a religious being with a personally motivated interest for the subject of my study and, therefore, possessing the necessary qualifications both to understand and to learn (about) Witchcraft. Without being a co-participant guided by empathy and compassion I would not have been able to conduct my study as intended. All in all, the benefits from a method of compassion are either visible in the present text, or there are no benefits. If the reader finds my research interesting and convincing, and agrees that I have managed to understand the phenomenon of Witchcraft deeply and more thoroughly through this method, I have reached an important goal. But I also hope the text reveals the vulnerabilities, not only the strengths, of becoming my own informant as well.

Fieldwork

Fieldwork in Reclaiming was formally conducted in the periods 1988-89 and 1990 for a doctoral dissertation, with a predoctoral research period in 1984–85, and several return trips in 1991 and 1994, a time span of 10 years. Every fieldwork and return trip has either been funded by the Norwegian Research Council or the University of Oslo.

When I first came to the San Francisco Bay Area in the academic year 1984-85, it was to study Witchcraft for my MA thesis in theology. Three years later, when I came back to conduct more regular fieldwork for a doctoral dissertation, I split the required year in two: eight months in 1988-89 (from mid-November to August) and four months in 1990 (from August to mid-November). During my first stay, I lived outside the San Francisco Reclaiming community together with my family and a woman friend I had met in 1984 (a practicing pagan who had moved toward New Age shamanism). In the second period, I lived with my three-year-old daughter in one of the Reclaiming-identified collective households in the Mission in San Francisco, Group W house. I returned in 1994 for two months in order to be initiated and to work. This time I also stayed in a Reclaiming-identified household in San Francisco, Flamingo Towers.

The foundation of my fieldwork was already established in my predoctoral research in 1984-85, when I enrolled in Reclaiming classes, participated in rituals and eventually became "a friend of Reclaiming", at the same time that I was a student at Graduate Theological Union in Berkeley. Early in the fall of 1984, the *Reclaiming Newsletter* announced a class called "Women's Magic". It addressed women "who have taken a Reclaiming class, or who have other experience in working magic in circle with women". Nine women were accepted to the class, including me, although I had just arrived in the US and had no previous experience "working magic in circle with women". In fact, I had no idea what "working magic" really meant. Yet the teachers were satisfied to hear about my work with feminist theology and liturgy back in Norway, and that became the entrance ticket to my first Reclaiming class and, from there, to the community.

A Witches' "coven" or "circle" grew out of this class, and I have been included as one of its members since the very beginning (1984) to the present. As mentioned earlier, a "coven" is the basic unit of Witchcraft: a small and intimate group of people who usually meet for rituals once a month. If I had not been accepted to the "Women's Magic" class in 1984, or if the women taking the class had not liked each other well enough to form a coven, I would not have belonged to any coven, and my fieldwork would probably have taken a very different turn. It is unlikely that any already existing covens in Reclaiming would have included a stranger like me for a year or so, and certainly no group would have done it to help my research or provided a role for me as "participant observer".[30] In other words, without the coincidences that made me a member of this coven, eventually named

"Gossip", I would not have found a way into the inside of daily ritual work, nor to the intimacy of feminist women's (and men's) magical communities.[31]

I met, to begin with, a rather reserved attitude from Reclaiming people, probably because I was a foreigner, was educated in the tradition of Christian (European) theology, knew no funny jokes (in my broken English) but asked too many questions (also in my broken English). When I did not understand something that happened in the ritual and asked "why", some took this as a sign that I was not "ready" to be taught. This led to my being excluded from certain rituals and conversations. When I finally learned to pose questions by expressing an opinion myself, the atmosphere slowly changed. But altogether, it took a long time until I gained Reclaiming people's trust, in fact not until springtime in 1985. Then I had been in Gossip for half a year, participated in all ritual events accessible to me, and socialized as much as possible with my coven sisters and the Reclaiming teachers I knew by then, including Starhawk.

When finally accepted, reservations faded away. Upon my return in November 1988, one of the Reclaiming teachers, as a joke, gave me a button to wear stating, "I have been sent here to study you people", implying that I was an alien, from an advanced civilization in outer space, sent to study "strange" people the way anthropologists used to study "primitive" cultures. Thus, since my presence was the result of supernatural intervention, it was perfectly okay. After this I was very much accepted even on my own premises: as a student in theology and social anthropology doing a piece of work and as a critical feminist on a religious journey. Yet my reputation in Reclaiming to this day is that my magical talents are poor, whereas my intellectual appetite is greedy.

For most people this acceptance lasted, while a few got tired of my questions and of being around a person who was *also* a continuous observer. Some dealt with my observer role by deciding that I was "off work" when we had coffee: then they felt I was just "one of them". Others realized I was always "on duty", just as I was always also "myself", an opinionated and compassionate woman, feminist, mother and Norwegian scholar, having no trouble with any of my roles.[32]

To be able to position Reclaiming on the pagan scene, but also in order to be acquainted with ritual language and behaviour, I took part in a variety of ritual events, including classes, available in the area (in 1984–85, 1988–89 and 1990). I ritualized with other feminist pagan spirituality groups (Ariadne, UU Pagans, Z. Budapest as well as independent feminist circles), with nonfeminist pagans and Witches (NROOGD, Ancient Ways, Corytalia/Bloodrose, Fellowship of Isis, Church of All Worlds) and ceremonial lodges like the OTO, as well as with New Age shamans and their Native American inspired rituals. Through this broad participation I discovered that Reclaiming had many features in common with groups invoking very different traditions and that ritual structures and elements probably originated from a common, though to me, at the time, indefinable source.

To be able to understand Reclaiming people's rigorous social and political engagements outside their own community, I worked, once a week, as a volunteer at Martin Deporres soup kitchen in San Francisco in the fall of 1990. I also participated in three direct actions, one at Nevada Nuclear Test Site, the other at Lawrence Livermore Nuclear Laboratory in California, while the third one took place in the streets of San Francisco: illegal needle exchange with poor drug users in order to prevent the spreading of AIDS.

In addition to the regular fieldwork in 1989–90, I conducted qualitative interviews with Witches, of which a majority was taped. The course of an interview was to a large extent determined by the fixed set of questions, which is included as Appendix A. But, since I also used the interviews to establish contacts, in addition to the information I was seeking, I often departed from the set-up questionnaire. In 1984-85 I conducted formalized, taped interviews with four Reclaiming women and three men, including Starhawk. In 1989-90, the interviews were less formalized, but still taped and with almost the same set of questions as in 1985. In this period I interviewed 26 women and 17 men in Reclaiming, and 11 women and seven men outside Reclaiming. The interviews were mostly done in people's homes or in cafés, and lasted about 1.5–2 hours each.[33]

During these years, pagans from all traditions have been very cooperative, and only one person asked refused to be interviewed. Those interviewed often expressed satisfaction at being able to talk about the history of their religious path with me. Because of the confidentiality of the situation, some people also used the interviews as a setting for gossip, or to voice their concerns about people or occurrences they felt uncomfortable with. I was informed about concealed conflicts, personal "wars", and the "shadow" sides of the "good" people, the kind of things that may happen in human interaction when a large number of people are cross-related through many different activities and through very challenging personal relationships.[34]

"Reclaiming" is not a fake name, but a real name for a real community. As long as I wanted to use Starhawk's texts in combination with my research on Reclaiming people's practices, there was no point in trying to hide the identity of the actual community studied. The advantage of this approach is that the community is left with an academic text that gives them a place in the historical records rather than in the history of anonymous case studies. The community and its people are named and acknowledged for their work, and readers who are eager to gain knowledge specifically about Reclaiming, and not about *one* Witchcraft community concealed behind a fake name, can be content. On the other hand, I need to protect individual identities. I have tried to balance these concerns by using public Witch names, that is, names that people are already known by publicly, when concerned with historicity, and fake names and identities when analysing cases, or whenever I find it necessary for protective reasons.

Those Reclaiming Witches who have read a draft of this book have voiced no objections to my analysis. Some are very happy with how the book has turned out; some have made it clear that parts of the book were hard to read, although they "believe I am right"; some are content to see the founding history of Reclaiming documented, but repeatedly tell me, "your perspective is only one out of several possible"; one woman is worried that I have included a chapter on initiation. Even though Starhawk and many other Witches have written at length about initiation, she feels that I take away its power by exposing a possible experience. This is always a dilemma, and I can only hope that a potential initiate in Reclaiming will not read this chapter until the process is completed or, if she does, that she will know that her experience and the one described will be completely different. But as long as Witches and pagans themselves continue to publish initiation narratives, I do not regard it as my responsibility as a scholar to end this practice. I have, however, put one restriction on myself: nothing is revealed about the secret part of the initiation ritual that is not already published, even though some people have told me in detail about it (and I finally also experienced it myself).

The thematic development of the book will, from this point on, follow the course of a typical apprentice to feminist Witchcraft. As she gains knowledge and skills, and as she enters more and more deeply into the Reclaiming community of San Francisco, she is given more and more information and insight. The textual representation of this journey is organized in two parts. Part I, *Guardians of the World* sets the scene by describing who the people are, where and how they live, their community-building activities, the myth of origin that holds them together and their similarities and differences from normative western spirituality. Part II, *Priestesses of the Craft* presents ethnographic description and analysis of several different rituals, including the efforts of the (predominantly) female priestesshood of the Reclaiming Witches' Craft to create a new symbolic order based on a transfiguration of the sacred within the ordinary and thus balance and regenerate human dilemmas of difference, unity and separation.

The first chapter in Part I, *The Reclaiming community,* introduces the political and spiritual visions (and conflicts) of these political and spiritual "guardians of the world", including Reclaiming's history and structure in the period 1984-94 and its reorganization in 1997 to accommodate the fact that this particular Witchcraft tradition has rapidly spread all over the US, Canada and western Europe.

In chapter 2, *Wicca revival,* I describe and analyze Witches' myth about a paradise lost as represented in Starhawk's writings. The myth – which in particular was significant to the first generation Reclaiming Witches – celebrates a time when "Goddess was worshipped and women respected" and thus claims to hold a cultural key to future bliss: a reawakening of the goddess is said to have the power to instigate a new non-patriarchal society – a vision highly criticized by historians and sociologists.

In chapter 3, *Utopian and generic Witches*, I illustrate ideological diversity among Reclaiming Witches and contextualize their joint Witchcraft tradition within a millenarian lineage, stretching back to the heretical Christian sects of medieval Europe. I discuss continuity and discontinuity in regard to western spiritual traditions and Reclaiming people's perception of Witchcraft as a "coming home" from spiritual exile. To be able to report an updated and personal response to heritage, I asked a handful of Witches to join me for Catholic Mass and here recount their subsequent comments. I also present a case in which a person is said to have found both "herself" and "home" through a ritualized performance called "processing".

In chapter 4, *Holy hermeneutics,* I analyze the ethno-hermeneutics of feminist Witches, that is, their notions of experience, truth, reality, sign, religion and magic ("sacred possession"). In my analysis I apply Starhawk's implicitly spatial distinction between the horizontal magic of everyday life and the vertical magic of ritual.

The first chapter in Part II, chapter 5: *Elements of magic,* introduces and discusses ritual theory and defines theoretical tools. By describing the proceedings of an introductory class in the Reclaiming tradition, I suggest how a person learns to ritualize and to interpret herself as a sacred being, that is, as a manifestation of the Goddess.

In chapter 6, *The Spiral Dance ritual,* I describe, in an emotionally marked narrative, the Witches' Samhain ritual (at Halloween) and the mythical and magical journeys of gendered bodily selves toward regeneration and renewal "conjured" by this ritual process.

In chapter 7, *Women's mysteries,* I describe women's community within the larger Reclaiming community as expressed in coven work, healing rituals and rites of passages, where the mysteries of women's bodies are celebrated as mirror images of the divine. I describe women's perceptions of themselves as gendered subjects of body and spirit and their efforts to gain "the power of womanhood", which also includes the painstaking labour – at least for the baby-boom generation – to balance the dilemmas of being woman and being man, of being joint and being separate.

In chapter 8, *Initiation,* I analyze in detail Catherine's initiation process, which covered a period of four years. The ritual offers a solution to the existential split between joint and separate through "rebirth", "regeneration", "personal growth" and "new knowledge".

In the concluding chapter, *Reclaiming Witchcraft and theology,* I recapitulate findings, outline some ways in which Reclaiming Witchcraft may contribute to and challenge the agenda of contemporary (feminist) theology and suggest further research.

A focused theological *and* ethnographic study of a single pagan community has not, to my knowledge, been conducted before. I hope that the reader will experience in my descriptions a meeting with real people and that these descriptive parts of the ethnography can suffice as an empirical foundation for further analysis, including to scholars other than myself.

Notes

1 Starhawk "Declaration of the Four Sacred Things", *Reclaiming Newsletter*, 38/1990.
2 When Gerald Gardner published the textual midwife of modern Witchcraft, *Witchcraft Today* in 1954, Margarat Murray wrote the preface. Here she supported Gardner's claims, legitimating his enterprise (cf. Gardner 1954:16).
3 Aleister Crowley's ideas and writings were not only a source to early Gardnerian Wicca but also a major influence on Anton LaVey's construction of Satanism (LaVey 1969). This common literary source, which still can be recognized in some symbols and ritual elements, is one of the reasons Witchcraft has been confused with Satanism. In Doreen Valiente's transformation of the Gardnerian tradition, a lot of Crowley-inspired occult ideology and high-flown terminology has been stripped away.
4 Trevor-Roper criticized the empirical status Murray gave to testimonies given under torture as scientifically improper (1970:121–46). Norman Cohn argued that the witch never existed, except as a sole product of the imagination. This image, then, was used strategically and psychologically by the Inquisition in its persecution of heretics (1975:104–25).
5 I present Linda Woodhead's viewpoints based on my own careful notetaking from listening to her: she read a paper on the subject in April 1996 at the Ambleside international conference on "Nature Religion Today".
6 The first "offshoot" came with Alex and Maxime Sanders. Although Alex supposedly was never accepted into a real Gardnerian coven, he nevertheless taught Witchcraft and initiated hundreds of people (Farrar 1971). Those Witches whose lineage derives from this couple are called Alexandrian Witches.
7 The notion "androcentric" (which is less comprehensive than "patriarchal") has in particular been developed by Kari Børresen, professor in Feminist Theology at the University of Oslo (Børresen 1995).
8 Since the mid-1990s, some of the more influential non-Gardnerian practitioners of the Witches' Craft in the US (such as Reclaiming's M. Macha NightMare) have very consciously decided to call themselves "Witches" (not Wiccans) and refer to their religion as "Witchcraft" (not Wicca). They have also (but without much success) tried to educate their other Witch friends about the correctness of this choice. To their dismay, Witches in the US have all come to be called Wiccans and a child in public school who is raised by Reclaiming parents will probably write "Wicca" as the family religion.
9 Pagan scholars themselves (e.g. Jenny Gibbons 1998) have also criticized simplified black and white narrative about the witch craze.
10 Who were the witches? The popular feminist image of the witch as a woman of independent power (an heretical thinker, a courageous lesbian, a benevolent healer or a skilled midwife) killed by evil men, was established in 1968 by a New York organization called WITCH: Women's International Conspiracy from Hell. In their manifesto they stated that Witchcraft had been the religion of all Europeans before Christianity, and thereafter of the peasants and independent women. The witch craze therefore represented the destruction of an alternative culture and, in reality, a war against feminism (Adler 1979:174). How many were persecuted? Mary Daly picked the number "9 million" from the old suffragist Mathilda Joselyn Gage and argued that it was a reasonable estimate (Daly 1981:183). According to historians, the number may be as low as 15,000 in all of Europe and America combined (Gibbons 1998).
11 This view is not derived from Gardner, but rather from the archaeologist Marija Gimbutas, who elaborated on this theory in her later works. She has been severely attacked by her colleagues for letting herself be "seduced" by a "false" feminist historiography (in which goddess-worshipping cultures are believed to have sparked

all civilization), and thereafter superimposing it on her own findings in Balkan Europe (cf. Renfrew 1992; Hayden 1998).

12 I will follow this convention and capitalize Witch and Witchcraft. The word "goddess" will be capitalized when I quote the Witches or refer to *the* Goddess as a proper name, while "pagan" will not be capitalized. It should be noted that in Witches' discourse G/goddess sometimes is used to apply to a number of goddesses, at other times a female version of *the* deity (like the Jewish and Christian God), at other times it is used almost adjectivally.

13 When I write "pagan", this classification includes the "Witch", but not the other way around. To become a Witch is in most Craft traditions like becoming a Druid: it usually involves initiation (self-initiation or traditional) and is often regarded as a more esoteric and committed act than just becoming a pagan. According to Gardnerian definitions, the name designates a priesthood, or a pagan population that exclusively contains priests and priestesses. It is, however, not used so strictly in Reclaiming since anybody can call herself a "Witch" if she so desires, regardless of whether she is an initiate or not.

14 Selena Fox and the Circle Sanctuary Community in Wisconsin publish *Circle Guide to Pagan Groups*. The guide is compiled from listings submitted by groups who choose to be known and accessible, besides meeting certain theological and ethical requirements set by Circle.

15 Until Starhawk's book became popular, the most widely read introduction to Witchcraft was *What Witches Do* by Stewart Farrar (1971). He was trained by Alex and Maxime Sanders, but the "Book of Shadows" on which the book is based, is of Gardnerian origin.

16 Her next book, *Dreaming the Dark. Magic, Sex and Politics* (1982a), had at the same time sold 100,000 copies, while the figures for her third book *Truth or Dare. Encounters with Power, Authority and Mystery* (1987) showed 53,000 copies sold.

17 From 1982 to 1990, Starhawk was a permanent staff member at the Dominican Holy Names College in Oakland in the Bay Area. In 1988 the Vatican silenced the college principal, Dr Matthew Fox, for a whole year for his refusal to discharge Starhawk from the staff. Two years later Fox was, for the same reasons, dismissed from his position. This received a lot of publicity in the US and made headlines in the major newspapers. Indirectly, it gave Starhawk and her branch of Witchcraft "good" publicity.

18 Cf. also Sarah Pike 1996:353, 355.

19 The suggested methodological movement text–theory–text does not imply that I dismiss the insights of the "hermeneutical circle": I do not believe that I am "without theory" when confronting a new text or a new ethnographic field. But, I do *not* believe that our cultural, semiotic predispositions are total, or that we can only learn what we already know. For further discussions on this topic, see Iris Marion Young (1997).

20 Like Reclaiming women, they regard the Jewish and Christian religions as intrinsically oppressive, to women and to men, and say they joined Reclaiming because this feminist community offers freedom from stereotyped role models. Although the personal and individual interpretations of Witchcraft among Reclaiming men are interesting, and add to the complexity of the tradition, this is not the focus of the book.

21 The notion "heterosexual matrix" is taken from Judith Butler (1990).

22 "Envelope" is a concept (or metaphor) developed by the French philosopher Luce Irigaray to signify the basic material structures that determine and support human life.

23 The notions "merger with the divine" or "merger with nature" as well as "transfiguration of the ordinary" were introduced to the study of contemporary Witchcraft by Dennis D. Carpenter in his PhD thesis from 1994. He and I may use these

notions slightly differently, especially when I use them to enter into dialogue with Caroline Walker Bynum's study of medieval women mystics. Nevertheless, I find them useful as designators of what is characteristic in Witches' spirituality.

24 Theologians like Uta Ranke–Heinemann support the Witches' concerns. She maintains that the *ideal* for the *pious life* of holy men in contemporary Catholicism has not really changed since medieval times: pious men are not encouraged to "mature and grow up", neither intellectually nor emotionally, but to remain "as children", both cognitively (by accepting "offending" dogma and Papal decrees) and sexually (by vowing to celibacy); cf. Ranke-Heinemann (1990, 1994). The lack of an initiation theme from immature adolescence to mature adulthood in the Christian rite of passage (i.e., baptism) is also the focus of the Rev. William O. Roberts Jr's work (1982) and has inspired him to construct a new initiation rite for Christian youth.

25 Grimes names the study of ritual "ritology", its scope reaching from "ritualization among animals through ordinary interaction ritual to highly differentiated religious liturgy" (Grimes 1990:9).

26 My choice of method is to a certain extent informed by McCarthy Brown's influential work (1991). Favret-Saada (1980) also ended as her own informant when studying malignant witchcraft in contemporary rural France. But this happened against her own will, out of fear of the spells people presumably made against each other. She became her own informant to the extent that she observed her own fear and realized that without her own emotional reactions she would not have discovered this magical, but hidden, discourse.

27 During Reclaiming rituals, tape-recording is not comme il faut. Continuous note taking is impolite and would also spoil the subjective experience of ritual. In later reconstructions, the informants are seldom of any help. My questions about ritual proceedings and meanings are experienced as intruding on their own personal experience in ritual, desacralizing it, and the answers are mostly, "I don't remember very well."

28 This theological "minimum" is as follows: I can relate to Reclaiming Witches' efforts to establish female symbolism to represent the face of God/ess, and to their dedication to create new patterns for ritualizing in western culture, although I do not necessarily agree with all its contents. I cannot relate to their non-christo-logical consensus as a final goal in theology, and I am deeply critical of their self-identification as "Witches", including their uncritical embrace of an occult lineage and its very problematic and mythological historiography. But I am not morally offended by how they misread the historical past or misrepresent Judaism and Christianity, or other institutions in western civilization. I believe that the invocation of simple, critical and imaginative approaches to social (and religious) reality by so-called ordinary people (nonexperts) has always contributed to, and been a necessary part of, ongoing cultural changes in the western hemisphere: they hold the key to powerful, rebellious visions and actions.

29 I started to change my mind after having been invited to and undergone a 10-day "Vision Quest" in the Inyo Desert in California in April 1989. This meditative quest was built on a model imitating the Lakota tradition, with four days in solitude on a mountaintop, fasting from food and shelter. For further reflections on this experience, which was meant to clarify a personal calling and induce growth in the participants (which it probably also did), see Salomonsen 1991 and 1999.

30 Such an act would have been regarded as spiritual "prostitution". As I have pointed out several times, there is no room for outsiders or observers in Reclaiming's circles. All circles and covens are built on mutual trust and equal commitment. Either you are in for personal (and not strategic) reasons, or you are not there at all.

31 For obvious reasons, the women in Gossip have become some of my best informants (as well as friends) and have guided my understanding and knowledge of Reclaiming in a profound way.

32 In addition to participation in Reclaiming-related social activities, classes, rituals, Witchcamps, direct actions etc., my activities also included (but were not limited to) Caradoc ap Codor's apprenticeship programme in the Faery tradition *Corytalia* (once a week from October 1984 to August 1985), Z. Budapest's six-week class *The Path of the Grey She Wolf*, one *Women's Music Festival* in Michigan, two women's solstice camps in the Nevada mountains called *Her Voice–Our Voices,* one *California Men's Gathering* in Santa Cruz, two *Ancient Ways* festivals in Harbin Hot Springs and, finally, several rituals arranged by *Church of All Worlds,* including the wedding rite for Anodea and Richard, as well as for Morning Glory, Otter and Diane, and the coming of age ritual for LeSarah. I went on a 10-day *Vision Quest* led by Sedonia Cahill, and participated in ceremonial circles led by the *Starmaiden Circle,* the *Blue Water Lodge,* and the *Council of Earth Lodges* in northern California.

33 The study material about Reclaiming community includes:
  • about 1200 pages handwritten fieldnotes (from 1984–85, 1988–89, 1990, 1994);
  • transcriptions of 63 (of the total of 68) taped interviews (the guiding question-naire is included as Appendices A and B);
  • *Reclaiming Newsletter,* 1980–94 (56 volumes);
  • Ritual manuals, including the Spiral Dance, for 1988 and 1989
  • Starhawk's books and articles from the period 1979–1993 (cf. bibliography).

34 Even though it is important in this study to also emphasize social tensions and discrepancies in Reclaiming, I have not exposed any conflicts confided to me, unless they were already public themes in the community. This has been very disappointing to some of my informants, who themselves have experienced painful conflicts. They find my ethnography too idealizing.

Part I

Guardians of the world

1 The Reclaiming community

A feminist, social construction

The public appearance of ritualizing women, men and children in urban areas in the western world is no longer unusual. For example, an occasional Sunday walker in Lincoln Park in San Francisco, California, may one day have observed the following: thirteen women of many ages, all dressed up in red party clothes, are gathered for the ritual celebration of a teenage girl's menstruation. As it happens, these women belong to the Reclaiming Witchcraft community. The girl, Sonia, has just had her first period. She is excited and nervous and keeps her mother, grandmother and friend Nicole close at hand. Nicole, who is now eighteen years old, had a similar celebration when she started menstruating five years ago.

The ritual begins as the women form a circle by holding hands, declaring the space to be sacred and "between the worlds". Starhawk holds a bottle of water in her left hand. She has gathered the water from different lakes, rivers and oceans around the world during her travels teaching the animist, egalitarian worldview of feminist Witchcraft: that divinity is a congenital (personal) power, birthing and animating all of life, and that the earth is "her" sacred "body". Now she anoints Sonia by lightly touching her forehead, breasts, belly and genitals, while declaring, "*Remember, nobody can give you power. You already have the power within.*"[1]

Then a cord is tied around Sonia's right and her mother's left wrist. Hera, Nicole's mother, says to Sonia,

> When you were born, you came to the world tied to your mother's body. As the umbilical cord had to be cut at that time for you to live, so the cord between the two of you has to be cut now. But the bond between you shall never be cut, because that is a bond by heart.

Mother and daughter are instructed to run tied together in the park for as long as they can. We watch them. Anna, the mother, does her best, but after a while she cries out that she cannot keep up with her daughter's speed. They are asked to come back to the circle. In the meantime, Hera has shown Sonia's grandmother how to cut the cord with a black-handled ritual knife called athame. When mother and daughter return, the grandmother cuts the cord between them. Later that day the knife is given to Sonia as a gift.

*   *   *

This passage from a ritual celebration for a young pagan woman, about to enter the first phase of adult womanhood, marks the beginning of a long ritual process that was completed in the evening with a large gender-mixed community ritual and party (described in full in chapter 7). It also marks the beginning of this chapter, which is an introduction to the Reclaiming community and to the people who have dedicated themselves to the path and rituals of "the Goddess".

The name, "Reclaiming", presently refers to a tradition of Witchcraft, a community of people and a religious organization. The Reclaiming *tradition* is a specific feminist branch of contemporary American pagan Witchcraft, while the Reclaiming *community* refers both to the local Witchcraft community in the San Francisco Bay Area (SF) of California and to the people, primarily in North America and western Europe, who identify with the Reclaiming tradition of Witchcraft. In fact, the tradition arose from a working collective within the SF community, naming itself the *Reclaiming Collective* in 1980. Thus, for almost 20 years, "Reclaiming" was the name of a small, founding community of approximately 20 people (the Collective), of a larger community of at least 130 Witches and pagans (primarily in SF) and, finally, of a distinct spiritual tradition, practised by thousands of people far beyond SF. In 1997, however, came a major shift: the SF Reclaiming Collective of elders[2] dissolved itself to give way to a new generation and a new social structure that could meet the needs of an emergent Reclaiming *movement* – not only spreading rapidly in the US, but also in Canada and western Europe (Germany, England, France and Spain) through so-called Witchcamps.

The SF Reclaiming Collective/community was organized differently before and after 1997, when "the Collective" was replaced with a local "Wheel" and a transnational "Spokes Council". Yet, the continuity in regard to basic ideology and structuring principles is obvious: no overall central authority, no implementation of dogmas or required beliefs, no formal hierarchy of priests and priestesses, no formal membership, no "church" that can be joined and no congregational building for worship and community gatherings. Reclaiming's social structure was and is founded on working "cells", which operate on a voluntary, nonhierarchical and independent basis, with a majority of active women. A small cell or circle may break down to an even smaller "circle within a circle" or expand to a large one when needed, for example, when performing rituals. People become involved in the organization known as Reclaiming by becoming involved in the work and activities of the various cells and circles.[3] For that reason, Reclaiming is not a regular church, but rather a network of like-minded people cross-related – socially, ideologically and emotionally – through common activities for common goals in a still evolving and living religious tradition.

The social structure particular to Reclaiming takes its point of departure from a radical analysis of power, while attempting to create a just alternative by combining an "anarchist political agenda" of equality, diversity and local autonomy with a "feminist liberation agenda" of empowering women, both in public and domestic spheres. In fact, Reclaiming as a movement may be regarded as a conscious effort to break away from the hegemonic sociological worldview that sexual asymmetry is trans-historical and universal and that a sexed dichotomy between public and domestic domains is inevitable as long as women continue to give birth and raise children.[4] Women in Reclaiming are instead encouraged to reclaim their authority/power within both domains: to re-form the structures of domestic life (division of labour, parenting, the marriage contract) and celebrate their reproductive capacities as life affirming and sacred; and to value feminist Witchcraft as a new public and social institution with the potential to change American society and instigate a new, nonpatriarchal culture.

The people who constituted this visionary, networking community in the period covered in this book (1984–94) primarily lived in the Mission District in the southeast area of SF. Most of their activities, such as rituals, actions, classes and meetings, also took place in, or close to, this area. Mission is the oldest neighborhood in SF. The city was founded here in 1776 as a Catholic mission to convert and "civilize" the Costanoan Indians. In the 1980s and early 1990s this area was considered one of the poorest working-class neighbourhoods in the city, with a predominance of Mexican American and African American citizens.[5] Street people, drug addicts, prostitutes and unemployed youths and older men marked the area. Crime rates were high, and the newspapers reported daily about robbery, assault, fighting and shooting. After dark it was unsafe for women to walk the streets alone.

But the Mission was also known to be picturesque, with old Victorian houses and a swarm of specialized shops, grocery stores, cafés, restaurants, bars, colourful murals and ethnic community centres. And because of low rents, the area also attracted a considerable number of white, middle-class "bohemians" such as artists, students and political activists. Street theatre, alternative bookstores, a Women's Building and radical Christian parishes were therefore integrated into parts of this neighbourhood's atmosphere, as were the possibilities for visiting a Catholic candle store (selling candles, incense, oils, crystal balls, amulets and figures of the Saints), a Voodoo supply store and the area's first Goddess-shop on the very same block.

The experimental lifestyles of the Mission bohemians and of those living in the adjacent vicinities of Eureka and Noe Valley, Bernal Heights and Potrero Hill, had some similarities to the earlier counter-culture in what is now the more fashionable Haight-Ashbury neighborhood northwest in the city, where the hippie movement reached one of its heights in the summer of 1967. Yet, two striking differences were that the Mission alternative scene was predominantly anti-drug and that its intentional communities were often committed to idealistic projects addressing bilingual, multicultural and working-class people. Also, while a majority of SF's gay men preferred to live in the Castro neighborhood, not far from Haight-Ashbury, the less wealthy lesbian women had at the time a large community in the Mission.[6] During the last decade, however, this typical Mission atmosphere is about to change.

Increasing commercial interests and upper middle-class people who buy old houses for renovation and profit have created a commercial culture that slowly transforms Mission into a more trendy and white neighborhood, forcing poor people of colour to leave.

Reclaiming represents one of the intentional communities in the Mission resisting these tendencies and which can still be recognized by some of the social (and moral) features that applied to the bohemian culture in general at the turn of the century. One basic feature characteristic is the value attributed to "individual diversity". Although Reclaiming is primarily a white, middle-class and well-educated community, it is composed of people from many different walks of life. It had room for women, men and children; gays, lesbians, bisexuals and heterosexuals; vegetarians, meat-lovers, drinkers and total abstainers; those of a Jewish heritage as well as former Catholics, Protestants and Buddhists. It includes people who are committed to being sexually monogamous and those who live with multiple relationships, people who shared income in a large collective household and those who choose to live as a traditional nuclear family. Some are deeply involved with politics, while others are primarily interested in Witchcraft as a spiritual practice. Some are mainly pagan feminists and perceive of the Witches' Craft as a simple nature and/or goddess religion, while others regard Witchcraft as a magical and secretive initiatory path. Some identify clearly as belonging to the Reclaiming community; others are more reserved and say they are only "friends" of Reclaiming. A majority participates in other communities as well, such as in the anarchist or direct action communities, in the twelve-step or performing arts communities, in the gay or lesbian communities, or in other pagan or non pagan spiritual traditions (many Jewish Witches do, for example, celebrate the Jewish holidays with non-Reclaiming friends and family).

I shall give a detailed description of how this community was founded and how its social order could be experienced in the early 1990s. A major goal is to provide the reader with a general idea of the social context for Reclaiming Witchcraft and the themes discussed in this book (such as human growth, ritualizing, and a female symbolic order). In addition to presenting Reclaiming's history, people and structuring principles, I will also discuss some of its struggles not to become esoteric, but to live up to its own social visions of practising freedom of thought and of welcoming all those differences of life situation, background and ability that increase human diversity.

The portrait given of work cells, classes, rituals, social dynamics and the Reclaiming way of thinking is still valid for today's community. The account of the Reclaiming Collective, including its structure and work tasks, applies less today since the Collective was dissolved in 1997. The different organization of Reclaiming in the SF Bay Area, including the new foundational "Principles of Unity" and the local SF "Wheel", must therefore be briefly presented as well. Yet the focus of this chapter is Reclaiming before this shift from local SF community to transnational movement took place. This is due to the fact that my data from the field cover the period prior to 1997 and were gathered with the intention of writing an in-depth study of one singular community, not of presenting a broad survey of a movement. Additionally, the historical period up to 1997, and the community it fostered, has been foundational to the development of Reclaiming Witchcraft and, therefore, essential to understanding both the ways in which it differs from other pagan and feminist spiritualities and why the unity of pagan spirituality and feminist, anarchist politics has become such a predominant feature of what is presently associated with the Reclaiming tradition.

The history of the Reclaiming Collective, 1979–1997

Reclaiming started in 1979 as a teaching collective for a "school" in Witchcraft. One evening in the early summer, Starhawk, at the time 29 years old, and her friend Diane Baker were sitting in the backyard of Starhawk's house in the Haight-Ashbury district in SF, talking about Diane's decision to move to New York. Diane was concerned that she did not know any Witches on the East Coast and wanted some tools with which to teach the Craft so that, eventually, she would be able to establish a coven, which is a small group of Witches celebrating lunar rituals and personal rites of passages together. They decided that to co-teach a class in SF in the fall would be the right thing to do and a way for Diane to acquire teaching skills. Also, Starhawk's book, *The Spiral Dance,* was due to be published later that year by Harper & Row, and to establish a "school" was an additional way for Starhawk to spread the "good news" about the "rebirth of the ancient religion of the Great Goddess".

Prior to that time, Starhawk had been teaching Witchcraft classes through the open universities and occult bookstores, and since 1976 had managed to mother three covens: Compost, Honeysuckle and Raving. Compost was a mixed coven, while the other two were women-only circles (Diane was Starhawk's coven sister from Raving). But, according to her own story, which conforms to an average Witch's conversion narrative, Starhawk (then Miriam Simos) "experienced" the Witches' goddess already in the summer of 1968. That summer, when she was only seventeen, she apparently lived so closely attuned to nature that she "began to feel connected to the world in a new way, to see everything as alive, erotic, engaged in a constant dance of mutual pleasuring, and myself as a special part of it all" (1989a:2). But she did not yet have a language to name her experience or a notion of a female deity.

Language came when she started college at UCLA in southern California and a group of Witches came to her sorority house to read them the so-called "Charge of the Goddess", written in the 1950s by Doreen Valiente. Starhawk's feeling was not that of hearing something new, but of finally being given names and interpretive frameworks for experiences she had already had. In addition she felt empowered by the concept of a religion that worshipped a goddess. By that time, Starhawk was already an active feminist and she instantly felt "a natural connection between a movement to empower women and a spiritual tradition based on the Goddess" (1989a:3).

She searched out Zuzanna Budapest in Los Angeles and started participating in the public rituals she offered. Budapest was at the time a lesbian
separatist who taught Witchcraft to feminist-lesbian-separatists as a pure
women's religion. She called herself a *hereditary* Witch because she claimed to
have inherited secret knowledge, magical spells and rituals from her mother
and grandmother in Hungary, practices which presumably go back to pre-
Christian pagan Europe. She identified herself as a priestess of the Roman
goddess Diana, and her Witchcraft was therefore called *Dianic*. [7]

Even though Starhawk was a feminist, she was neither a lesbian nor a
separatist. She therefore did not really fit in with Budapest's Dianic Witches.
The summer she turned 23, she decided to take off with her bicycle and travel
in the US for a year. This year turned out to be a sort of a "vision quest": she
was challenged by people and the natural world and learned to trust her
intuition and let it be her guide. As part of her "initiation" she claims to have
had a series of powerful dreams in which she met the Goddess, and was given
the names "Star" and "Hawk". To mark this point of "no return" and to name
her new being, she decided to change her Jewish birth-name, Miriam Simos,
to Starhawk – mainly for the purpose of teaching Witchcraft. Teaching and
writing now became her vocation. It also became her method to deepen her
knowledge of the "path of the Goddess" and meet with soul mates.

In 1975, Starhawk decided to move to Berkeley (near SF). At the time,
Berkeley and the Bay Area already had a small networking community of
nonfeminist Witches and pagans, consisting of groups such as *Corytalia (Faery)*,
Church of All Worlds, The Fellowship of the Spiral Path and the *New Reformed
Orthodox Order of the Golden Dawn (NROOGD)*, as well as traditions imported
from Britain, like the *Gardnerians* and *Alexandrians*. Although magical communities are characterized by their overlapping membership structure, a
majority of the Berkeley Witches did at the time belong to the NROOGD.
This group did not claim to have inherited any tradition but openly admitted
to having made it all up from reading (amongst others, Gerald Gardner) and
from experimenting with ritual.[8] In 1976, this networking community joined
together with some solitary Witches to form an umbrella organization, the
Covenant of the Goddess (COG), which soon incorporated as a legally recognized church.[9]

After Starhawk had taught Witchcraft her own style in Berkeley and SF for
a year, she finally decided to approach a well-known hereditary male Witch in
the area: Victor Anderson. Since the late 1960s he had offered initiations into
Faery Witchcraft, a tradition that claims heritage from African Shamanism,
Celtic paganism and Hawaiian Kahuna Magic. He claimed that this mix was
not his own brew but partly passed on to him by his grandmother in Virginia
as an oral, secret tradition, partly revealed when he was initiated into the
Harper coven in Ashland, Oregon, in 1932 (cf. Kelly 1991:21). According to
Starhawk, she wanted to be trained by him and initiated into this supposedly
hereditary, fixed tradition to acquire a deeper understanding of Witchcraft, to
develop her own curriculum when teaching, and to be acknowledged as a

priestess of the Craft within the larger pagan community. She was indeed accepted and in 1976 elected first officer and public spokesperson for COG.

But Starhawk's feminist, nonseparatist interpretation of Witchcraft, which became more and more important to her, needed a different audience from COG people to prosper and take form. In 1977, she even broke with her first coven Compost, of which she was a high priestess and founder, because it included women and men who did not share her growing political concerns. She moved to SF and decided to concentrate her work exclusively on women, at least for a period. The first result of this priority was Raving, a coven for women only. It had no position for a high priestess and put greater emphasis upon personal and inner experience (in contrast to inherited tradition) as religious norm and authority than was common in more traditional Witchcraft covens at the time.

So, when Starhawk discussed co-teaching with Diane Baker, she had both been trained in the Faery tradition, been initiated a "Witch and Priestess of the Goddess" and had taught Witchcraft (disguised as feminist spirituality) on her own for three years. This, she felt, was a foundation on which she both could build a "school" (Reclaiming) and publish a "curriculum" (*The Spiral Dance*).

Starhawk and Diane called their first class "The Elements of Magic". It was a six-week introductory series directed toward women. Classes were taught within sacred space and focused on different aspects of magic associated with one of the elements air, fire, water and earth. In addition, students learned about goddess spirituality, the ethical foundation for the practice of magic, and how to create their own rituals. The class was a success, and the students pleaded for more. With help from members of their coven Raving (Kevin and Lauren), Starhawk and Diane created a second series of "Elements" as well as a more advanced class called "The Iron Pentacle". Its main focus was meditations on the five-pointed star (the points being sex, self, passion, pride and power) and discoveries of the healing powers of the human body through breathing exercises, visualization techniques and trance work. Again, success generated another class called "The Rites of Passage". This third class taught the students about the structure and symbolism of rites of passage cross-culturally, and how myths, fairytales and personal stories could be incorporated into pagan celebrations of birth, puberty, marriage and aging, and, not least, to make religious initiation happen. The class ended with the students initiating themselves as "Witches" and starting their own coven, the Holy Terrors, followed soon thereafter by Wind Hags.

From there, more classes were formed, more covens arose, more people began teaching, and more people kept gathering for solar rituals to celebrate the Witches high holidays in a so-called Reclaiming-style. Starhawk describes their style of ritual with the acronym EIEIO: Ecstatic, Improvisational, Ensemble (many priest/esses take different roles at rituals), Inspired, Organic.[10] The first public ritual arranged by Starhawk and her friends was the Spiral Dance. Starhawk wrote the ritual script herself to celebrate and promote her first book (with the same title). It took place at Samhain (Halloween) in November 1979 and has, since then, become a permanent institution. The ritual itself (described in chapter 6) is regarded as Reclaiming's annual gift to the larger pagan community.

Since 1979, public rituals and the three core classes mentioned above have been continually offered by the Reclaiming Collective, so naming itself in 1980. In fact, when Raving made the transition from coven to working collective aimed at teaching and ritual facilitation, it needed a new name. The name "Reclaiming" was picked because Starhawk, Diane, Lauren and Kevin were convinced that contemporary Witchcraft was the claiming back of an ancient goddess religion, although reinterpreted through the lenses of feminism. In alignment with this ideological stance, they decided to make decisions through a consensus process model, to always have two teachers in every class, and to run all classes in private homes – mainly to counteract people's urge to make an exclusive authority of *the* teacher and to keep a low monetary profile. They also made a policy to teach within the structure of ritual so that the class itself could become an experience of how a coven (ideally a community of equals) might function. The ritual form in Witchcraft is the circle. People sit, stand, lie down or hold hands, always in a circle. There are no chairs, tables or pulpit, only an open floor with altars set up around the walls. By choosing this structure also for teaching, the women hoped to increase the chances that people would form covens when the classes ended. These principles are still guidelines for most classes offered by Reclaiming, even after 1997.

To announce their classes and public rituals, the four women decided to put out a small bulletin, the *Reclaiming Newsletter*. This is their mission statement and self-presentation as printed in the first issue in 1980:

> RECLAIMING – a centre for feminist spirituality and counseling.
> RECLAIMING means:
> We reclaim the Goddess: the immanent life force, the connecting pattern to all being.
> We reclaim the creative and healing power of women.
> We reclaim the God/ess: the source for nurturing, feeling, healing ways of being male.
> We reclaim our visions, our personal myths, our heritage and lost histories.
> We reclaim our magic: the "art of changing consciousness at will", the art of training intuition and awareness in order to shape reality.
> We reclaim our personal power, and transform blocked energies into freedom, intimacy and strength to change.
> We reclaim our culture through art, poetry, performance, music, dance, writing and ritual.
> We reclaim political and social power to counter the destructive and oppressive forces in our society.
> We reclaim the human community of all races and classes, and the

interconnected community of plants, elements, animals, energy and resources . . .
RECLAIMING is a collective of four women who combine spiritual and political visions . . . We use the word "Witch" as an affirmation of women's power to shape reality.

Early in 1981, the Collective expanded by taking in new members from the two covens it had fostered: Holy Terrors and Wind Hags. These were Rose, Cerridwen, Sofia, Bonnie Bridged, Bone Blossom and Thyme. At this point, the Reclaiming Collective numbered ten women. The notion of a community separate from the Collective was not yet born: Starhawk's circle of goddess-worshipping friends who were looking for a new pagan community was still fairly small.

This changed during the fall of 1981, which in many ways became a turning point for Reclaiming: Starhawk and Rose (now coven sisters in Wind Hags), participated in a large nonviolent civil disobedience demonstration at Diablo Canyon in California to stop the opening of a nuclear power plant. Together with several thousand other American leftists and alternativists, they were arrested. It was the first time they did ritual and magic in a politicized field and the first time they met the anarchist community in SF, which also demonstrated at Diablo Canyon (cf. also chapter 3). From that point on, Reclaiming's feminism was extended to include anarchism and direct political action, and the first men were accepted into the Collective: Feather, David Kubrin, and Raven.

After weeks and months of discussion, the Collective that constituted itself after the Diablo Canyon action wrote an updated mission statement about their visions for Reclaiming. Since 1982, this statement has appeared in each issue of the *Reclaiming Newsletter*:

Reclaiming is a collective of (San Francisco Bay Area) women and men working to unite spirit and politics. Our vision is rooted in the religion and magic of the Goddess – the immanent Life Force. We see our work as teaching and making magic – the art of empowering ourselves and each other. In our classes, workshops, public rituals and individual counseling, we train our voices, bodies, energy, intuition and minds. We use the skills we learn to deepen our strength, both as individuals and as community, to voice our concerns about the world in which we live and bring to birth a vision of a new culture.[11]

The unexpected alliances formed at Diablo Canyon opened a new epoch for Reclaiming: large numbers of SF anarchists and political activists, with no former experience with Witchcraft or paganism, started to take Reclaiming classes. Some worked their way into the Reclaiming Collective; others were satisfied to belong to a growing Reclaiming community. By 1990, the Collective counted 19 people, and most new members had been recruited from this new coalition between paganism and political activism. In fact, only Starhawk, Rose, Bone and Macha represented the times before the Diablo Canyon action, meaning that Diane, Kevin and Lauren were gone, as were Cerridwen, Sofia, Thyme and Bonnie.

The result was a working collective consisting of two paired generations: older feminists (women) and younger anarchists (both women and men), ranging between 57 and 22 years of age. While the older women represented experience and knowledge, also about the larger pagan community, the younger anarchists represented new ideas and new networks. To them, Reclaiming was *the* representative of Witchcraft, and they had a rather vague idea of actually belonging to a large, new religious movement.

As many as 52 people were members of the Reclaiming Collective for long or short periods of time between 1980 and 1997 (when it dissolved). They composed an autonomous, self-recruiting body of people who never represented a larger assembly, at least not formally. Membership in the Collective was an organic process. New people were not voted in, but suggested by mentors and invited to join. The primary criteria for being accepted were commitment to and experience in the ongoing work cells, the need for more people in the Collective and, most importantly, everybody's like and trust of the prospective member. A person who only wanted a place to discuss Witchcraft and politics, or to socialize and find community, was not welcome, for the Collective met primarily to do business (four times a year): to make decisions about teaching policy, public rituals, money matters and the newsletter's editorial profile. But once inside, membership was unlimited by time and many long-lasting social friendships and personal relationships were formed.

That a modern "mystery school" came to be headed by such a large, multigenerational, multigendered and mutable group of people, who also attempted to be equally influential in terms of decision making, was and is unique to Reclaiming. Common practice in magical communities is to have only one teacher, or two if they are a (married) couple. Everybody else is put in various positions of "the adept", admitted to inner circles exclusively by the teacher-guru, either to receive secret knowledge or move up the ladder of initiation. This more or less authoritarian style is also the case with many other Witchcraft traditions, be it a Californian Dianic or a British Gardnerian coven.

Yet this is not to say that decisions in Reclaiming were always reached without conflicts or that a covert hierarchy between insiders and outsiders did not exist. Conflicts surely existed and, as could be expected, they often centreed on the seniority of the elders versus the inexperience of younger members. But people have left the Collective for other reasons as well. Some have wanted to charge more money for teaching classes and decided to turn toward New Age and Shamanic traditions instead. Some have disagreed with the anarchist bent, beginning in 1981–82, and felt that the feminist intention of empowering women was put to the side. Some have left because of personal conflicts with others in the group or because a new family situation required more time at home. Some have just left because they wanted the

Collective itself to focus more on building and being community. In 1990, one person was asked to leave because of drug abuse, while four others took a leave of absence for an unspecified period due to overwork and unresolved conflicts. Leaving the Reclaiming Collective was not, however, equivalent to leaving the Reclaiming Community. So, in spite of people's moving in and out of the Collective, the Community continued to grow.

A major reason for the growth of the community has been Starhawk's influential writings and the spread of the so-called Witchcamps. In 1985, Reclaiming offered its first week-long summer intensive apprenticeship. It was mainly directed at people who lived out of city or state but who were willing to travel to SF for the occasion. This week-long "summer school" became a big success and was soon to be known as *Witchcamp* (it was held in camping retreat facilities). Two additional camps were taught in Mendocino, North California, the following year. In 1987, Witchcamps spread to Vancouver, BC, and to Ben Lomond, Michigan. In 1989, Reclaiming teachers were invited to Europe, and the first Witchcamp was held in Germany.

The people trained in those camps in turn trained others in their communities. Today, Reclaiming tradition Witchcamps are organized throughout the US (Georgia, California, Florida, Michigan, Missouri, Pennsylvania, Texas, Vermont, Virginia), Canada (Vancouver) and western Europe (Germany and England). They are run autonomously, although some SF Reclaiming elders are usually asked to teach together with local people. Between 50 and a hundred people attend each one of these Reclaiming-identified camps. This means that more than a thousand people go through Reclaiming's "educational system" every year without becoming identifiable members of the SF community. In fact, more than 15 communities in the Reclaiming tradition have been established around the world as a result of the expansion of Witchcamps.

The Reclaiming Collective and its working cells in 1989–1990

In 1990, the Reclaiming Collective started the process of incorporating as a nonprofit religious organization under state and federal law and writing by-laws based on a consensus process model of decision making. Incorporation was a reality in 1994. Shortly thereafter the Collective gained 501(c)(3) tax status with the US Internal Revenue Service. This was the first step in formalizing themselves as a religious organization, which eventually happened in 1997 when the Collective wrote the "Reclaiming Principles of Unity" and reorganized from a working Collective (a cell in its own right) to a representative Wheel (or spokes council) for all the actual working cells. By that time it was clear that there were perhaps thousands of Reclaiming Witches in the US and also many abroad. And more importantly, as time passed, a new generation of SF Bay Area Witches was knocking at the door, wanting to have a say and take leadership. Formalization and reorganization had become unavoidable. Let us therefore turn toward the SF Mission vicinity and recollect activities and struggles emblematic of Reclaiming in these crucial years, just before the SF community expanded exponentially and the Collective dissolved.

*   *   *

In 1989–90, the Reclaiming Collective counted 19 people (13 women and six men).[12] They represented a diverse body, and not only in terms of age. For example, only eight of the 19 identified as heterosexuals (five women and three men) whereas four women identified as lesbians, two men as gay, while four women and one man said they were bisexuals. Seven were married or lived with a domestic partner and five were parents. When the Collective started in 1979, the founders (Starhawk, Diane, Kevin and Lauren) were all of Jewish heritage. In 1990, only three were Jewish, while seven were ex-Catholics, seven were ex-Protestants and one raised as an atheist. Except for one African-American man, all of them were white. When interviewed, six told me they came from a working-class background, nine from the middle class and three from the upper-middle class. Their educational level was higher than that of an average American: two had taken a PhD (in History and English Literature); two had a Masters Degree (in Psychology and Literature); one was a Juris Doctor and Lawyer; and one was a graduate student in Biology. Of the remaining 13, all had either a BA or at least three years of college. Except for Starhawk, who makes a living from her writing and teaching Witchcraft and feminist spirituality outside of the Reclaiming community, all had ordinary jobs.[13]

These statistical findings from the Collective in 1989–90, conform with the demographic data I gathered in the same period when interviewing 68 Witches and pagans (41 women and 27 men) who either were part of, affiliated with or friendly toward the Reclaiming community.[14] An interesting pattern is that a relatively high percentage of the people interviewed reported having a working-class background (39 per cent), high education (80 per cent) and skilled work (84 per cent), middle income (40 per cent), Catholic (35 per cent) or Jewish (21 per cent) upbringing, were bisexuals (27 per cent) and practised multiple relationships (37 per cent), were from the East (38 per cent) or West (33 per cent) Coast, and lived collectively (47 per cent). To this we may add that a majority of Witches and pagans in the US are women (60 per cent), which also conform to Reclaiming's profile. This social profile fits fairly well with my impressions from doing fieldwork and conforms with the research literature.[15]

The time-consuming labour performed by this Collective of people was planned in work cells, defined according to tasks: teaching, newsletter, and bookkeeping. In addition, they organized ad hoc committees to help plan and facilitate public rituals and other short-term projects. Such committees were usually open for participation by any pagan. A Collective member could belong to all three cells or to only one of them, and to as many ad hoc committees she wanted. The more cells she participated in, the more influence she had. Authority was also gained with age, experience and personal charisma. Being its founder, Starhawk was the most influential person in the Collective, closely followed by Rose, Pandora and Raven.

The most prestigious group in the Collective was the Teaching Cell. This was the only formal cell with a limited membership since, essentially, the teachers themselves controlled membership by deciding whom they would allow to student teach. Teachers not only taught classes and Witchcamps, but "priestessed" (or led) most public and communal rites. They were therefore regarded as more skilled with rituals than others and acknowledged for spreading the "word of the goddess" through teaching and active dedication. Through these functions, some of them were highly respected, and given a lot of power. The ideology behind Reclaiming's classes and Witchcamps was to teach spiritual practices, not theological dogma. This way the students might learn that ultimate spiritual authority is within themselves and stop turning to taken-for-granted authorities. They were, for example, not given lectures about the goddess, but taught meditations in which to "meet" her. The policy of having two teachers in a class was meant to strengthen the students' individual autonomy, independent thoughts, self-confidence and engagement with the world. The teaching couple was expected to demonstrate disagreements and diversity in the Craft and stand out as embodied examples of how symbols can have multiple meanings, all of which may be true. The couple was ideally a woman and a man or two women, but never two men. This "prohibition" was meant to counter the students' predisposed attitude of seeing men as religious authorities. When a class or a summer intensive (Witchcamp) was completed, the students were expected to feel at home with Reclaiming-style public rituals, able and confident to facilitate simple rituals on their own, and ready to participate in the ad hoc committees to help prepare public rituals.

The curriculum in the Reclaiming school of Witchcraft always included the earlier mentioned core classes: "Elements" (I), "Pentacle" (II) and "Rites of Passage" (III). Additional classes and teaching tracks (at Witchcamp) were offered, depending on the individual teacher's skills and concerns. A woman, Cybelle, was a body-worker and incest survivor who regularly offered *Breath and Body for Survivors of Incest and Abuse* (women only). A man, Bird, whose background was black working-class Catholicism and Voodoo, liked to teach *Spellcrafting and Mundane Magic* (mixed class). He claimed to have learned magic and spells from his grandmother. Vibra, who had had several abortions, led healing workshops called *Abortion and Feminist Spirituality* (women only). Macha and Bone were skilled herbalists. On and off they offered *Herbs for Food and Healing* (mixed class). In these non-core classes the teacher was free to ask whoever she wanted to co-teach, also somebody who was not a part of Reclaiming, as long as she/he was skilled and sympathetic to Reclaiming's mission statement. In that case, she/he would automatically become a member of the teacher's cell. Nearly half of the classes offered in SF were for women only and, on request, Reclaiming taught a Pentacle class for men.[16]

Traditionally, Witches do not actively proselytize, and neither does Reclaiming. It was therefore expected that the students would find them, and not the other way around. If people complained about how difficult that was, the teacher's attitude would be that this was "healthy". They believed that some consistency in the effort to learn magic was pertinent on the part of the seeker, so that the not-serious could be weeded out early in the process. But once inside, the students were informed about the opportunity to subscribe to the *Reclaiming Newsletter* (after 1997, the *Reclaiming Quarterly*), which was actually an option for anybody.

In 1989 the Newsletter was published quarterly in 1,500 copies, of which 500 were mailed to subscribers outside of SF. Sample copies ($2 a copy) were distributed and sold through the alternative bookstores in the SF Bay Area and other major cities. The newsletter size varied from 30 to 60 pages and according to the Newsletter Cell, which functioned as editorial board, its main function was to inform about classes, workshops, Witchcamps, Starhawk's teaching schedule around the world, and public rituals (the eight solar sabbats). Advertisements from other pagan "mystery schools" recognized by Reclaiming were also printed, as were notices or reports from ongoing political actions. The newsletter was also an important forum for discussions. Since most groups in the community were work- and goal-oriented, people lacked the time and opportunity to voice different opinions beyond a small circle. This need was to a certain degree made up for by the newsletter, which might include articles, poetry and book reviews on feminism, gender, the symbolism of goddess and god, magic, ethics, New Age, Neoshamanism and money policy.

In 1988, the Collective decided to expand their business to include the production of tapes, CDs and books.[17] By 1994, they had produced four different tapes: two with chants and songs to be used in rituals, one with songs from the Spiral Dance Ritual, and one with a trance-journey-meditation read by Starhawk. Another outreach service created was the Reclaiming Events Line. This was a phone number (listed in the Newsletter/Quarterly) connected to an answering machine. In 1989, a caller dialling the number, would hear a message about happenings on the pagan scene in general (in the SF Bay Area) and in the Reclaiming community in particular. The Events Line continues in a similar format today, although most people probably get information about Reclaiming through the internet, from reading Reclaiming's web site (http://www.reclaiming.org).

The Reclaiming Collective and Newsletter were supported by money earned from teaching, the sale of music tapes, CDs and books, fundraising at Spiral Dance rituals and individual donations. The Spiral Dance could raise as much as $15,000, tapes/CDs/books $1,000, and donations $2,000. The Bridged or Candlemas ritual was also a fundraising event, not for the Collective but for responsible social projects and direct actions, such as the "Prevention Point" needle exchange action for AIDS and HIV-positive drug users in San Francisco, or the support network for political prisoners in El Salvador. At fundraising rituals in 1989–90, people were asked to give at least $5.

Money matters and communication with the mundane world were in 1990 administered by a Triad: Rose, Vibra and Pleiades. Pleiades was paid for doing part-time office work, including bookkeeping and handling mail. She reported to the whole Collective on the status of their money and the whole Collective would decide how it was spent. In between scheduled meetings, the Triad was empowered to make small financial decisions that could not wait. The Reclaiming Collective receives mail to a post office box. In 1990 Pleiades collected 50 to 60 letters a day. The most common questions were about classes, rituals, Starhawk's books, how to subscribe to the newsletter, and how to find other Witches in their neighbourhood.

Money brought into the Collective by any Cell was allocated to the work of the Collective. In principle, everyone in the Collective was entitled to payment for their work, but most donated most of their time. Teachers paid 13 per cent of the student fees back to the Collective and could keep the rest. This practice was intended to prevent a teacher with a full class (15 people) from earning a lot more than a less successful colleague. Income from teaching was in any case low and only meant to compensate and add to a person's professional salary, not to replace it. Every year, the Collective donated surplus money to help support political actions or humanitarian work.

Reclaiming's money policy was distinctly different from the New Age movement: a six-week New Age course in 1990 would cost at least $200. Reclaiming therefore called its money policy an "option for the poor". Another reason to keep the fees low was to avoid attracting teachers who wanted to become professional Witches/clergy and who would therefore be prone to pushing Reclaiming in the direction of what Witches associate with "church". Three earlier Collective members left because of conflicts over money. They wanted to charge more, and for a whole year (1984–85) this was a subject of lively debate in the *Newsletter*.

Students paid for their classes on a sliding scale, depending on income. The minimum course fee for a six-week class in 1990 was $45, in 2000 $75. Unemployed and others with meagre financial means could pay by doing work exchange for the Collective. Reclaiming did not normally charge money for public rituals or community rituals, although the celebrants could be asked to contribute financially to cover expenses, such as the renting of space and equipment.

Ritual circles: sabbats, esbats, coveners and initiates

The Reclaiming community celebrates three different types of ritual: rites of calendar (solar and lunar), rites of passage, and rites of crisis or celebration. Lunar rites of calendar ("esbats") are usually celebrated in small, gender-segregated covens, preferably on the nights when the moon is dark or full. Only the solar rites are public. They are celebrated according to a "Wheel of the Year" as eight so-called "sabbats":

1. *Yule* (or winter solstice), 21 December
2. *Bridged* (or Candlemas), 2 February
3. *Eostar* (or spring equinox), 21 March
4. *Beltane*, 1 May
5. *Litha* (or summer solstice), 21 June
6. *Lammas* (or Lughnasad), 1 August
7. *Mabon* (or fall equinox), 21 September
8. *Samhain* (or Halloween), 1 November

Samhain and Bridged are the largest public rites and in the 1980s and early 1990s they were usually arranged in the Women's Building or at Martin Deporres Soup Kitchen in the Mission District. They were open to anyone, whether a "member" of the Reclaiming community or not, and could have several hundred celebrants. In the fall of 1989, when celebrating both the tenth anniversary of Starhawk's book *The Spiral Dance* and Reclaiming's Samhain ritual "The Spiral Dance", the Collective rented Herbst pavilion at Fort Mason at the SF harbour. Twelve hundred pagans and Witches attended the ritual, which was planned by a small ad hoc committee from the Collective, but with a core group of at least 150 volunteers working on it to make it happen. In addition to priestesses and priests for the strict liturgical tasks, this core group included dancers, choreographers, musicians, songwriters and composers, mask designers, dressmakers, prop people, media people, and childcare people. When celebrating the twentieth anniversary 10 years later (in 1999), the same ritual gathered 1,500 people. The other (six) Witches' sabbats were usually celebrated as smaller community rites with an average attendance of about 30–50 people, including children. They usually took place outdoors, on hilltops or at the Pacific Coast beaches. Today these rituals easily get twice as many participants.

If a person wanted to become more deeply involved in Witchcraft, the next step after having taken classes and attending public rites was to become a member of a coven. The concept of a coven is shared by all Witchcraft traditions. Gerald Gardner imagined, from having read Margaret Murray and encountered what he claimed to be surviving Witches in England, that the practitioners of "the Old Religion" gathered for secret ritual celebrations in small groups called *covens*. Each coven supposedly had thirteen members, symbolizing the phases of the moon, and was headed by a high priestess and a high priest. Ideally it included an equal number of females and males who performed the rituals naked or "skyclad", as Gardner writes. A coven was independent, both in terms of rites and mythology, and educated new people inside its own structures. Graduation was equal to initiation into the coven secrets. Covens were, in other words, the smallest assembly and basic ritual unit in the Old Religion, and initiation its educational form.

Reclaiming has reformed Gardner's historical projections of what a coven might be. In accordance with their egalitarian ideology, the notion of a *high* priest/ess has been omitted. All coven members are regarded as ministers, and most covens only have four to seven members. They do not stress the polarity between women and men; and, except for one circle, all Reclaiming covens in 1990 were either for women or men only. But covens are still treated as theologically independent, an attitude which fits well with anarchist and feminist ideologies. New covens are not off-shoots from older covens, but are generated by people who have met in class and share the same basic knowledge. A coven's first year is regarded as critical to whether it will prosper and continue or fall apart. Once established, the covens in Reclaiming do not easily break up; and in 1990 there were nine covens (or circles) in the community.

Covens usually meet once a month to ritualize according to the rhythms of the moon. Since lunar cycles are documented to influence human as well as natural life, Witches believe that certain kinds of magic are more successful if performed when the moon is full or dark. The lunar cycle also corresponds with women's menstruation cycles, a reason in and of itself for Witches to stress its importance. The covens meet in private homes or outdoors and are primarily concerned with the participants' daily life affairs in regard to work, partners, household matters and children. A coven also celebrates a variety of rites of passages for its members and their significant others, such as birth, puberty, marriage, menopause and aging. On these ritual occasions, a coven may invite a large group of people.

A stated goal for a coven is to cultivate personal and spiritual growth in each individual and bring about "perfect love and perfect trust" among themselves. An obvious result from coven work is intimate friendship and deep emotional bonding. A coven may, to some extent, resemble a long-term therapy group or, rather, a consciousness-raising group from the early women's movement. But, a coven also goes beyond the concerns of such groups by interpreting daily life as part of the sacred, as manifestations of goddess, and, further, by bringing people's ordinary life experiences into a spiritual circle for healing, prayer or celebration. The multiplicity of the coven's tasks has been formulated thus by Starhawk: "The coven is a Witch's support group, consciousness-raising group, psychic study centre, clergy-training programme, College of Mysteries, surrogate clan, and religious congregation all rolled into one. In a strong coven, the bond is, by tradition, 'closer than family': a sharing of spirits, emotions, imaginations" (1979a:35).

In addition to the self-initiation performed in connection with the "Rites of Passage" class, Reclaiming also has a tradition of secret initiation for one to be made "Witch and Priestess of the Goddess". Initiation is regarded as the ultimate option for personal growth and healing and requires hard work and deep commitment from both the initiate and her initiators. In order for initiation "to happen," the candidate is asked "to willfully give up her own will" for a limited period of time and to submit herself to be acted upon by initiators, spirits and goddess herself.

This requirement is, of course, a hot topic in a community which otherwise adheres to nonhierarchical structures and equal access to knowledge.

Between 1979 and 1989, only 23 people had been initiated. Of these 19 were women and four men, and 10 were members of the Reclaiming Collective. But the trend has been changing, and by 1990, eight more people (three women and five men) had asked for initiation. The initiation ritual as such is based on Starhawk's initiation into Faery Witchcraft, although radically reformed into what is now recognized by other Witches as a separate Reclaiming initiation.

A hallmark of the Reclaiming tradition is that initiation does not lead to any sort of entitlement. Neither is it required for teaching or priestessing at public rituals, an attitude unique to Reclaiming in comparison to more traditional magical communities. Yet, according to some informants, there was in 1990 a status hierarchy between those who were initiated, those who belonged to a coven and those who only went to public rituals. The initiates were said to represent "first-class" Witches, those who presumably had gained access to special knowledge and magical powers. Coveners thus represented the "second-class" Witches, whereas those who only went to open rituals represented the eternal novices. But this status hierarchy was constantly fluctuating. Someone who had low status in one circle because she lacked magical skills, could in another have high status because she had been involved in, for example, direct political action. Another aspect to coven life was its contribution to social integration: people from different households and work projects created intimate bonds and networks across various segments of the community by virtue of being coveners.

The Reclaiming classes and the solar and lunar rituals constitute the spiritual "trunk" of the Reclaiming community. All other rites are only "branches" grafted onto "the trunk", adding depth, complexity and options for personal growth. The earlier mentioned rites of passage and rites of crisis or celebrations are "branches" of that kind. Rites of passage include *coming of age* rituals (such as the puberty rite for Sonia, initiation to adulthood, menopause and aging), rituals that mark change in *social rank* (such as graduation, handfasting/wedding, childbirth/baby welcoming, parenthood and dying), and the secret *initiation* ritual. Rites of crisis and celebration are typical ad hoc rituals. They comprise rituals for personal healing as well as magical spells to influence political decision making, like those performed at Diablo Canyon. A celebratory ad hoc ritual can simply be a housewarming or birthday party ritual.

Reclaiming is a community founded on shared visions and common goals: to evolve a pagan version of feminist spirituality that, in essence, is inseparable from radical leftist politics. In daily life, unification unfolds as a rhythmic alternation between public and private domains: large communal rituals, work projects and actions on one hand, and intimate, autonomous circles of close same-sex friends on the other. To a majority, this alternation is also a materialized expression of a viable, nonhierarchical social structure, which in and of itself bucks the notion of a universal, gendered dichotomy between public and private. An alternative angle from which to perceive the totality of what Reclaiming is, may perhaps be found in Victor Turner's famous distinction between "communitas" and "structure": since liminality, which is the hallmark of communitas, is unrestricted by conventional binary oppositions, communitas may be said to cut across the static differentiation between public and private and create new social grounds for experimentation and trans-formation. Reclaiming is "communitas" when re-modelling the theological notions and gendered personalities fundamental to western religiosity, and "structure" when interacting with the institutions of the world in order to effect cultural and social change.

The Reclaiming community: "circles within circles"

Where is the SF Reclaiming community and how does it become visible to seekers? In 1990, some informants insisted that the whole "Reclaiming community" was a fiction and that what existed was only the "Reclaiming Collective" plus some people who were affiliated with members of this Collective through friendship. They had become friends by attending Reclaim-ing classes and rituals over a number of years, from living in the same household, or from doing joint political actions. Especially people from the Collective itself were eager to delimit the concept of community to their own circle of friends. One reason was that they were repeatedly confronted with questions from newcomers in their classes, formulated as applications for entry: "Where is the community, and how do I become a member?" They were usually answered that the so-called community could not be pinned down geographically, had no membership list and was not located in any one "house". It was not an organization or a church which could be joined. What existed was a network of people bonded together through love, work and shared visions. To become part of this community was possible only through friendship. A way in was to offer oneself as a volunteer to one of the work projects or by being accepted into a collective household as a new resident. Otherwise, people were encouraged to build small-scale community networks in the areas where they already lived.

But this restricted use of the concept of community did not prevent people from identifying with their Reclaiming-related activities to such an extent that they stated that they were part of the "Reclaiming community". When, for example, in 1990 I asked Rose, a long-time member of the Reclaiming Collective, how many people belonged to the community, she said 50, and started to name former members of the Collective, her friends and friends of her friends. She added, however, that her small community surely overlapped both with the anarchist community and the broader pagan community. "So it depends," she said, "on where I stand and what I am looking for." When I asked Hannah, who lived at Paradox House, about the size of the community, she said that, if we referred to the anarchist, pagan community in SF as *the* Reclaiming community, it included at least 200 people. But then, she had not counted people affiliated with Reclaiming who did not identify as anarchists.

She believed she would have to add another 50 to be fair to them. Both estimates were wrong, the first being too low, the second too high. But both women took one thing for granted: The Reclaiming Collective was at the time the heart of the Reclaiming community. It was *the* inner circle, from which they counted outward, "circles within circles". Rose stopped at the second circle, while Hannah added maybe three more.

In connection with his study of the gay community in San Francisco, Manuel Castells, defines a community as an "urban movement in search for cultural identity through the maintenance or creation of autonomous local cultures, ethnically based or historically originated" (Castells 1983:319). A movement, to Castells, is first of all defined by its goals, and the goal of community is "defense of communication between people, autonomously defined social meaning and face-to-face interaction" (p. 320). The cultural identity sought in Reclaiming is that of being a practising Witch in contemporary American society and, at the same time, a person who takes responsibility for the world in which she lives. This identity is historically originated and manifests itself through the creation of a new, autonomous culture and social arena. But this culture is not really local or based on the idea of territory or ghetto, nor is it self-absorbed. Focusing on the Mission District was a construction I used for practical reasons. Since the community has no official building where members gather and can be counted, I needed some criteria to delimit Reclaiming in order to have a context for further description. When I point to the Mission, it is because most Reclaiming people lived here in the time period under study. But many also lived in the more affluent areas of the SF Bay Area or in adjacent towns and counties. Living in adjoining neighbourhoods can strengthen the feeling of belonging, but it is not essential. Reclaiming is rather an ideologically founded culture, open to anybody who has the skills to work her way in. To understand Reclaiming's social grounds, we have to supplement with the term "network".

If, for example, we look at Freya and her 1990 network, we find that she was engaged with ten groups and committed to steady relationships with at least 60 different people: she lived collectively at Dragon House in the Mission, with seven other adults and two children. She was a member of the Reclaiming Collective, and on the board for two of the three cells. She taught magic and ritual six evenings each semester and Witchcamp in the summer and participated regularly in appointed ad hoc committees to plan public rituals. She was a member of the coven Wind Hags and the Circle A affinity group and one of 15 volunteers in the illegal "Prevention Point" needle exchange in SF.[18] From time to time she helped out at the Martin Deporres Soup Kitchen, run by the Catholic Workers. One Saturday a month she went to the social gathering/happening called "Anarchist Coffeehouse" and on Friday nights she socialized with her pagan and anarchist friends at the El Rio bar in the Mission. Professionally, she worked in the AIDS prevention programme for Hispanic women under the State of California.

These activities and the Reclaiming community were never identical. Some of the groups were not even run by Reclaiming, or included people far beyond the community. They were nevertheless equally important in Freya's identity as a Reclaiming Witch. Further, cross-affiliation in other communities was not specific to Freya, but was typical of Reclaiming people in general. Groups constantly formed and dissolved and most of them worked as concentric, fluid circles, deeply interacting with the circles of other intentional communities as well. If I map Reclaiming in 1990 as a network of circles within circles, spreading out from an inner core circle, it looks like this:

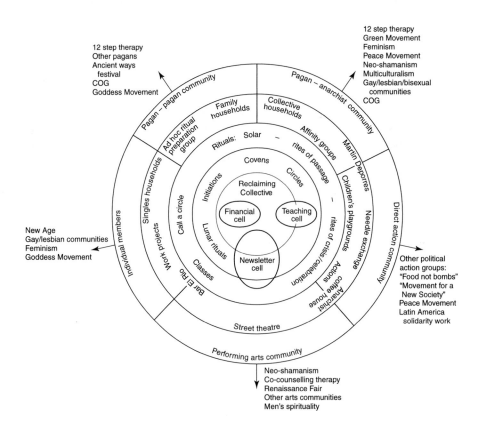

Underneath this network of groups and circles, which were all clustered around one core, centre cell, the Reclaiming Collective, was another social order: interrelated households. This social web was more invisible but equally important. Furthermore, it contributed a functional criterion by which to count Reclaiming people that at least conformed with the community's unofficial agreement about where Reclaiming was located and who its people were.

In 1990, I lived in a collective household named "Group W" in the southern part of Mission. This household of four women had a community list with phone numbers to 123 other households (collectives, families and singles), including a total of 281 people. The list was made and distributed to other households in the larger pagan–anarchist community, both in the SF Bay Area and in neighbouring towns by my roommate Vivianne, who loosely identified with Reclaiming. When I asked where I could find her community, she gave me this phone list.

Most of the households I regard as core to Reclaiming in 1990 were of course on Vivianne's list. On the basis of interviews, visits to a number of households, and my own counting and impressions from being an active participant observer in the community, I suggest that the Reclaiming community in 1990 numbered approximately 130 people spread between 42 households. Of these, 23 were collective households, 13 nuclear family households, and six composed of a single person.[19] This small community in turn served a much larger community of maybe 2,000 people through classes, workshops and public rituals, but also through political projects, like training circles for civil disobedience direct actions, needle exchange or the soup kitchen.

The conclusion is that the SF Reclaiming community in the 1980s and early 1990s was a network of people who were personally and emotionally bonded due to common activities for common goals and who recognized each other as belonging to the same community network. People who merely attended public rituals and otherwise remained anonymous to their fellow celebrants (which was also possible when attending Sunday services in large Christian congregations) were not part of the community in this sense. They had to have some social links, either from class, via friendship or from commitment to a work cell, to be included in this definition. But since community in this organic sense is primarily built on personal work relationships, there is a limit to how large it can grow (two to three hundred people). When the Collective reorganized into a "Wheel" in 1997, one reason was that the community was growing too large, splitting up people in subgroups who no longer knew each other. In order to foster the new, independent communities which were forming, a new structure proved necessary also for the founding collective in SF.

Conflicting circles: magical houses, feminist politics, and insiders versus outsiders

As stated above, Reclaiming's social vision is to treat any human being as a unique manifestation of the goddess, to welcome any serious seeker into their classes and to help those who ask to find their way among ritual circles and work cells. How does this seemingly horizontal pattern of circles within circles actually materialize socially, and why is a newcomer to Reclaiming more likely to experience this pattern as a hierarchy and as a structure representing insiders versus outsiders? The Anarchist Coffeehouse organized at Dragon House in October 1990, is an exemplary case to start with since both gatherings and houses could participate in the creation of this structure.

The two single most important social scenes in the pagan community in SF were in 1990 the Reclaiming public rituals and the Anarchist Coffeehouse. Coffeehouse was a monthly cultural gathering organized by Urban Stonehenge, but hosted by different collective households (a normal situation for a community lacking common space). It was open to any anarchist, pagan or not, and gathered between one and two hundred people.[20]

They came to socialize, discuss, watch shows and performances and help raise money for various political projects. The performances were the most popular part, and favourite pieces were comic sketches in which pagan or anarchist lifestyles were made fun of. A highlight was when Pandora and Starhawk entered the scene in dialogue as "Hannah Clancy" and "Mimi". Hannah was an urban village hag, who gave magical advice about such things as cleaning toilets while twisting the lofty, quasi-academic language of Witchcraft. Mimi was a New Age hippie-like pagan, overloaded with jewelry and politically correct clichéd opinions. Nobody made more fun of Starhawk than Starhawk herself, and people respected her deeply for that quality.

The location for the gathering, Dragon House, was one of the most active Reclaiming households at the time and, with a square area of about five hundred feet, it could pride itself on being a perfect place both for Coffeehouse and for small rituals. The residence was a huge Victorian house in the heart of the Mission, beautifully renovated by its ten inhabitants. It had three floors and twelve rooms. People had separate bedrooms, while other rooms were common space. The combined kitchen and living room on the second floor was the main room. It was huge and originally consisted of three separate rooms. By the eastern wall was a house altar. The altar decoration changed according to the Wheel of the Year. Anarchist Coffeehouse was held in late October, close to Samhain. The altar was therefore covered with symbols representing decay, death and rebirth, including pictures of beloved dead. The private altars, for private magic, were in the bedrooms. On the third floor, there was a large attic. It had been newly renovated into a space that alternately could accommodate rituals, classes, meetings and parties. A wooden staircase was built on the outside, from the backyard garden up to the attic. At each floor, the staircase had a little deck and an entrance door.

The official programme for Coffeehouse took place in the attic. Snacks, bagels, refreshments, beer and wine were sold in the kitchen-living room, which was also a place for socializing. Smokers hung out on the decks and in the outdoor staircase. Others visited the private bedrooms. Everybody paid $1 as an entrance fee, and altogether AC collected $280 that evening. The money was a benefit for organizing the "500th Anniversary of Columbus Invading the Americas" (which took place in 1994).

There were 15 performances in the attic that night and many received high applause. Starhawk and Pandora (from Avalon) played their comedy; Neil (Treat Street) spoke humorously about mental depression and explained how it is supposedly related to monotheism. Three people (from New Moon and Urban Stonehenge) performed an ironic act about promiscuous relationships, showing how difficult it is to make them work ethically. Ann (Treat Street) read intimate passages from her diary, from the time she was a prostitute. Max (Group W) entertained with Jewish folksongs and told a dramatic story about a strip search when she was arrested for squatting in Berkeley.

In the listening crowd I saw many young people and many unfamiliar faces, people who were probably anarchists but not pagans. Some of the Reclaiming elders and a majority of those living as singles or in family households were missing. But the people present still represented most of the circles in the community. People who felt at home constantly moved between the attic, the kitchen and the decks, while the newcomers observed the performances until they were finished. All the group conversations in the kitchen and on the staircase outside the attic were carried on by inner-circle Reclaiming people (those active at plural levels). Especially the young and the newcomers tended to stay the whole evening in the attic. Downstairs on the first floor, in Freya's room, a group of inner-core people (those affiliated with the Reclaiming Collective's teaching cell) was gathered. The door was locked. They opened when I knocked. The people inside exchanged news and gossip.

Not only Dragon House, but any Reclaiming household, was divided into spaces of public and private character. The social status of a guest became visible through watching what area she was allowed to enter. At Dragon House, the attic was both the most public (when having meetings) and the most private (when doing rituals). This room could be transformed according to purpose. Furthermore, the kitchen-living room was semi-public and the bedrooms were private. A person who was let into the attic at meetings could still be an outsider in the community. Whether she belonged depended on whether she was welcomed to socialize in the kitchen, or knew people at that level. A person who, in addition, was invited to Freya's bedroom was about to enter the inner circle. In this room, Freya had altars, spells and all her magical props exposed. It was not for everybody to see.

The double character of the attic, and its potential to be transformed from public to private, was expressed in the fact that the actual night a huge carpet covered up a certain painting on the floor:

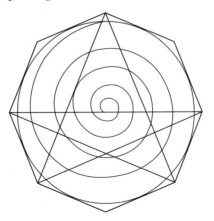

This painting is a magical symbol, a so-called "power vortex". It consists of a red circle, a golden spiral within the circle, a black octagonal figure wreathing the circle, and a black pentagram within the octagonal figure. All these symbols, except the octagram, are used separately in Witchcraft rituals. The octagram symbolizes the "eightfold path of initiation" and is used only in that context. To cluster them together in a painting on the floor is an effort to express the "natural power" that has apparently been accumulated at this spot. Feather, a former member of Reclaiming Collective, had dowsed the house to find out how the earth energies ran underneath and had pointed out this spot as a powerful and natural energy reservoir. The vortex was first painted in the basement, just above the earth, and then later in the attic. It was not meant to be visible to the public eye, that is, to those who only came to meetings or parties. On these occasions, the painting was covered, as it was at Coffeehouse.

Witches believe that a physical house not only has power spots within it, but that the house itself constitutes an energy body. As such, it is a living substance with its energy peak in the power vortex. Therefore houses have names, families and persons have names, and a collective household is listed by its house-name in the phonebook and on the community list. To choose a name is to designate both the energy of the material building and the earth it stands on. It also names the spirit of the household, of a joint group of people. The name "Dragon House" points to some of the Witches' words of wisdom: "Where there is fear there is power." The dragons of European fairy tales are awe-inspiring creatures at the same time as they may be enchanted princesses. Also the Sumerian primordial mother, the goddess Tiamat, was/is a dragon. Her image arouses fear, but is really an expression of the Creatrix. To live in her "House" (or belly) is to be nourished by the female powers of birth and creation.

Not everybody who belonged to the Reclaiming community in 1990 went to the Anarchist Coffeehouse and not everybody was welcome to see and feel the power vortex at Dragon House. It depended on whether they sought a "total identity" of having come home to their "true tribe", or if they were content with the less involved "religious identity" of practising feminist Witchcraft. Only those with a "total identity" were reckoned as inner-circle people in the community. Michael was a typical example. He grew up as a run-away child and spent some time in jail in his early youth. All his life had been a search for home, until he found Reclaiming, "My challenge has been to learn to accept love and to trust it . . . . Then I met the Witches; it was like coming home. Like tying together all the previous stuff I have done, and finally focusing it . . . . This community is my family". Michael became involved in rituals, a coven, teaching, political actions and communal living. He got many friends, was invited to most parties (including Sonia's blood rite party), and managed to bond with several women through sexual relationships. He became a close friend of Rose and Starhawk, and his age and experience gave him a position close to an elder. Reclaiming had indeed helped Michael fulfill his needs: he was provided with an identity of being a valuable and successful person, with a place and a purpose for his life; he even found a "home" *within* himself.

Everybody connected to the community in 1990 would agree with Michael that the particular spiritual practices they had learned from the Reclaiming Witches provided them with an opportunity to find a spiritual family. They would not necessarily agree that they had found a social family. One of those who didn't go to Coffeehouse or El Rio bar, lived collectively, did direct actions, or received invitations to parties was Fallon. Thus, she disagreed strongly with Michael in his positive affirmation of Reclaiming as "home".

Fallon was a lawyer and worked as an attorney. Fallon was Macha's friend and work fellow and was introduced to Reclaiming through her. She was 38 years old, was married and had a daughter 5 years old. Her husband accepted her religious quest but did not participate himself. The three of them lived an ordinary family life in a flat in Noe Valley, west of the Mission. Since 1984, Fallon had taken five Reclaiming classes. She regularly went to the Sabbat rituals and often brought her daughter, whom she tried to raise as a pagan. For a year she belonged to a mixed coven, which dissolved because people started growing in different directions. She was a very competent attorney and had a sweet and friendly personality, although quite reserved. When I asked her to describe her particular magical skills or healing gifts, she answered, "love".

Fallon was a committed worshipper of the Goddess and told me that

> To be a Witch is to honor and revere . . . the earth as a living, breathing being. And also to use that energy to work change in different ways in my own life and in the lives of people around me, in positive healing ways. This knowledge and this practise is a gift I have received from the Reclaiming teachers.

In 1989, she decided to ask for initiation, both to symbolize the commitment she already had and to take a step toward a deeper connection. The tradition recommends that one ask at least three initiators to perform the ritual for her, and since initiation in Reclaiming (which is customized to the individual seeker) involves very exposing and personal challenges, it is a requirement that the candidate already know her initiators intimately as friends. They have to know her weak points, and still accept her, to really be able to challenge her. The problem was that Fallon, after all these years, did not really know anybody as a friend except for Macha. All the other women she asked to be her initiators therefore answered "no"; they did not know her well enough. They suggested instead that she became more involved in the community and asked again later.

These women gave Fallon a hard time because they were right: she did not really belong to the community; she said, she was only associated. She explained her distance partly with reference to her commitment to family and work, partly with reference to the difficulty of being locked into the inner circle of initiated Witches:

Reclaiming is notorious for having an inner circle which is very hard to break in to. I just haven't wanted to put out the energy to try to do that. Also, I think you need to have an "in" . . . . My experience with these kinds of groups in general is that if you have something, a particular quality, or a particular experience in your background, or you just happen to connect on some level with someone in the group who can bring you into the group, then you are in. And if you don't have any of those things, then you are not. That was true in high school and in college. This group dynamic is not unique to Reclaiming, but it is very strong in Reclaiming. And I think it is ironic because of the values that Reclaiming represents, which are community, openness, tolerance. But these are not practised; it is exactly the opposite. And that leaves me with a bad feeling too.

Fallon was here making a vertical and normative distinction between "outsiders" and "insiders" in relation to a particular circle: the influential core members of the Reclaiming Collective. And she was slowly moving from the self-identified position of being a voluntary "outsider" to the position of an *in*voluntary "outsider", the position of those who lack something. When identifying herself as a victim of exclusivity (Reclaiming is here interpreted as representing exactly the opposite of community, openness, tolerance), she ignored her close friendship with Macha, who was in the inner circle and who had kept the door in open for Fallon all those years.

But Fallon did not resign herself to this situation. Her determination to be initiated "forced her" to act counter to her identity as shy, modest and loving: she insisted on relationships with people. She took initiative and demanded to be seen and heard and taken into account. She started to work in ad hoc committees to prepare public rituals. She went to parties and made an effort to talk with people, to bond and be involved – for example in the community ritual celebrating Sonia. In Witches' terminology, Fallon "claimed her power" when she stopped complaining and took charge of her own life in order to reach her goals.

Witches regard everything a person experiences after having asked for initiation (whether she gets a "yes" or "no") as part of her initiation process. The women's rejection of Fallon ended up as her challenge to change her relationship with herself and become a more outspoken and "needy" person. In Witches' language, Fallon had been challenged to cultivate the element "fire" (involvement and will) and balance her "water" (emotional tenderness and loving attitude). For Michael the challenge had been the other way around, to cultivate his "water" (learning to accept love) and balance his "fire" (restless activity and running away). Fallon succeeded and eventually she was initiated.

Michael and Fallon are examples of two people who both belonged to the community, but for a long time with two different positions: as insider and outsider to the core circles. Fallon, though, worked hard to change her position and finally did so. A majority of my 1990 informants agreed that classes were fairly easy and welcoming places to meet Reclaiming and that the teachers gave a lot of themselves at that level. But as soon as they stopped being in class and tried to approach the mysterious Reclaiming community, for example, by going to Coffeehouse or parties, that level of intimacy was gone. Now there was no more interest in getting to know new people; rather the opposite. Some thought that was perfectly acceptable; others complained about the same fact. They were disappointed over the experienced gap between welcoming classes and beautiful rituals and the elitist interaction pattern in the community at large.

It is obvious that the construction called "Reclaiming" was not as welcoming and inclusive in 1990 as intended on a social level, no matter how alternative and good-intentioned. Instead of representing "paradise lost", Reclaiming was rather a community of ordinary people who gossiped, hurt each other, had loud discussions and insisted upon humour and irony as primary criteria for belonging. At the same time, they made a lot of compassionate demands on each other in terms of experimenting, caring, speaking up, processing, forgiving and helping each other grow. But passion has a tendency to take sides, to differentiate between likes and dislikes, between friend and not friend. Sometimes people did not manage this process of "growth". They simply ended up as enemies, and somebody had to leave the larger group for peace to be restored. Those who stayed and those who left showed the power balance within the community.

Why is it that the elitist structure of insider–outsider became such a deep reality in the Reclaiming community? At least four factors seem important: first, an explicit redefinition of the traditional roles of females from being *caretakers* to being *powerful*. Women in Reclaiming had consciously disconnected themselves from traditionally gendered expectations and proclaimed that their task was not to create a cosy community, but to effect changes in the American culture. Nothing less. In Reclaiming's first mission statement, the word "Witch" was even invoked as "an affirmation of women's power to shape reality". The second factor was the extensive use of consensus decision making, and the authority attributed to experience and, therefore, to age. This ethical universe was double-edged because it could invite power games from those who actually had experience and age. Also, where there is no explicit leadership and open hierarchy, a covert hierarchy is likely to develop, at least in a large group. The third factor was the goal of unifying politics and spirituality. As long as politics was defined as direct action, this goal would inevitably establish a creed demanding continuous involvement from its followers and implicitly value people differently according to time and resources invested. Fourth, Reclaiming people offered no distinct keys to enter their informal, organic community, except for "hanging around" or starting to work in a work cell. Although this was an intended strategy in order to stay small and intimate, it was still frustrating to many.

Consequently, the *ideal* associated with the Reclaiming community, which was to empower the individual and build nourishing social and spiritual relationships, could be experienced as just an ideal by a person who did not easily meet these requirements. A defender of Reclaiming's social order would say that the ideal as such was the problem: people were drawn to feminist Witchcraft because they felt that institutional Judaism and Christianity had betrayed them; and now they wanted to create a politically correct religion that conformed with their utopian visions about "paradise lost" but forgot the fact that humans are still complicated beings, and visions always ambiguous and preliminary.

The Reclaiming Wheel in SF (since 1997)

Although Reclaiming has tried over the years to deal with failure, and a less intimate strategy for household arrangements started to evolve in the mid-1990s, the elitist structures in Reclaiming continued to flourish. These were, in the long run, dissatisfying to all. New people complained that they did not get a chance to become involved. Old people, who held tremendous power, felt burned out and tired from hyper-activism. If younger adults and a second generation of those born and raised in the community were to come into leadership, and those who continued to yearn for inclusive community were to be heard, time was ripe for a change.

After Reclaiming in 1994 became a tax-exempt, nonprofit religious organization, many felt the need to create "a home" for the community, a place where people could come together and express themselves apart from the household network. With a central space, information would be more accessible and structures feel more inclusive. They started to look at how churches and synagogues raise money as a model for how Reclaiming might be able to afford a space. But the more they looked, the more they realized that Reclaiming is no regular church, that they were creating a new structure for which there were no models. The idea of a house was thus frozen.

In order to open up the perceived central authority of Reclaiming to the many who, by the mid-1990s, identified as Reclaiming Witches, the Collective started instead a process of reformation by creating a statement called "Reclaiming Principles of Unity" (cf. Appendix B). Here they tried to answer the following questions: what is the Reclaiming tradition, and what entitles somebody to say that they teach in this tradition? The result was a statement of core values, for example, that all of life is sacred and inter-connected, and that ultimate spiritual authority is within each and every person, not of propositions of faith. A Reclaiming *tradition* was thus defined for the first time, not in terms of a theology, but in terms of a worldview and methodology. By this carefully configured move, those among the Reclaiming Witches who always had argued (in opposition to Starhawk) that Witchcraft was not a religion, but merely a magical and spiritual practice, seemed to augment their position.

This configuration of the Reclaiming tradition happened at a retreat for the Collective in November 1997. At the same retreat, the Collective dissolved itself, creating basic suggestions and guidelines for the structure of Reclaiming in the Bay Area which exists today: the Wheel and the various working cells. Today, this Wheel of Reclaiming holds the legal identity of Reclaiming as a tax-exempt religious organization. It is the only assembly empowered to act in the name of Reclaiming in a legal context, to make policy decisions and recognize new cells. It works as a council with representatives from each cell and makes decisions by consensus. Reclaiming cells now number fifteen (Teaching; Advisory; Prison Ministry; E-Cell (website); Community Building; Spiral Dance; Special Projects; East Bay, North Bay and SF Ritual Planning; North Bay Teachers; SF/East Bay Teachers; Quarterly Magazine; Administrative; and Youth), but a procedure in which a new self-appointed work cell can apply for recognition and membership in the Wheel after a year and a day has been developed. Each cell sends one or two representatives to the Wheel, which, like the former Collective, meets at least four times a year. A representative must be chosen by her cell and it is preferred that she sits for a period of two years, which is a major difference from the life-time membership in the old Collective. The members of the former Collective constitute an Advisory Cell, which has two representatives on the Wheel. Some former Collective members are present on the Wheel as chosen representatives from their work cells, but most representatives are young people. If we compare this reorganization with the figure on p. 53, the inner circle called "Reclaiming Collective" has been replaced by the "Reclaiming Wheel", and the three cells "financial", "teaching" and "newsletter" have been extended to fifteen cells, related to the Wheel as independent suns around a shimmering, although highly dependent moon.

Reclaiming Witches in other places organize themselves (or not) as they will. We find Reclaiming-identified communities in Los Angeles ("ReWeaving"), Oregon ("Strand by Strand"), Missouri ("Diana's Grove"), Texas ("Tejas Web"), and in the Mid-Atlantic region ("SpiralHeart"), although they are not incorporated as religious organizations. The Teaching Cell for Witchcamps, however, was separated out from the local Wheel structure and organized as an autonomous transnational Spokes Council. It has representatives from the local Witchcamp organizers and teachers in North America and western Europe and meets twice a year.

The reorganization of Reclaiming also affected the *Newsletter*, which in 1997 transformed into a magazine and became the *Reclaiming Quarterly* (printed in 2,000 copies, $5 for a sample). The self-presentation "Reclaiming – a center for feminist spirituality", followed by the old mission statement, is still printed on the cover page. But, since the magazine now addresses Reclaiming Witches all over the world, the four words "San Francisco Bay Area" have been omitted. Fifty per cent of the magazine's total volume is authored by SF pagans. The other half are articles and announcements from Reclaiming-identified communities throughout the US, Canada and Europe. The editorial policy is to feature anything that will inform Reclaiming's work and meet the needs of a new generation of Reclaiming Witches. A teenage column has therefore been started, as well as a kids' page for those up to the age of eight.

Although Starhawk is one of Reclaiming's founders, and a most important architect behind the new Reclaiming structure, she renounced a position as nonelected leader-guru at the top. In fact, she is not on the SF Wheel at all, only on the Spokes Council for Witchcamp. Her action is not typical for leaders of magical communities and new religious movements, but maybe is for feminist visionaries: instead of mummifying herself and "the old days", she gave up her power and handed over the leadership of the Reclaiming Collective and community to a new generation of young people.

Although the Reclaiming community in SF has a new organizational heart and has refocused from the friendship circles of the household to that of public, representative space, its activities still revolve around classes, public rituals, covens, initiations, work projects and parties. But restructuring has made the informal networks less important and helped to integrate a new generation of Reclaiming Witches. Restructuring has, in fact, made the Reclaiming community in SF more open and inclusive to all parties, both young and old, and helped to revitalize the old visions from the early 1980s.

In the following chapters, I shall describe the pre-1997 Reclaiming community in present tense. There are two reasons for why I take this liberty: first, it adds more life to the narrative and the analysis. Second, it reminds us that the San Francisco Reclaiming community before and after 1997 are not two different entities. Reclaiming's mission statements in 1982 and 2000 are for example almost identical – as are the core values stated in the Principles of Unity from 1997 and those anticipated in every single issue of the *Reclaiming Newsletter/Quarterly* since 1980. Present day Reclaiming Witches obviously identify with the mythological past and the ritual practices invented in the 1980s and early 1990s. Through this book they also get a chance to be acquainted with its larger contexts and meanings.

Notes

1 Quotations by Witches taken from my field notes are written down *after* the ritual process was completed. Thus, some words and phrases may, in fact, have been spoken slightly differently as the ritual took place.

2 Since Reclaiming has no authorized body of elders, this is not a Reclaiming term. But the expression "elders" is sometimes used with reference to "experienced and respected Reclaiming teachers who have been active for many years". To the extent I use the term, it is in this latter sense.

3 My description of the community is primarily based on interviews, newsletters and fieldwork notes. But I have also found and used valuable information in recent *Reclaiming Quarterly* articles written by Reclaiming elders, such as Vibra Willow ("A Brief History of Reclaiming"), M. Macha NightMare ("Reclaiming Tradition Witchcraft"), Starhawk ("A working Definition of Reclaiming") and Jody Logan and Patti Martin ("Reclaiming: History, Structure, and the Future"). These articles can be found on Reclaiming's web site: http://www.reclaiming.org

4 Feminist scholars believe that the universal division of (sexed) labour between public and domestic activities stems from the fact that women give birth and raise children. Therefore, the most egalitarian societies are those in which men value and participate in the domestic life of the home and where women "are able to

transcend domestic limits, either by entering the men's world or by creating a society unto themselves" (M. Rosaldo 1974:41).

5 According to a US census from 1980, SF had then a population of 678,974, of which 42 per cent belonged to the Black, Hispanic, Chinese and Filipino ethnic groups. About 50,000 people lived in the Mission District (Godfrey 1988:3, 146).

6 Castells 1983:138. San Francisco had in 1980 an estimated 115,000 homosexuals, about 17 per cent of the city's population. Two-thirds of the total were men, one-third were women. The Castro ghetto were primarily populated by white, middle-class gay men. According to Deborah G. Wolf (1979), lesbians tended not to concentrate in a given territory or to give priority to spatial communities but rather as loose social and interpersonal *networks*. On the whole they were poorer than gay men and had less choice in terms of work and location. Their Mission community was at the time centred around a feminist bookstore, the Women's Building, two women-only cafés and a women's bathhouse. Cf. also Castells 1983:140.

7 In the early 1970s, Budapest founded the "Susan B. Anthony Coven no. 1" (named after a famous suffragist) and opened a Goddess bookstore in Los Angeles. In 1976 she published *The Feminist Book of Light and Shadow*. Ten years later, Budapest moved to Oakland, close to SF. There are other branches of Witchcraft also identifying as "Dianic", but they are neither lesbian nor separatist.

8 NROOGD was already established in 1967–68 and their name was meant to be a humorous twisting of the famous British occult order "The Hermetic Order of the Golden Dawn", established in 1887. The rituals of the latter group probably influenced Gardner's creation of Witchcraft (cf. Introduction and chapter 2).

9 The magical communities in the SF Bay Area are still characterized by their overlapping membership structure, a feature also documented by T.H. Luhrmann (1989) when she studied magical communities in London. My experience from having participated in rituals in many different magical traditions confirms Luhrmann's assertion that magical groups are highly interrelated. Except for the feminists, it is not unusual that people belong to several communities simultaneously or frequently visit each other's rituals.

10 "A Working Definition of Reclaiming", taken from Reclaiming's web site, 25 August 2000.

11 The words "San Francisco Bay Area" were the only ones omitted when Reclaiming reorganized in 1997.

12 Listed chronologically from the year they joined (with their 1989 age in parentheses), members included *Starhawk* (38) since 1979; *Rose May Dance* (41) and *Bone Blossom* (41) since 1981; *Deadly* (36), *Pandora O'Mallory* (38), *M. Macha NightMare* (45), *Judy Foster* (57), *Raven Moonshadow* (29) and *David Kubrin* (50) since 1982; *Rick Dragonstongue* (42), *Roy King* (43) and *Roddy* (33) since 1984; *Cybelle* (34) and *Vibra Willow* (42) since 1985. In 1989, they decided to take in more young people. *Pleiades* (28) and *Rosemary* (26) came in that year, while *Jody Logan* (22), *Suzanne* (22) and *Beverly* (24) became members in 1990.

13 Of those with a BA or less, two worked in an AIDS/HIV educational program, two were secretaries, two were dancers, one was a computer programmer, one was a bank data analyst, one was a body-worker/healer, one was a cook, one was a carpenter and two of the younger were unemployed. Their income varied considerably, largely determined by their educational level.

14 I have taped interviews with 68 Witches/Pagans, 41 women and 27 men. A total of 50 of these interviews are with Reclaiming people, 30 women and 20 men. The interviews were fairly organized, although I did not asked the same standard set of questions of everybody (the question guide for the 1989/90 interviews is included as Appendix A). Information about life histories, therefore, varies from sparse to very rich. But there is certain core information which is repeated: a total of 61

gave information about age, 60 about religious upbringing, 60 about housing situation, 60 about sexual identity, 59 about civil status, 59 about present work, 58 about education, 57 about income, 57 about class background and 41 about birthplace. Of the people I interviewed, two were Black and one was Latino. Most of the Catholics reported having Irish ethnic backgrounds. All together, the people interviewed had 32 children. A reader who wants to go into the statistical data in more detail can consult my PhD dissertation "*'I am a Witch—a Healer and a Bender'. An Expression of Religious Woman in Contemporary USA*" from 1996 in the University Library in Oslo, Norway.

15 Loretta Orion (1995) writes that of the total US population, 39.4 per cent are Protestant, 36.5 per cent are Catholic, 4 per cent are Jewish, 0.1 per cent are Unitarian and 20 per cent are Other. In 1991, J. Gordon Melton reported the religious background of (neo)pagans to be: 42.7 per cent Protestant, 25.8 per cent Catholic, 6.2 per cent Jewish, 25.3 per cent Other (Melton 1991:467). In 1995, Loretta Orion reported their religious backgrounds as: 59 per cent Protestant (32 per cent in Reclaiming, compared to 39.4 in the US population), 26 per cent Catholic (35 in R. compared to 36.5); 9 per cent Jewish (21 in R. compared to 4), 4.2 per cent Unitarians (5 per cent in R. compared to 0.1), 3 per cent Other (7 in R. compared to 20). Orion's reports on education were: PhD 4.2 per cent (9 in Reclaiming); MA 22.8 per cent (31 in R.); BA 31.7 per cent (40 in R.); 1–3 years of college 11.5 per cent (19 in R.); High School only 23.8 per cent (1 in R.). Reclaiming does, in other words, score very high on education. Carol Matthews (1995:345) writes that 40 per cent of Americans have attended college whereas in Reclaiming 80 per cent report having completed a college or graduate degree. Orion reports that of (neo)pagans 61 per cent are heterosexuals (55 in Reclaiming); 11 per cent are homosexuals (18 in R.); 28 per cent are bisexuals (27 in R.). The national average is 10 per cent homosexuals and 13 per cent bisexuals. Regarding age, Orion refers to a San Diego study that found the highest percentage of (neo)pagans to fall between 31 and 40 years (50 per cent are between 30 and 40 years in R.).

16 How many people were educated in Reclaiming's "mystery school" annually? In the spring term of 1989, Reclaiming offered 22 classes in SF with a total of 14 teachers. If we count approximately eight students in every class (which is a low estimate), it means that 176 people in the SF Bay Area were educated in the "religion and magic of the Goddess Reclaiming-style" within this period only. In addition come a couple of thousand who sign up for 10 to 12 Witchcamps and participate in workshops given by Starhawk and other Reclaiming teachers outside of SF (Starhawk carries out extensive travelling in the US and Europe every spring).

17 Books published by Reclaiming people are listed under Starhawk in the bibliography since she, so far, has figured as the main author.

18 "Prevention Point" was started as an illegal direct action in November 1988 by pagan anarchists and members of the Reclaiming Collective. The goal was to prevent the spread of AIDS among drug abusers in the streets of SF caused by addicts sharing the same needle by exchanging old needles with new. The new needles were sent to them by anarchist friends in Canada, where needles could be bought at the pharmacy. Once a week drug users in SF could exchange an equal number of used needles for an equal number of new ones, and during the first two years of the action, 200,000 needles were exchanged. Before "Prevention Point" entered the streets, they held hands in a circle while grounding and bonding. In their homes people burnt magic candles to help the activists be invisible to the police. This was a highly successful action, resulting in the legalization of the action by SF city and county governments. Since 1993 the action has been financed by the city. It has a director, several full time officers and 200 volunteers

to do the street work. In 1994, they gave out 65,000–70,000 needles per week, interacting with around 4,000 drug users. Legal needle-exchange programmes have also been started in many other large US cities.

19 At the time there were 15 households in the Mission, seven in Noe Valley, Bernal Heights and Potrero Hills, eight in the Haight-Ashbury and two at the Golden Gate Park. Each house was named, for example Urban Stonehenge, New Moon, Black Cat, Casa Sanchez, Group W, Avalon, Castle Discordia, Paradox House, Garlic Moon and Suburban Palace. In 1990 there were four Reclaiming affiliated houses in Berkeley, four in Sonoma County, one in Santa Cruz and one in Grass Valley. Some of these out-of-city-members had earlier lived in collective households in SF.

20 Several of my 1990 informants maintained that the anarchist political scene in SF at the time included 2,000 active people, of which 200 were believed to be pagans as well – but this number was not restricted to those active in Reclaiming. By "anarchism" in America I mean a political ideology inspired by writers such as Emma Goldman and Dorothy Day. Many European anarchists immigrated to the US in the early twentieth century, and Goldman was among the more influential. Today's anarchists have local government and decentralization as their basic political guidelines. They believe societies can be organized on premises other than the nation state, the judicial system, the institutions of private property, the army and the police. Consequently, they distance themselves strongly from traditional communist or socialist politics in which state economics replace market economics.

2 Wicca revival

Starhawk and the myth of ancient origin

If we ask Reclaiming people how the Witch movement came into being, the sceptical and ignorant will say it was invented by Starhawk and other feminists. The sceptical and well read will say it was invented by Gerald Gardner on the basis of the European esoteric traditions. The non sceptical lovers of myth, who represent the majority of feminist Witchcraft, will refer us to a certain myth of ancient origin. This myth, in different versions, is met with in all variations of the Witch movement (Adler 1979:45). In fact, it is not really a myth, but a genealogical account which, when clothed in terms of the history of religions, describes how some of the Witches themselves understand their origin and evolution. The Reclaiming version of the myth is formulated by Starhawk. She claims to have inherited it from the Faery tradition, although its narrative elements are similar to Gardner's accounts.[1] Briefly, Starhawk's version is as follows.

Witchcraft has its spiritual roots in the tribal religions of Europe some 10,000 years ago. Therefore, in spirit it is related to the surviving shamanistic "Earth religions" of the contemporary west, including those of Native Americans, African Americans, the Sami and the Inuits. The old Europeans originally worshipped the "Great Goddess", as divine giver of life and fertility, and her son–lover, the Horned God. These tribal peoples celebrated the cycles of the seasons, and their religion provided tools to establish bonds between individuals, the community and the earth. Just as religion was goddess-centreed, society was woman-centreed and organized around the mother and her kin as a basic social principle. These matrifocal and matrilineal cultures were egalitarian, peaceful, just and creative, and laid the foundation of our civilization. In time, the cultures were invaded by patriarchal warriors from the east. They conquered or drove out the matrilineal goddess-worshippers and laid the foundation for patriarchal and oppressive societies in Europe. The invaders worshipped a male warrior-god as the supreme godhead and they degraded the indigenous worship of the goddess and her consort. In the British Isles, the invading Celts conquered the goddess-people by adopting and assimilating many elements of "the Old Religion", which later became the Druid Mysteries. But the "Goddess religion", or now, Witchcraft, also continued to live in folk customs, esoteric traditions and in the covens of the

Faery people, led by women, or now, Witches. Later, during the Church's persecution of heretics, the Witches were forced underground. Many of the traditions were forgotten, but some of them lived on in great secrecy in certain families. With the European immigration to America, some families also brought the Craft with them. When England repealed the ban on the practice of Witchcraft in 1951, the Witches' Craft emerged from hiding, first in England, then in the US.

The true genesis of Wicca is not the topic of this book. In this chapter we shall, therefore, trace the historical roots and recent revival of Witchcraft according to their own indigenous exegesis. While scholars emphasize the literary and folklorist sources, most Witches also insist upon a spiritual continuity with the past in terms of magico-religious practices. Claims of historicity are very important to the Witches since the past is a major resource on which the Wiccan identity is built. To most Reclaiming people, Starhawk's books, and not Gerald Gardner's, are the primary source for answers about the origin and revival of Witchcraft. Her books are also extensively referred to in interviews. I shall, therefore, give an extract of her position, which differs from Gardner by her typical feminist interest in prehistory and archeology.

However, parallel to her interpretations of the historical lineage of Witchcraft, Starhawk also formulates a cultural theory of "Paradise, Fall, Persecution, and Regeneration". This theory is of great importance since it is used both to explain and legitimate Americans' current search for an identity as Witches. In addition to describing mythical-historical outlines, we must, therefore, investigate the rationale Starhawk uses when producing such a theory, specifically her concept of the natural, and her interpretations of the assumed link between religious symbols and social reality.

In the Introduction, I described some features that seem to be characteristic of women's religiosity. One of them was how women use religious symbols in continuity with social life. Regarding feminist Witches, we must expand the continuum: they also argue to create a religious symbolic order in continuity with natural life as well. When they regard Jewish and Christian religions as patriarchal and oppressive, it is exactly because they believe they are based on wrong perceptions of the natural world and therefore, inevitably, lies about the nature of reality. First, they lie about humans' fundamental relationship with nature. Second, they resist any experience of nature as animate. Third, they deny that the elemental power that gives birth is female. Consequently, patriarchal religion is said to make use of symbols which represent natural reversals, as when "Dea Creatrix" is symbolized as God and not as Goddess, although it is the females of the species who, in fact, give birth to everything living.

Hence, the first and basic question to a Witch is not, "how do we create new life-affirming symbols?" but, "what is true?" As is the case with any religious path, theirs is a search for the Real, as they understand it, and an effort to approximate their lives to it. The Real to Starhawk is what is expressed through notions like "immanence" and "interconnection": the earth is alive, and all living beings are interconnected manifestations of the divine life force. When composing such a view of the world, she is leaning on a western occult tradition that has already reformulated ancient, pre-Socratic concepts into a so-called esoteric cosmology. According to Antoine Faivre, this cosmology has six phenomenological characteristics, of which I shall briefly mention three: (1) the Universe is *alive* and the natural world "bound together" through a network of elementals, of which the basic four are air, fire, water and earth; (2) because of elemental *correspondences* between all parts of the visible and invisible universe, microcosm can be said to mirror macrocosm; (3) the universal net of elemental correspondences can be mediated and manipulated by the human *imagination,* an activity often labelled "magic" (Faivre 1992: xv–xx).

Esoteric cosmology is of course only a symbolic expression of human assumptions about the Real. But, to Starhawk, this symbolic discourse represents objective ground, an ontological platform necessary for any apprentice to Witchcraft. After reformulating them in her own language and clothing them with her own favourite metaphors, Starhawk contends that the essential principles, which are the true basics of nature and operative in all human cultural activity, are to be named *energy, spirit* and *matter.* This knowledge stems from a magical consciousness

> that sees the world itself as a living being, made up of dynamic aspects, a world where one thing shape-shifts into another, where there are no solid separations and no simple causes and effects . . . . Magic teaches that living beings are beings of energy and spirit as well as matter, that energy – what the Chinese call Chi – flows in certain patterns throughout the human body, and can be raised, stored, shaped and sent. The movements of energy affect the physical world, and vice versa.
>
> (Starhawk 1987:15, 24)

The world or cosmos "as a living being" is ultimately symbolized as "the living body of the Goddess, in whose being we all partake, who encompasses us and is immanent within us" (Starhawk 1987:7). The Goddess is regarded as the great life-force. The energy and spirit embedded in nature are only manifestations of her breath and soul. But energy and spirit are not only contained within what we traditionally conceive of as nature. According to Starhawk, they dwell in *all* matter, whether a human body or a work of art.

In this magical worldview, everything seems to belong to the domain of "nature". And in her writings, Starhawk seldom distinguishes between "nature" and "culture"; rather she distinguishes between the physical and nonphysical worlds. They are believed to be mutually influencing parts of a system, a continuous feed-back loop. In fact, Starhawk regards the hierarchical opposition between nature and culture as an expression of patriarchal dualism. Instead she seems to operate with a distinction between natural and unnatural. When Starhawk advocates Witchcraft as a "natural" religion, it is not in opposition to "cultural", but to "unnatural" religion.[2]

In the origin myth Starhawk's discourse implies that a social utopia/paradise must express the natural order of the universe and be a mirror of those cosmic laws mentioned above. Thus, Witchcraft is understood to be in alignment with cosmic laws and to represent both a natural religion and a true cognition about matter, energy and spirit. This knowledge is regarded basic to fostering a just social organization. The natural has thus become ethically normative: "natural" is made identical with organic, normal and good (feminist), "unnatural" with inorganic, abnormal and evil (patriarchal). Accordingly, the combination of true knowledge of and reverence for the universe gives rise to natural religions (meaning paganism), natural societies (meaning egalitarian and matrifocal), and natural people (meaning healthy/happy) in a moral sense. Patriarchal religions, such as Judaism, Christianity and Islam, on the other hand, are examples of unnatural religions and function to legitimate social oppression, sexism and ecological/personal estrangement. Patriarchal religious symbolism represents a distorted imagery of how the laws of nature *really* work and an ignorance of nature's constitution as matter–energy–spirit.

Aided by this analytical distinction, we shall now investigate how Starhawk unfolds her theory about the natural beginnings of time, cultural fall and possible resurrection, and how the unnatural patriarchal culture built on symbolic reversals and misrepresentations in regard to social life and the natural world came into existence. I shall base the examination mainly upon Starhawk's books, *The Spiral Dance* (1979a) and *Truth or Dare* (1987) and also signal the development of her thinking from the first to the second book.

Paradise lost

Starhawk's paradise is characterized by what she terms a "consciousness of immanence", as opposed to a patriarchal "consciousness of estrangement". The consciousness of immanence is holistic and sees the world as interrelated and interconnected. This is the natural perception of reality, which people appropriate when they live attuned to and in harmony with the natural world. Starhawk believes that the context for the rise of Witchcraft thousand of years ago was a Paleolithic culture in which

> gifted shamans could attune themselves to the spirit of the herds, and in so doing they became aware of the pulsating rhythm that infuses all life, the dance of the double spiral, the whirling into being, and whirling out again. They did not frame this insight intellectually, but in images: the Mother Goddess, the birthgiver, who brings into existence all life; and the Horned God, hunter and hunted, who eternally passes through the gates of death that new life must go on. Male shamans dressed in skins and horns in identification with the God and the herds; but female priestesses presided naked, embodying the fertility of the Goddess. . . . As isolated settlements grew into villages, shamans and priestesses linked forces and shared knowledge. The first covens were formed . . . villages grew into

the first towns and cities . . . The year became a great wheel divided into eight parts: the solstices and equinoxes and the cross-quarter days between, when great feasts were held and fires lit . . . Within the [stone] circles . . . priestesses could probe the secrets of time and the hidden structure of the cosmos. Mathematics, astronomy, poetry, music, medicine, and the understandings of the workings of the human mind developed side by side with the lore of the deeper mysteries . . . The covens, who preserved the knowledge of the subtle forces, were called Wicca . . . They were those who could shape the unseen to their will. Healers, teachers poets and midwives, they were central figures in every community.

(Starhawk 1979a:3–5)

This extract is from *The Spiral Dance* and according to Starhawk is to be read as a legend, although she refers to a variety of "scientific sources" like Joseph Campbell, James Mellaart and Margaret A. Murray, to prove the validity of her reconstruction (Starhawk 1987:15). Legend or not, her goal is to establish a normative image of a natural culture. Its hallmark is that symbolic representations are metonymical rather than metaphorical: every symbolic act is understood to be in continuity with its social meaning and natural function.

Goddess, femaleness and that which constitutes the essential principles of fertility and procreation are associated through their embodiment in the woman, the priestess. God, maleness and the animals that die in the hunt, sacrificing their lives as food in order to feed life, are associated through their embodiment in or with man, the shaman. Natural death does not reverse life; it transforms life into new forms and is, therefore, nothing to fear. Both life and death are understood to be a continuous stream of stages through which life is reincarnated, again and again. The ritual cycle of the year mirrors the natural cycle. People are able to receive and understand the secrets of cosmos directly. Magicians can shape the unseen to their will and for the best of the community.

A natural culture's evolution from a simple social organization (tribal) to a more complex one (urban) does not generate war and oppression. It is exactly when a society lives in attunement with the laws of nature that it develops high culture and peaceful civilization, city-states and a unification of science and religion. In other words, in a natural culture there is deep continuity between the symbolic, social and natural worlds, a state of being which Starhawk labels holistic and whose central figure is the Witch, *the* symbol of continuity and balance.

This ideal, holistic society is not located anywhere specific and, in *The Spiral Dance*, Starhawk seems to grant universal validity to its embodied evolutionary pattern. Eight years later, in *Truth or Dare*, Starhawk wants to be read literally. Her historical reconstructions are no longer advocated as legends but as research. Now she limits herself to one geographical area, of which we have the oldest written sources available, namely, the rise and fall of Sumer in Mesopotamia 3000 BCE. She chooses this area because she considers it to contain the roots of western culture (Starhawk 1987:33). Starhawk's study materials are edited secondary sources, containing poetry and myths as well as summaries of royal lineages, food supplies and utensils, crops and herds, the production of clothes and ceramics – all listed and preserved by Sumerian temple accountants. Her focus is the symbolic and social position of women and how it changes when the social and natural worlds are split apart, distorting a natural culture's conceptualizations of sexuality and fertility and divinity. In this enterprise, Starhawk does not discuss different theories but refers only to those scholars who support her own perspective. Primarily, these include Ruby Rohrlich (1980), Gerda Lerner (1986), Samuel N. Kramer (1963), James Mellaart (1967) and Marija Gimbutas (1982, 1989).

Once again, Starhawk starts out with what she calls the "matristic times" or "mother times", a previous golden age in pre-Sumerian Anatolia in which the society was presumably matrifocal and matrilineal and the supreme deity was the Great Goddess, a goddess of nature as well as a goddess of culture. Starhawk maintains that this goddess represented both life and death, fertility and decay. The aim of religion was to ensure the continuity of life, and the characteristics of a civilization worshipping goddesses were that "women were leaders, priestesses, revered and respected members of the society" (Starhawk 1987:36). Starhawk holds that the imagery of art and objects did not reflect structures of domination. There were no images of war, no indication of animal sacrifice, and little differentiation was present in grave goods to indicate class divisions. In the later, more stratified Sumerian culture, writing, education, science and account keeping were still the domain of a goddess, and women continued, according to Starhawk's sources, to be scribes and scholars, poets and composers of religious texts.

What seems to intrigue Starhawk the most is that "gender as a category . . . was not seen as a necessary or natural correlative of power or powerlessness" (Starhawk 1987:39). She finds this fact explicitly demonstrated in the mythic representations of the sexual relation between goddess and god, representing woman and man. In the Sumerian myths about Inanna and her consort Dumuzi, the renewal of the world is enacted "through the life-sustaining power of the erotic" in the rite of the sacred marriage. Through these myths Starhawk is convinced that she finds a religion that is concerned to

> celebrate the presence of immanent power in the natural and human world, in the seasonal rhythms of renewal and withering, in food and in sexuality. The erotic power of woman is venerated, seen as a force that generates good for all the community, and as a power that woman herself takes pride in.
>
> (1987:43)

According to Starhawk, the erotic metaphors in the Sacred Marriage texts centre on milk and cream. Inanna asks Dumuzi to make the milk yellow – that is, creamy and fat – for her. She praises her vulva and compares it to a field ready for the fertilizing seed plough. She praises her own body parts with metaphors from the natural world:

> (My crescent-shaped) "Barge of Heaven,"
> so (well) belayed,
> full of loveliness, like the new moon,
> my untilled plot,
>   left so fallow in the desert,
> my duck field so studded with ducks,
> my hillock land, so (well) watered,
> my parts, piled up with levees,
>   (well) watered. [3]

Starhawk points out that Inanna never gets pregnant and that Sumer was a society in which the erotic, not only motherhood, was seen as sacred. Additionally, male sexuality was associated with fertility and procreation. Male sexual power was symbolized as lifesustaining, as food itself; and nowhere in the myths does she see any suggestions that male eroticism is linked with the power of conquest, or force, or violence, or rulership, or suffering. Inanna sings for Dumuzi:

> He has sprouted, he has burgeoned,
> He is lettuce planted by the water,
> He is the one my womb loves best . . . .
> Make your milk sweet and thick, my bridegroom.
> My shepherd, I will drink your fresh milk. . . .
> Let the milk of the goat flow in my sheepfold.
> Fill my holy churn with honey cheese. [4]

Starhawk's message is that goddess worship is the oldest religion in the world, flourishing when women still had important influence and power in society. In her reading, Starhawk has confronted no split between the social world, as portrayed in sacred myth, and the social world of actual women and men. There was balance and equilibrium, and religious symbols functioned to enhance and sacralize social life. Early Sumerian religion is portrayed as a fertility cult in a broad sense, dedicated to the continuity of natural and social life. Its basic worldview was erotic: the coming together of goddess and god, of planets and stars, of women and men in an eternal pattern of polarity; its proper rituals were fertility rites for the fecundity of people and their land.

Then came a shift. Goddess worship was slowly suppressed during a 2000-year-long patriarchal war against nature, women and female sexuality, resulting in male dominance and female subordination – well-known attributes of western culture. Let us now turn to how Starhawk interprets this fall from the originally good life, from paradise. First we shall discuss her explanations of the driving forces that create an unnatural culture, and then her analysis of the core ideology that maintains it.

Patriarchal fall

Starhawk's theory about the development of unnatural cultures is formulated as a cultural critique. Its function is to explain why a culture in dissonance with the founding principles of cosmos has come to be normal in the human perception of the world. The foundation she wants to establish for her critique is that the unnatural is the result of social and historical construction, not of metaphysical origin. The fall is not due to human sinfulness, or the result of an inner, existential failure in the human constitution; neither can it be explained with reference to an evil creator-god or to evil spirits who have possessed and blindfolded the human mind and her good will. Starhawk's optimistic rhetoric states: since the fall has a social origin, it can be counteracted by social means and human invention.

Starhawk tells two different stories about the development of unnatural cultures. In the first story, published in *The Spiral Dance,* Starhawk explains the unnatural as resulting from invasion. In the second story, in *Truth or Dare,* the unnatural culture is due to degeneration, meaning a real fall within society itself (cf. Dyrendal 1993:28–30). As we shall see, Starhawk does not fully succeed in avoiding metaphysical explanations in her dual effort to establish the fall as socially constructed since she cannot elucidate the causality of its happening – whether as invasion or as degeneration. Actually, she comes close to turning the traditional Jewish and Christian paradisiacal narratives in the book of Genesis on their heads, making of the male, instead of the female, the generic weak spot.

In Starhawk's invasion theory, what she describes as the peaceful, prospering goddess cultures in Neolithic Europe were suddenly attacked from the outside. Since these people were innocent to the phenomenon of war, having no defence or weapons, they became an easy prey. In the origin myth, the invaders are simply called "conquering patriarchs" from the East.

> But in other lands [as opposed to the peaceful Wiccan societies], cultures developed that devoted themselves to the arts of war. Wave after wave of invasion swept over Europe from the bronze age on. Warrior gods drove out the Goddess peoples from the fertile low lands and fine temples, into the hills and high mountains where they became known as the . . . Faeries.
>
> (1979a:4)

Through the invasions of Indo-European warrior tribes, the old era of goddess worship slowly came to an end. The mythology changed to legitimate a new social structure and a new religion, and the Indo-European male-dominated pantheon as expressed in Greek and Roman, as well as Norse, mythology became authoritative. But it was not before Christianity came to power, and gained a position as state religion all over Europe, that the Old Religion and goddess-worship were interpreted as devil worship and forbidden. According to Starhawk, it is at that point that the persecution of pagans became aggressive, with a special interest in the punishment of the women–goddess analogy, of women's bodies as sacred symbols, and of women as representative of the earlier mentioned erotic worldview:

> The persecution was most strongly directed against women . . . . The asceticism of early Christianity, which turned its back on the world of flesh, had degenerated, in some quarters of the Church, into hatred of those who brought the flesh into being . . . . The terror was indescribable . . . . The Witches and Faeries who could do so, escaped to lands where the Inquisition did not reach. Some may have come to America . . . . In America as in Europe the Craft went underground, and became the most secret of religions. Traditions were passed down only to those who could be trusted absolutely, usually to members of the same family . . . . Parts of the tradition became lost or forgotten. Yet somehow, in secret, in silence, over glowing coals, behind closed shutters, encoded as fairytales and folksongs, or hidden in subconscious memories, the seed was passed on.
>
> (1979a:5–7)

When the persecutions were put to an end in the eighteenth century, the seed-carriers could again emerge and "counter the imagery of evil with truth" (1979a:7). As mentioned earlier, Starhawk herself learned the Craft from Victor Anderson, whom she believes is a seed-carrier of the Faery tradition surviving in America. She concludes her reconstructions of the past with an ethical and political programme:

> The word "Witch" carries so many negative connotations that many people wonder why we use the word at all. Yet to reclaim the word "Witch" is to reclaim our right, as women, to be powerful; as men to know the feminine within as divine. To be a Witch is to identify with 9 million victims of bigotry and hatred and to take responsibility for shaping a world in which prejudice claims no more victims.
>
> (Ibid.)

A Witch is a shaper, one who bends the unseen into form. It is the responsibility of these few "shapers" and "benders" to give a true account of history, of the patriarchal ideology and of the means to create a better society, that is, of Witchcraft.

As we have seen, in the invasion theory presented in *The Spiral Dance*, Starhawk operates with two simultaneous societies, existing independently of each other, representing antagonistic social principles. They are both created by humans, although one is a social paradise and the other an evil patriarchy, characterized by disrespect for natural laws. The question of *why* this is the case is never answered. In reality, Starhawk leaves the reader with no explanations as to how and why patriarchy developed. The existence of and contradiction between natural and unnatural therefore become permanent, because the unnatural cannot be understood and analysed within the conceptualized framework of the natural (cf. Dyrendal 1993). In such a theory the unnatural becomes identical with impure and alien, constituting an element that cannot be changed except through cleansing and exorcism. The evil element is naturally constituted as evil for mysterious and unknowable reasons, splitting the world between organic good and evil.

This black-and-white fairy tale of Europe's cultural history can perhaps be accepted as a legend but not as history. Criticism even emerged among the Witches themselves, and to meet this new attitude Starhawk changed her perspective when writing *Truth or Dare*. As was the case in the paradise tale, she now labels her work research and wants to be taken seriously by feminist scholars. She dismisses the invasion theory and substitutes for it a theory of fall and degeneration within the society itself – without blaming intruders for the misery. She still believes that the fall is due to war, not so much because of conquistadors as because of a slow distortion of a society's own, internal value system, splitting the human Self.

Starhawk tries to describe the rise of patriarchy by going back to Sumer in Mesopotamia. She makes diligent use of Gerda Lerner's and Ruby Rohrlich's historical research. Starhawk compares the parallel developments of society and religion in this region, and the key concepts in her theory are "centralization/kingship" and "militarization". She makes them represent a change in mentality from egalitarian to stratified, from matrilineal to patrilineal, from an attitude in which nature is worshipped as giver of life to a new attitude which states that nature represents chaos, forces that destroy life and that must be controlled. She sees this shift as the result of an increased accumulation of power and wealth by the two parallel – and closely linked – social institutions: the temple and the priesthood; the castle and the kingship. Traditionally, the temple and the castle represented a gender-segregated power structure. The head of the temple was a female priestess, while the king was male. They were both elected and did not inherit their positions. As the mundane representatives of Inanna and Dumuzi, they united once a year in a sacred marriage rite. The kingship lasted only one year for each. Then the king was replaced and the cycle was repeated.

According to Starhawk's sources, the mentality shift came when the king increased his power at the expense of the temple high priestess. First he prolonged his rulership from a year to his lifetime, introducing heritage to the throne through bloodlines and to property through patrilineal descent. His daughter, now subjugated to his law and authority, became the new high priestess of the temple. Her inferior and vulnerable position gave the male temple priests more power. The material foundations for these changes were, on one hand, increased crop production and, on the other, increased involvement with warfare. Both crop production and herding were the domains of the temple and its properties. Improved, extensive agricultural irrigation, resulting in larger crops, demanded stronger and more centralized organization. City-states developed slowly and increased tax collection strengthened the material power of the temple. At the same time, the king's involvement with warfare demanded a different form of social organization and leadership. Starhawk believes that, in order to be recruited as foot soldiers, the males had to be raised with a new set of values.

To analyse these new values Starhawk reads the *Gilgamesh* epic, probably dating back to 2100 BCE and written down 1600 BCE, and the creation myth *Enuma Elish* from about 2000 BCE, including its story of Tiamat and Marduk. Her aim is to name these values and to see how sexuality, gender and the natural world were affected by new perceptions.

Gilgamesh was a king in Uruk who spread fear amongst his people because of his constant hunt for young virgin maidens. He refused to engage in the sacred marriage rite or, according to Starhawk, to submit himself to the power of the erotic. Instead he made a lifelong commitment to comradeship with his friend and companion in wars, the wild man Enkidu. Starhawk states:

> In the Gilgamesh epic the view of the erotic has changed. No longer is sexuality the source of fertility, joy and abundance. Now the erotic is linked in the same breath with war and conquest. Sex has become a prerogative of the ruler . . . . Now, women belong to men. Where the erotic once linked the human and natural worlds, now sex is seen to separate the wild man from nature.
>
> (Starhawk 1987:49–50)

According to Starhawk, male comradeship came to supersede the old rites of love and fertility, and the nonsexual love between Gilgamesh and Enkidu replaced the sexual love for women. Gender relations were reduced to pro-creation and the satisfaction of pure sexual drives, while men loved passionately as comrades in war and undertook heroic adventures together. In a passage where Enkidu feels fear, Gilgamesh answers him,

> Dear friend, do not speak like a coward . . . . hold close to me now and you will feel no fear of death . . . . When two go together each will protect himself and shield his companion, and if they fall they leave an enduring name.[5]

Starhawk maintains that we here find the ideology and psychology of warfare. She makes a distinction between tribal wars and "civilized" wars and holds that "civilized" warfare, from Sumerian times on, is characterized by the need for masses of soldiers to act together as parts of a whole, to face danger and relinquish the right to make an individual decision about whether to stand or run. These wars require a level of organization, obedience and discipline that "runs deeply counter to instinct". The value gained by being one of the company of warriors is a substitute for the "lost value of the self". As warfare became chronic, Starhawk believes, Sumerian society was restructured in the image of war. Myth, epic, religion and customs changed to perpetuate a new ideology of control.

Dumuzi's power had been a power-from-within, the erotic power inherent in his magically rising penis associated with food and not with violence. By the time of Gilgamesh, the erotic had been diminished for men. According to Starhawk, the male body instead became a weapon, no longer a source of nourishment, comfort and delight. The ideology of warfare is founded on contempt for women and associates sex with violence and control.

In the religious realm this shift in ideology became partly visible through the introduction of sacrifice. To Starhawk it symbolizes human subordination and the separation between humans and the gods: "The appearance of sacrifice marks the erosion of women's power and the shift from the celebration of the Goddess of life, to glorification of the divinity of rulers" (Starhawk 1987:47).

But more importantly, the natural world was degraded and associated with women, while men came to represent culture and the agency transforming nature. This ideology Starhawk claims to read in the *Enuma Elish* creation myth. In this myth the god Marduk creates the world by fighting and dismembering the body of his mother (or grandmother), the goddess Tiamat. She is the chaos water out of which he creates form and order, and thus gains kingship.

> He split her like a shell fish into two parts:
> Half of her he set up and ceiled it as sky,
> Pulled down the bar and posted guards.
> He bade them to allow not her waters to escape . . .
> He spoke, and at his word
> the constellation was destroyed . . .
> The Gods, his fathers,
> seeing (the power of) his word,
> rejoiced, paid homage: Marduk is king.[6]

Starhawk reads the myth as a reflection of the triumph of the patriarchal order over the older "matristic" order, represented as the battle between Marduk, champion of gods, and Tiamat, original progenitrix, primal sea. Being defeated, Tiamat is now turned into a demon, a dragon of the waters, something that bears no resemblance to humans' common being. The old snake symbolism of life-renewing female power is twisted to make female power seem dangerous and destructive.

Starhawk finds the imagery of the supreme godhead as king and the sole creator of the universe to be repeated in the later Hebrew scriptures and in the attributes given to Yahweh. She writes that everywhere patriarchal cultures and values were moulded, "the work of Marduk was continued by those who dismembered the ancient Goddess religion" (1987:65). In fact, Starhawk's favourite imagery to describe the misery of the present world is the myth of Tiamat's dismembered body.

According to Starhawk, Marduk's splitting of Tiamat not only expresses how a male god gained superiority over a female or how women lost social status long ago in Sumer. The message given in metaphorical language is that the roots of western civilization are based upon control and mastery of nature; control, "dismemberment" and "demonizing" of women are an integral mythological part of controlling nature. Starhawk often uses the story of Tiamat and Marduk in her workshops, and in a ritual meditation called "Remembering Tiamat", she asks the participants to go beyond time and space and become Tiamat, helping to re-member her dis-membered body. Starhawk's educational point is to remind women that the world existed for thousands of years before Marduk and Yahweh gained rulership and destroyed the goddess and that patriarchy is a relatively new cultural invention from a historical perspective (we shall return to the Tiamat meditation in chapter 4).

If we now compare the invasion theory with the degradation theory (the internal fall), we find that war, and the social values connected to war, are the primary explanation for why and how patriarchy and unnatural cultures developed: "power-over is ultimately born of war and the structures, social and intrapsychic, necessary to sustain mass, organized warfare" (Starhawk 1987:9). In the first theory, the unnatural culture of war was imported from aggressive invaders; in the second, this culture developed within society by a complex and long process. In Starhawk's account, Sumer is made an exemplary model to understand the mindset and social structures of patriarchy in *all* societies.

I shall now describe how Starhawk understands the characteristics of a patriarchal ideology and theology, regardless of any particular society, and how they become internalized in the individual. I shall no longer make explicit distinctions between her theorizing in *The Spiral Dance* and *Truth or Dare*. In addition, I shall include arguments taken from *Dreaming the Dark* (1982a) since in that book she explicitly turns her criticism against the Christian culture.

Disease: patriarchal consciousness

Patriarchy is, according to Starhawk, characterized by a mindset she names a "consciousness of estrangement". Its creative force is to divide and split apart, and its first manifestations were seen when people allegedly changed from worshipping the divine as immanent, and feeling a bond to all beings, to worshipping the divine as transcendent, and feeling separated and alienated:

> The history of Patriarchal civilization could be read as a cumulative effort to break that bond, to drive a wedge between spirit and flesh, culture and nature, man and woman . . . and impose[d] . . . a mechanistic view of the world as a dead machine. That rupture underlines the entwined oppressions of race, sex, class and ecological destruction.
>
> (Starhawk 1982a:xii)

This fundamental splitting apart into not only opposing but also contradictory categories Starhawk calls "dualism" (1982a:19). Dualism starts the moment humans no longer consider themselves as part of nature but divorce value from organic life and project it onto a transcendent deity. Humans thus become alienated from the world, from other people and from themselves.

Starhawk maintains that patriarchal dualism and the consciousness of estrangement can be recognized in certain cultural narratives and internalized thought-forms about sacredness (1), knowledge (2), morality (3) and gender (4). The cultural dualism expressed in these themes is given an almost ontological status since it possesses every new individual born in patriarchal societies. To become de-possessed from patriarchy is the struggle of feminism; and, in fact, the Witches' ritual magic is a significant means in this struggle.

The contents of these themes are all related to religion and religious symbolism, although it is difficult to say which concrete religion Starhawk has in mind. In her discourse, the expression "patriarchal religion" refers not only to the monotheistic traditions but also, to a certain extent, to the pagan religions of ancient Greece and Rome.[7] Nevertheless, the concept of god that she criticizes is a certain interpretation of the Jewish divinity, Yahweh, although she takes it for granted that this theistic, transcendental figure also represents Christian versions of the godhead. Let me briefly present her criticism.

1 *Sacredness*   The most important characteristic of patriarchal religion is, according to Starhawk, that the sacred as such is removed from the world and located in a separate, transcendent reality. Since one of the attributes of deity is to represent ultimate value, this value is thus removed from the world, from nature and from human beings. When deity is no longer manifest in the world, nature also becomes desacralized: "when nature is empty of spirit, forest and trees become merely timber" (Starhawk 1982a:6). The separation of the divine from nature and natural life creates attitudes in which nature is regarded as a dead machine that can be manipulated without any knowledge of its inner organic life. Starhawk maintains that the Jewish and Christian traditions have been driving forces in this development in western culture because they reject nature as something sacred. Patriarchal religion creates a consciousness "modeled on the God who stands outside the world, outside nature, who must be appeased, placated, feared, and above all, obeyed" (Starhawk 1987:9). The existential consequences of emptying the world of its inherent value are confusion and depression. People experience a constant loss of the Self and their endless search for the unattainable object of desire, always outside of the Self, will only bring temporary satisfaction and healing.[8]

2 *Knowledge*   According to Starhawk, the meaning of divine transcendence is not only to locate ultimate value spatially and structurally; it is also to claim exclusive access to knowledge of its contents. Since god does not dwell inside human beings, the knowledge about ultimate value cannot be available to individual humans through their experiences, senses or bodies. Instead, people

are taught that truth is revealed to certain chosen, great Men and confined to their Word. This Word – which mediates between the godhead and the humans – becomes ultimate authority.[9]

The belief in the unity of a transcendent truth creates fundamentalists. They preserve the unity by purging out heretics and declaring war on lies. The war between truth and lies is identical with the war between rulers and oppressed, men and women – as well as between good and evil, light and darkness, culture and nature, soul and body, god and devil. The goal is always to control and eradicate "the other", the polluted. Starhawk believes that both sexism and racism can be traced to this way of thinking.

3 *Morality* Starhawk believes that "the imagery of religion shapes the self by defining what value is" (1987:64). By projecting ultimate meaning outside the world of the living, mundane life is deprived of value; it becomes inauthentic and alien. In their inauthentic lives, humans are unable themselves to distinguish good from evil, and ethics becomes a set of laws and rules which are laid down by an outside agency through its representatives on earth. This way, all humans are retained in a childlike relationship to all authority. Therefore, they do not easily develop moral integrity, which, according to Starhawk, is a result of listening to the god(dess) within and taking responsibility for one's own actions and choices, which, in turn, is the moral code of the Wiccan initiation.

This is the story of success and failure, in which value is not something inherent by birth: "a person who lacks value gains it; a person who has value loses it. . . .[the story] reinforces a consciousness and a power structure in which some people have value and others don't" (1982a:22–3). The structure of Paradise and Fall in Jewish and Christian traditions is, according to Starhawk, different from her own analysis of a lost garden and its succeeding historical degeneration: the Jewish and Christian paradise is a perfect natural place from which people have been cast out because of their sins and to which they are denied entrance because of their shortcomings (unless they are reinitiated through baptism).

4 *Gender* Starhawk believes that the degradation of the body, the senses and sexuality – which is implicit in the "god against nature" ideology – is an expression of the same historical process that has created patriarchy and generated a gender shift in the symbols of divinity from "goddess" to "god". Control of nature and hatred of women are two aspects of the same dualistic way of thinking. Dualism categorizes by opposing values, and extensive use of analogies implies that the association god/male degrades its opposite pole: the world/female.

Starhawk maintains that by degrading nature, changing the limits of nature's domain and worshipping transcendent gods, humans have achieved the illusion of power and control over life itself. A model where a male deity governs the cosmos from outside serves to legitimize men's control of social institutions and the subordination of women.

Since the consciousness of estrangement determines how people in general are valued, it also has negative consequences for men. It creates attitudes of psychological "splitting" toward other fellow human beings, an attitude which she defines as "the inability to see people or things as wholes containing both desired and undesired elements . . . . In the split world, spirit wars with flesh, culture with nature, the sacred with the profane, the light with the dark" (Starhawk 1982a:19).

In *Truth or Dare,* Starhawk gives a more detailed psychological description of how people "lose their Selves", thus becoming alienated from themselves. Her theory is that the unnatural culture is reproduced through unconscious internalization: the religious–cultural deep structures force themselves upon every individual and take possession, although not completely because then change and resistance would be impossible. She names this culturally conditioned person the "self-hater". Her/his character is to underestimate her/his own value and to identify negatively with a mirror image of god, the King. The self-hater may "possess" humans with masks that mirror the five roles of the King: Judge, Conqueror, Master of Servants, Censor, and Orderer of the Universe. Starhawk's strategy for moving beyond this inculturated personality structure she calls the magic of de-possession, a strategy to which we shall return.

Dualism

Starhawk believes that profound social changes are deeply linked to profound changes in religious symbolism and religious language. This is so because, "Religion is the soil of culture – in which the belief systems, the stories, the thought-forms and all other institutions are based" (Starhawk 1982a:72).

She has been able to identify the structures of domination by comparing religious narratives, social institutions and human relationships. The most significant deep structure considered is the separation between god and the natural world. This split is regarded as foundational for the unnatural culture's worldview, for example in modern science, where objects are regarded as separate and existing in linear time, and in modern psychology, where humans are defined irrespective of their natural surroundings. Transcendence is, therefore, not only a metaphysical concept. Inherent in the image of a transcendent god is the principle of social transcendence over nature, women, body, sexuality and emotions. This process of splitting up Starhawk labels "dualism".[10]

Let us now summarize the basic principles she has identified in a dualistic way of thinking: first, reducing and categorizing the diversity of the natural world into pairs of opposites, A–B. The problem arises when these categories are not defined as binary or polar, but as contradictory. Dualistic contradiction is something other than recognizing a binary structure that causes something to move or to have meaning by being different from something else. "Dualism" as used by Starhawk implies an *essential* contradiction between A and B; they are not included as poles that are complementary to each other or to a third dimension.

The second principle entails attributing different moral value to A and B and then making hierarchies by naming A positive/good and B negative/evil. This is the most important step because until good and evil are separated as incompatible moral dimensions, we cannot really talk about dualism. Contradiction between A and B is not enough as long as they are not measured within a hierarchy of moral values. Initially, evil is not defined as immoral actions but as an unclean state of being. Evil is constructed by judging parts of the physiology of natural life as polluted and, thereafter, sinful. When statements like "the body is unclean", "death is an enemy", "nature is cruel" have no room for ambiguities, chastity becomes only good, carnal lust becomes only evil. To protect the purity of "the good", grayness, uncertainty and fluidity are not welcomed. A is symbolized as white and light and morally good while B is black and dark and morally evil; and they are not to be mixed.

The third principle involves finally degrading or annihilating B in the sense that A alone has the power. The dualistic thinking in terms of opposites does not stop at a hierarchical system of moral values; the very fact of recognizing the negative pole's right to existence is to accept sin. Therefore, dualism declares holy war on evil and tries to eradicate it, either literally, for example, by burning witches or by ideological control. Because of this fusion between "the evil" and "the other", "oneness" becomes the highest good. Oneness is a quality that characterizes the monotheistic concept of god in orthodox Judaism, Christianity and Islam. Implicit in dualism's ultimate desire for oneness is the concept of a fall from the original oneness which, in the eschatological future, will be reestablished. Although dualism is defined as separating the world into irreconcilable twos, it understands this split to be ontologically determined: it can only be repealed in a new world. "Holy war" is an aid to opening the door to the new world's lack of differentiation here and now.

Implied in Starhawk's definition of dualism, and in the way I have structured its basic pattern above, there is a crucial distinction between *complementary* and *contradictory* binarity. She does not deny that humans think and order the world in terms of opposites or poles. In fact, the erotic worldview of Witchcraft is founded on polarity and attraction between "female" and "male" energies. Her critique is rather directed toward the moral value judgement put upon these opposites and their internal relationship: one of harmony or one of war.

Starhawk's concern that we ought not to confuse polarity with contradictions can be illuminated by consulting Lévi-Strauss's cognitive theory. He finds "thinking in terms of polarity" to be a pan-cultural pattern, from which he draws the conclusion that binarity is universal and a reflection of how our brain works objectively (Lévi-Strauss 1979:10–13). Starting with the basic couple nature–culture, he states that a part of our brain's cognitive equipment is to arrange opposed concepts in binary series of correspondences to produce meaning, like cold–warm, death–life, woman–man, etc. According to Lévi-Strauss, the decisive difference between cultures is not binarity but whether they classify social status and identity by reference to metaphors from the natural or from the cultural domain. To this we may add: whether they classify according to polarity or contradiction.

Starhawk's solution, within Lévi-Strauss's conceptual framework, is to transgress the either–or division between natural and cultural categories. The social identity claimed in "I am a Witch", is an effort to undermine this distinction. The Witch represents neither "culture" nor "nature"; she is both. She comes from the animal kingdom, not metaphorically but substantially, meaning that she *is* nature, constituted by the substances matter–energy–spirit. She has the ability to communicate with other animals, the plants, the whole cosmos, because "these powers live in us, as we live in them. The mysteries are what is wild in us" (Starhawk 1987:6). She is also a human being, with the specific human ability to bend the energy–spirit embodied in her for a cultural purpose, as well as to transform matter into cultural artifacts. Ideally, she is not a prey to the forces of nature; nor is she a victim of the forces of culture because she has power within both domains.

If women shall understand their true natures and their history and be able to take agency and the responsibility for shaping the world "in the image of the Goddess", Starhawk claims that they must reenter the position of the "witch". In her opinion, Witchcraft represents a realistic (natural) worldview about the interconnection between nature and culture that is true and valid for all people, not only for the Witch. The reason Starhawk can be so optimistic about the possibility of creating cultural change is that humans are not seen as totally conditioned or possessed by an unnatural culture. There is a vestige of the wild in every being, a place inside symbolized as "the child", from which new power and new knowledge can be drawn. Magical ritual is seen as a unique tool for entering the domain between nature and culture, inviting nature as essence and as domain to be represented simultaneously.

Medicine: the return of the Goddess

As her claimed ancestors did, Starhawk believes in some form of reincarnation theology that every human spirit or soul is born from goddess in the beginnings of time. It never dies but is physically reborn in new forms in time. This spirit is identical with the Deep Self, which in fact is the immanent aspect of goddess. In her worldview, humans are thus twice born: of goddess first (their spirit) and then by a woman (their bodies, minds and feelings). Further, humans do not enter this world as a *tabula rasa*; they are imprinted with inner knowledge about the source of their beings, as well as with an ethical programme stating a will to life on earth. So, even though Starhawk's theory is that patriarchy has permeated every inch of society, it never was and never can be completely in control:

We are not machines. We are not infinitely programmable, endlessly reshapable. The self has demands of its own, and the body has needs that cannot be denied. The Orderer's belief that all can be known and controlled is a delusion . . . . The Orderer's false knowing keeps us from seeing and understanding the true order inherent in our bodies, in nature, in the ways we interact . . . . What needs to be reclaimed from the Orderer is our own ability to create an order grounded in organic reality and connected to the natural world, the order of the body's own needs and processes, pains and pleasures.

(Starhawk 1987:233)

Starhawk's goal is a society "grounded in organic reality" that can heal the "dis-membered" world and recognize the inherent value of each person and the elemental life that makes up the earth's living body. She believes that her vision is not radically new and refers to the values preached – but never practised – in the American Constitution. But, the old dream about "liberty and justice for all", proclaimed by the Founding Fathers, is not enough: "A society that truly recognizes the sacred manifest in the living world must go even further. For the earth herself becomes sacred to us, as do all her creatures" (Starhawk 1987:315).

Starhawk's vision is rooted in the knowledge and experience of "the Goddess". Toward the end of *Truth or Dare*, before introducing the chapter on "Resistance and Renewal", she repeats the myth of ancient origin, stating that at one time, the Goddess, who is the spirit-soul of the earth and of all living beings, was awake in everybody. All knew and honoured her and lived in balance and harmony. Then the patriarchal fall came. People turned away from the Goddess and created a "culture of death". Suddenly confronted with the possibility of final ecological destruction at the turn of the twenty-first century, women and men began to remember the Goddess:

The reborn dead walked the earth in new forms; the Witches arose and danced in the open. The peoples of the earth began to forge new links of friendship. They reclaimed the sacred places and with them the sacredness of the earth . . . they learned again the ancient knowledge and the mysteries, and used that knowledge not to build weapons but to evoke the will to life of the earth herself that burns in every living being . . . . But the ending of this myth has not yet been written. Has the Goddess reawakened only to preside over the destruction of the earth? Or will our awakening come in time? For unlike other deities, the Goddess does not come to save us. It is up to us to save her – if we so choose. If we so will.

(Starhawk 1987:310–11)

The return of the Goddess and the abilities of her devotees to re-create a new natural culture, or a sustainable culture in Starhawk's terminology, are therefore an open-ended question, the outcome of which she is hesitant to describe –

although she proclaims a complete political manifest for the fictitious year 2040 in her novel *The Fifth Sacred Thing*. Her basic argument is that a goddess-centreed culture must be holistic, growing organically from a consciousness that is radically different from the consciousness of dualism and patriarchy: "This is the consciousness I call immanence – the awareness of the world and everything in it as alive, dynamic, interdependent, interacting, and infused with moving energies: a living being, a weaving dance" (Starhawk 1982a:9).

Immanence is also a primary characteristic of the Goddess, defined in opposition to the transcendent, patriarchal male god. The Goddess, therefore, becomes *the* symbol of a new culture, and to worship her – through ritual and right living – becomes *the* medium to cultural and personal transformation.

Starhawk's optimism about the cultural effects of resurrecting the Goddess is founded on a specific theory of symbols developed by certain feminist scholars. From reading Mary Daly's *Beyond God the Father* and Carol P. Christ's famous article "Why Women Need the Goddess", Starhawk has learned that the nature of religious symbols is to constitute the values of the human social world. According to Christ, religious symbols and rituals create a cultural ethos that defines the deepest values in a society and in the persons living there. She supports her argument with Clifford Geertz's definition of religion as "a system of symbols which acts to establish powerful, pervasive and long-lasting moods and motivations . . . ." (cf. Geertz 1979:79). Regarding the power of symbols, she asserts that "symbols have both psychological and political effects, because they create the inner conditions [deep-seated attitudes and feelings] that lead people to feel comfortable with, or to accept social and political arrangements that correspond to the symbol system" (Christ 1982 [1979]: 72, 79).

Even if people no longer believe in "God" as defined in the Jewish and Christian traditions, or participate in the church's institutional structure, they are, according to Christ, still bound by the power of the God–Father symbolism. The effect of a symbol does not depend on rational agreement. It works in the unconscious mind and makes it possible for people to deal with frontier situations in life, such as death, evil, suffering, birth, sexuality. Therefore, "symbol systems cannot simply be rejected, they must be replaced" (Christ 1982:23).

The God–Father symbol has, according to Christ and Daly, been shown to have disastrous consequences for women. The symbol not only legitimizes hierarchy between men and women, with men as the superior, but it also legitimizes the oppression of women's bodies and their sexuality. This is so since a woman may see herself as created in the image of God–Father, meaning in his likeness, only by denying her own sexual identity, affirming instead God's transcendence and sexual "identity" (cf. Christ 1982:73).

Religious symbols, then, are both models *of* divine existence and models *for* human behaviour and identity, an interpretation that today permeates both the Goddess Movement and feminist Witchcraft. Since religious symbols are so powerful, both these movements argue that "the seeds" of a new society are sown by creating new stories, myths, images and symbols. One of the tasks of "Goddess thealogy" is, therefore, to develop "Goddess symbolism" that can give new models of identification.

In the myth of ancient origin there is an assumed link between goddess worship and a high social value attributed to women. Since Starhawk takes it for granted that the link between religious symbols and social values is deterministic, the resurrection of the old goddesses can be made equal to a political programme for a futuristic, feminist society. But implied in this link is a hidden argument about the priority of the natural, meaning that the symbol of "Goddess" is not chosen because it is morally better than "God", but because it holds more empirical truth about the natural world: it symbolizes that the birthing power is female and proclaims that humans are born of women, not of men. As stated earlier, Witches believe in the occult (and ancient philosophical) creed "as above so below", which means that forces operative in the human microcosm mirror the universal macrocosm – or vice versa. In the human microcosms, women are empirically those who bring life into the world. But if the human life-generating powers are of a female nature, so must the cosmic life-generating powers be. To highlight this truth, Starhawk suggests a female symbol for the divine creator:

> We call her Goddess, not to narrowly define her gender, but as a continual reminder that what we value is life brought into the world.
>
> (1987:7)
>
> She could just as easily be called *God* . . . . Yet the female nature of the ground of being is stressed – because the process of creation is a *birth* process. The world is born, not made, and not commanded into being.
>
> (1979a:24)

That women give birth is a cosmic and not a cultural law. When a culture values this cosmic fact by giving women high respect socially, it mirrors natural laws and opens the door to the possibility of creating a social paradise. When a religion expresses this fact through its system of symbol it supports the social validation of women.

Starhawk is not fully convinced that people will retrieve this knowledge unless they make a conscious choice; it is not likely to burst forth spontaneously. We find a similar argument when she states that it is not enough to know the laws of nature in order to create justice. Nature must also be revered from a strictly chosen ethical position, an ethics which gives life value above death. For since death feeds life in the reproductive chain of natural life, it is *not* a given from mere observations of nature that life should be valued more highly than death, or that "life brought into the world" – as represented by the goddess–women analogy – is of the highest moral order.

Since humans are born from the earth, which is the Goddess, they are imprinted by her in their deepest state of being and, ideally, in no need of rituals to be connected to her. But, given the conditions under which they live, the Goddess has been suppressed and denied by patriarchal culture for centuries and is in deep need of resurrection. To "reconnect" with the Goddess is, therefore, for modern people equal to rebirth in a mystical sense, that is, to entering the consciously chosen path of the Goddess. However it happens – either by ethical choice or by mystical experience/revelation – Starhawk promises great rewards for those who take the oath of initiation:

> She is the bridge, on which we can cross the chasms within ourselves, which were created by our social conditioning, and reconnect with our lost potentials. She is the ship, on which we sail the waters of the deep self, exploring the uncharted seas within. She is the door, through which we pass into the future. She is the cauldron, in which we who have been wrenched apart simmer until we again become whole. She is the vaginal passage, through which we are reborn.
>
> (Starhawk 1979a:77)

In Christianity, it is not common to perceive people as born twice (by God/ess and by woman), with an additional third possibility of rebirth. Although *created* by god, human beings are not generally regarded as *born from* God/ess prior to their physical birth. They are first born by women; later, owing to the fall, humans are offered symbolic rebirth by the Holy Spirit through the rite of baptism. But this second birth is not generic; it is an option for choice, a rebirth similar to Witches' third birth (initiation). This is an important difference.

Also, within the theological framework of the baptismal ritual, birth from woman represents a birth to death, meaning a life limited by death, while the second birth by the Holy Spirit is a birth from death to life, meaning eternal life unlimited by death. In Starhawk's goddess theology, death is not an absolute division line since she believes that death, by its very nature, continually makes room for new life to grow. In her universe, every human being is, therefore, granted the spirit of the Goddess as a gift of creation. This is so because humans are regarded as a specific *modus* of the divine: at a deep level humans are divine, made of the same substances (matter–energy–spirit) as the divine, part of the cosmos and connected to all life. But as humans they are primarily separate, with a mere provisional understanding of their deep nature. The alienated, nonreligious human is therefore unnatural because humans' basic natural condition is to walk the path of the Goddess (cf. Dyrendal 1993: 88,102).

Summing up, we may conclude that Starhawk's long perspectives on the European and Semitic cultural developments, from matrilinear to patrilinear kinship systems and from worship predominantly of goddesses and gods to worship predominantly of one male god, are to some extent in accordance with prevailing research. But her claim that these changes mirror changes in women's actual lives and social positions from influential and egalitarian to marginal and oppressed is greatly disputed and criticized. Also, her filling in of empirical dates and explanations in this long perspective must be regarded as closer to mytho-poetry than to historical research.[11]

A crucial point of her misconceptions is her moralistic reading of history. Prehistorical pagan society, of which we know very little except from more or less interesting archeological interpretations, is conceived of as good; ancient Greek and Roman pagan societies, of which we know a whole lot more, are less good since these already represent militarism and patriarchy; while contemporary "Christian" society is the incarnate evil since, amongst many horrible things, it constructed "the witch" in an early modern phase to identify its enemy and burned her as scapegoat.

The problem is, according to historians like J.B. Russell, that Christianity did *not* invent the witch; paganism did (Russell 1985:25). Long before the Inquisition started its witch hunt, she was produced as a social scapegoat by pre-Christian pagan cultures, causing individual charges of witchcraft to be raised according to the regulations of the civil law. This witch was not regarded as a healer but as an antisocial, destructive element who needed to be neutralized. In fact, the Christian Church initially dismissed pagan beliefs in witchcraft as superstition. It was first when the Inquisition, in its hunt for heretics in the fourteenth century, developed a comprehensive demonology that the pagan witch was resurrected by theologians in order to serve as a diabolic co-creator to the Devil. Anthropologist Andrew Sanders has documented how the witch is constructed as scapegoat cross-culturally and not only in western countries. This figure was common in both the Navaho and Ndembu societies, and Navaho people did admit that witchcraft accusations could be used politically in order to destroy political competitors. In some instances, the accused witch was sentenced to death (Sanders 1995:124, 143). The difference between tribal pagan societies and Christian Renaissance Europe is, therefore, not the creation of the witch as a scapegoat but of the demonic powers attributed to her and the extent to which she was exorcised: by the purgation of death during a time span of 300 years (p. 152).

Starhawk, pagan modernists and *Wicca Revival*

Starhawk is not alone when claiming historical lineage for her beliefs. As pointed out, this is characteristic of Witchcraft as religion and social movement; and, until the 1970s, Witches' historical claims were not in severe conflict with an academic viewpoint. As I wrote in the Introduction, many historians believed that the people persecuted as witches in the European witch hunts were members of a surviving pagan religion (Hutton 1996:3). This view had been established as acceptable early in the century, in particular through the immense influence of egyptologist and ethnologist Margaret A. Murray. When the thesis of an Old Religion collapsed, it made the plausibility of Murray's reconstruction of this religion, as well as Gardner's claims about its survival into the present, also collapse. All of a sudden, there was no social heritage to a living religion, only folklore, folk customs, literature and ceremonial fraternities.

The collapse of the theory of a surviving Old Religion has caused great distress to the Witches' identity, and during the last 20 years they have developed different strategies to cope with this fact. One strategy is orthodox, devotedly believing in Gardner's story, insisting upon a real historical lineage to the past in spite of the scholarly arguments. The other strategy is modernist, conforming to the updated research published, maintaining that living connections with the past are impossible to prove historically and, therefore, renouncing the whole idea as really unimportant to legitimate contemporary paganism. The middle group makes a hermeneutical distinction between content (spiritual roots) and form (historical roots);

> "The roots of the *spirit* of Wicca are the fundamental nature and the needs of the human psyche in its relation to the universe. The roots of the *form* of Wicca are many and various. A great deal of misunderstanding and irrelevant criticism has arisen from confusing the two. By separating form and content, it is possible to claim a lineage back to pagan spirituality, even though the historical roots are shown to be fairly recent.
>
> (Farrar 1983:19)

Starhawk takes a middle position of her own. As I have attempted to document above, she considers the consciousness and spirit of Witchcraft akin to ancient paganism, having survived into the present as "seeds"; historically, she alternates between two different viewpoints. On one hand, she regards Witchcraft as a religious path arising from experience, not dependent upon traditions to survive or to be authentic. Even though Witchcraft is the "Old Religion", it has undergone so many changes that, in reality, it is recreated rather than revived (Starhawk 1979a:8). On the other hand, she does not completely give up the idea of historical lineage, since the pagan spirit was obviously kept alive by something or somebody until it resurfaced. In fact, Starhawk does not demonstrate a great interest in the recent history of Witchcraft from the time it went underground until it was reclaimed by Gardner. Her focus is rather toward prehistory and ancient history, and her ultimate goal is to answer her own questions concerning *why* European cultures gave up the goddess and instead encouraged a patriarchal social development.

When Starhawk turns to the past, it is in order to "root" the identity of contemporary, feminist Witchcraft. Apart from this, Starhawk is not interested in origins. Neither in her writings nor in conversation does she give any explicit account of the sources of her theology and ritual teachings. She will refer to her own experience, to what she has learned from coven work, or to her teacher and founder of the "orally preserved" Faery tradition, Victor Anderson. Her authority of reference is usually stated as, "In my tradition we say . . . ., we do . . . ." or, "Witchcraft teaches . . . ". Her disengagement in naming her sources and her apparent lack of interest in how modern Witchcraft was really created have been adopted as a common attitude in the Reclaiming community. They often rely on, and refer to, Starhawk's version of history and cultural development in order to meaningfully explain the choice of Witchcraft as their spiritual path. In the fora in which I participated – whether in classes, circles, ritual planning groups, political meetings or social gatherings – I never experienced a discussion of the roots and recent development of Witchcraft or Wicca beyond the level of mythopoesis. I also met this ahistorical attitude within non-Reclaiming feminist groups, and it seems to be a characteristic of the feminist branch of Witchcraft.

In more traditional Wiccan groups there is often a lively debate regarding the contemporary roots of Witchcraft, and people take pride in being well read and arguing consistently. Some of them have also contributed substantially to the academic research record, for example Aidan Kelly, the founder of *NROOGD*. By means of comparative textual analysis he has tried to prove that contemporary pagan Witchcraft was invented fully-fledged by Gerald Gardner from sources such as magical lore and grimoires, in particular *The Greater Key of Solomon* (1888) and Aleister Crowley's *Magick in Theory and Practice* (1929). Although he keeps the door open for the possibility that pre-Gardnerian, coven-like groups might have existed, also in the US, he dismisses that these groups had access to any other or older sources than what Gardner had, including Victor Anderson's Faery tradition. Kelly blatantly states, "I call all Neopagan witches Gardnerian witches, because, as far as I can tell [. . .] all the current activity derives from widespread imitating of Gardnerian practices, and from no other sources." [12] Modernists, such as Kelly, do not agree that the new-ness of Witchcraft is diminishing since all religions by necessity begin as new religions. He simply regards the coming-into-being of Witchcraft as a response to a Christianity not fulfilling people's needs: "If the Roman Catholic church were actually as [Andrew] Greeley describes it, there would be no need for the Craft" (Kelly 1991:4).

Although Witchcraft was created under solid influence from ceremonial magic, it also differs distinctly from this occult tradition, for the theological ideas specific to Witchcraft are inspired by sources other than the mainly Christian and Kabbalistic heritage of western occultism. As Kelly states,

> the "ceremonial" or "high" magic of the grimoires and secret societies were inherently Judaeo-Christian in concept and vocabulary [. . . .] Gardner began with a Judaeo-Christian ritual that he later "paganized," by removing the obviously Judaeo-Christian terms, and replacing them with terms that appear more neutral.
>
> (Kelly 1991:36,50).

However, the Jewish and Christian heritage still shines through, for example in the determinate gender relationship between divinity and priesthood, most rigidly expressed in the Catholic Church, where God is exclusively represented by a male priesthood. Accordingly, when divinity in Witchcraft is extended with a female side, the Goddess must be represented by a female priestess. When the Goddess is elevated, so also is the position of the priestess. If we now recall the theory of religious feminism about a supposed interdependence between religious gender symbolism and social gender position, we can conclude that this whole idea is not a theory but a theology. It is based on the occult, but nevertheless also Christian, doctrine "as above, so below". It projects an ancient western idea as a universal given, presumably implied in the nature of symbolism as such. But it is only in the western world that heavenly gender prescribes social gender as a mirror image. In many other cultures a male god will be served by a female priestess, and vice versa.

The Craft itself can bear witness to how difficult it is in western traditions to break with Christian culture and, for example, introduce femaleness as the primary principle of divinity or of leadership. Gardner and Valiente split up in 1959 because Gardner's success as a religious inventor "was going to his head". He suggested a new set of Laws for the Craft, which Valiente considered sexist. The Laws set forth that

> the Gods love the brethren of Wicca as a man loveth a woman, by mastering her . . . . [The High Priestess had to recognize that all power came from the God, who had only lent it to her] . . . . And the greatest virtue of a High Priestess be that she recognizes that youth is necessary to the representative of the Goddess. So will she gracefully retire in favour of a younger woman, should the coven so decide in council.
>
> (Valiente 1989:70)

What Valiente failed to see is that Gardner's sexism was not his individual problem; his way of thinking is simply representative of the sexism embedded in the western occult traditions, wholesale. When Gardner portrays the goddess through her representative in a lovely, "sweet" woman, who is "Man's ideal" (cf. Gardner 1959:128) and with whom he seeks reunion, he only reveals his dependence on a fundamentally androcentric western spiritual tradition. The Kabbalah may be a nice, non-Christian mystical tradition to lean on for pagans, but its whole raison d'être is to reconcile a man with his god, manifesting as the Shekinah, the lost feminine who is believed to graciously descend into the man's wife every Friday night in order for him to merge, not with her, but with the godhead manifesting in her (cf. Scholem 1946:225, 235). The very same theme is repeated in the romantic tradition, which ultimately restores the feminine in order to save the Man and return him "back home" (Abrams 1973:255).

Valiente disdained Gardner's sexism and broke away. Since this, a series of new Witches' covens have branched off from the original covens constructed by Gardner (and Valiente) in England in the 1950s, and in the 1960s, the movement spread to the US via Raymond Buckland, a Gardnerian Witch (Adler 1979:90). Except from what has been hinted at in the Introduction, I shall go into no more detail about how the Craft then split, spread and flourished, but refer readers to Adler (1979), Eller (1993), Orion (1995) and Hutton (2000).

Reclaiming and *Wicca Revival*

How do we position Reclaiming and the Faery tradition within the framework and history of *Wicca Revival*? As stated earlier, when confronted with questions about the truth-value of their claimed historical lineage, most Reclaiming Witches will resort to a position in which it is of no consequence whether the myth of ancient origin and its recent revival are true or not; Witchcraft as they practice it is perceived as a feminist religion of *experience*. Although Starhawk supports this view to a certain extent, her basic attitude to this approach is that she finds it possible and likely that Gardner's Witch tradition was created by him, while her Faery tradition relies on other historical sources. What these sources might be she never states. As far as the occult influence is concerned, she admits that Witches may have adopted some of the ritual procedures of the Jewish Kabbalah, for example, in the way Witches create sacred space for the ritual. She writes that this probability is enhanced by the "fact" that it was common for witches in the Middle Ages to hide Jews from the Christian persecutors (Starhawk 1979a:58). In this argument, Starhawk turns toward orthodoxy, holding on to the myth of "The Wicca Revival" and referring to her own initiation in the Faery tradition in order to legitimize the claim that the religious path she presents is not "invented".

Why is it that the occult heritage and the kinship with Gardnerian Witchcraft, to the extent that they are known, is denied by Starhawk and most Reclaiming people? I find two plausible answers. The first is the sexism syndrome we already encountered in the conflict between Valiente and Gardner. Reclaiming people are bored with, and do not want to be associated with, what they regard as male chauvinism and the "obsession with sex, drugs and rock 'n' roll", which in periods they have seen flourish within some of the more traditional Witchcraft traditions. When I asked one of the long-term members in Reclaiming why she did not go to pagan gatherings anymore, she answered that she was fed up with non-feminist (neo)pagan Witches, "The only reason they are into the Craft is because of a chance to get laid and have free sex. I don't go to festivals because I am sick and tired from listening to how they boast of their orgies at breakfast." This very emotional answer does not really portray paganism and traditional Witchcraft as I have come to know them, including at the festivals. But regarding the lack of a feminist consciousness within these traditions, there are, in fact, tendencies toward sexual games and manipulation, which are *not* found within Reclaiming.[13]

The second answer is that Reclaiming Witches insist on practising a feminist religion and, therefore, try to hide their western occult and patriarchal roots, both from themselves and from others. This is because of the dilemmas that may arise when a feminist spiritual path has to admit to inheriting important elements of its cult from such a male-dominated and dogmatic tradition as the privileged men's secret societies from the turn of the century and their main pillar, the Kabbalah. Even though "unclean" heritage lines seem to be the fate of all reform movements, Starhawk herself has an understanding of Witchcraft as a break-up with all patriarchal traditions, including Jewish and Christian, and as a return to a pure, natural prepatriarchal religious practice. Having to admit that they cannot fully escape their Christian and Jewish upbringing, which shows up in the Witches' ideological luggage disguised as occult philosophy, would probably be experienced by many as too ironic and felt as a restraint on their visionary optimism about the potential of Witchcraft to create a new nonpatriarchal culture. It is extremely important to draw attention to this dilemma in order to undertake a serious analysis of the religious practices of the Reclaiming Witches. It also indicates the complexity of their religious symbolism, pointing to constant underlying tensions between segments of the Witches' theology and that of anarchism.

Notes

1 Starhawk starts both The Spiral Dance (1979a:3) and Dreaming the Dark (1982a:xii) by telling her own version of the myth about "the Wicca Revival", as she has inherited it from the Faery tradition.

2 In western culture the category of nature (or the natural) is commonly used in two distinct fashions: either to designate a *class of objects,* such as trees, animals or human bodies, or to designate the *constitutive principles* (or essences) underlying all objects. In the last case we cannot really separate between nature and non-nature. A difference set up against nature (as chaos or culture) is necessarily a difference *in* or *of* nature. Culture as cultivation and transformation of natural things is not an opposition but a prolongation of (and included within) the category of nature. In her theoretical constructs, Starhawk refers to nature both as domain and as essence (cf. Dyrendal 1993).

3 Thorkild Jacobsen 1976:45–6, quoted in Starhawk 1987:43.

4 Diane Wolkstein and Samuel N. Kramer 1983:38–9, quoted in Starhawk 1987:44–5.

5 N.K. Sandars 1960:76–7, quoted in Starhawk 1987:51.

6 James B. Pritchard 1958:35 and 32, quoted in Starhawk 1987:51; Jacobsen 1976:176, quoted in Starhawk 1987:63–4.

7 By also presenting the old pagan religions as patriarchal, Starhawk differs significantly from nonfeminist Wiccan authors (e.g. Jones and Pennick 1995).

8 Starhawk regards Christianity's devaluation of nature as a primary cause for the process of secularization, a fact of modernity which she resents (cf. Starhawk 1979a:190; 1982a:23).

9 Starhawk does not believe that Witchcraft is the only radical alternative to patriarchal religion and says she hopes that the religions of the future will be "multifaceted, growing out of many traditions" (1979a:196).

10 The contents of Starhawk's critique of western religion are in particular inspired by Mary Daly (cf. York 1995:107) and resemble viewpoints that are also shared by other feminist theologians – although her form is more poignant and biased. Ruether, for example, displays from *Sexism and God-Talk* (1983) onward viewpoints largely similar to those of Starhawk regarding the question of religious dualism. Ruether's own quest for the God/ess includes, according to McCance, "a critique of the dualistic, hierarchical thinking which she argues has informed the western theological tradition, including its God-language and imagery . . . . Ruether

suggests that 'God/ess' language draws its imagery, not from models of kingship and hierarchical power, but from female roles and experience" (McCance 1990: 173).

11 Starhawk has been heavily criticized (e.g. by Eller 2000) for the theoretical and historical constructs that she and other goddess worshippers have inherited from miscellaneous feminist scholarship. The critical voices argue that we cannot take for granted that female cult figurines symbolize *deities*, and not simply women or clan mothers; the alleged existence of an ancient, unified religion of *the* goddess is rejected as a historic fallacy; the view that historical evolution shows a linear development from matrilinear to patrilinear, which should be irreversible within patriarchy, is discarded; the Indo-European migration from east to west was not a conquest but more likely a slow, peaceful integration; there is no uniform evidence for deterministic correlations between values expressed in religious symbolism and those functioning in social life; those who read mythology as historical documentaries in search of historical identity have misunderstood the whole genre; the search for a historical golden age is unfounded in any historical material except in myths; the duo-theistic concepts of *a* goddess and *a* god are foreign to ancient cultures and only an ideal projection onto history of a romantic, modern notion of love.

The thesis of religious feminism, that there is a positive correlation between religious gender symbolism and social gender hierarchies, has in particular been contested. According to Caroline Walker Bynum, the thesis stems from a misreading of C. Geertz in which the interpreters make too tight a relationship between social fact and symbolic meaning. She finds no historical evidence that female god(dess) language leads to higher social status for women, or a more affirming female identity (Bynum 1986:9, n. 15). The problem with Bynum's criticism is, however, her purely formal categories for male and female. A consequence is that individual qualities attributed to the deities become irrelevant. But isn't there indeed historical evidence that the religion of Yahweh and the early Jesus movement had radically different social implications for both men and women, not because Jesus was male (as was Yahweh) but because he differed from the conventional male icon? A common example used to substantiate Bynum's argument is Mary, Jesus' mother. She is venerated in all Catholic countries without having "caused" a higher social status for women. Again, the problem with this argument is that the identity the female figure of Mary points to is completely conventional. It does not offer a break with the culturally accepted gendered discourse. We may assume that if such were the case, she would have instigated a breakup from patriarchal role models, as Jesus has done, again and again. Bynum fails to notice that Mary's gender is irrelevant as long as she does not transcend the traditionally gendered (and heterosexual) western matrix.

A more balanced viewpoint is offered by anthropologist Peggy Reeves Sanday (1981). She maintains, on the basis of extensive cross-cultural comparisons, that arguments similar to Bynum's are only partly to the point. Sanday tries to demonstrate that people are more apt to antagonize and "turn literal", making sexual difference a key part of their struggle, in times of severe social pressure, harsh competition over short supplies or during warfare. Values conferred to gendered symbols of the sacred are then read literally and transferred directly to social reality (and vice versa). Under such circumstances, divine maleness will more easily become incitement for male dominance and for social subordination of women, just as female deities are more likely to be conquered by their male siblings. Times of peace, prosperity and abundance do, on the other hand, make people's symbolizing abilities more sophisticated and less literal. They are, according to Sanday, able to worship a male god as divinity without reducing the worthiness of females in the social world (e.g. modern Europe); they are able to worship female goddesses as representative of deity without enhancing the worthiness of females in the social world (e.g. traditional India).

12 (Kelly 1991:x). Kelly has a PhD from the Graduate Theological Union in Berkeley.

13 The fear of sexual orgies has always lingered with the Witches, and the researchers are accordingly mindful to tell that they have never experienced them (cf. Matthews 1995:341), and neither have I. But my oldest informants tell another story. They say that sexual orgies could happen during the 1970s, just as they also can tell about occasions of sexual abuse. During my fieldwork there was a new incident in the pagan community: a 40-year-old man and 12-year-old girl had kissed intimately, laying on the ground within circle space, after the ritual was completed. I talked with many who attended that gathering, and all had different opinions. Some were upset and took it very seriously; others smiled and called it "a silly little episode". Such minimizing would not have been tolerated in Reclaiming, and, in fact, the sexual safety one feels as a woman in Reclaiming was one of the reasons I chose to study this explicitly feminist community.

3   Utopian and generic Witches

Revitalizing western spiritualities

In the previous chapter, I presented the cultural theory of Reclaiming Witch-craft as interpreted by Starhawk. Contending that western culture suffers from severe social and spiritual disease, she argues that a revival of paganism and goddess worship is necessary to heal people, save the planet and restore cultural sanity. Oppressive society is identified with Jewish and Christian traditions and the force of social regeneration with contemporary paganism and Witchcraft. This cultural theory is, however, a simplification of the Witches' belief, even in regard to the community of which she is the founder. Starhawk's utopian discourse is not the only norm in the Reclaiming community, and I shall deliberately contrast two analytical options: *utopian* and *generic* Witchcraft.

Those I call "utopian" Witches interpret Wicca along Starhawk's lines as a religious and social gospel for the emancipation and rescue of the world. They have chosen Witchcraft as their religion because it presumably conforms to their politics: it represents an acceptable spiritual path for those dedicated to creating an ideal society. Community is therefore understood to be a space of commoners who have consciously chosen a certain worldview and a certain lifestyle.

Those I call "generic" claim that Witchcraft is solely a position of personal belief. They have not chosen this religion for ideological reasons; they have been chosen by it, almost as if they are Witches by birth and constitution, realizing it now. If so, their new identity is in fact an old identity finally let out of the closet. The Witches' craft is almost to be regarded as a genetic disposition, their desire to join the pagan priesthood almost an obligation. Community, therefore, is not understood as a common lifestyle, but as common psychic ground for shared communication, despite differences in lifestyle.

Both utopian and generic Witches describe the choice of Wicca as a spiritual path to personal growth and the path itself as a "coming home". A major difference involves notions of human nature, the relationship between the human and the divine self, and the potential of Witchcraft to transform people. Also, while utopian Witches represent a self-understanding of con-sciously having broken all bonds with Jewish and Christian religions, generic Witches are more likely to admit some form of ideological continuity or, rather, similarity, between former and present religious beliefs. They distance themselves from Starhawk's unilateral and biased critique of western religion, claiming instead that the tradition has marked them permanently, in both a positive and negative sense.

When describing utopian and generic Witches I shall, therefore, emphasize how they build a Wiccan identity in contrast and conciliation to their perceptions of the Jewish and Christian traditions. Even though there are no historical-genetic relationships between Christian communities of the past and Reclaiming, there are plenty of ideological affinities; for in its utopian and social representation, the Witches' emancipatory project cannot be said to be linked to ancient paganism. It rather resembles the eschatology of the "counter-cultural" Christian Church.[1] Although Witches also go beyond this heritage line, a certain continuity to this sub-branch of western religion in terms of ethical and spiritual values can easily be read in Starhawk's books, in the interviews given by informants and in their actual communal living.[2]

An important way in which Reclaiming Witches actually diverge, representing discontinuity with western Jewish and Christian traditions, is in their persistent acceptance of a variety of interpretive trends along the continuum "utopian/generic". The *conscious* celebration and acceptance of differences and plurality is not a quality inherited from western religion, but rather from western modernism and, perhaps, from encounters with non-western cultural traditions. This attitude conforms to the Witches' self-understanding of leaving behind an old religious paradigm and creating a new one and is fully expressed within ritual space. In order to contrast heritage with new inventions, I shall contrast the act of forgiving with the art of processing.

When in the following I describe how some typical Reclaiming Witches manifest combined spiritual and political ideals in daily life affairs, the narratives refer to the time period 1989–90. The information was gathered from informal conversations and taped interviews conducted in June and July 1990.

Utopian Witchcraft: intentional living

Susan (35) is one of the Reclaiming Witches of a utopian bent. When she encountered Reclaiming in September 1981, she was already identifying herself as a feminist anarchist and anti-nuclear activist, and at that time was involved in civil disobedience and direct action to stop the opening of the Diablo Canyon Nuclear Power Plant in California. Together with several thousand other American leftists and alternativists, she camped with her friends outside the plant area in one of the largest non-violent civil disobedience demonstrations in American history. The action did not stop the Diablo Canyon Nuclear Power Plant from opening, but it influenced the future of many other US plants, preventing them from opening. Concerning the building of a new political community and strong emotional bonding between demonstrators, this particular action was summed up as being highly successful.

Here at Diablo Canyon, Susan confronted Witchcraft for the first time. Starhawk and Rose were active in the demonstration, and one day they went around the camp, drumming and shouting, trying to gather people for ritual. It was a simple ritual: the holding of hands in a circle, singing and drumming, calling upon divine forces. The ritual goal was to work out frustration, helping the activists to keep the focus of their intended work. Susan was intrigued with the Reclaiming women's ritual skills and ability to "work energy", and with their combination of politics with spirituality.[3]

Later that week, Susan encountered the real Witchcraft, the ritual working of magic, and not only a simple circle gathering. She was invited to join some Reclaiming Witches and other Pagans to do combined protest actions and magic in the backcountry around Diablo. She was told that when Jews and Christians intend to affect the world by means of spirituality, it is called "prayer". Witches call this intended formatting act "magic". After arriving at the hillside, they split into three groups. The first group called up "chaos energy" in the ritual circle with the intention to protect the second group, which was sent off to break through the fence lines. "Chaos energy" is believed to be protective by confusing the police. Because the people who entered the grounds managed to complete their action without being discovered, the ritual action was interpreted as successful and the magic as working. The third group did what is called "deep magic", meaning that the ritualists went into a group trance and visualized themselves inside the nuclear reactor, trying to prevent it from going online.[4] When the newspapers some days later reported that Diablo had to slow down the construction of the nuclear energy plant due to problems in the blueprints of the reactors, the trouble was interpreted by Witches as caused by their joint magical actions.

Susan was so thrilled to meet women like the Reclaiming Witches, who combined politics with spiritual practices and beliefs, that she decided to join the pagan community in San Francisco (SF). For years, she lived in a pagan–anarchist collective household in SF, took Reclaiming classes and went to the annual Witchcamp. In 1984 she became a member of a women-only circle – which she still is – and worked for a while in the Reclaiming Collective. In 1989 she "returned back to the land", meaning that she moved to Sonoma County to help build a small pagan commune, the Compost Ranch. Once a month she drives to SF together with her friend Artemis to participate in their women's circle. They also continue to join the SF anarchists for political actions and celebrate many of the sabbat rituals with the Reclaiming community in the city. On these occasions, Susan usually stays at Barbara's BQ with her "circle sister" and close friend Ruth, whom she also met at Diablo Canyon. This is a collective household of five adults dedicated to somewhat similar utopian values as those held by Susan and her commune.

Susan is of Jewish descent. Although she holds on to the ethnic side of her Jewish identity, she claims to have broken all bonds with Jewish religion. To her, Witchcraft represents something totally new, a religious path for the future. Susan considers herself to be primarily a political person, secondarily a spiritual one, and ranks politics before spirituality within her own value system. Over the years she has merged Witchcraft and anarchism into one great utopian union; Wicca fits into her already held anarchist norms:

> When I was introduced to Witchcraft I thought, this makes sense; this is what I already believe . . . . I think to be a Witch for me is like being part of a new paradigm, a new consciousness in which we see the earth and nature as sacred and as alive. I was brought up in a cultural paradigm in which you were disconnected from the earth. God was way up in the sky, and if you were good you could get to go to heaven . . . . To be a Witch is to see through a different lens, to have a whole different world perspective, which is that all of life is a web. We can tune in and work magically with it. I really like the rituals, the songs, dances, the altered states. But to this day I have a hard time with the concept "religion" or "worship": it is too hierarchical. The words "goddess" and "god" give associations to something outside myself. And I don't believe that; I think it is all inside, in all of us. I'm a free spirit: I don't like theological dogma.

Susan lives at the Compost Ranch with two children and five other adults, three men and two women, one of them being Artemis (40). Their adult lifestyle is in accordance with typical utopian values. They do, for example, identify as bisexuals and practice nonmonogamy. To manifest their sexual independence, they live in small, separate cabins, spread out on the land. The children live with their mothers. The cabins function as private space and sleeping areas, whereas all other activities take place outdoors or in the main building, an old trailer. Here we find the kitchen, the living room, a temporary bathroom and the guestroom. Food wastes are composted and metal and paper recycled. Their electricity is produced by solar panels and a generator is started whenever they need to pump water. The Ranchers mostly cook vegetarian meals, are non-smokers and consume very little alcohol. Some of them use mild drugs occasionally.

The community tries to keep its participation in money economics at a minimum. In addition to what they earn on gardening, they run a printing business. They design and print T-shirts on commission. Artemis has a part-time job at the local pharmacy. They have very low personal budgets and share all their goods, property and income as equals. Money policy is discussed weekly in their housemeetings, which function as "parliament". They have no formal rules in the commune, but anything can be put on the housemeeting agenda. Then they discuss and listen to each other until they reach consensus.

The children do not attend public schools but are enrolled in a home schooling programme. This means that the parents have the main respon-sibility for their education. Teaching the children is a shared task between the adults. The commune has no television because the parents do not want their children exposed to TV commercials and war figures. They want to raise their children as pagans, within the context of a commune, and protect them as much as possible from what they regard as destructive influences and attitudes in mainstream society. The reason for choosing home schooling is not the curriculum, but the socialization of the children.

The Ranchers do not intend to withdraw from society and interact actively with people outside their commune. New relationships with Sonoma residents are mainly built through cultural work, such as dancing and chorus, ritual circles, political actions, socializing and parties, but also through the home-schooling programme and Artemis's wage labour. They often have Reclaiming friends visiting from SF, but only for recreational purposes. All the adults have practical skills and take turns doing the different tasks necessary in a large household. It is very important for them to be committed to and sustain an egalitarian structure within the group.

As is common in all Reclaiming-affiliated collective households, the circle and the principle of consensus are ruling norms in the commune. Every morning, before breakfast, they make an outdoor circle. Adults and children hold hands while singing an old Quaker song:

> It's a gift to be simple, it's a gift to be free,
> it's a gift to come 'round where we ought to be.
> And when we find ourselves in a place just right,
> we will be in the valley of love and delight.
> When true simplicity is gained,
> to bow and to bend, we will not be ashamed.
> To turn and to turn, it will be our delight,
> till, by turning and turning, we come 'round right.

After the singing they "check in": everybody tells how they feel and what work they plan to do during the day. This morning Karen (55) asks the other women if it is okay to have a women-only meeting in the afternoon. They close their circle by hugging each other, while repeatedly singing, "I just want to tell you that I love you. I am so glad you are here and helping me grow."

Although these are Quaker songs, they use them because they represent the emotional and political values of their commune. Their goal is to build a combined communal and psychic space where they can live a simple life, free from material bonds and oppressive traditions, free to love and grow as people according to their beliefs, being "beacons" and "seedcarriers" for a new society. But ideals and reality do not always coincide, and they spend hours in housemeetings processing disagreements or conflicts. This is not regarded as a sign of weakness for the commune but as a necessary step in everybody's growth, because, as stated in the song, "by turning and turning, we come 'round right". The processing is part of the so-called consensus decision making, a practice American alternativists have also learned from the Quakers.

In the afternoon meeting Karen asks the other women for advice. She has met a new man and feels that Philip (33) does not really handle it well. He wants her attention and comes on to her more strongly, as if he is jealous. Susan and Artemis suggest that she make it clear to herself what she wants and that she states it to Philip, to the new man, and to the new man's lover. She does not want to create insecurity, either for Philip, the new man's lover or for the community. Karen is, therefore, encouraged to reassure Philip emotionally that he is number one and to give him more attention, and to tell the new man's lover that her intention is not to intrude in their committed relationship. She only wants "to have fun", nothing more.

Later Susan tells me that for nonmonogamy to work everybody has to be honest and open and continually work on and process his or her own jealousy. She believes in free love and regards jealousy as a culturally conditioned feeling. It is not something inherent in human nature and, therefore, it can be worked on and changed. She has chosen her sexual lifestyle because she believes that every person should have the freedom to do with her body what she wants to and to be with whomever she wants to be with – as long as it is mutual and beneficial to all parties. Sexual politics she regards as a fundamental part of nonhierarchical, egalitarian anarchism. Also her friends at Barbara's BQ have adopted Emma Goldman as a political role model and live in separate bedrooms. To advertise that they practice sexual freedom and that their ethical standard is "safe sex", they keep a big bowl of condoms on the table by the entrance door.

Susan believes Witchcraft is inherent to her lifestyle and that the prosperity of the community and the personal changes she has been through could not have happened without it. The name "Compost" is a reminder of the principle of recycling and organic balance, both materially and personally.

> I am always aware of the earth and the living creatures around me. I am conscious about what I use from the earth, what I throw out, where it goes, like being conscious of the cycles of life. Being a Witch, I also believe that I, as a person, have a lot of power and that I can change things. I can change the way I think, I can change the way other people think just by my own process and by the way I come across to people, and I can use ritual and I do use ritual and circles to help myself change and to help other things change. And I think it works. Circle and commune is to me a configuration of people who are trusted completely and loved, helping me and helping each other in whatever we are going through in our lives. In that atmosphere I was able to change – change myself. And the magic we did was not at all mysterious. It was kind of a method to focus energy and intention.

Susan and the Ranchers are utopian, idealistic Witches. They have not chosen this religion due to personal revelation or an intense religious experience. They are Witches because it fits with their already chosen political values. They are also idealistic in a literal sense, meaning that the flow of movement goes from imagination to action. They imagine the ideal life and then try to live it. To reach their goal, they will incorporate into their lives whatever tools are considered necessary. If multiple sexual relationships are the goal, processing of jealousy and magical circles may be tools. If a lifestyle in ecological balance is the goal, the worldview of Witchcraft is a tool to raise and incorporate a new consciousness. If protection of children from violence and TV commercials is the goal, home schooling is a tool.

Susan is well educated and believes that reality is socially constructed. Her attitude is formed by appropriating anthropological knowledge and its documentation of an "infinite" number of global, cultural forms, created and chosen by human beings in order to construct social life and social norms. Therefore, since lifestyle and sexuality are not subjugated to natural law, they are open choices, limited by nothing except the self and her cultural possibilities. But, even if one has been raised with the attitudes of jealousy, greed, ownership, violence or racism, there still is hope, because deep inside, everybody carries a pure and natural self, a self which already knows the difference between good and evil since it, by birth, is connected with goddess. In order to tend the good seed in every individual, the pagan communities need to cast off the chains of oppressive religion, oppressive childbearing, oppressive family structures, etc. In Susan's life, the power of magic is a new and optimistic tool that has already demonstrated its ability to instigate change and transformation.

Many pagan anarchists in SF believe that their combined spiritual and political visions were kindled in the past by late medieval heretics, such as the Brethren of the Free Spirit, and their Renaissance siblings, the Diggers. Since these movements renounced the priesthood and other authorities, they are considered historical role models for anarchist lifestyles. They are also identified with because people like the Ranchers need to convince themselves that the efforts to create a society built on community, egalitarianism, non-hierarchy, nonproperty and nonmonogamy have already been made in human history before with some success and are, therefore, worth the struggle.[5]

In the early 1970s, one of the anarchist publishing houses in SF called itself the "Free Spirit Press." Frank (39), who now lives at Compost Ranch, formerly worked there. I asked him if the name of the press was chosen with reference to the medieval movement, which he confirmed. He also told me that the Brethren of the Free Spirit was a heretical, anarchist movement in the fourteenth century, preaching that divinity was immanent in humans and that all people already had direct access to knowledge and wisdom from within. Frank takes it for granted that members of the Free Spirit were burnt as heretics. He parallels both the Free Spirits and the Diggers – a group reviving the "free spirit" in seventeenth-century England – with today's anarchists since the latter also believe that every individual is knowledgeable and ethically responsible and, therefore, in no need of laws and ruling authorities. Similar to many anarchist households in SF, the Compost Ranch has a poster with a poem about the Diggers called "The World Turned Upside Down":

In 1649 to St George's Hill[6]
a ragged band they called the diggers came to show the people's will.
They defied the landlords, they defied the law,
they were the dispossessed reclaiming what was theirs.
We come in peace they said, to dig and sow.
We come to work the land in common and to make the wastegrounds grow.
This earth divided we will make whole,
so it will be a common treasury for all.
The sin of property we do disdain.
No one has any right to buy and sell the earth for private gain.
By theft and murder they took the land,
now everywhere the walls spring up at their command.
They made the laws to chain us well.
The clergy dazzle us with heaven or they damn us into hell.
We will not worship the gods they serve,
the god of greed who feeds the rich while poor folks starve.
We work, we eat together, we need no swords.
We will not bow to the masters or pay rent to the lords.
We are free people though we are poor,
You diggers all rise up for freedom, rise up now.
From the men of property the orders came.
They sent the hired men and troopers to wipe out the digger's claim.
Tear down their cottages, destroy their corn.
They were dispersed, but their vision lingers on.

The poem is written by a contemporary anarchist songwriter and was printed in about two hundred copies in 1989 by a pagan anarchist in SF. The songwriter has interpreted the Diggers' revolt from a modern perspective, being antimilitaristic ("we need no sword"), antiauthoritarian ("disdain the law"/ "bow to no master"), antiproperty ("sin of property") and antichurch ("clergy dazzle us"). He reclaims their utopian vision and carries it on.

Susan, too, sees herself as a contemporary carrier of these old, utopian visions, both socially and religiously. But since she is not only a pagan but also a Witch, she makes a point that those who *really* embodied the freedom, egalitarianism and healing powers she yearns for were the Witches of "the burning times". Like Starhawk, she has deep faith in the powers of Witchcraft and of communities like Reclaiming and Compost Ranch and their abilities to move both the world and the individual in a much-needed new direction.

In Starhawk's novel, *The Fifth Sacred Thing* (1993), some of their ambitious utopian goals are played out as fiction. We are introduced to SF in the year 2040 and now, finally, every citizen is a pagan, a healer or a Witch, and magic is taught in schools. The year is divided by the pagan holidays and every hill is a sanctuary for multiple religious paths. People share the land, the food, the water and the air in common. Pollution is eradicated and, instead of cars, people commute in gondolas. There are no split subjects, no criminals and no prisons because no children are neglected and nobody oppressed. All have plural sexual identities and practice nonmonogamy. Jealousy is not a problem because they always "work it out". Governmental power is not structured hierarchically but as a network of concentric circles. Every worker is organized into guilds and every neighbourhood has its own community council. These are all run by consensus decision making and take turns sending representatives to the highest city council. The highest council is headed by a majority of women and advised by women elders. In this utopian society, Reclaiming's community ideals have finally materialized.

Utopian Witchcraft and counter-cultural Church

Is the social utopianism of Witchcraft a revival of ancient pagan or Renaissance Christian practices? As pure idea, without any goal-oriented practices attached, utopianism can be traced as far back as the prophetic movements of Judaism and to philosophers of the ancient world. But as social practice, it does not reach further back than medieval times: utopian dreams were not converted into social action until the millenarian movements arose, writes historian Norman Cohn. Thus, it is within the ideological lineage of millenarianism that I shall seek the first roots of Starhawk's basic concepts – community, interconnection, immanence – as well as of the social forms experimented with at the Compost Ranch and Barbara's BQ.[7]

The notion of the millennium is, according to Cohn, derived from the belief that God, with the active help of elected holy women and men, was soon to eliminate the existing social order of inequality and papal hypocrisy and restore upon earth the original and natural state of affairs in the Garden of Eden: equality, communality and sexual innocence and freedom (1981:19). He describes the medieval movements as responses to social crises provoked by poverty, class differences and social and spiritual oppression. Concerning their intent to purify and redefine community and interhuman relationships, they may be regarded as social revitalization movements.

Long before millenarianism converted utopia into action, the ideas were developed both in Greek and Roman literature in the form of a myth about the "original state of nature" that had existed on earth in some lost Golden Age. The myth provided a theme for philosophical speculation: especially the Stoics of the third century BCE stressed that all "men" were "brothers", and that all men were by nature free and equal. Cohn asserts that the version of the myth as contained in Ovid's *Metamorphoses*, in particular, was echoed in later literature, exercising important influence upon communistic experimentation during the Middle Ages. According to Ovid, at the beginning of human history

> men used to cultivate good faith and virtue spontaneously, without laws. Punishment and fear did not exist, nor were threatening phrases to be read from fixed bronze tablets . . . . Earth herself, untroubled and un-

touched by the hoe, unwounded by any ploughshare, used to give all
things of her own accord.

(Quoted in Cohn 1981:187)

In order to emerge as social theory, the myth needed support from "natural"
examples. Seneca developed the myth/social theory by pointing to how the
sun is beneficent to all and how humans are equally dependent upon the air,
the water and the gifts of the earth to live. When this thought figure was
adopted by the Church Fathers, it turned into a doctrine in which the
original state of nature was interpreted as divine law, later undermined by
man-made law. In their writings it becomes "God's will and decree" that the
sun shines for rich and poor, for ignorant and wise, for men and women. God
also made the vine and grain and all other fruits for the charity of all. It was
human laws that created the distinction between "Mine" and "Thine"; and it
was this violation of community and equality that gave rise to theft and all
crime. Cohn argues that, from the third century CE onward, it was agreed by
most of the Fathers that inequality, slavery, coercive government and private
property had no part in the original intention of God and had come into
being only as a result of the Fall.[8]

Since these egalitarian and communistic ideals were acknowledged among
many clerics long before medieval times, why is it that they were not
automatically projected into the future as ideals for building community here
and now? According to Cohn, this is because the ideals were regarded as
lost ideals, and necessarily so. Once the Fall had taken place, people were
irrecoverably corrupted by Original Sin. From that time on human nature
demanded restraints that would not be found in an egalitarian order.
Inequalities of wealth, status and power were not only consequences of sin,
but also arrangements for combating sin. The Golden Age was not simply lost,
but necessarily lost. Neither Ovid, Seneca, or the Church Fathers were
concerned with social and economic change. The only recommendations they
gave on behalf of the lost ideals were directed toward individuals, dealing
solely with problems of personal conduct, for example, that a landlord ought
to behave reasonably toward his labourer, and that a rich man should refrain
from using his wealth for evil purposes. The original state of nature was only
regarded as providing guidelines and ideals for *individual* life. The Church
maintained, though, that voluntary poverty was the more perfect way. It also
insisted that in a corrupt, fallen world, the original state of nature was an ideal
that should only be pursued by the elite. The institutionalized expression of
this attitude was found in the orders of monks and friars (Cohn 1981:197).

It was not until the end of the fourteenth century, with the outbreak of
the millenarian movements, that this changed. These movements called the
egalitarian state of nature out of its past and projected it into the future as an
ideal society. According to Carolyn Merchant, their vision was "the complete
overthrow of the established social order and its replacement by an egalitarian
communal society and state of nature like that anticipated during the millen-

nium – a thousand-year period when Christ would reign on earth and Satan would be banished" (Merchant 1983:79). The movements had a historical continuity dating from the medieval crusades of the poor (thirteenth century) to the religious sects of the English Civil War (seventeenth century).[9] Merchant also connects the naturalism of these communal movements with the outburst of occultism within the same time period.

Their revolutionary eschatology was based upon a paradisiacal notion of "the *real* state of nature" as the original state of affairs in which all people were equal in status and wealth and nobody was oppressed or exploited by anyone else. It was also characterized by universal good faith and brotherly love, and sometimes by community sharing of property and even spouses. They argued that the original Golden Age was not irrevocably lost in the past but, instead, predestined for the near future. To work toward its manifestation, either peacefully or through revolt, was in their view an act of piety: now was the time when God himself prepared to descend heaven upon earth and humans and divinity would meet face to face within joint time and space, "finally at home". According to the adepts of the Free Spirit, they only prepared its way by living as if "the Kingdom" were reality.[10]

Because of their communistic ideals and their actual obliteration of man-made law, Cohn calls the Brethren of the Free Spirit "mystical anarchists" or "revolutionary anarchists". They left their ordinary occupations and obliga-tions behind and gathered together in a new "perfect commune". Cohn claims that the adepts of the Free Spirit never formed a single church, but rather a number of independent, like-minded groups (Cohn 1981:172). Each group had its own particular practices, rites and articles of belief. But the groups kept in contact with each other and were recognizable by a common corpus of doctrine.

Like other counter-cultural movements of the time, the Free Spirits were accused of so-called deification theology: the basic feature of their faith was pantheism, developed within a neo-Platonic framework of successive emanations from a first source.[11] The Free Spirits stated their beliefs in sentences like, "God is all that is", "God is in every stone and in each limb of the human body as surely as in the Eucharistic bread." "God is me and I am him." Anything with a separate existence had emanated from God, but was no longer God. On the other hand, whatever existed was compelled to find its way back into the Origin, and at the end of time everything would, in fact, be reabsorbed into God. Since divinity, through the spirit, dwells in each human being, they were not dependent upon Scripture or sermons. They were taught by the spirit directly and no other teachings, either by Scripture or otherwise, were of any use to them (Cohn 1981:293).

Their spiritual goal was to be completely transformed into God. This they believed was possible by the "subtle in spirit". To reach this state, the novice had to practice various techniques, from self-abjection to the cultivation of absolute passivity, for several years. The reward was a state of mind known as the "spirit of freedom", or the Free Spirit, attained when a person experienced being entirely transformed into God. In this state one is restored to one's original state before flowing out of the deity; the concept of sin no longer has any meaning. The Brethren of the Free Spirit were free to engage in all human activities without restrains. "The free man is quite right to do whatever gives him pleasure." "Nothing is sin except what is thought of as sin." "I belong to the Liberty of Nature, and all that my nature desires I satisfy . . . . I am a natural man."[12]

The movement included men and women and, whether married or not, they were considered free to have as many sexual partners as they wished.[13] They regarded exclusive monogamy as a result of the curse. The brethren were free from the curse and, therefore, free to mate as naturally and promiscuously as animals or as innocently as Eve and Adam in the Garden of Eden. They also attributed transcendent, mystical value to the sexual act itself. Some regarded it as a sacrament, called "Christerie" (Cohn 1981:180). Cohn interprets their libertine sexual activity as an affirmation of emancipation. The adepts also at times practised ritual nakedness, arguing that "one ought not blush at anything that was natural". To be naked and unashamed they saw as an essential part of the state of perfection on earth. Promiscuity and nakedness were thus remedies in the effort to establish an earthly Paradise, beyond the cursed knowledge of good and evil. Merchant writes that sexual freedom for both women and men was also brought up among Ranters and Quakers, and in their meetings it was not uncommon that people stripped naked in church. It was, according to Merchant, a symbol of resurrection (Merchant 1983:124).

If we now recall Starhawk's cultural theory of paradise-fall-regeneration, as presented in chapter 2, as well as the philosophical themes and narratives deduced from the theory, it becomes apparent that many of the ideological elements in the ethos of feminist Witchcraft are similar to those expressed in the utopian strands of western religion in general. In addition, many Wiccan beliefs, as well as some communal and ritual practices – such as the immanent god, the astral movements of the soul, ritual nakedness, sexual freedom, the autonomous coven, the idea of brotherhood or community, egalitarianism and naturalism – resemble the utopian eschatology of the counter-cultural Church, in particular the ideas of the Free Spirit movement and their successors.[14]

In fact, when Catherine Albanese (1990) presents the history of American nature religions, including paganism, from the eighteenth century onward, she argues that these movements, in their advocacy for naturalism, were deeply influenced by what I have called "counter-cultural Church". The communitarianism of European utopianism developed new forms after immigrants imported it to the US. One example is the earlier mentioned consensus decision making process, developed by the Quaker society and appropriated among others by Reclaiming.

Feminist Witchcraft does, of course, also resemble occult ideas, which materialized as social movements during the Renaissance. But this has already been argued for in earlier chapters and is today well established knowledge regarding more traditional forms of Witchcraft.

Generic Witchcraft: the priesthood of the goddess

Although most Reclaiming people are utopian Witches, a substantial number have a more generic bent. They do not believe in Witches' extraordinary talents for creating a perfect community, a paradise on earth. They do, however, still believe that they are among the Guardians of the world – if not communally, then individually. As initiated Witches they have access to a privileged place where they can see what others cannot see; they can sense what others cannot sense, or induce change on the material plane through ritual and magic. To them, the people of the world represent the laity, whereas Witches are the priesthood with secret and special knowledge, serving the people.

As chosen or gifted individuals, a certain moral responsibility for the well-being of the world is bestowed upon them. Some believe that magical gifts, such as clairvoyance and healing power, have been part of their natural constitution since birth. Accordingly, their self-understanding is simply to have been born Witches. To others, magical gifts are regarded as something anybody can acquire through learning and ultimately through initiation. A generic Witch will often make a clear distinction between those who are initiated as Witches and those who are not, emphasizing the important function of the initiation process. Even if this attitude is not announced publicly, it nevertheless exists inside the initiates' own circles. A generic Witch believes that only initiates' can contact "the other side" and call the Mighty Dead.

We shall use Aradia (36), who lives in SF, and her circle of friends as examples of generic Witches, although they inevitably also have some utopian inclinations. In contrast to Susan, and typically for those she represents, Aradia is an initiated Witch *and* she has taken a new name, a goddess name.[15] She is a long-term member of a coven and of the Reclaiming Collective, as well as a teacher and a ritual facilitator. She is a highly respected elder and one of the most important contributors to Reclaiming's version of Witchcraft. Aradia works as an intellectual, presently as an editorial manager in a large publishing house. Her sexual preference is lesbian. She lives a quite ordinary, mono-gamous, nuclear-family life in Bernal Heights south of Mission with her lesbian Witch partner and their pets. Their house is full of books, although a huge altar, decorated according to the "wheel of the year", commands all the attention in the living room. Aradia's working altar is in her bedroom. Here she keeps coloured candles, incense, imagery of the goddess, as well as ritual tools: athame, wand, cup and pentacle. When she first entered Witchcraft in 1981, Aradia did magical spellwork to achieve practical goals. When I interviewed her in July 1990, she considered herself to be solely a devotional Witch.

Unlike Susan, Aradia did not choose Witchcraft for intellectual or political reasons. Even though feminism is a fundamental platform to her life, she endorses Witchcraft exclusively because she considers it true. In fact, already in 1980 she was told by her inner voice that this was her true path. A year and a day later (in 1981), she was initiated Witch and Priestess of Bridged, the Irish goddess. To symbolize her new status and being, she took a new name, a goddess's name. Aradia recalls that she has always been a psychic, and as a child she could simultaneously be in several realities: she could think of things and they would happen. She also believes that she, in her core Self, has been a priestess of Bridged in many earlier lifetimes. At least she feels completely dedicated to her vocation. According to her, she did not choose Bridged but was chosen by her; "I am hers, and she gets to do with me whatever she wants", says Aradia.

When teaching Reclaiming classes, Aradia emphasizes that she is an urban Witch. She wants to teach her students to see everything that exists in three dimensions as sacred and to understand that *this* outlook is the real political power of Witchcraft. She regards Witchcraft as a religious path that in and of itself sanctifies, which means that it calls holy that which exists in three dimensions. Witches normally proclaim the land as sacred, the air as sacred, the sky as sacred, the water as sacred, the animals as sacred, humans as sacred. Aradia says:

> But I go further and say the sidewalks are sacred, the buildings are sacred, the telephone poles are sacred, the ground everywhere is sacred. Every thing that exists in three dimensions is sacred. I don't use this expression geometrically but metaphysically. Not nature or "the other place" is sacred but all places are sacred. That kind of thinking changes your political basis. When we are brought up in a system that puts ultimate value somewhere else, in another world, it is a political act to say that this very world of life and death and decay is sacred. It is not the only one sacred, but it is the one I'm focusing on now. Addiction is a way of being somewhere else: in the past, in the future, some other reality, just not here. Healing from our escape into other realities is a political act. I am a human here and now, and I am not supposed to be anything else, or anywhere else.

In Aradia's terminology, utopian Witchcraft can result in addictive behaviour because the utopians often long to be somewhere else, in a better world. Aradia, therefore, dislikes the utopian bent in Reclaiming. She finds it dangerous to think – as so many Witches do – that a certain religion can save the world, or that Goddess religion is inherently something that will help people not abuse other people.

> I think evil exists, and that the desire to abuse power is something human. So, religion is not going to change the world: humans are in it. You know what I mean? Please, give me a break . . . . I really think it's a dangerous sort of thing to think. It can lead you to start believing that the Craft is what is going to save the world, which is such bullshit. It can turn right into another Catholicism. We are not perfect and neither are we allowed to be. Spirituality is not about fixing the world and feeling good about yourself. It's about trusting in something larger, giving yourself over to

something larger, exactly because you cannot fix it yourself. A spiritual path has to entail some sense of willingness to surrender. I think the Craft is one way to do that, but not the only one.

Aradia also differs from Susan by not being willing to dismiss her Catholic Christian roots. In fact, she has become famous in the community for calling herself both a Witch and a Catholic. This explicitly dual religious identity is not very common among Witches who were raised as Christians. If a Witch celebrates Christmas, she is likely to make it an extended part of Winter Solstice. If she finds the ethics ascribed to the concept "love your neighbour as yourself" to be normatively valid, she will immediately point out the tenet's universality or what she considers its pre-Christian roots.

If we compare this situation with Reclaiming people of Jewish descent, we find an interesting difference. Many Reclaiming Witches, including Starhawk, are strongly attached to their Jewish ethnic identity. In addition to pagan practices, such as celebrating the pagan cycle of the tangled lunar and solar rituals, some also observe the Jewish holidays, like Passover and Hanukkah. The main argument for holding on to dual identities, as Witches and Jews, is that Judaism is not only a religion, but also – and primarily – an ethnic identity. To distance oneself from an identity as Jewish would be equal to suppressing one's own ethnicity. To claim this identity involves claiming the sacred history of the Jewish people and its sufferings.

This dual identity is not questioned or criticized by non-Jewish Witches. Jewish Reclaiming Witches are "allowed" to communicate their dual identity in the open, while Witches who are raised as Christians seem to under-communicate theirs. A plausible explanation is that, although both Judaism and Christianity are considered patriarchal religions, Christianity is regarded as much more negatively loaded. It has a heavier "karma" stemming from its aggressive conversion politics: crusades, persecutions and witch trials.

During fieldwork I realized that this generalization is not quite true. There seems to be a difference between those of a Catholic and those of a Protestant upbringing. While the Protestants are more likely to "trash" their religious heritage, many Catholics more closely resemble the Jewish Witches, consciously taking at least a partly dual identity. They do not fully identify with Starhawk's critique of western religion, but claim that the traditions they were brought up with have marked them permanently, positively as well as negatively. They admit to somehow carrying on western religiosity and recognize it as a cultural heritage, although they also diverge from it, having created new forms, searched out new beliefs.

Re-Attending Catholic church

To better understand how these Catholic Witches balance a dual identity between the religion of their childhood and their adult choice and why they after all prefer Witchcraft, I invited Aradia and five of her ex-Catholic

Reclaiming friends and elders to an ordinary 10 a.m. Sunday Mass. We decided to visit *Mission Dolores* because of its location, age and aesthetics: the church is located in their neighbourhood; the parish is the oldest in SF; its architecture as well as interior decorations are very beautiful. The basilica has two arches. One is dark blue, symbolizing the cosmos with a glowing light at its center. The four directions of the universe are marked with different signs. In the other arch Mary is painted inside the sun, holding the seven crosses of the heart. The room is decorated with stained glass windows and small chapels and altars for the saints, and smells of incense.

The Witches have all dressed up for the occasion and observe the proceedings of the Mass with both interest and respect. Except for Aradia, who attends Mass regularly, none of them have been to church for many, many years. The church is one of the largest in San Francisco, and they are all surprised to see it so crowded, with people from many cultures and different social classes. The service is reformed. In his sermon, the priest addresses the social reality of the people present but also makes people laugh. In the final announcements, people are informed that the church serves free meals to victims of AIDS. The priest then reads the menu for the meals in the week to come and asks for monetary contributions.

After the Mass, we go to a café to discuss the experience. I am aware that had I asked them to come with me to a fundamentalist Christian meeting, they would have answered no in addition to having interpreted and judged their Christian heritage very differently. I believe, however, that a positive encounter with Christian religion provides for a more sober evaluation and, therefore, one which is more interesting. The sobriety of their evaluation is also supported by the fact that I interviewed them collectively and taped our conversation. Their feelings about Christian religion were not secret confessions to me but open statements meant to be heard by other Witches as well.

Aradia opens the floor by telling us that she is a Catholic but not a Christian, and that she has a profound belief in Christ:

> I deeply believe in all those miracles: that God descended in Jesus; that the body of Christ is in the wafer and wine. The problem is that the codification says there is a boundary here, and that nothing exists or is true except for these events. And I don't believe that. So I fit Catholicism into my Goddess religion, not the other way around . . . . I believe that the deities operate in an infinite number of ways, and this is one of them. I am a priestess of the Goddess, and I am allowed this mutual path.

One of her friends, Andrew, a lawyer, says he used to be an altar boy both before and after the Vatican II reform, and that he has many good things to say about the Mass we just observed. He felt a lot of positive emotions around shaking hands, calling in political events, and parts of the ceremony where people were getting involved. "And yet, my overwhelming feeling is boredom.

They still do not know how to raise energy. That amazes me . . . . Also, what I feel most uncomfortable with in Christianity is the cross. I walked into the church and saw that cross again, and thought that for the twentieth century it should have been the electric chair."

Hera, a midwife, agrees with him that this is the reason why she is not a Christian anymore: the cross and the concepts of suffering and martyrdom are not central to her spirituality. She believes that we continually have to deal with the mystery of pain and death and human shortcomings, finding meaning in suffering,

> but my problem is that it is made the centre, the exclusive centre, which everything else is hierarchically descended from. Although it is important in life, I simply do not believe that sacrifice, pain and suffering, is the root of life. As a Witch I do not worship death, but life.

But Hera also agrees with Aradia and says that she still considers herself a Catholic. To her it seems impossible to divorce completely from something that was part of her formative years, from something she was raised with. So, "the catholic" is still a part of her core being. She also admits to having enjoyed the mass,

> I really enjoyed it, even if I actually was not prepared to enjoy it. I was noticing today that there are a lot of anchors that I have, that I am not aware of till I step into a church that is structured like the one we were in today. The architecture, the high ceilings, something about the visual still hold a connection for me. I made peace with some parts of the service today. The singing, the chorus, something inside me, some very good parts of myself, a feeling of good will toward humanity, a very giving place that I think developed in the Catholic Church.

They all agree that Christianity at different historical points has got lost from "good will toward humanity", which they equate with the teachings of Christ. Instead it became a political instrument to conquer land and people. Regarding such a central Christian doctrine as forgiveness for sins, they believe Jesus had in mind something like, "you don't have to pay for karma, or be totally worn down in it. I am coming to cancel out a whole lot of karma so we can have a fresh start". But his gospel was twisted to mean "all you need is a sacrament".

Pan, a computer analyst, is very clear that he is looking for a bridge between what he was raised with and the pagan spirituality that he practises today:

> Many people, including Starhawk, often talk of paganism as the popular religion until the burning times, and then it was wiped out, and now we are returning to it. There is some usefulness in the ideas, but I don't think

of that as a historical reality. I think of paganism these days as being part of western culture and spirituality, and that it has a relationship to nature. So you can have pagan Catholics or whatever, if they do have a spiritual relationship with nature . . . . I don't think you can say that Christianity only is patriarchal and in search of control over magic and mystery, because a majority of western spirituality has been through Christianity. Those who won, and took control over time, have revised the history. The cult of saints, for example, is not what won in the conflicts inside the church, and yet it existed all the time.

When I explicitly ask why they are Witches, not Christians, they all agree to Freya's statement: "The reason why I am a Witch is that I have found a way to really have the ecstatic, the singing and the shaking, and also with an extremely intellectual faith. I don't see the Christian service satisfying any of these concerns for me."

To the extent these Witches agree with Aradia and differentiate between Catholic and Christian, the term "Catholic" comes close to representing an ethnic category, loaded with tradition, identity and "blood ties". They perceive of themselves as linked to their western ancestors and deceased family members, honouring the positive ethical teachings and selected spiritual practices handed down by these beloved ancestors, claiming that this heritage has played a determinant role in their formative years. They seem to have an overall good feeling for the liturgy, although they also complain that it is too boring and nonecstatic for their adult taste. They identify strongly with the doctrine of love and with Christianity's social gospel and positive involvement in the world. In this respect, they judge the Jewish and Christian traditions very differently from the way Starhawk does. They honour it for caring about individual people and social, worldly affairs; she criticizes it for emptying the world and all life of inherent value. To make room for both statements to be true, Pan invites a differentiation between the many traditions of Christianity and the leading authorities. In order to explain the errors made by the Church, the Witches also separate between "what Jesus had in mind" and the doctrines developed by those in charge.

Christianity has disappointed them, but some of its basic teachings and ideals still seem to be norms and guidelines. Have they moved to Wicca from a feeling of betrayal, so that Witchcraft becomes what Christianity should have been? By this question we immediately touch upon the dynamic tensions between utopian and generic Witches. The first group believe that the Jewish and Christian traditions must go because they cannot hold the truth about the nature of Reality: they resist the experience of divine immanence and of nature as animate; they deny that the elemental power that gives birth is female. Therefore, they need to be replaced by a new cultural paradigm.

The other group sees more continuity between now and then. According to ex-Methodist/Unitarian Anna in the Reclaiming Collective, she has not converted to a totally new worldview through Witchcraft, but primarily broken with a patriarchal institution:

> I think that as far as the morals go, and the connection between the political implications of religious beliefs of what is sacred and what is valued – that has always been there. The difference is the external practices. I mean, I just couldn't stand being in the Christian church any longer. All the patriarchal language, the patriarchal imagery . . . just no . . . I couldn't be a woman in that context and just be ignored. Because the fact is that even though people have practised it in a variety of ways, the institution is abominable. The formal teaching is not so bad. But, certainly the traditional and majority interpretations of the formal teaching are just . . . they are worse than irrelevant.

Another difference between the two positions pertains to human nature. Utopian Witches believe that humans are another modus of divinity. Evil is not part of the human constitution but culturally constructed. People are conditioned through upbringing and society, for good or for bad. But the inner-core being is pure and innocent and can be restored through cultural deprogramming and ritual cleansing. These utopian Witches also have greater faith in the possibility of restoring "paradise lost" by means of intentional living than have the other group.

Generic Witches are more cynical about the possibilities of changing the world and do not automatically interpret the image of an inner divine Self, which they also embrace, in ethical terms or as a guideline for action. They believe humans are in constant need of help from a higher power and from fellow humans to face their inner shadows and take responsibility for their own actions. Generic Witches believe not as much in narratives about a social fall from original bliss, but rather in the idea of a fundamentally split subject who can never be all pure and good. In this respect they can be considered ideological heirs to western psychologies and talking cures – with their precursor in the Christian confession. In contrast, when utopian Witches emphasize community and the idea of an original, undivided, deified Self who can act according to divine will, they should be considered heirs to utopian ideas also recognizable in the western counter-cultural Church.

However, as stated earlier in this chapter, a division between utopians and generics is primarily analytical and a way to sort out and expose different beliefs, attitudes and practices within a large, heterogeneous community. Let me now end this hermeneutics of "splitting apart" by presenting a case in which many of the beliefs just discussed are blended together in a highly innovative social practice embraced by all Witches: the ritual circle. In this particular circle, the meanings of Self and of "unconditional forgiving" inherited from western and Jewish and Christian traditions are reinterpreted in accordance with the karmic ideal of taking responsibility for one's own actions, of using every mistake as an opportunity for growth.

Case: forgiving and processing a rule-breaker

All my informants have opinions about what they regard as the "set-up" in the Christian obligation to forgive unconditionally and the twisting of the gospel to mean "all you need is a sacrament". On one hand, they believe it stages a scene in which both aggressor and victim lose their "selves": the aggressor by being treated like a child, the victim by being asked to accept abuse and victimization. On the other hand, they have observed that the shadow side to "unconditional" forgiveness is a daily practice in which transgressions are not allowed at all, and the transgressors, therefore, are scapegoated and shamed instead of forgiven.

Leila (28), a co-student in one of my Reclaiming classes, was the first to teach me on these matters. As a child, Leila was sexually abused by her Baptist minister father. She says she cannot forgive him because he has no consciousness of what he really did. Leila does not forgive unconditionally but demands change and emotional growth from the abuser. This is not only a moralistic claim on her part, but she seriously believes that his actions will continually stick to his karma unless he repents within himself and makes up for his deeds. This is the only way he can forgive himself, which she believes is a primary requirement for change. If she forgives him without demanding any internal changes, he will only continue to hurt her and others in new and subtle ways. The result is that he is kept in a spoiled child-like relationship to the world, whereas she becomes the eternal masochistic victim. By not forgiving him, she takes responsibility for herself and for not becoming another passive female victim.

Leila strongly believes that a real possibility for the aggressor to forgive herself/himself is lacking in the Christian demands about forgiveness that she was raised with. The alternative is to be given the gift of a real chance to forgive oneself. Then the aggressor might move on from only feeling shame – to actually sensing the other person's hurt. Without this empathic, emotional act, there is no change – and without change, no forgiveness of self by self.

The Witches' alternative and gift is to offer "processing" of individuals if they have broken common rules. This process will hopefully get them back on the right track, and it may give both the aggressor and the offended a real opportunity to forgive and forget and move on. This method is eagerly practised at Compost Ranch and in other Reclaiming circles when serious conflicts arise. To illustrate this method and to highlight the interaction between ideas of human growth, definitions of the sacred and the importance of community immanent within the processing itself, I shall present a case where a person had violated moral rules and cultural codes within the community and was worked on in a psychodrama ritual to induce internal change. She was regarded as a person who, through her actions, had lost her "self", and the community's task was to help her gain it back. As we shall see, shame and hurt were central feelings in the drama.

The person in this story is myself. To use oneself consciously as informant within the framework of an academic text is always difficult, although it is a method that is increasingly being called for (cf. Staal 1975; Favret-Saada 1980). Having dealt with methodological considerations in the Introduction, I shall not enter this discussion again. So even if this story also illuminates the peculiar and sometimes risky position of the participant observer in a research process, we shall bracket that here. In the present context I choose to use the story as a case because it so well illustrates our topic.

The social context for my case was Witchcamp, an event that took place in the forests outside of Vancouver, Canada in 1989. This week-long apprenticeship programme included 100 participants, and lectures, workshops and rituals were offered from early morning to late evening. The overall theme for the camp was "Building Community". At this social arena I made a serious transgression while in the position of fieldworker: the very last night I tape-recorded parts of a ritual without permission – and was discovered while doing it. This immoral action gave me an opportunity to experience full membership in the Witchcraft community: my action was interpreted and dealt with according to their – and not my – worldview. I was punished, forgiven and "worked on" in the ritual called "processing." Afterward the whole happening was given a symbolic interpretation as my human growth, being part of my healing from shame and detachment, ultimately bringing me onto the path of the Goddess.

I shall try to record what happened as if I experienced it as a native. By this I mean that I shall weave together the narrative with an account of my actual feelings in the situation. My feelings are important in the processing ritual and, therefore, an important key to understanding this therapeutic setting. Consequently, I have to share my feelings to the best of my memory when narrating the story. When Witches interpret growth, that is, emotional development and the gaining of new insight, their interpretations are to a large extent founded on the honest sharing of feelings. Without my expressing feelings the processing would not have succeeded and the final symbolic interpretation would have reached a different conclusion.

*   *   *

In Witches' rituals, permission to record must usually be explicitly granted beforehand. Otherwise, both tape-recording and taking photographs are regarded as violations of ritual space. The use of recording instruments is believed to disturb the energy called forth in ritual and to invade other people's sacred space – in addition to making the photographer/tape-recorder an observer. Witches have no place for observers at their rituals and provide no back seat for the detached and passive sceptics. Their ritual structure demands active participation. When ritual is about to be performed, cameras are always out of the question, though taping is sometimes permitted.

My problem at Witchcamp was that I had not asked permission to tape and had, therefore, put myself in an extremely embarrassing situation. I felt both shame and anger at being discovered: anger at myself for taking the risk and not asking permission, and anger at the woman, Amanda, who detected the tape-recorder, for not accepting my explanation. I wanted to persuade Amanda that my behaviour really was reasonable and have her pardon me immediately and put an end to the whole situation. I told her that I had taped parts of the three-hour-long ritual to help me remember its structure and contents; it was strictly for my own use when doing research. I had not asked permission because I knew that the object itself might be regarded as alien and disturbing to some participants. I had also learned that certain campers associated tape-recording, as such, with the FBI and with potential "persecution" due to their identities as Witches – an irritating and self-important attitude in my opinion. I had not asked because, under these circumstances, I was afraid of getting a "no". It was selfish of me, but I was so tired from one week of intense ritualizing and continuous notetaking that I felt I could not handle a refusal.

Amanda was not convinced that this was a plausible reason to break common rules. She was angry and more concerned with the community than with my so-called repentance. She said she felt betrayed by me and claimed I had abused everybody's trust. She wondered what kind of "student of Reclaiming" I really was, and she wanted to bring it up publicly in the closing ritual circle the next morning. Then it could be dealt with by everybody, including me, and processed there. With this judgement upon me, there seemed to be nothing I could do to prevent the forthcoming punishment.

It was a very difficult situation, and I worried about the negative feelings my trust-breaking action would create in the five Reclaiming teachers who formed the leading team at the camp. I was studying their community in San Francisco, partly with their permission. They were all valuable and supportive informants and responsible for the decision to make room for my research at Witchcamp. During the entire fieldwork I was told, over and over again, that they let me study their "thing" because I was "trusted" and "loved". Now I was afraid of losing trust and friendships. I could see how hard it would be for them to forget such a violation and to continue our confident cooperation as if nothing had happened. I prepared to be either fully or partly "exiled", meaning that I would either be asked to end my research or to accept a more restricted fieldwork situation. I tried to imagine their disappointment the next morning when my "inner self" in their eyes would be revealed, and I was angry with myself for having created the situation.

Amanda informed the Reclaiming teachers and camp organizers about her discovery. Early next morning a few of them came to see me. They expressed disappointment and asked how I could have done what I did. I explained again why, and their response was repeatedly, "But you could only have asked, why didn't you ask?" Their words made me even more worried for the proceedings at the forthcoming morning circle. One of the premises, though, had been changed: now Amanda wanted me, not her, to inform everybody at the public ritual.

Shortly thereafter we went to the outdoor ritual space, where I was to face my fate. Rumours of my actions were out – everybody already knew. Almost in complete silence, one hundred pairs of eyes watched me arriving. I wished for a little miracle to end this embarrassment, but, of course, nothing happened. Some of the women saw how I felt. They came over and said they wanted to support me so that the whole task would be easier for me. Everybody else was standing in a circle, waiting for me to speak. So I spoke and explained, and offered my apology and expressed my willingness to destroy the actual tape.

When I was finished, Starhawk opened the floor to processing. This means that people can express their emotions, but they may not comment upon reactions from the others or start discussions. Neither could I respond or defend myself. No emotion expressed is regarded as better or worse; and as the word itself says, "processing" is a process and does not end with negotiated and voted-for solutions. It is a therapeutic method to open a channel for feelings to be heard and "worked on". It addresses people's "heart-level", not only their intellect. This method is also fairly common among political grassroots activists in the US, and it is often utilized in consensus decision making. It is believed that, in and of itself, processing is a cleansing and fosters growth. It will eventually make people forgive each other, reassert mutual positive feelings and rebuild community. To let go of what is "bad", through speech (or symbol), is regarded as necessary to let the "good" feelings prosper and develop. Good feelings and close bonding are seen as necessary for a joint action (or ritual) to be successful.

The processing had started. First there was silence and then people started to talk, one at a time, in spontaneous succession. One woman smiled and said, "It's OK, Jone; it doesn't matter." A man said, "I think you are really brave, making this statement here in front of everybody." A third one said, "Even though you have explained the situation, you have lost my trust. I experienced something similar in my work as therapist, and I know that this will be a learning experience for you." Another said, "I get very angry with what you did, and I am not prepared to forgive you easily. I have experienced espionage from the FBI during the Vietnam War, and have strong feelings around things like tape-recording." This went on for five or ten minutes, then Starhawk suggested that people finish the processing with me after the ritual.

The theme for this leave-taking ritual was "Celebrating our Community". The structure and basic elements of Reclaiming Witches' rituals will be described in chapter 5. In this specific ritual the most challenging part for me was participation in the ritual dance at the end – the so-called Spiral Dance, which was led by Starhawk. The dance leader is like a snake's head; the participants holding hands in a circle form her body. In the inward circling the participants build a tight spiral pattern; in the outward movement, circling out of the spiral, everybody must pass each other face to face, and all are expected to meet the other person's eyes. The dancers are building a metaphorical "body" through weaving their bodies in dancing, a key ritual element when celebrating community. I normally find the Spiral Dance very energizing, and to Witches it gives a strong feeling of community and belonging. Meeting eyes while singing in a sacred dance in a sacred space is interpreted both as "looking at the Goddess" and as meeting your "Self" in the other person. In that situation I felt uncomfortable. I was still in a state of shame and wanted to protect myself. Instead my body was surrounded by people who, in the dance movements, were coming closer and closer. In the outward circling I had to meet all these people's eyes at a very short distance and receive all the subtle energy they sent me. I tried to interpret eyes: Who accepts me? Who dismisses me? Do they see the Goddess? Do they see themselves? Do they see me?

When the ritual was done I felt better, even though I was still confused as to the non-conclusion of this processing. Was I trusted by Reclaiming and the extended Reclaiming community, or was I not? Suddenly Starhawk came toward me. She smiled, and her eyes were twinkling. She said, "Well, since you made this terrible mistake and tape-recorded the ritual, I would like to listen to it. So don't throw it away!" She gave me a hug and left. I felt relieved and appreciated her humorous comment. Other people came and expressed their feelings: some positive and some negative. But now I was starting to anticipate the situation and really listen to what they said. I felt accepted and was able to see their hurt and not only my shame. I was still being processed, but it was okay – I was learning something new.

But what did they want me to learn? And what did they learn themselves? Rachel, who earlier in the week had offered to be my hostess when we returned to Vancouver, was the first to teach me. In the processing she had expressed strong anger and disappointment with my trickery. I therefore took it for granted that the invitation to be her guest was no longer valid, that she would feel uncomfortable with my company. When I said this, she looked at me really surprised and said, "No, Jone, it is not your person I don't validate; it is your behaviour. When we are done with 'processing' we are done, and the you who acted out this behaviour is forgiven. I will be delighted to have you as my guest." To confirm her statement, she nicely prepared a bedroom for me while I enjoyed a hot bath.

Since Rachel had opened the door to conversation and interpretation, I decided to share some of my spontaneous thoughts and feelings with her. I told her that the whole incident had been an unusual experience. I had never before tried this method or been transformed publicly from feeling shame and regret to feeling acceptance and peace. The experience also contrasted with my upbringing, through which I had learned that I was a sinner – meaning an imperfect human being dependent on the grace of God – with no chance of ever really improving and growing. On the other hand, I was not allowed to be who I was: an imperfect human being. I should not fail, and if I did, it had costs. To help me learn and shape up, something would be "taken away" from me – trust, privileges, things. I could ask God for forgiveness. Then, theoretically, everything would be okay, even if it were not okay with people. In my up-bringing, God and people were separate; in Witchcraft they merged.

Rachel, who has an Episcopalian background, was very pleased with my "confession". She decided to give me additional teaching:

> We are building a spiritual community that is different from the ones we had when growing up. At the camp we were all struck by your behaviour because we are bonded emotionally and communally. When doing "processing" we are helping each other to really forgive you. Not as a polite saying, but as a real doing. And not only that, we are helping you to forgive yourself and accept who you are. This we have never learned before, how to forgive ourselves, or that it was even necessary. But without forgiving of selves by selves there is no growth and no learning. Instead you will repeat the same mistakes over and over and never change. With self-acceptance you open up for your inner sacred being to come forth, and you reconnect with the Goddess. When you feel shame you cut yourself off from her. We help you to reconnect, to heal, to change and become whole again. And when we dance in ritual the Goddess is manifesting and helping us out. We can't do it without her. We have to open our hearts, just as you have to. We have to re-learn to see you as a sacred being, you have to see us, as well as yourself. Repentance and change can only take place when you see the other. And this "seeing" can only be done from a place of love for self, which is love for the Goddess inside. When this happens the "processing" becomes a healing ritual for all of us.

Back in San Francisco, every teacher in Reclaiming was informed about my transgression. In our conversation, one of them, Freya (who also participated in the Catholic Mass at Mission Dolores), asked me how I felt after Witchcamp. I gave a very short answer but made sure that my message showed that I was troubled with what happened. She brushed me off, saying:

> Listen Jone, Witchcamp always brings up a lot of 'shit' in everybody; that is the way it is constructed. And not only in the students, but in the teachers as well. Without making contact with your shadow, you can never change. This is the work and path of the Goddess. So listen to her and make it a learning experience.

Freya gave the response I naively had hoped for from Amanda. She did not ask for explanations or show disappointment – she only stated reality and invited me to use it as an opportunity to change.

The interpretation of my experience at Witchcamp was taken even one step further by another generic Witch, Aradia. She told me that she saw the whole incident as an initiatory experience, that I had touched upon a process of death and rebirth. This was a signal, meaning that I was called forth by the

Goddess to enter a new level of experience and commitment: it was time for me to ask for initiation. She added that she was waiting for me to ask. I was very surprised by this openness because usually initiation is not something easily acquired – especially not by a scholar. But I knew that if a Reclaiming Witch said it was time for me to be initiated, it was not meant technically to help my research: it was because she believed I had experienced something that qualified me personally to enter the secret circle.

In contrast to these thoughtful and educational responses were those of my six circle sisters, who did not give any verbal interpretations. They only listened to my story, comforted me as if I were their wounded child by reassuring me of their feelings for me, agreeing fully that Witches are hysterical about tape-recorders out of fear of the FBI. Whether my action was immoral or not was not commented upon. They expressed no disappoint-ments and no doubts as to whether I still might be trusted to be in a circle/coven and share their most intimate experiences. I was very surprised and very pleased to experience an acceptance so close to being unconditional. This coven ritual of "thoughtful listening" to one individual is the opposite of the processing of a whole group. But the "ethics of immanence" are the same. In processing the group itself holds the focus, and I was not supposed to comment or judge the emotions being expressed about my behaviour. In thoughtful listening I am the focus, and the others shall not comment, correct, analyse or judge my action or emotions. All in all, the incident which I feared could have ruined my whole fieldwork ended with the Witches integrating me even more strongly into their community.

*   *   *

From the Witches' point of view, my immoral act was an expression of "power-over". I acted as if I were above the stated common rules and made other people the object of my manipulation. To Witches this is an act of alienation: I severed myself from the community, and in this process I was regarded as having lost my Self and the immediate contact to my "inner voice" that is believed to separate right from wrong. After being caught, I continued to act from this place of achieved "power-over": I was concerned with not losing face and jeopardizing my fieldwork. I was not dealing with having lost myself, having violated my own moral standards.

To cleanse the situation, the Witches orchestrated processing. This is regarded as a method for restoring "power-from-within", creating emotional balance and moral integrity in a person and inducing growth from temporary, symbolic childishness to adulthood. The method is basically to force the transgressor to see "the other", to leave her severed position and recognize in herself the emotional suffering of "the other". A Witch shall not lie, not because it is forbidden by moral law but because it disconnects her from her inner Self, from others and from harmony with the Goddess. The punishment is, therefore, believed to be embedded in the action itself.

Also, I identified my behaviour with my self and with my value as a person. In Rachel's worldview the only way to forgive transgressions is to temporarily separate self and behaviour. It is not the behaviour that is forgiven, but the person who displayed it. Abuse is wrong and can never be forgiven, but the person who does wrong can be forgiven. This distinction is, to Witches, the only way a person can handle facing her wrongs, her shadows, "her shit". And without facing "the shit" they do not believe there is any chance for improvement. Rachel, Freya and Aradia each offered an interpretation in which I could distinguish between my self and my behaviour. My behaviour was wrong, but in and of itself it created an opportunity to connect with my divine inner being and to grow. This paradox, that something painful and immoral can create something good, is highly valued by Aradia when she names it an initiatory experience from death to rebirth. As stated earlier, this way of giving spiritual value to daily life events and including them as themes for ritualizing are typical features of women's religiosity.

Processing is a practice shared by Witches of utopian and generic bents. But the case illustrates well how the generic concept of the human subject defines the context: humans are fundamentally split, with the ability to repeatedly act counter to their claimed norms. This ability is not judged as evil in itself but stated as a painful part of reality, constitutive of the human condition. It manifests outwardly as a constant tension between the values of estrangement, commonly experienced in lived reality, and the values of wholeness, represented ideally as the core self, the so-called Deep Self. However, this inner split in a person is not static. On the one hand, it may be turned into a subject for healing and growth. On the other hand, the split can freeze or increase through negative reinforcements from the social world. Did not "Jone" confess how she was socially conditioned to alienate herself from her Self in her upbringing? This split within a person is regarded as *the* challenge when someone is called forth to grow and mature from child to adult, seeking to balance the inner self with the outer world.

The Goddess is identified with the true nature of Deep Self and, in my processing and the following ritual, this deity was actually called forth to restore balance. She is believed to always dwell in me, but she manifests only through actions. Anybody can alienate herself from the Goddess and lose her sense of right living. But the Goddess can be restored again through ritual action. Ritual, then, has the function of integrating a person more and more into the values of wholeness and the harmony of Deep Self.

My "confession" to Rachel about my upbringing was a signal that the processing was successful. Rachel evaluated my new attitude to be in harmony with my inner Self, and once again I was credited with the ability to listen and learn. I was reintegrated into the community when she educated and interpreted for me. When I contrasted my upbringing with Witchcraft, my speech also functioned as reinforcement of the truth-value of Wiccan hermeneutics and ritual. My transgression was not only being turned into a positive lesson for me, but everybody could use my mistake and its processing as subjective mirrors for a positive validation of Witchcraft. Their worldview was confirmed: 1 The Goddess is indeed identical with the deepest power of inner Self (she transformed Jone). 2 Humans are indeed split subjects (even the trusted Jone failed). 3 Humans can therefore alienate themselves from the Goddess and behave badly (Jone focused only on her own ego, alienating herself from her Self, and it had terrible consequences). 4 By means of ritual and the support of community, wrong-acting can be forgiven and the Goddess restored (my confession was a signal that this had happened). 5 A process leading from emotional alienation to integration is structurally equivalent to existential rebirth and is, therefore, a process of literal growth (Jone was believed to never again be able to tape-record without permission; she actually changed and was, therefore, offered the chance to continue this changing process through the death-and-rebirth ritual of initiation). 6 Finally, Witches are confirmed in their belief that they are in control of human behaviour and know the tools for emotional modelling and growth. Freya's statement that "Witchcamp always brings up a lot of 'shit' in everybody; that is the way it is constructed" implies that my mistake, as well as others, was almost calculated and arranged for with the educational function for the campers to "meet themselves" and grow.

Generic Witches display a close association between concepts of the sacred and definitions of human nature. As humans are split and ambiguous, so is divinity. The Goddess can be incarnated in humans, making the self an *object* for divine programming. The Goddess can also be an external relationship, making the self a *subject* for encountering the sacred in ritual. In the processing ritual at Witchcamp, the human subject and the Goddess are perceived as separate beings. The goal of ritualizing is to slowly merge the two. In the thoughtful listening ritual in the coven, the Goddess is perceived as incarnate in me, manifesting in my voice and being. The characteristic feature of both rituals is that their initial themes are gathered from daily life, and not from myths. The second stage of the ritual process, though, is precisely to reinterpret daily life in terms of mythological imagery, as happens when my experience is being interpreted as a spiritual death and rebirth.

This act of processing can also be regarded as an example of how feminist Witches create a religion which is a "politically correct Christianity": they are finally able to accept wrongs, change them and forgive them, but without necessarily reviving utopianism, for the goal in this context cannot be said to be the perfection of human beings – understood as beings who in time will never fail in relation to claimed norms – but rather self-knowledge and growth in accordance with the principle of power-from-within. The distinction between "power-from-within" and "power-over" as an overall norm in Reclaiming is, to a certain extent, visible in this case. The community does not act from a position of power-over with restricting punishment or ostracism; rather, they confront truth in the open, contrasting with my attempt to conceal my acts. The case also illustrates Witches' methods for healing of culture "at home", at a community level. The individual, her community and the extended ecological family are believed to be intimately interconnected. My healing is, therefore, regarded as a healing of the body of the *whole* community.[16]

Witchcraft and western traditions

For the first time in history, people raised as Christian Catholics, Christian Protestants and Jewish Jews have found each other in a joint spiritual path – which is mainly evolving as they go along. Some of these worshippers dismiss their essential first names while keeping their family names and ancestral heritage, ending up calling themselves Catholic Witches, Jewish Witches, but not yet Protestant Witches. Due to a certain positive identification with parts of their religious heritage, many of them cannot possibly keep up a concept of religion as identical with one social institution. Instead they turn Christianity (and Judaism) into multiple traditions of internal contradiction. Implicitly in this manoeuvre, my informants support the option of positioning the Witches' emancipatory project within western spirituality, not totally outside of it.

On the other hand, the religious innovations characteristic of Witchcraft, such as those emphasizing human growth and the power of magical ritual, are also striking. In exactly what respects, then, do I claim modern Witches to be in debt to Jewish and Christian traditions? First, through the belief that life is no accident but derived from an ultimately divine, beneficent source (the Creator God or the Great Goddess); and second, through the adoption of the concept of a holy spirit (or goddess) within the Deep Self, which can be listened to beyond, and in opposition to, the context of tradition. Witches have not inherited this concept of spirit from paganism or any other religion, but from Christian theology and heresy.

Iconoclasm in reference to an autonomous, veritable voice – potentially present in everybody, without regard to rank and deeds and not in reference to God's commandments or to the way of the ancestors – is, in western civilization, genuinely Christian.[17] The same is true of the enlightenment movements, whose existence definitely is unthinkable without the tradition of the anarchist Holy Spirit[18] and the belief in God as a beneficent creator. When embracing radical political projects, Witches place themselves within this western heritage line. Whatever beliefs Witches might share with their acclaimed pagan ancestors, these ancestors' spiritual aim was not the emancipation of people from form and custom, but was, rather, to pay homage to tradition. Witches do not pay homage to any tradition and discount any once-and-for-all "ten commandments". They also reject the eastern tradition of noninvolvement, where an individual is left to interpret suffering as personal, bad karma, generated through bad deeds in an earlier life. As real western radicals, they take responsibility for human fate globally and put themselves in a privileged position as the guardians of the world, as its "healers and benders".

But Witches also go several steps further. Unlike their counter-cultural Christian predecessors, they do not settle for a new Church, a new priesthood, a new and, finally, correct interpretation of the Book of Scripture or the Book of Nature. In accordance with the ideals of late modernity they simply renounce this finite concept of truth and insist that viable religion can be created from lived experiences by ordinary people, similar to the creation processes of other cultural institutions. In so doing, Witches push the modern idea of democracy one step further and suggest that the "institution of the sacred" be fully incorporated into modernity, debarred from its premodern and privileged authority structure. By this suggestion they take away from theology and educated priesthood the exclusive authority to interpret the will of God and perform ritual.

When studying Reclaiming Witches, we are obviously left with an ambiguous tradition that holds conflicting views of the human Self. On the one hand, a human person is regarded as a rational being who may create her own life and her own religious forms autonomously, aided solely by her own experiences and an inculturated inner voice, the conscience. On the other hand, she is constructed from divine sources as a person with an indwelling spirit. The notion of spirit represents a different voice, not coming from the ego or the unconscious but from divinity – and it asks to be served. The modernist slogan, "being my own authority" is modified by a mystical slogan, the "authority of the spirit within". When Witches claim to be in service of "the Goddess" and her magical religion, as well as of "Democracy" and modern rationality, they enter the domain of paradox.

Notes

1 This notion shall broadly refer to those (heretical) movements which challenged the authority of interpretation after the Church ascended to power in the fourth century CE.

2 Taking on the western utopian discourse inevitably means taking on the genre and logic inherent in the discourse itself. New religious innovations like Witchcraft will, from pure hermeneutical necessity, have to stand on the shoulders of their rejected forerunners while, at the same time, stretching forward. Nobody can create new forms by inventing or imagining *tabula rasa,* by completely stepping outside the culture in which one was born and lives. Continuity is also reinforced by the very acceptance of personal and plural interpretations, so characteristic of modern paganism. To a certain degree these interpretations will, in all their diversity, be based on and determined by previous religious configurations. The first Christians interpreted their new personal experiences and beliefs on the basis of various branches of Judaism and Greco-Roman paganism, just as modern Witches interpret on the basis of both their Jewish and Christian and classical cultural heritage – as well as going beyond it. Witchcraft is inevitably a product of modernism and its "illness" and was unlikely to have come up in any other time period.

3 By that time Starhawk had already established a reputation as facilitator for large political groups organized through the philosophy of consensus decision making, as well as being known as a practising Witch. She was also well known in the San Francisco Bay Area for being instrumental in organizing (together with her Witch friends) the Three Mile Island Memorial Parade in 1979. She had also been involved in rituals for the National Conference of Women and Violence (1976),

the Take Back the Night March (1978) and Inviting the Light Celebration (1979). Today (2001), Starhawk is active in the anti-globalization movement ("Attach") and with permacultural farming.

4 Witches believe that any object, person or event has its invisible duplicate on an energy level. This energy body of an object can be sensed, although not seen, and is believed to be accessible within the framework of ritual, a space where ordinary time and space dissolve.

5 One reason is that well known scholars, like Norman Cohn and Carolyn Merchant, call these groups the first revolutionary anarchists and communists. Their scholarship gave a major input to Starhawk when she wrote Appendix I, "The Burning Times: Notes on a Crucial Period of History" in *Dreaming the Dark* (1982a). This is obvious from her bibliography. The feeling of being linked spiritually to the European heretical movements has also been reinforced by David Kubrin's work (1981, 1987). He holds a PhD in the History of Science, and since 1981 he has been an opinionated and influential activist in Reclaiming and the broader anarchist pagan community. Kubrin (1981) is listed among Starhawk's literary sources in *Dreaming the Dark*. Carolyn Merchant started out as Kubrin's student and attributes her *Death of Nature* to his inspiration. Since the two are not independent sources of historical analysis, I shall only use Merchant's (not Kubrin's) work.

6 According to Cohn (1981:288) and Merchant (1983:123), a certain Gerrard Winstantly founded the Diggers in the 1640s as an anarchist community. In 1649 they took possession of St George's Hill in Surrey and began to cultivate the common and waste grounds until they were defeated by military troops.

7 In my presentation of this lineage I will rely solely on Cohn and Merchant.

8 Cohn 1981:192, who here refers to Augustine and Cyprian.

9 They included: the continental Free Spirit movement, dating back to the beginning of the fourteenth century; the English Peasant Revolt, presumably organized by the legendary John Ball from around 1380; the Amaurians and radical Taborites, organized in Bohemia after the burning of John Hus in 1414; Thomas Munster and the Anabaptists. As mentioned, the Free Spirit re-emerged in Cromwell's England in the seventeenth century as the Diggers. In the same period religious enthusiasts known as Ranters, Seekers, Levellers and Antinomians multiplied rapidly (Cohn 1981:151; Merchant 1983:123). Also, in the early seventeenth century, two utopian drafts were published: Tommaso Campanella's *City of the Sun* (1602) and the Lutheran pastor Johann Valentin Andreä's *Christianopolis* (1619). They formulated a philosophy of communal sharing and egalitarian distribution of wealth and were both serious about making the utopian plans social reality.

10 The medieval imagery implied in the notion of the state of nature, could be supported by *Genesis* (all are descended from one father and mother, Adam and Eve, etc.), *Acts* (the first apostles apparently lived communally, sharing all their common goods) and the *Book of Revelation* (the Kingdom of God is soon to come).

11 They held some values in common with the Church and the monastic orders, for example, voluntary poverty and the sharing of land, food, properties and commodities. But they disagreed strongly on the sharing of spouses and on the deification theology.

12 Cohn 1981:178. According to Cohn, this freedom from sin took on certain abnormalities, which gave the movement a reputation of being amoral. He argues that certain members maintained that to murder a man was not sin as long as the action came from a pure heart.

13 Some scholars include the *Beguines* as part of the Free Spirit spirituality, a lay monastic movement led by women (cf. Neel 1989; Bowie 1990).

14 Some Witches identify with the heretical, Christian Gnostics and would have set the date for comparisons to the first century. This identification is based on the fact that Gnosticism was also regarded as heretical, that its spiritual path was a search for gnosis from within, and that female imagery of the divine (Sophia) was included in their theology. But, objectively, Witchcraft beliefs are *not* compatible with Gnosticism. This tradition is fundamentally dualistic and degrades the body, and the earth in general, by attributing them to an evil creation god, the Demiurge.

15 "Aradia" is the name of the Italian Queen of the Witches, as described by Leland (1897). To take on a new name, and renounce one's birth name, is a common practice within the new religious movements. To be called "Aradia" means that the goddess Aradia is invoked in the person every time the name is uttered. The woman's intention, when changing her name, is either to rename a quality already present within herself or to pledge to manifest more and more of Aradia in her daily life.

16 When one of my informants, let us call him "Bryan", read a draft of this chapter, he became very angry. He was, himself, involved in a severe conflict with some of the leading Reclaiming women: eight years ago he said something extremely offensive and deeply hurtful to one of them and, although he apologized, he was never forgiven. When reading my draft, Bryan expressed anger at Reclaiming for applying such high principles of "redemption" in my case, and not in his, and anger at me for presenting my case as if it were what is generally done within the community. He tried to figure out the differences that might explain the different treatment of our respective transgressions in our two cases. He roughly ended up with two possible reasons: that he already had a "weak social position" due to previous conflicts with one of the women – which I had not; that he was a man – I was a woman. His last guess implied that Reclaiming has a gendered morality that discriminates against men. Bryan may be right: it is possible that my illegal tape-recording would have been treated differently had I been a man. On the other hand, it is hard to compare the two cases: I broke the law; he broke somebody's heart. I believe I too would have been punished differently had I broken somebody's heart. Furthermore, the conflict he initiated *was* actually processed by the aid of two chosen mediators. The problem is, rather, that the offended party in Bryan's case felt that processing made no difference, whereas in my case it was felt to make a difference.

17 The acclamation of this new authority *beyond* Scripture, priesthood and tradition was also an ingredient when the first-century Jewish community in Jerusalem decided to expel the "Jesus people" from their midst. It was this act that initially forced them to create a new religion, Christianity. The Holy Spirit, believed to be infused in every individual through baptism, is, therefore, the most anarchistic principle in the Christian tradition. In reference to the voice of the spirit – against the voices of pope, bishop, father and mother, tradition and custom – new Christian traditions have continually been created.

18 According to Ronald Grimes (1990:25), the Holy Spirit refers to human experience before language and narrative. It is a deep source of renewal in human life – including in the art of ritualizing. The Holy Spirit is also Peter Berger's criterion when defining the church–sect typology: in the former, the Spirit is considered as remote; in the latter, the Spirit is believed to be immediately present (cf. York 1995:321).

4 Holy hermeneutics

How to find truth

Sofia is one of the Jewish founders of Reclaiming. When I asked her why she became a Witch, she referred to a religious experience she had in 1974, when 23 years old. She lived by the ocean and usually walked on the beach in the evenings. One evening she suddenly felt a presence. She looked around and saw nobody. She finally looked at the moon and felt an intense stream of communication, almost as if she merged with the moon. She heard a voice from inside the moon, talking to her, telling her that it had saved her and protected her from all kinds of dangers throughout her life:

> What happened was that I was being picked out by the Goddess to hear her message. She told me to meditate every full moon and said I would start meeting women that would show me what I needed to know. The Goddess also asked me to take back Sofia, my birth name – which also is one of her names – and told me her creed, the "Charge of the Goddess", It almost had the same form as the traditional one.

This extraordinary experience changed Sofia's life. She believed she had been elected as a subject for divine revelation, and from that day she started meditating every full moon, while waiting for the women who would teach her to show up. First she met Z. Budapest in Los Angeles, and through her she was in 1977 introduced to Starhawk. Sofia learned that the goddess who had revealed herself at the beach was exactly the same divinity who was worshipped in the religion called "Witchcraft". She then, of course, joined this religious path and is presently still a Witch.

This story is not unique to Sofia, and among generic Witches it is fairly common to refer to one's religious path as some kind of selection, a waking up or even conversion, sparked by an extraordinary experience or revelation. Francesca, a Faery initiate and friend of Reclaiming, told me that:

> The sheer physical presence of the Goddess captured me and changed my being. You get chosen; yes, Goddess kidnaps you; that's it, and that's how I have experienced a lot of my path. But I cannot tell you that this is

objective reality. We do not believe in such a concept. If you are going to understand something, you get involved with it. You get involved with your whole being, with your God spirit, with your sacred animal nature, with your passion – you bring all parts of you and experience it. If you bring that being to your observation of nature, you will truly see nature for what it really is. You will see the Goddess in it and understand her mysteries. Anybody can find her mysteries if they just look with their whole being and live it. Witchcraft is not a belief system which you adopt intellectually. It is rather our understanding from being alive and interacting with things.

One of the functions of stories like this is to assure the believers that their religious path is not made up, in a fictitious sense, but refers to something Real. My informants would repeatedly tell me "Even though we make up this religion, the Goddess is not made up. She is more than a chosen metaphor; she is real and she is alive." "Experience" becomes a key concept to explain the existence of the Goddess and her religion. To Francesca, experience means total involvement, an embodied way of thinking, and is a fundamental hermeneutic principle to "read" reality. Francesca's reference to experience resembles the Aristotelian notion *empeira*, meaning knowledge received from interacting with things, being involved and skilled, in opposition to *theoria*, which means knowledge from looking at, observing at a distance, as when astronomers study the planets.

To Sofia, the concept of experience is a way to legitimize the possibility of living with a consciousness of inventing religion but not of making up that which religion is essentially about: the experience of divine reality. Witches invent, while at the same time insisting on religion's truthfulness. In Sofia's religion, people have decided that the moon is one of the normative symbols of female divinity, and the core understanding of the essential being of this divinity has been expressed in a creed called the "Charge of the Goddess". This creed is formulated as two speeches, one given by the Great Mother, the other by the Star goddess, thus revealing their "essence(s)" to the reader: *For I am the soul of nature that gives life to the universe. From Me all things proceed and unto Me they must return. Let My worship be in the heart that rejoices, for behold—all acts of love and pleasure are My rituals.*[1] Doreen Valiente (and Gerald Gardner) originally wrote this speech act of the goddess, but most Witches – among them Starhawk – claim it to be both ancient and traditional. This information, as well as the whole discussion on whether a religious element is ancient or modern, whether it is a chosen metaphor or a true expression of reality, is irrelevant to Sofia's conversion narrative. She invokes another reality, in which the moon itself speaks and tells the truth directly to her. Like Francesca, she regards her own experience as her highest authority, and according to this experience the creed is authored by the Goddess herself. It may also be true that it was written down in the 1950s, but in her opinion this information is only true in the reality of science and visible facts.

To cope with multiple realities and several concepts of truth, the Reclaiming Witches depend upon an implicit hermeneutic distinction between what they understand to be presymbolic experience and cultural symbols. This indigenous distinction between natural "truth" and cultural "invention" is crucial to an understanding of their self-proclaimed authority and cultural mission, as well as their worldview in general. Witches may disagree strongly on certain beliefs, but they all agree on method: to contrast experienced reality continuously with representations of reality.

However, the Witches do not claim the notion "hermeneutics". It is solely an etic category, which I utilize in order to develop a descriptive terminology and to come to terms with presumably confusing, interpretive strategies and multiple realities invoked by Reclaiming Witches. To be able to do so, we must start by delimiting hermeneutics as a theoretical concept and then proceed to contextualize the ethno-hermeneutics of Witchcraft in relation to the ways in which prevailing academic theory reads reality and its signs. My presentation of hermeneutics is based on Engdahl (1977), Daniel (1986), White (1987, 1988), Ricoeur (1988) and Petersen (1996).

Religion and hermeneutics

The word "hermeneutics" is derived from the name of the Greek god Hermes. He was believed to be the carrier of divine messages from the gods to the humans. Later he also became the mythical inventor of writing. Hermeneutics, then, was originally the art of understanding holy messages from the gods as these were revealed directly and experientially to a human medium, that is, of bridging the divine and the mundane. It was a tool to mediate between two kinds of reality, to overcome the gap between divine speech and human reality and make them one (a vertical interpretive move), while its contemporary meaning has become the art of interpretation in general (a horizontal interpretive move).

In the classical period, hermeneutics was developed further as the art of interpreting divine discourse that was already encoded in sacred text. The sacred text in classical Greece was the Homeric Epic. But Homer's anthropomorphic portrait of the gods was considered all too human and amoral for classical taste. The solution to this problem was not to question the authority of the narratives as such and write new sacred text, but to find an interpretation that was not literal, that created another, more acceptable meaning. This "translation" is a metaphorical interpretive process, a prototype of horizontal hermeneutics.

The tension between direct experience (revelation) and encoded message (text) in medieval times was expressed via the imagery of God revealing godself through two kinds of books: the "Book of Nature" and the "Book of Scripture", representing respectively an immanent and a transcendent aspect of deity. Each of "the Books" was true, or carried Truth. The way for human beings to understand both divine (macrocosmic) and human (microcosmic) reality was to interpret these books, one by means of the other. This reciprocal interpretation was possible because the human microcosm was believed to be a reflection of the divine macrocosm. Accordingly, the goal was not only to read the sacred Books but also to be read by them.

The duality between nature (revelation) and scripture (text) eventually received a this-worldly interpretation in Romantic hermeneutical theory: divine duality was transferred to human psychology as a duality between direct experience (nature/revelation) and indirect reflection (scripture/text). In fact, the duality itself came to be understood as the basic dilemma in *all* religious discourse (cf. Smith 1981). A Romantic theory of religion, going back to Schleiermacher and Goethe, invokes several parallel realities. It regards fundamental religious experience as mystical, since it belongs to a reality beyond language. According to Thomas Aquinas's brief definition, mysticism is *cognitio dei experimentalis,* or "knowledge of God through experience". But mysticism is also bound to the paradox of language. The mystical knowledge, which cannot be told, must be spoken and symbolized to have meaning. Romanticism acknowledges both the power of language and that of experience, but it does not subsume the one under the other.

In post-Romantic hermeneutic theory this is exactly what happens. The duality between the realities of experience and language/reflection, between nature and scripture is synthesized and reduced to a secularized oneness. The most influential historical figure in this process was Feuerbach. First, he transformed metaphysics into naturalism by merging the "Book of Scripture" and the "Book of Nature" into one sacred reality immanent in the profane world. Second, he completely merged the sacred with the profane, with the consequence that the notion of the immanent sacred became lost in time. Third, he proclaimed the institution of religion and the elevation of the sacred to another reality to be a human projection (cf. Widmann 1989).

Feuerbach's unification of heaven and earth has been essential to the sociology of religion. In the positivist, empirical tradition going back to Comte, the unified sacred–profane reality was reduced to empirical daily life. Durkheim proclaimed religion to be nothing but society writ large, and Mauss described the hermeneutics of sociology as completely horizontal: first a description of facts, which are people's actual beliefs in spiritual beings; second an interpretation of these beliefs by placing their entire foundation in social organization, not in a meta-human reality (Mauss 1985:31).

In the symbolist neo-Kantian tradition, reinterpreted by Durkheim and later developed through influence from literary criticism, the formula "human projection" became a norm for all kinds of cultural phenomena. The interesting approach to religion was no longer to see it as a human illusion (which it is, *de facto*, also to a symbolist) but to regard it as a system of symbols conferring meaning upon human reality. The context is still human sociality, but the focus has changed from social facts to social meaning.

In contemporary post-Romantic hermeneutical theory, in social sciences as well as in the humanities, we still find these two major positions. From a

Romantic point of view, they are both reductionist. The empiricists emphasize ordinary experience and claim to study the empirical reality of daily life. The symbolists emphasize language and cognition and claim to study the symbolic reality of human culture. To the empiricists, language is not part of reality but simply a medium to represent experienced reality. To the symbolists, language itself is the problem. They regard language and signs as fundamentally arbitrary in relation to reality. Language never represents reality; it creates reality and interprets reality. Consequently, there is no nonlinguistic reality available for direct experience. While the empiricists ultimately interpret meaning to understand reality, the symbolists have totally given up on the concept of reality (White 1987:281).

The goal of hermeneutics is to transform something foreign to something familiar by the "bridge-building" act of interpretation. But what needs a bridge? What is to be united? According to Ricoeur, the unification process in religious hermeneutics is a translation of presumed divine reality to make it relevant to this world of ordinary, daily life, overcoming experiences of alienation from a human being's point of view (Ricoeur 1988:55). But even Ricoeur turns into a symbolist when he goes on to interpret this bridging as a metaphorical, horizontal process in which language is discontinuous with the things (that is, divine reality) it represents. Acceptable meaning, to him, is created solely through interpretations and new names, by metaphorical translation of one universe of meaning into another.

None of these post-Romantic hermeneutical strategies is able to encompass Sofia's sensory experience of being addressed by extra-ordinary divine reality without reducing it to a nonsensory, symbolic representation within ordinary reality. In order to develop a language for Witches' ethno-hermeneutics that may comprise the magical and experiential aspects claimed, we need to go back to an older notion of hermeneutics, extending the one unification axis to include two. In addition to a *horizontal*, metaphorical interpretive process on a cultural level, Witches may be said to operate with a second unification, which is *vertical*, magical and individual. This axis is about the unification of supernatural and natural, of sacred and profane, of emotion and thought, of extra-ordinary and ordinary, the merging of "real substances" in the experience of a single person beyond ordinary language and narrative. Reshaped through this transformative experience, the individual is now (ideally) made capable of invoking a magical language of action, not only of signification. This magical language is, in contrast, conceived as continuous with the things it represents.

We may say that the ethno-hermeneutics of magical religion unifies both horizontally and vertically. But in order to name reality and position religion, it also comprises symbolic and empirical positions. This presumed inconsistency is due to Witches' nonsynthetic, plural concepts of reality. Let me make this explicit by presenting their dual definitions of religion, which eventually lead to a third notion: magical reality.

Religion as symbol, experience and magical reality

As stated earlier, Witches confess to a Romantic distinction between pre-symbolic experience and cultural symbol. This is integral to their acclaimed cultural mission and to their argument concerning why it is worthwhile to re-create dead or dormant traditions and invent religion. One argument is existential, the other political and pragmatic. As existentialists, they are focused on what is true. As politicians, they are concerned with strategies and necessities and firmly believe that it is not possible to change western culture without changing western religion. Therefore, it is only in accordance with the differentiation between existential (what is true to the individual) and political (what is necessary to create a better society), that we may say that Witches separate functionally between religious experience and religious symbols. Experience is viewed as authentic and true in a prelinguistic sense, symbols and forms as secondary inculturations of those experiences. When defining religion on a cultural level, they adopt symbolic anthropology, embracing among others Clifford Geertz and Victor Turner. When defining religion existentially, they adopt an esoteric version of Romanticism. Thus they operate simultaneously with at least two different concepts of religion. In Starhawk's recreations of Witchcraft, this duality becomes rather visible.

First, Starhawk relies upon Clifford Geertz and maintains that religion is constitutive of culture because it creates a cultural ethos that defines the deepest values in a society and in the persons living there (cf. chapter 2). Religion, in Starhawk's language, is empirically "the soil of culture – in which the belief systems, the stories, the thought-forms and all other institutions are based" (Starhawk 1982a:72). She claims that there is no way to accommodate cultural change without changing religion: not rejecting it, but replacing it with another symbol system and structures that evoke other values. At this argumentative level Starhawk accepts that religion as form is a human pro-jection or construction. But it is a most powerful and necessary construction. The question, then, is not whether this construction is an illusion; it is whether the construction is life-affirming and nourishing to human beings or life negating and oppressive. Metaphysics is measured by ethics. What is considered true "dogmatically" cannot be true "in fact" if it does not liberate people and sanctify all of life. The explicit goal of Witchcraft at this level is to unite spirit and politics, to unite the values attributed to divine reality and the values circulating in social reality: to realize religion as social utopia.

Second, Starhawk depends upon esoteric Romanticism and opposes Geertz and symbolic anthropology. She states that religion is constitutive in human life not only due to the power of symbols, but also because it deals with substance, with real powers, life-generating powers, that can actually be "tapped" by the art of magic (such as ritual invocations, prayer, meditation). When talking about religion inside this realm of real powers, Starhawk defines religion essentially, not empirically, as "a matter of re-linking, with the divine within and with her outer manifestations in the entire human and natural world" (Starhawk 1979a:186). Divinity is ultimately defined as "life-generating powers" in a very literal sense, even though "Goddess" can also be symbolized conventionally as deity. Divine reality is not divided between immanence and transcendence but between *visible* reality, as experienced in ordinary life, and *invisible* reality, as experienced extra-ordinarily, abruptly as in revelation, in ritual space or in altered states of consciousness (trance). Correspondingly, we find two fluctuating meanings of the concept of experience. One refers to ordinary life, the other to a mystical, extra-ordinary experience.

The double floor in Reclaiming Witches' conceptualizations of reality and the twofold definition of religion places them in the category that sociologist Peter L. Berger calls "inductive strategy" in the renewal of religion: going back to experience and, from there, assessing tradition. In *The Heretical Imperative* (1980), Berger displays a Romantic theory of religion that, to a certain extent, echoes Witchcraft. It is based on the thesis that the individual experience of the supernatural is not coextensive with the social phenomenon of religion: "Religion can be understood as a human projection because it is communicated in human symbols. But this very communication is motivated by an experience in which a metahuman reality is injected into human life" (Berger 1980:52). Berger claims that the distinction between experience and reflection is crucial if the study of religion is to become something more than a history of ideas and if we shall have any chance of understanding the strong energies playing in religious fields, or say, new religious movements. From there he defines religion empirically, but not essentially, as a human attitude that conceives of the cosmos, including the supernatural, as a sacred order (Berger 1980:53; 43). Both the sacred and the supernatural must be present for Berger to call a phenomenon "religion".

If we apply Berger's terminology to the Witches, "sacred" refers to a horizontal interpretation of unity between self and cosmos, in which goddess is experienced metaphorically as visible, ordinary reality itself, meaning that she is manifest and present in all life forms in a nonpersonal form. "Supernatural" designates, according to Berger, "the radically, overwhelmingly other, referring to an experience of something being out there . . . having an irresistible reality that is independent of one's own will" (Berger 1980:42). Applied to the Witches, "supernatural" refers to a vertical invisible reality in which goddess may be experienced as substance, as life-generating powers or, personally, as "the other", as deity.

However, this is not all there is to say about the Goddess. She is also believed to "exile" herself from transcendent supernaturalism and *materialize* in a magical sense: to incarnate and descend into people – an act named "sacred possession" by Starhawk. In order to understand how language is used for such a possession to happen and to grasp the symbolic complexity of Witchcraft, we need to deepen the Romantic theory of religion summarized above and linger with the fact that Wicca is also a magico-mystical religion within western esotericism. As such, it attempts to restore a magical worldview and to seek extraordinary mystical experiences. A simple differentiation between experience and cultural symbol does not fully comprise the "possessiveness" of the Goddess and this other magical reality. Within a more esoteric frame of reference, Witches no longer understand the function and meaning of symbols exclusively as signifiers, as the "clothing" of experiences into cultural languages. In addition, symbols are, in themselves, regarded as literal vehicles and pointers to other realities. Within this magical–mystical framework we may ask: how do they now read signs? How do they comprehend magical reality and position themselves in relation to a more realist view of language?

Just as Starhawk operates with two concepts of religion, so she assumes, simultaneously, two corresponding sign theories. One is metaphorical, nominalist and horizontal, suiting her feminist, post-Romantic symbolic pro-gramme. The other is magical, realist and vertical, suiting her personal–spiritual transformation agenda and occult lineage. On one hand, Starhawk claims that language, as such, is basically metaphorical and arbitrary, irrespective of whether it is expressed through explicit metaphors (poetry) or implicit metaphors (scientific concepts): "Scientific knowledge, like religious know-ledge, is a set of metaphors for a reality that can never be completely described or comprehended . . . . Religion becomes dogmatic when it confuses the metaphor with the thing itself" (Starhawk 1979a:190). On the other hand, Starhawk adopts esoteric realism. In order to grasp the mystical meaning of symbols, she recommends that as part of the initiate's training she is taught to visualize symbols, to meditate on them and play with them in her imagination until they reveal their meaning directly (Starhawk 1979a:81). The meaning referred to here is not metaphorical and arbitrary, but arche-typal. Archetypal knowledge is eternal knowledge that "inhabits things", independently of the human subject, but it may become known to the subject as "embodied thoughts" through her active involvement, play, emotionality and meditation.

But then, at a certain point in the sign process, divine knowledge and the question of semantics (whether archetypal or metaphorical) abate altogether, whereas the symbol as a mediator for divine substance, for *power* in a realistic sense, takes over. Within this linguistic framework, very different from meta-phorism, Starhawk maintains, "The symbol tells us, look at this. Experience this thing; become this thing; open a channel so the power can flow through you" (1979a:74). In this context, the symbol is "of the object", the trans-cendent has become present as real forces, and the symbol acquires a literal, almost material, magical character.

The sign theory confronted here is probably derived from esoteric neo-Platonism, according to which language itself is constituted by cosmic, divine law and activity, not by human creativity. Neo-Platonic language theory maintains that some phonic archetypes are eternal, constituting a realm of "phonic ideas" that underlies the phenomenal reality (Bakker 1990:295). Such a realist view of language is necessarily part of all magical worldviews because of the very fact that magic originates from belief in cosmological correspondences: that there are real, invisible physical or energetic relationships between the elementals of nature as well as between words and things, that is, between symbols of people and people, between sacred symbols and that to which the symbols refer. According to Starhawk, magic opens the door to a reality that is just as valid to human experience, as is the tangible, visible world, only it has a different quality:

> The tangible, visible world is only one aspect of reality. There are other dimensions that are equally real, although less solid. Myths and metaphors are maps to other dimensions. Tir-Na-Nog, the Land of Youth in Irish mythology, is not a metaphor nor an archetype, it is a real place that can be visited. But its reality is not a physical one and the visits do not take place in the physical body. Beings also exist in those other realms, for the gods are more than symbols. They are real powers . . . . When we reach for Goddess, she reveals herself to us.
>
> (Starhawk 1987:25)

In order to integrate a notion of multiple realities, Reclaiming Witches have developed a corresponding concept of multiple selves in the individual: the divine Deep Self, the emotional Younger Self and the rational Talking Self.[2] Deep Self represents the core of the human body/mind, reflecting a funda- mental aspect of divine reality, while the culturally conditioned person includes the emotional body/mind of Younger Self and the rational body/mind of Talking Self. The structure of human consciousness is also believed to be organized according to these three selves: the ordinary consciousness of the Talking Self; the unconscious or dream state of the Younger Self; and the extraordinary consciousness of Deep Self. While Younger Self experiences the world, Talking Self structures it by arranging, categorizing, classifying and giving names. Deep Self, however, is "the Divine within, the ultimate and original essence, the spirit that exists beyond time, space and matter" (Starhawk 1979a:22) and is only accessible through Younger Self. It is not the rational "I" that communicates with the divine (although this "I" may communicate *about* the divine), but the intuitive Self. The content of this communication cannot be categorized as rational knowledge, but is rather spontaneous awareness, a discernment of the way things really are.

In *A Rumor of Angels* (1970), Peter Berger indirectly supports the Witches' position when he argues that reality is never experienced as one unified whole, neither by ancient nor by modern people. Rather, it is perceived as multiple, as containing zones or strata with greatly different qualities. The realities that differ from being wide awake in ordinary, empirical reality he calls "sub-universes" and points out that these may be based on physiological processes, such as the dream state, or they may be experienced as a radical emotional rupture from daily life, such as in ecstasy. Starhawk's conscious rotation between different modes of being, then, is not a sign of irrationality or regression. The fact that these sub-universes are questioned at all Berger ascribes solely to the process of secularization: the social plausibility structures supporting magical beliefs are weakened or gone. But secularization does not mean that the consciousness of modern people has changed and developed *en bloc* from irrational to rational.

In order to approach magical reality and the literal qualities of language, I shall combine Berger's concept of sub-universes with the Reclaiming Witches' concept of the three selves, and investigate the magico-ritual framework for the experiential category associated with "reaching for the Goddess" and entering realms like Tir-Na-Nog, the Land of Youth in Celtic mythology.

Trance-induction: *Remembering Tiamat*

As elaborated by Starhawk, the sacred can be perceived and experienced at two different levels: either as an awareness of divine presence immanent in the visible reality of empirical daily life, or as an extra-ordinary experience of the presence of divine reality within a "less solid", invisible sub-universe. Witches make use of ritual trance techniques in order to induce an extraordinary consciousness of divine presence. Trance is a controlled form of hypnosis, which alters the ordinary consciousness to a mode close to the dream state by the conscious manipulation of fantasy and emotions (Goodman 1988:6–7). It is, in fact, to enter the dream state while being awake. In Reclaiming, this is regarded as a major magical tool. It helps a person to "leave" the sensual body and travel somewhere else in her consciousness. This journey is believed to take place on the astral plane, a place beyond time and space and the limits of the physical body. In dream state a person can journey to a mythological universe, enter the narrative and become simultaneous with narrative time.

In shamanic traditions this journey to another world is often induced by strong sensory stimuli: fasting from food and drink, flagellation, exhausting dancing or – most commonly – the monotonous and steady beat of a drum.[3] The essence in trance work is not the drum, but guided visualization. The medium is taken to another reality by a narrator's voice. The body position of the medium is that of lying down on the floor or walking slowly in the room, in both cases with her eyes closed. She is taken into an altered state of consciousness, into the dream state of her Deep Self, by letting her imagination and feelings follow the guidelines of the narrator.

The goal of ritual trance is to arrange for people to have a deep experience of truth, believed to be accessible through this journey to another reality. Here they can find answers to important questions, meet their ancestors or another part of themselves, merge with the elements or deep forces in nature, or ultimately, meet the goddess and become "possessed". The experiences in trance are considerably heightened if the dream state is built to a level of ecstasy. This is most commonly done by ecstatic techniques such as exhausting singing and dancing. According to Reclaiming Witches, "letting oneself trance" requires deep trust in the narrator as well as in one's fellow ritualists.

This mental journey to a place where historical time and space dissolve into mythical present is regarded as possible because Witches believe that some part of them, some part of their Deep Selves, *actually* reaches back to the beginning of time in an unbroken line. The memory of the beginning of time is literally stored in their DNA cells and can be called forth in every new reincarnation of a human being. Trance is an aid to healing and becoming depossessed from oppressive culture and imagery and is a means to dispense with *time* and remember through the body, as Starhawk puts it, "that the Goddess lives in us as we in her as in each other" and that she has been incarnated in humans since the beginning of time. Ritual trance may, therefore, also help the participants to "remember" their former lives, for example, as hunters and gatherers in prehistoric Africa or as Witches burned during the inquisition. In trance, the history of evolution and all time lags can be merged into the memory of a single person.

Let us now enter the Witches' ritual space to explore how trance can be used. The following example is from Witchcamp in Vancouver in 1989, where the Goddess was invoked by this method. The trance work was jointly led by Starhawk, Raven, Deadly, Cybelle and Pandora. Approximately 100 people participated. The ritual sequence lasted probably half an hour.

*   *   *

The ritualists are asked to slowly move clockwise in circle with their eyes closed. Starhawk enters the centre of the circle while beating a certain rhythm on her Palestinian doumbec drum. Raven moves counter-clockwise at the circle's edge, also beating his drum. Gradually people adjust their movements to the rhythm of the drums. After a while Deadly starts speaking, slowly and evocatively:[4]

> *Long ago, there once was a time when people knew that the earth was a living being and that all of life was holy. They knew the Goddess and they worshipped her as Tiamat, as Inanna, as the Goddess of many names and guises. This harmony was interrupted when her sons all of a sudden wanted the power. They came together in Babylon, cut her body into pieces and made the world as we know it today, dis-membered and scattered . . . . Now, we who are alive in her as she in us as we are in each other will go back to this time and remember Tiamat. We shall re-member the Goddess, shed her old skin and re-create her anew.*

Starhawk now starts singing, and people follow.

> *Snake Woman, shedding her skin, Snake Woman shedding her skin,*
> *Shed, shed, shedding her skin. Shed, shed, shedding her skin.*

The song is repeated again and again, building up energy. Then it fades and ends, and only the drumbeat is heard. After a while, Starhawk continues the trance induction.

Remember as you imagine how we who are alive in her as she in us were fettered, beaten, raped, tortured, burned, and poisoned. Remember how we were dismembered and scattered, almost destroyed. Remember the feeling of being lost and lonely, how you are hurt and wounded by other people. Now, remember the times when you feel that you fail, how you hurt and wound others . . . . Breathe deep, feel the pain – where it lives deep in us (as salt), burning. Flush it out! Let the pain become a sound, a living river on the breath. Raise your voice – cry out. Scream. Wail. Keen and mourn for the dismembering of the world.[5]

As the ritualists start to embody the images and the sound of the narrating voice, they cry out, wail and mourn. After quite a while, Starhawk continues.

Remember, there is a place within us all, deep within, where we still are whole and can feel the wholeness, before we were cut into pieces. Now, reach for that sacred place, which always has been there. Reconnect with Deep Self and remember that you are a whole being and always have been.

The chanting starts again, builds up and fades.

Snake woman, etc.

After a while Cybelle continues to talk.

We are remade; we are whole; we are healed. You do not any longer feel lost or scattered. Feel that place of peace and rest deep within, stretching back in time, and make a vision for the future . . . . Now, imagine that every child on this planet is fed and cared for. Imagine that we cultivate the land in harmony and respect for its internal balance. Imagine a city in which women can walk the streets in peace, without any fear. Imagine a culture in which the Goddess again is worshipped and sanity restored . . . . What is your challenge to re-create the world? . . . Listen to your inner voice; what do you hear, what is your challenge?

The chant starts again, and energy is slowly built into an ecstatic state, raising what Witches call "a cone of power". This energy is meant to actualize and give an energetic form to the vision created by Cybelle, transforming it from image to reality on the astral plane, which again can manifest on the mundane. Pandora continues to talk.

Reach out and feel the energy in the centre of the circle. Place your hand on the lower part of your belly, and feel the place deep within where the Goddess is re-membered . . . . Now, bend and place your hands on the ground and give back to the earth the energy you do not need. Reach for your challenge and keep it in your hand . . . . When you are ready, return to this room. Stamp your feet hard on the floor. Open your eyes and look around you. Clasp your hands three times, and say your own name out loud . . . . Find two other people in this room, and form groups of three. Share your experience of dismemberment, of wholeness and of your challenge.

*   *   *

The mythic imagery used in this trance work is taken from *Enuma Elish*, the Babylonian creation epic. As stated in chapter 2, it tells the story of how the cosmos was created by defeating chaos, symbolized as the goddess Tiamat, the primeval snake.

Starhawk does not read *Enuma Elish* as a creation story, but as a symptom of the displacement of a prehistoric goddess religion and the subordination of women by male warriors. As observed in the ritual sequence above, the participants are asked to investigate and experience the mythical event by entering the sub-universe of mythical time in their imagination and becoming Tiamat, the snake woman; they are asked to unweave history by depossessing or shedding their skins and being reborn; they are asked to remember what they cannot possibly remember, the deep centre of their being that was never cut in pieces and destroyed by priests similar to Marduk's and to reconnect with it. They are asked to remember the time before men where rulers and gods were champions, to remember that women's bodies and sexual power are the oldest imagery used to symbolize divine creation. It is taken for granted that the Goddess is a power manifesting in Deep Self and that merging with the Goddess "who is alive in us as we in her as in each other" is conducive to healing common cultural heritage as well as to psychological healing of individuals.

The word "re-member" has double meaning; it refers both to "recall" and to "put something together". This putting together within a ritual context is not only a symbolization but is considered a magical act with real impact upon people and the state of affairs in this world. But, for healing actually to take place, it is obviously equally important to leave the trance state of collective merger and undifferentiation, to reenter the ordinary reality of separation and individuality, and, then, to complete the healing process by re-experiencing it at this level through the acts of communication, sharing and putting into metaphorical language.

The energy experienced and raised in ritual trance belongs to rhetoric as well as to the field of psychophysical emotional exercises. Energy is set in motion by the compelling force of symbolic language, certain body postures and the art of imagination. But energy is also affected by the materiality of language itself: since the word is voiced as speech or song, it becomes a bodily thing, not only a rhetorical sign. In addition, the symbolic figure Tiamat is perceived by Witches as a living entity, concealed simultaneously, so to speak, as linguistic tropes in the mythical text and as a virtual being in the Deep Self. When retelling the myth as a ritualized trance induction, Witches maintain that the Goddess becomes alive within the experience of the trance mediums; they meet her as substance, as "the great powers" taking possession. In accordance with a worldview of living nature and cosmological corres-pondences, Witches believe in the possibility of real, although invisible relationships between words and things. Therefore, as the transcendent "becomes" present as real forces in the subject, the narrative of Tiamat is not only regarded as a pointer to the thing (that is, divine reality), but emerges as an indexical sign: the symbolic figure "Tiamat" is perceived as contiguous with the divine subject/object Tiamat. The made-up sacred narrative is believed to be "of the thing": it is the material and medium through which Goddess takes possession of the Deep Self.

Why is it that the range of experience reported in magical religion cannot be grasped through the hermeneutics of symbolic analysis? Because of its reductive sign theory: it trivializes questions regarding the existence of the object and, in particular, the existence of the extra-ordinary.[6] On this background, anthropologist E. Valentine Daniel has questioned the entire enterprise of the study of religion as merely a system of symbols. "From the analyst's point of view, a culture may be a system of symbols and meanings. But from the native's point of view, his culture is constituted of indexical and iconic signs in addition to symbols" (Daniel 1984:32). Daniel differentiates between symbol, icon and index according to how the sign is constituted: in the symbol, "image" and object are arbitrarily related by convention; in the icon they are related by similarity (some actual resemblance or quality of the object is represented in the image); in the index, "image" and object are related by contiguity (for example, smoke may be an index of fire), giving "a fluid and potentially alchemical relationship" (Daniel 1984:29).

This is relevant to Witches: in their world, icons and indexical signs may be perceived as pointers and doorsteps to magical reality and sacred possession. They make the experiential category of magic more plausible, and bridge the distinction between Witchcraft as an invented human symbolization on the one hand, and as a truthful experience of extra-ordinary reality on the other.

Witchcraft in relation to *unio mystica* and esoteric sign theory

When Witches emphasize the authority of experience over dogma, using symbols and myths as pointers and mediators *to*, and indexical signs *of*, divine reality, they appear as seekers of the *unio mystica*, for the mark of mystical religion is its emphasis on extra-ordinary experiences of the divine and the effort to "merge with" the deity. The particular mystical tradition that has most profoundly influenced Witchcraft and its occult lineage is an esoteric version of the Jewish Kabbalah.[7] According to the Jewish scholar Gershom G. Scholem, a Kabbalist desires to "taste" God, not only "listen" to divine words. This tasting can occur through ecstatic immersion in inner experience, intuition, contemplation or ritual, but *not* through intellectual work. Neither can mystical knowledge about God be expressed by the intellect using ordinary language: "By its very nature, mysticism is knowledge that cannot be communicated directly, but may be expressed only through symbol and metaphor" (Scholem 1946:4).

The Kabbalah is, however, characterized by being mystical and esoteric simultaneously. That is to say, mystical knowledge, which cannot be communicated, exists side by side with a highly developed esoteric teaching that seeks to reveal to the intellect exactly those mysteries surrounding the hidden

God and the relation between deity and creation that can be communicated, if only to the initiated (Scholem 1974:3). An important part of esotericism is knowledge about the magical techniques used to achieve union with God: prayers, meditation, spell work, trances, ritual performance or the correct utterance of God's secret name. In western esotericism, such magical acts are divided into two groups: "high magic", which seeks union with God, and "low magic", which uses the same magical techniques to achieve things in daily life, such as good health, prosperity or a lover. In the Kabbalah, this latter kind of magic is called "practical Kabbalah" (Scholem 1974:5).

The tension between the mystical and the esoteric parts of the Kabbalah is to a certain extent similar to the Romantic distinction between presymbolic experience and cultural symbol; for whereas mysticism represents silence, seeking individual, immediate experience of divine reality, esotericism represents doctrine and the desire to discover and formulate *the* truth about the universe and the being of God in cultural language. Scholem points out that the Kabbalists themselves experience a sort of paradoxical congruence between these elements: intuitive experience (mysticism) on the one hand, and cultural reflection (esoteric doctrine) on the other (Scholem 1974:3).[8] An effort to explain the paradox is, however, offered in the theory of the hidden and manifest aspects of the divine. God is said to be both hidden (transcendent) and manifest (immanent), and the seekers of *unio mystica* are invited to experience the transcendent, hidden godhead through God's manifestations in something tangible and mundane.

Starhawk's dual definition of religion as "mystical experience" and "soil of culture", resembles the Kabbalistic tension between experience and reflection, or that between mystical encounter and esoteric mediumship. In theory Starhawk dismisses dogma and religious tenets intended to generalize the experience of the divine and establish Truth. In practice, however, there is tradition and a need to teach newcomers and distinguish Reclaiming from other Craft communities. Therefore, in the wake of its occult heritage, there is a large amount of literature competing to present the esoteric teachings of Witchcraft "correctly". Starhawk's writings must be included in this series of explanation where dogma is replaced by tradition.

The fact that Witches embrace this Kabbalistic paradox is also pertinent to understanding how they can combine the tradition of anarchism, revolt and the autonomy of experience, together with the tradition of initiation, secret knowledge and esoteric teachings. The dilemma is, however, solved by inventing a depth–surface discourse for the concept of experience: to the extent that human experience of the Goddess may be interpreted as a confrontation with "life-generating powers", it is, at its deepest level, universal. The encounter only appears to be differentiated and diversified at a surface level, when it is individualized and inculturated by means of language and the social environment.[9] This topical structure also holds true for the concept of divinity, which is interpreted in alignment with the idea of the hidden versus the manifest divine.

In order to explain the paradoxical nature of the Jewish Kabbalah, Scholem invokes a sign theory in which the distinction between metaphor and religious symbol is crucial. He maintains that while a metaphor is descriptive, translating one universe of meaning into another, a religious symbol is representative. A metaphor can be replaced by any of its numerous meanings. The religious symbol, on the other hand, cannot. It can represent or make something else transparent, but this "something else" cannot substitute for the symbol and make it superfluous.

To explain the peculiarity of mystical language, Scholem expands the notion of symbol from religious to mystical. The mystical symbol is regarded as different from the religious symbol proper in that it does not carry a meaning, only an expression (image, sound/word or gesture) and a hidden referent (object). It is more like an empty pointer/mediator in relation to a reality which cannot be expressed in any other way: "The symbol 'signifies' nothing and communicates nothing, but makes something transparent which is beyond all expression . . . the symbol is intuitively understood all at once – or not at all" (Scholem 1946:27).

The vertical interpretive process implied here is different from a horizontal, metaphorical translation of divine discourse already encoded in sacred texts. The mystical symbol has no specific prescribed meaning and is not a manifestation of something hidden, but reveals the hidden, makes it transparent and clear. The symbol is like a doorstep to the invisible, pointing us to another world. The Kabbalistic Tree of Life (beyond the doctrine of the sephiroths), the symbol of the circle, encapsulating a point or a hexagram, the letters representing God's name (YHWH) – all are mystical symbols. The mystical symbol is therefore closer to an icon: the expression (image, sound/word or gesture) points to the object, that is, to transcendent (or invisible) reality due to some mystical similarities between it and the object.

Although Scholem's sign theory may be profitable for describing the mystical aspects of Witchcraft symbolism, it does not really help us penetrate the experiential category of magic and sacred possession. This is so because Scholem hesitates to elaborate on the indexical aspect of the mystical symbol operative in magic. When the hidden, transcendent object becomes manifest in the symbol as magical power, the mystical symbol may be said to transform into an indexical sign. This may, for example "take place" when God, according to the Kabbalists, becomes fully present *in* the tetragrammaton (the four letters YHWH), or when meditation upon the ten sephiroths of the Tree of Life actually restores the universe and reconciles God from God's alienation within godself. Then, the object dissolves into the symbol and we are left with (1) expression and (2) meaning: the symbol no longer has a separate object/referent! For terminological consistency I shall refer to this new, magical presence filled with meaning as an *esoteric symbol*.

Esoteric symbols are the real *axis mundi* between this world and the invisible realms of the divine. In Witchcraft we will find that the Goddess, the Deep Self, the four elements and the ritual circle have the potential to fulfill this function. When deity is called into ritual space, incarnating *as substance* in everybody present, the circle is transformed from a mystical to an esoteric symbol. When the Witch says "I am Goddess," she confirms that deity is herself. The people holding hands have become an index of divine presence. At this point, the sacred circle represents and means what it refers to.

It is in order to grasp this magical and sensual dimension inside a theory of symbols that I suggest splitting between mystical and esoteric symbols. In contrast to the mystical symbol's function of pointing to something hidden, the hidden, in actual fact, becomes manifest in the esoteric symbol as power or divine presence. This may happen in the Witches' ritual circle, at the orthodox altar (behind the iconostasia) believed to represent God's indwelling presence, and when Christ is proclaimed as fully present in the bread and wine on the altar.

Interpreting divine indexicality: Goddess as deity and other-than-deity

The goddesses of Witchcraft are obviously multidimensional symbols: they are metaphorical; they point and reveal; they mediate real forces. Tiamat is both a religious symbol and more than a symbol. To call upon her is to call upon certain forces that are different from "what comes" if calling upon Inanna. And finally, these forces are said to be more than archetypes: they are considered to be real, separate entities.

Witches themselves may or may not experience all these levels of the goddess symbol, or their relationship with her may be totally anarchistic. In an interview given to Carol P. Christ in 1979, Starhawk insisted, "It all depends on how I feel. When I feel weak, She is someone who can help and protect me. When I feel strong, She is the symbol of my own power. At other times I feel Her as the natural energy in my body and the world" (Christ 1982:76). To Sofia, the Goddess is the moon but also an invisible agent who picks out people "to hear her message". To Francesca she is someone with a "physical presence" who justs "kidnaps you". In addition, Francesca speaks of the Goddess as representing immanent reality and the "mysteries" of nature.

Nevertheless, the Witches' goddess symbol seems confusing and difficult to comprehend to many feminist scholars. Most frequently she is reduced and defined as either a pantheistic principle or a psychological concept.[10] Yet some of the difficulty arises precisely because she is neither a purely pantheistic principle nor a transcendent deity but a manifest goddess. And as Starhawk points out, it is very difficult for westerners to grasp the concept of a manifest deity (Starhawk 1979a:77). In fact, in order to comprehend this concept and desist from reductionism, we must apparently claim two opposing theories at the same time: that the Goddess is both deity and other-than-deity simultaneously.

Theologian Robert P. Scharleman has argued that most western people carry an internal concept of the divine that is formed by a theistic notion of

YHWH and its implied opposite, *a-theism*. The problem, however, is that theism's image of God includes only two entities: *Creator* (God as subject and deity) and *creation* (the object created by the deity) (Scharleman 1982:89). This concept of God, says Scharleman, is incomplete because it does not include God as other-than-deity, that is, it does not include God as part of creation: "What cannot be thought, in the tradition of this picture, is that the world itself is a moment in the being of God, what cannot be thought is that the world is the being of God when God is not being deity" (Scharleman 1982:90). If the symbol of God is to contain the manifest divine in the world beyond God's historical incarnation as Christ, then "God" must, according to Scharleman, be represented and understood both as deity and as other-than-deity.

I find this differentiation very helpful since it provides a tool to move beyond various reductionist interpretations of the Goddess and also include the reflections already made on the mystical and esoteric aspects of the symbol. As other-than-deity, the Witches' goddess may be perceived as "internal force": a metaphor for life-generating powers and the principle of creation throughout the universe. As deity, the Goddess may be perceived as "external force": an anthropomorphic symbol believed to mediate and express divine action and being. But since we are dealing, in addition, with a mystery religion that distinguishes between the manifest and the hidden, Goddess as deity and as other-than-deity must be divided into another two levels. We thus get four levels of the goddess symbol, which can be illustrated by the following diagram:

		Goddess	
The Living Universe/other-than-deity (metaphor *for life-generating powers*)		*The Great Mother/deity* (anthropomorphic symbol)	
1 Manifest other-than-deity	2 Hidden other-than-deity	3 Hidden deity	4 Manifest deity
Goddess as immanent being in all creation	Goddess as incomprehensible ground of being	Goddess's many names and guises	Goddess's virtual incarnation in all human beings
Goddess as countless *metaphors*	Goddess as *mystical symbol*	Goddess as *conventional religious symbol*	Goddess as *esoteric, indexical symbol*

As *manifest other-than-deity*, the Goddess represents the principle of creation and is immanent in all beings. She is the earth and the world in all its diversity and visibility. In this connection she is not a symbol that represents something hidden, but a metaphor for those life-generating powers that constitute the universe: "To Witches the cosmos is the living body of the Goddess, in whose being we all partake, who encompasses us and is immanent within us" (Starhawk 1987:7). Countless names and images can describe Goddess, such as "river", "chair", "Starhawk", etc. endlessly. The human experience of the Goddess as manifest other-than-deity may take place anywhere – in cultural or natural landscapes, in interhuman relationships, as a sudden awareness of the sacred "given" in the cycles of life and death. Goddess is thus a metaphor that may be replaced by its numerous meanings taken from all these encounters.

As *hidden other-than-deity*, the Goddess is the ultimate mystery, indefinable, before words, nameless, the fundament of being, the silent part of Deep Self. In this aspect, the Goddess may also be described as "She whose name cannot be spoken because she is the circle before it is broken by a name that separates out" (Starhawk 1982a:73). As explained earlier, the mystical symbol has no meaning in itself. It is an empty mediator for a hidden reality that reveals the hidden without manifesting it. But in contrast to the metaphor, there is no meaning evoked by the symbol that can substitute for it. The goddess symbol points to an otherness that cannot be represented unless the symbol continues to point. To "taste" the mystical Goddess as hidden other-than-deity is only possible indirectly, as "recognition, in the midst of pleasure, of its deepest source" (Starhawk 1979a:84). Goddess may be revealed in disguise in human experience, but is not manifested.

As *hidden deity*, the Goddess separated herself from the all-inclusive categories of nature and mystery, entered the circle and become available *in* language *as* subject through the act of naming. Since she of necessity is also created *by* the human languages, Starhawk proclaims: "She exists and we create Her" (Starhawk 1979a:81). As life-generating powers or mystical ground of being, the Goddess is One. But as personified, hidden deity, the Goddess appears as plural goddesses with "a thousand" personal names, shapes and guises. The deities are often represented with the formula "I am Tiamat", "I am Inanna", etc. Traditionally the word "I" has no reference outside the speaking subject itself since it is impossible to say the word "I" without being the person it refers to (Scharleman 1982:91). But the speaking voice of a hidden deity does not yet convey real forces; it has not yet manifested in substance; it still belongs to otherness, to Tiamat. As hidden deity, Goddess is therefore perceived as a mighty subject who represents otherness to the human subject. She may also be addressed as a "You" in relation to an "I", with a series of personal qualities such as love, mercy and forgiveness projected onto her.

As *manifest deity*, Goddess and humans are able to meet, merge and become as one. The Witches' mystical insight is that the Goddess is virtually present in all beings. Every time a person says, "I am," she reiterates the hidden existence of the Goddess in her own being. The very moment she says, "I am Goddess" she confirms that the Goddess's otherness has incarnated in her, which is indicated by the negation of the subject's own name. The symbol now represents what it refers to: "I" represent Tiamat in actuality. Tiamat is no longer a metaphor or a pure, religious symbol, but an esoteric, indexical

symbol that makes the absent present as distinctive forces.[11] This takes place in ritual when the Goddess is invoked in persona as external being but "in reality" incarnates in the Witch as an awakening of the Deep Self: "To invoke the Goddess, is to awake the Goddess within, to become, for a time, that aspect that we invoke" (Starhawk 1979a:55). By means of various trance techniques, the Goddess gradually transposes into a manifest deity, and ultimately in the act declaring "Thou art Goddess." When a priestess or a single person enters this "bodily state of mind" on behalf of a larger group, it is referred to as "aspecting" or "drawing down the moon".

This particular experience of manifesting the Goddess as deity usually happens in extra-ordinary consciousness in ritual and is essentially different from the horizontal, everyday consciousness that the Goddess is "in me", just as she is in every thing, because she *is* the world. Furthermore, in "sacred possession" we are confronted with an empirically felt reality of how a religious symbol may transform into an esoteric, indexical symbol. But, indexicality is not only a property of the sign or symbol. In fact, it is a fundamental feature of religious ritual as such, being the foundation of its efficacy, uniqueness and importance.

The hermeneutics of space

In the above I have tried to show the ways in which Starhawk and other Reclaiming Witches perceive of and systematize ultimate Reality: by means of sub-universes, multiple selves and plural states of the human consciousness corresponding to plural meanings of "experience", "goddess", "religion" and "language". Since they take an interest not in developing a consistent meta-theory, but rather in creating a symbolic universe in which the existence of multiple realities can be true, their ethno-hermeneutics appears to be paradoxical.

But as we saw when analysing the goddess symbol, there is an elementary order in the paradox in terms of an implicit hierarchy and interpretive matrix. This matrix is constituted by a depth–surface discourse or, more accurately, by the "hermeneutics of space": symbolic movements from one level of reality to the next according to a vertical and horizontal axis, resonating with the horizontal magic of everyday life and the vertical magic of ritual. For example, Starhawk's arguments develop along both axes as three successive hermeneutical steps: she starts in the visible, ordinary reality of Talking Self in which the Goddess is represented as countless metaphors, and language said only to describe reality indirectly (1). This is Starhawk's nominalist and symbolic position. Her Nietzsche-inspired criticism is that metaphor in our culture has turned into dogmatic concept, confusing the metaphor with the thing itself. To cut loose from this language trap, the only way out is to dive experientially into the source of invisible, extra-ordinary reality, that is, into the bosom of the Goddess who conveys real truth (2). The path to the Goddess or the divine within goes through Younger Self, and the status of language is now magical. This is Starhawk's magico-empirical, or realist, position. After knowing truth from diving into the source, she returns to visible reality and Talking Self, where language again is metaphorical.

This whole process I place on a vertical axis, whereas the next one I place on the horizontal one: now Starhawk is free to choose new metaphors for ordinary reality depending on values implicit in names, not on whether they are true or not in a conceptual sense. She is also ready for the horizontal movement in the world to practice the magic of everyday life, where "talk" is equivalent to "walk" (3). In this reality, she constantly moves between an empirical-experiential and a symbolic position. Let me fill in this sketch by describing Starhawk's hermeneutics of space as matrix for personal and social transformation.

Horizontal magic of everyday life (I): possessed reality and oppressive metaphors

Starhawk's hermeneutical programme in regard to cultural analysis takes its point of departure in empirical daily life, in the reality of Talking Self, in how the world actually is perceived, named and valued through language. She maintains that language is political and that the hallmark of power is to define realities: "The root question is, how do we define the world? For it is an old magical secret that the way we define reality shapes reality. Name a thing and you invoke it. If we call the world non-living, we will surely kill her. But when we name the world alive, we begin to bring her back to life" (Starhawk 1987:8).

In this context Starhawk is concerned with the values invoked in meaning and not with referential truth. Her emphasis on the power of language and symbols stems from a metaphorical theory of language in which meaning is arbitrarily conferred upon the world. But, since meaning also embodies values, the power of language is not a superficial question of naming, but of social-ization. According to Starhawk, we live in a patriarchal world and experiences power as forces of domination and control, as "power-over". We are possessed, so to speak, by the language of this culture:

> Culture provides us with a "language" – a set of internal rules and expectations for combining things and acts . . . . These patterns are never accidental; they are the concrete manifestations of a culture's deepest assumptions, structures, and power relationships . . . . The patterns of patriarchy become literally embedded within us. We are possessed.
>
> (Starhawk 1987:96)

How is it possible to become depossessed and liberated, or even to reflect upon one's own oppression, if the human subject is totally conditioned by society? The answer is that we are not *fully* conditioned. Deep within all human beings is a precultural, natural core of "divine descent". Moreover, due to the structure of the three selves and the human consciousness, people are forever split subjects and will never be completely continuous with the dominant culture.

Vertical magic of ritual: sacred reality and indexical symbols

Starhawk's medicine for becoming "desocialized" and confronting "power-over" and the values of oppression is to turn inward by means of meditation or ritual and make contact with the Goddess. It is to merge totally with divine reality for a limited time period and experience sacred possession. This state of mind is induced by the ritual techniques already presented, such as trance work and exhausting singing and dancing. "Sacred possession . . . . is an ecstatic state, and ecstasy reminds us that the sacred is immanent. When the great powers are moving through us they also bring knowledge, abilities and healing that go beyond our ordinary limitations. Equally important, the knowledge of how to become possessed is also the knowledge of how to become unpossessed" (Starhawk 1987:96). In this quotation Starhawk calls up an esoteric reality in which knowledge is not conveyed through the symbol system of language but directly from the divine source, from the things them-selves. She leaves the manifest level of meaning and invokes a fundamental "deep semantics": the realm of archetypes, magic and esoteric, indexical symbols.

Starhawk insists that her ability to define and delimit power-over comes from calling upon another kind of power, a power from within the natural world. She states again and again that "those powers live in us, as we live in them" (1987:6) and maintains that nobody can control them or disconnect from them. But they may be invoked to cleanse, rebuild and heal, and this is what Starhawk defines as magic:

> The technology of power-from-within is magic, the art of changing consciousness, of shifting shapes and dimensions, of bending reality. Its science is a psychology far older than Freud, Jung, or Skinner. And its motivations are erotic in the broadest sense of the deep drives in us to experience and share pleasure, to connect, to create, to see our impact on others and on the world.
>
> (Starhawk 1987:15)

It is to reach these sources of power of another kind that Witches conduct magical ritual and work with energy. According to Starhawk, it is only the magical language of the dream state that can call forth the power-from-within whereby people can become unpossessed by power-over and start the process of healing themselves and culture. The language of "power-from-within" is poetry, metaphor, symbol, ritual, myth, "the language of magic, of 'thinking in things', where the concrete becomes resonant with mysteries that go beyond its seeming solid form. Its language is action, which speaks in the body and to all the senses in ways that can never be completely conveyed in words" (Starhawk 1987:15).

Even though magical language is made from metaphors, its ability to name reality truthfully is regarded as basic: when the Goddess is called, she will arrive. The symbol becomes identical with its referent, transforming into an esoteric symbol. In this realist, neo-Platonic view of language, linguistic meaning is archetypically, not arbitrarily, conferred upon the world. The things themselves are understood to reveal their essence and names to us if we are open to this experience.

Horizontal magic of everyday life (II): depossessed reality and liberating metaphors

After diving and cleansing herself vertically in divine (or supernatural) reality, Starhawk returns to her Talking Self and ordinary daily life. Still, she is not outside the realm of the sacred, which is believed to be immanent and ever present. She has only changed consciousness. In magical reality the divine encompasses her completely; in ordinary reality she carries the divine inside as Deep Self and confronts it in "the other". In Starhawk's theology it is not desirable or possible for human beings to merge permanently with the divine. If they did, there would be no individuality and no creativity. An important part of this creativity is the freedom to name according to certain values. This is the area of the consciously chosen, liberating metaphors that name life-generating powers "the Goddess": "We call her Goddess, not to narrowly define her gender, but as a continual reminder that what we value is life brought into the world" (Starhawk 1987:7).

This is an example of Starhawk's position as symbolist. Again, language is basically seen as arbitrary and metaphorical. It does not represent reality, and there are no true names for the Goddess. But, even if one metaphor is not closer to reality than another, words have values. This is why the world must be renamed in the image of the Goddess: "as a continual reminder that what we value is life brought into the world."

"Power" in the realm of depossessed, ordinary reality, is not defined as power-from-within but as *power-with*. In the consciousness of power-from-within, every being has the same value. In the consciousness of power-with, people are valued as having a higher worth than worms. Politics is impossible without rating and choosing one alternative before another (Starhawk 1987:15). To take on the name "Witch" is also an act of choosing, of ethically separating out from immanent reality an identity more noble than another. For to be a Witch is "to make a commitment to the Goddess, to the protection, preservation, nurturing, and fostering of the great powers of life as they emerge in every being" (Starhawk 1987:8). In fact, it is to choose life before death. This is pertinent since, in the realm of undivided divinity that en-compasses the whole circle of life and death, there are no immediate criteria available with which to rank one lifeform above another, or one social structure as more desirable than another. This is how Starhawk explains her biased choice:

> I am on the side of the power that emerges from within, that is inherent in us as the power to grow is inherent in seed. As a shaper, as one who practices magic, my work is to find that power, to call it forth, to coax it out of hiding, tend it, and free it of restrictions. In a society based on power-over, that work inevitably must result in conflict with the forces of domination, for we cannot bear our own true fruit when we are under another's control.
>
> (Starhawk 1987:8)

The goal of Witchcraft is eventually to liberate people, sanctify the world, and unify spirit and politics. This means to unite the values inherent in divine reality and the values circulating in social reality.

If divinity in its totality is understood to be cut off from this world, isolated in a transcendent realm that is radically "other" to daily life, then the unification will inevitably be a disqualification of earthly life. If the principles of radical transcendence shall guide the politics of and hopes of daily life affairs, Witches fear that the underlying message will be that this life is truly of little value.

But if divinity is defined as cited above, as immanent in the world, permeating every cell of every living being, they believe the hierarchies of values will turn upside down: if this world is the home of the gods, then the unification of spirit and politics will be the ultimate sanctification of this life. Union, therefore, is not sought "outside the world in some heavenly sphere nor through dissolution of the self into the void beyond the senses. Spiritual union is found in life, within nature, passion, sensuality – through being fully human, fully one's self" (Starhawk 1979b:263). Instead of loosing the self, Witches seek merger with nature and the manifest Goddess. Instead of referring spiritual experiences exclusively to a nonordinary realm, the path of the Goddess leads toward a spiritual transfiguration of the ordinary.

Summing up, we may say that the Witches have three hermeneutical programmes: to call forth and connect with life-generating powers; to rename the world and redefine value; to walk their talk and live in accordance with their beliefs and visions. Each programme invokes different realities, world-views and theories of language/symbol. Although these realities are held to be equally real, they seem to constitute a hierarchy, both in terms of profoundness and semantics. This, however, cannot be known spontaneously from daily life affairs or direct perception; only deep experience and hermeneutical interpretation can convey the profoundly sacred dimension of ordinary reality: that the Goddess constitutes its very being.

Notes

1 The "traditional" *Charge of the Goddess* is quoted in full in Starhawk 1979a:76–7.
2 The three selves were initially developed by the Faery tradition. In *The Spiral Dance,* Starhawk talks about a "High Self". But, in line with her increasing political consciousness (in the Talking Self!), the name of the third self has been changed

from *High* to *Deep.* According to Starhawk, the three selves correspond to three types of subtle or invisible energy: 1 *Raith* energy is the energy in the elements, maintaining human beings' physical bodies and bodily memories, and is the body of Younger Self. 2 *Astral* energy consists of the conscious mind, thoughts and fantasies, and is the body of Talking Self. Raith and astral energy together make up a person's aura or energy field. 3 *Divine* energy is that which comprises Deep Self and the gods. This is the most powerful energy, and when the Witches invoke the gods in ritual, they connect themselves to this energy. The theory of the three energy bodies is a typical occult inheritance, a fact that Starhawk does not try to conceal (Starhawk 1979a:134).

3 Cf. Eliade (1964) and Harner (1980). The shaman usually lies down on the ground with her eyes closed. While listening to the drum, the shaman is trained to find – in her imagination – a place in nature, like a rock or a tree, unto which she can "enter", to travel either to the underworld or the upper world. This technique is also used in healing ceremonies. Illness in a shamanic worldview is often explained with soul loss. When the shaman journeys to another world, accompanied by a drumbeat, it is exactly to search for the lost soul and bring it back to the patient.

4 The actual ritual was not taped, and my retelling of it is primarily based on field notes and memory. Even though all the words may not be exact, I choose to write in present, as if I am quoting the ritual process word by word, to give a better impression of "trance journey" as a magical method. A substantial part of the words "said" by Starhawk are directly copied from her book *Truth or Dare* (1987: 28–31).

5 The lyrics of the invocation "said" by Starhawk in this context are taken from her trance poem in *Truth or Dare* (1987: 28–31).

6 Symbolists usually define a symbol (or sign) as a binary correlation of two sets of differences: signifier (expression) and signified (meaning). What is missing is both a notion of the sign itself as substance, as materiality, and a triadic perception of the sign, which – in addition to signifier and signified – can include the "native experience" of the category of the Real: the actual object to which the expression refers.

7 According to Aleister Crowley, Kabbalah is the foundation of modern magic, including Witchcraft: "The whole basis of our (magical) theory is Quabbalah. The method of operation in magic is based on this" (Crowley 1987:9). Kabbalah, which means tradition, is the most commonly used designation for the Jewish mysticism practised from the Middle Ages onward. The occult version of the Kabbalah is a Christianized and paganized interpretation.

8 Antoine Faivre criticizes Scholem's phenomenology as outdated for studies of contemporary esotericism since the major difference between mysticism and esotericism is no longer "experience" versus "reflection": today esotericists also seek experiential union with God. In contrast to mystics they do, however, prefer *mediators* such as rituals, symbolic images, mandalas, and spirit-helpers to aid them in their quest (Faivre 1992:xvii). "Real" mystics, on the other hand, tend to see such intermediaries as hindrances, and this is, says Faivre, the main difference between the two.

9 Starhawk 1979a:82. This is, however, not a very convincing statement considering how Witches position themselves in opposition to interpretations of "life-generating powers" in other religions, like Christianity, Judaism and Islam.

10 Naomi Goldenberg is a representative of this position when she in her famous book, *Changing of the Gods*, defines feminist Witchcraft and the goddess symbol in purely psychological terms (Goldenberg 1979:89).

11 Scholem writes that, in the Kabbalah, being able to speak God's name means becoming God/acquiring power with God, just as being able to speak a language is being able to control it. The Kabbalists can draw the tetragram on a robe and put it on, thus taking over the power from YHWH's name, and carry out "practical Kabbalah", that is, perform magic (Scholem 1946:77; 96; 131).

Plate 1   Starhawk at the goddess camp *Her Voice – Our Voices* in America's Nevada mountains, June 1989. (Image: Jone Salomonsen, 1989.)

Plate 2 Goddess-worshipping women gathered for ritual at *Her Voice – Our Voices*, Nevada, June 1989. Starhawk facilitated the ritual, although only some women identified as Witches. (Image: Jone Salomonsen, 1989.)

Plate 3 Goddess-worshipping women in the act of ritualizing at *Her Voice – Our Voices*, June 1989. (Image: Jone Salomonsen, 1989.)

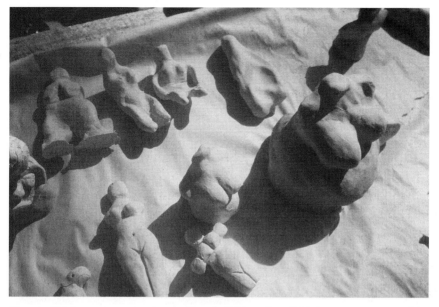

Plate 4 Witches and pagans often prefer paleolithic and neolithic images to represent "the Goddess". These homemade clay figures are for altar use, labyrinths or private gardens. (Image: Jone Salomonsen, 1989.)

Plate 5 Detail from the northern altar at Reclaiming's Spiral Dance ritual in November 1990. Four ritual altars are usually erected, representing each compass direction. The northern altar represents the earth, and therefore death and rebirth. (Image: Jone Salomonsen, 1989.)

Plate 6 Detail from the northern altar at Reclaiming's Spiral Dance ritual in November 2000. This is the main altar, erected in honour of the dead. Published with the kind permission of Ewa Litauer.

Plate 7 A baby doll in a coffin, symbolizing death and suffering among children, is placed at the northern altar at Reclaiming's Spiral Dance ritual in November 2000. Published with the kind permission of Ewa Litauer.

Plate 8 On special ritual occasions, Witches and pagans may adorn themselves with masks and body painting. The masks usually portray animals or ancient goddess imagery. (Image: Jone Salomonsen.)

Plate 9 Detail from a street parade in San Francisco's Mission district on *El dia de los muertos* (Day of the Dead) in November 1990. Representing the dead by dressing up, celebrating and dancing with them is an old Latino tradition. Celebrants at Reclaiming's Spiral Dance ritual may also wear death-costumes. (Image: Jone Salomonsen, 1990.)

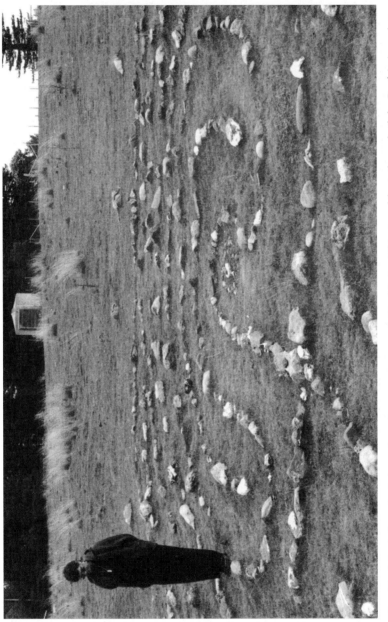

Plate 10 Labyrinths and spirals are favourite energy patterns in Reclaiming. This stone labyrinth was built by Reclaiming priestess Mer DeDanan on her land in Sonoma, north of San Francisco, and has often been used as ritual space. Originally published in *West by Northwest* online magazine, June/July 2000. Published with the kind permission of Mer DeDanan.

Plate 11 A maypole with ribbons is erected in downtown San Francisco as part of the Reclaim May Day demonstration in 2000. Starhawk leads a ritual dance around the maypole in order to conjure fertility for just political causes. Published with the kind permission of Ben Read.

Plate 12 Reclaiming organized the annual Reclaim May Day demonstration in San Francisco on 1 May 2000. All over the world this day is celebrated as a festival or as Labour Day. For Witches, 1 May is also a major holiday (*Beltane*), and celebrated as a fertility rite. Published with the kind permission of Bob Thawley.

Plate 13 *Beltane* is one of the Witches' eight sabbaths and traditionally celebrated with dances around the maypole. Coloured ribbons are woven around a large tree trunk in this celebration north of San Francisco, organized by the pagan Church of All Worlds in May 1989. (Image: Jone Salomonsen, 1989.)

Part II

Priestesses of the craft

5 Elements of magic

Learning to ritualize

Ritual has hermeneutic primacy in Reclaiming. When a person approaches this spiritual community, she is taught their "mysteries" by being introduced to ritual and magic. This usually takes place in the introductory "Elements of Magic" class. By giving a thorough description and interpretation of the ritual proceedings in this class, as well as of the meanings implied in the basic ritual outline taught, I hope to construct a basis for analysing magical ritualizing among contemporary Witches. This account will also yield knowledge about how a person is directed into the identity of actually *practising* Witchcraft. But, before I carry out the goals set, it is necessary to present both the ways in which Witches understand ritual, and the theoretical perspectives I use to interpret this activity.

Witches' understanding of ritual

In one of her definitions, Starhawk proposes that religion is "a matter of re-linking with the divine within and with her outer manifestations in all of the human and natural world" (Starhawk 1979a:186). To be able to "relink" requires a belief in somebody or something in here or out there with which one may be, and probably once was, connected. Connection and linkage are implied as desirable; disconnection and separation are apparently not. So, the question is, how may one be "linked up again" and reenter the path of the Goddess? Some people will explain that it happens spontaneously and as a completely internal event. To others the Goddess is almost experienced as a social agent, as happened to Francesca when she was "kidnapped". But for the majority, who probably never will experience immediate divine visitation (or revelation), learning the art of ritualizing may be an option, for this is how many Witches understand ritual, as a "technology" to evoke the Deep Self and become "familiar with power-from-within, learn to recognize its feel, learn how to call it up and let it go" (Starhawk 1989b:326). In a very short definition, Starhawk maintains that ritual simply is "a patterned movement of energy to accomplish a purpose". "Energy" is a condensed, somewhat technical term for "life-generating powers", which is the mystical aspect of the Goddess. This emphasis on "moving energy" and "purpose" may just as well be a definition of *magic;* and to many Witches, ritual is nothing but a pattern for working magic and adding to the transformation of the world.

But there is another aspect to religious ritual in Starhawk's definition, just as important as the subjective experience of relinking with the divine and moving her energy: to relink with "her outer manifestations in all of the human and natural world". This cannot happen in solitude or independence from other social bodies and is in particular believed to take place at the eight annual community rituals or sabbats:

> The Sabbats are . . . the interstices where the seasonal, the celestial, the communal, the creative and the personal all meet. As we enact each drama in its time, we transform ourselves . . . . We are not separate from each other, from the broader world around us; we are one with the Goddess, with the God.
>
> (Starhawk 1979a:169)

It is obvious that Starhawk's understanding of ritual is deeply linked to her notions of human and divine nature and that she regards "connection versus separation" as a basic ontological and psychological theme dramatized in ritual. In her interpretation of this theme, she is strongly influenced by transpersonal psychology and object relations theory, being trained – as she is – a psychologist in an alternative environment (Antioch Community College in San Francisco). In opposition to classical Freudian instinct theory, which is more focused on a person as an individual entity, a separate subject, determined to a large extent by instincts and drives – object relations theory rather depicts a person in her radical interconnectedness to other people, to her love objects. A human being is said to evolve from infant to adult along the axis unity–separation, and the key to psychic health and maturation is whether bonding and separation in early childhood were successful. Although separation is inevitable, if unsuccessful, it may inflict a life-long mourning process and a feeling of alienation that will trigger an endless search for transitional objects as replacement of the original maternal union.[1]

This antithetical side to human existence brings a lot of confusion and pain into people's lives; and according to most object relations theorists, mystical religion and magical ritual contribute significantly to increase it: When focused on the bliss of divine union and on rituals that attempt to effect merger with an original love object, the adult is said to simply return to childish fantasies of omnipotence. But this criticism does not take into account the fundamentally temporary, mimetic and symbolic character of ritual as such, nor that its point of departure is a conviction that the emotional conflict of merger and separation not only dominates infancy and childhood, but extends into adult life as a permanent existential conflict immanent to the human condition. [2]

This existential conflict revolves, says object relations theorist Margaret Mahler, around the struggle to become an autonomous separate person, differentiated and distinct, and at the same time connected and bonded with the love object, with significant others (Faber 1993:34). Although the struggle may be different for women and men, the fact that they have to struggle is regarded as essential to their shared humanity. Starhawk, who in *Dreaming the Dark* (1982a) explicitly refers to Mahler (p. 233, n.8), believes that a resolution to the struggle in terms of the solitary quest, of breaking free and discovering one's unique, individual self, really is modeled on an image of the tribe, of a fundamental first belonging, where the individual self mirrors the collective, the group mind, and where the break-up is necessary to bring something new back to the group. Starhawk's point is that this existential imagery does not match western culture, in which both women and men "are raised separately – to the point of pain" (1982a:48). Unless the journey toward individuation is grounded in a relationship with "living, breathing, human beings", people will only end up confirming their own isolation. In other words, Starhawk does not accept any conceptualizations of individual, autonomous life in opposition to living in interdependence with the world as relevant to the agenda of growth and self realization – neither to women nor men.[3]

Yet, when the rituals of feminist Witchcraft restage this classical existential scenario of heteronomy versus autonomy, it takes place within a larger interpretive context than object relations theory. The particular context offered in ritual is a worldview in which the first human bonding is not perceived as union with the biological or social mother, but with the Goddess, the mystical source of the Self prior to individual birth. In alignment with this worldview, humans may be said to be twice born: of goddess first and primarily (their Deep Self/spirit), and from a human female secondarily (their body/mind/soul). Witches claim the importance of acknowledging this primary "ground of being" and of regularly "re-turning" to the *real* mother of life in order to mature and grow as human beings. The primary aim of re-turning is sacred possession or spiritual bonding – not only with the deity but also with her living creatures, including any representative of the four elements air, fire, water and earth. The secondary aim of re-turning is the accomplishment of a magical purpose by means of healing, meditation, prayer or trance work. To deny this dependency upon a larger power and reality may result in human feelings of estrangement and a perpetual search for its replacements. Hence, to recognize this dependency is believed to be the true path to freedom and creativity, as well as to the embodied confidence of being at home on this planet (cf. also Keller 1986).

Instead of being regressive, ritualizing in Reclaiming is claimed to be a major method to actually induce change and establish new feelings of belonging, as well as a medium to relate the present to the past and mark the progression of time and transformation – personally, socially and mythologically (Goldenberg 1990:193). Magical ritual also challenges the notion of a linear development from union to separation in the human growth process when suggesting that this process is, rather, cyclical; for an individual will need again and again to be nourished by the bliss of reunion – not with her biological or social mother, but with her spiritual kin. She will also need, however, to learn to let go, that is, to end the ecstasy of ritual and divine merger and reenter ordinary consciousness in which she is a separate person in authority of language, history and agency. In order to stress how important the temporary aspect of ritual is, Starhawk equates ordinary consciousness with experiences of the Goddess as she who creates structure and division (in opposition to the extra-ordinary consciousness of the unifying circle):

> *Ordinary consciousness is a marvelous thing; it allows us to live in the world, to think, plan, create, work, and do. Practicing magic, we respect our ordinary boundaries: our goal is not to escape them, not to destroy the separations and divisions, but to slip in and out of them at will, with flexibility. For the boundaries, the separations, the names themselves are, no less than our experiences of oneness, manifestations of the Goddess, who is that-which-creates-structure.*
>
> (Starhawk 1982a:56)

The most efficient and comprehensive restaging and recontextualization of the human conflict between unity and separation, and of the paradoxical need of an adult to be simultaneously joined and separate, related and independent, autonomous and connected, is the initiation ritual to become a "Witch and Priestess of the Goddess". This particular Reclaiming ritual is also said to make visible the continual importance of transitional love objects in the process of emotional growth, whether in children or adults. But the path toward initiation is long and crooked, and a first required step is learning the Craft of the Witches: magical ritualizing. To the adept, this powerful Craft – which she enters classes to study and pays money to achieve – represents a different mode of knowing, being and relating to the world.

Theories of ritual, ritualizing and ritualization

Although academic ritual studies is a large and expanding interdisciplinary field, there is no scholarly consensus defining this object of study. Presently there seem to be as many definitions as there are researchers. The reason for this confusion is, according to Ronald Grimes, that the essence of ritual is misunderstood in definitions similar to Starhawk's: as an essential and delimited "what". In her efforts to define a precious object, she has probably imitated well-known "what" scholars, such as Victor Turner in his famous definition of ritual as, "formal behaviour prescribed for occasions not given over to technological routine that have reference to beliefs in mystical beings or powers" (Turner and Turner 1978:243). This definition is, however, misleading since ritual according to Grimes is not a formal "what" (a thing), but a fluid "how" (a quality) of which there are different degrees: "Any action can be ritualized, though not every action is a rite" (Grimes 1990:13).

The weakness of formal "what" definitions is that they from necessity will exclude some expressions as not belonging to ritual proper. For example, Turner's definition limits ritual to religious ritual, to liturgy, and implies that ritual is linked to religious belief. Also, when differentiating ritual from "technological routine", he excludes magical rites aiming at "empirical results such as making crops grow or healing patients" (Grimes 1990:13). As an alternative to "what" definitions, Grimes suggests a turn toward ritual understood as "how" and offers a list of qualities (the "how's") scholars seem to find in ritual action: performed, formalized, repetitive, patterned, symbolic, dramatic, mystical, etc. Grimes's point is that none of them is unique to ritual, but together they compose a chart that makes it possible to explore boundary-like activities such as ritual drama, civil ceremony, military parades and museum openings, as well as religious ritual and liturgy.

Catherine Bell goes one step further by linking the distinction between ritual as "what" and "how" with a sharp differentiation between "ritual" and "ritualization". She has observed that the notion "ritual" refers to an experimential, folk-category and to an abstract category of academic analysis. In order to differentiate these two levels of activity and meaning, Bell suggests that "ritual" ("what") be reserved for indigenous naming and description, while "ritualization" ("how"), is a more fruitful focus for theoretical analysis (Bell 1992:ix). While *ritual*, then, refers to a set of special practices and *ritualizing* to the art of cultivating these particular practices, *ritualization* means a social strategy or activity "that is not culturally framed as ritual but which someone, often an observer, interprets as if it were potential ritual" (Grimes 1990:9–10).

One of the reasons that Bell suggests a move from "what" to "how", is the underlying problems she sees in the Durkheimian heritage in contemporary ritual theory. In the Durkheimian conceptualization of religion (which is the same as mainstream Protestantism's), beliefs are regarded as primary and rites as secondary. The function of ritual is to legitimize and reinforce beliefs by "dramatizing or enacting prior conceptual entities in order to reaffirm or reexperience them" (Bell 1992:38). In critical opposition to this theoretical tradition, ritual may be seen as a legitimate means of knowing in its own terms, as an embodied, incarnate means of knowing, and not primarily as a reinforcing interpretation of something else, of another way of knowing (Grimes 1990:169). This view was eagerly expressed by Roy Rappaport already in 1979 when stating that "ritual is not simply an alternative way to express certain things, but that certain things can be expressed only in ritual" (Rappaport 1979:174).

Another problem in the Durkheimian conceptualization of ritual as a secondary derivative is the theoretical branching off of ritual from the context of ordinary social life and its implicit power games regarding insider–outsider, privileges and hierarchies. This critique has in particular been aimed at Victor Turner and Clifford Geertz and other symbolic schools that interpret ritual as expressions of mental orientations in analogy to textual meanings.[4] When Bell redefines ritual from isolated symbolic practice to paradigmatic cultural acts, she also contextualizes these "strategic ways of acting" in relation to the power dynamics of social relations and socialized bodies (Bell 1992:8).

Since my aim also is textual exegesis, that is, to analyse the basic symbolic meanings implied in Reclaiming's ritual, I cannot totally give up the notion of ritual as also being an analytic construct. I shall therefore use a charter developed by the Danish theologian Anders Klostergaard Petersen (1996) when listing the qualities (following Grimes) that *I see* in magico-religious ritual and ritualizing, although I regard ritual both as "what" (A) and "how" (B):

A Ritual as "what"

1. A specific ritual is a *local* symbolic expression and a *contextualized* mani-festation of a worldview of a general order (a Witchcraft ritual is a manifestation of Witches' worldview). If not, ritual would be self-absorbed and self-contained and fundamentally meaningless.[5] Ritual is also an independent expression of a worldview, an embodied means of knowing, also expressing things that can only be expressed in ritual. When ritual is not seen as a blueprint of, or an acting out of, belief or myth, it becomes obvious that ritual may also be an arena for conflict and for reconciliation. For example, ritual is a place to practice living with dissonance between things said and things done (Grimes 1990:166). It may also, through its symbols and spatial organization, express neglected and displaced segments of an otherwise hegemonic worldview (the "hidden" occult heritage in Witchcraft is more visible in ritual than in other symbolic expressions).

2. Ritual is not only metaphorical or symbolic in a self-referential sense, but has an important *indexical character*, meaning that it refers to circumstances or powers outside of ritual, leaving traces in ritual itself or even becoming magically present, as discussed in chapter 4. This feature is one of the main reasons ritualization is used in *religious* contexts (Petersen 1996:12). Within the present theoretical outline, religious ritual only differs from non-religious ritual by its reference to a religious worldview – including extensive communication between what are regarded as human and non-human actors – and by the importance of indexicality.[6]

   Petersen argues that the indexical function of ritual is to create a reversed, realistic foundation for symbolic processes of signification (1996: 13–14). Petersen uses Charles S. Peirce's triadic sign theory, in which all signs are said to consist of *representamen* (word, thing, image, gesture), *interpretant* (meaning) and *object* (that which the word, thing, image, gesture refers to). The letters h-o-r-s-e are representamen for a concrete, living animal (object), evoking a semantic, cultural meaning equivalent to the English notion horse (interpretant). We may, in addition, differentiate between symbol, icon and index according to how the sign is constituted. The representamen in ordinary symbolic communication often consists of an abstract, non-substantial sign, while the object will appear to be real, material, substantial, as with h-o-r-s-e and the actual animal.

   Petersen's point is that in indexical (magical) rituals this relationship is twisted. Now it is the representamen instead (for example, the bread and wine in the communion) that receives a "real" material, present character, while its reference, the object (for example, the body and blood of Christ) is "unreal", intangible and presumably absent. But, by virtue of the material character of ritual, symbols/representamens create an "aura of factuality" to the absent object as well. Petersen also mentions baptism, in which the water represents the inner transformation from death to life. The inner transformation is invisible; the water is visible and its visibility and materiality help to guarantee the credibility of that which is signified. We find a parallel in Witchcraft in the five material symbols (knife, wand, cup, pentagram, cauldron) representing sacred space, the four+one directions, the four+one elements, the three human Selves, divine life-generating powers or vital energy. These symbols are manipulated in the context of ritual in order to induce an embodied experience of merger and oneness between macrocosm and microcosm within the ritualizing human subject. The actual unity is invisible; the material symbols (and their associated meanings) are visible and present. If we now recall chapter 4 and the characteristics of the indexical, esoteric symbol, we find that in this symbol, the object/reference dissolves into the representamen, leaving us with only representamen and meaning.

B Ritual as "how"

3. Ritualization is a *social practice* and, therefore, also a form of social control. It constructs and appoints limited and limiting power relationships (as in initiation rituals and other rites of passages) as well as deconstructs non-appointed power positions (as in my processing at Witchcamp). As social praxis, ritual is a particular cultural strategy of differentiation between acts, working either to confirm (preserve) worldviews or to transform them; to confirm social beings and their social worlds or to transform them. Typical qualities of the ritualizing strategy are performance (verbal or gestured doings), formalization (organized, not spontaneous), repetitiveness (not happening once but repeated according to cycles), pattern (the ritual proceedings always follow the same basic pattern), and symbolic language (including objects, imagery and words). But the most important feature of ritualization is that all its strategies are rooted in the body, or rather in "the interaction of the social body within a symbolically constituted spatial and temporal environment. Essential to ritualization is the circular production of a ritualized body which in turn produces ritualized practices" (Bell 1992:93). It is this bodily strategy that produces an incarnate means of knowing, and that makes possible effective confirmation or transformation. The primacy of the body in a ritualized environment is what, in fact, distinguishes ritualization from other social strategies.

4. Through ritualization of the body, ritual (that is, a ritualized environment) effect a *change of being* in the ritualists (shedding off old nature or social position; embodying new nature or social position). It happens in baptism

when the ritualist is marked with water, words and the sign of the cross to "make happen" (or to confirm) that she now is dead and resurrected with Christ, and has received the Holy Spirit. It happens in trance rites such as Remembering Tiamat when the ritualists, by internal means, "decompose" and shed the present pain-struck body and re-create themselves as a new healed being. It happens in rites of passages when the ritualist is transformed from one social being to another by virtue of bodily acts in a ritualized environment. In this reciprocal process the body becomes a mediator between the individual and deity, between the individual and the social environment, or between her social world and a greater cosmos by virtue of communicating between the two or merging them completely (Petersen 1996:8). According to Pierre Bourdieu, it is in the dialectical relationship between the body and the space structured according to mythico-ritual oppositions "that one finds the form par excellence . . . which leads to the em-bodying of the structures of the world, that is, the appropriating by the world of a body thus enabled to appropriate the world" (Bourdieu 1991:89).

One of the reasons for the success of this dialectical process between body and space is that physical acts may have indexical character. For example, a kneeling human being not only symbolizes submission, but she becomes submissive within ritual space through the act itself. By kneeling, the ritualist merges with the system of symbols to which kneeling refers, expressing this system indexically. When the act of having kneeled in submission also has effects outside of ritual, stretching into the future, it is, according to Bell, because the ritualist gains "ritual competence" that qualifies her to apply the internalized values and meanings also in other social contexts, in order to redefine and restructure reality.

However, what is missing in the theoretical outline above (and in the theoretical approaches of Grimes, Bell, Bourdieu, and Petersen) is a more specific suggestion as to *how* the apprenticeship between a ritualized body and a ritualized space leads to individual embodiment of a certain worldview, or rather, of the structures of the world. In order to explain "a body thus enabled" I shall add perspectives from the anthropology of emotion.

First, ritualizing is an intentional act and a conscious decision: prior to any paradigmatic acts that may be observed by Bell, a potential ritualist decides to ritualize or, at least, to partake in an ongoing ritualization. This change of consciousness is according to Caroline Humphrey and James Laidlaw (1994) a must and can be compared to the fictional contract which is automatically entered when one or two or more people decide to play on the field or perform on the stage. If the autonomous decision to ritualize is absent, we are talking about neurotic behaviour or social coercion (or convention).

Second, if ritualizing shall be efficient in terms of transforming/confirming the ritualist and giving ritual competence ("a body thus enabled") with which to redefine social reality, it seems to involve some form of emotional participation. The rhetorical intention of preaching the Word in Protestant congregations is to move the heart and induce/confirm faith in the ritualist (Aune 1994). In Witchcraft, emotional honesty and sensitivity are required of any person who wants to learn their craft and engage with the existential agenda of being joined and being separate – let alone to learn anything from this work and establish an identity as Witch. Subjugating oneself to the intentional and conscious manipulations of emotion and imagination is also regarded as *the* method to alter one's mind and enter into an extra-ordinary consciousness or trance state, or to evoke energy and "magically" accomplish a purpose. When people feel frustrated with "working magic" they often blame it on themselves and their inability to get in contact with their own feelings.[7]

But emotions do not manifest themselves in a cultural vacuum. They involve both physical feelings and cultural meanings, all derived from cultural experience, knowledge and thought. According to Michelle Rosaldo, emotions are about the ways the social world is one in which *we* are involved. They are "thoughts that are felt" or "embodied": "embodied thoughts . . . bespeaks the difference between a mere hearing of a child's cry and a hearing felt – as when one realizes that danger is involved or that the child is one's own" (Rosaldo 1984:143). In regard to ritual space, "embodied thoughts" imply a linking together of thinking and affect, of the active narration or exegesis of myth combined with deep emotional responses that involve physical feelings and cultural meanings. Emotional discourse is, therefore, part of the language through which ritual transformations are marked and new identity formed (cf. Larsen 1995:40).

Summing up ritual as "what" (A):
- ritual is a local symbolic expression and a contextualized manifestation of a *worldview* of a general order;
- ritual always has an indexical quality which, in particular, is important to religious ritual;
- the aim of ritualizing is to cultivate rites in order to induce a different mode of knowing and being in the world.

Summing up ritual as "how" (B):
- ritualization is an intentional social practice and a strategic, paradigmatic way of acting that depends upon the interaction of a culturally situated body and ritually defined space;
- through ritualization of the body – including the intentional manipulation of emotions and the indexicality of symbols – ritual works either to confirm or transform social beings and their worlds. While ritualizing refers to an indigenous method with which to reach ideological and magical goals, ritualization denotes what actually takes place from the stance of socio-logical meta-analysis.

A Reclaiming class: learning magical worldview and the art of ritualizing

In order to illuminate the hermeneutic primacy of ritual among Reclaiming Witches and analyse ritual both as structure and as symbolic expression ("what") and as a culturally defined social strategy ("how"), I shall start by describing a teaching session that took place the second night of an "Elements of Magic" class. It was open to both women and men and taught by Aradia and Bird in San Francisco in the spring of 1989. To make the descriptions as rich as possible, I will in addition add elements that were taught in the same course offered at Witchcamp in Canada in the summer of 1989. By the time I asked to join and observe the SF class, it was already full. Instead it was arranged that I participate as a student teacher. Because I had been a member of a Reclaiming coven since 1984 and believed to be somewhat experienced, Aradia and Bird offered me this opportunity to study their teaching from the inside. I was, however, also expected to participate actively. In order to stress the inevitable experiential perspective of this account, then, I shall use the pronoun "we", not "they", when suitable.

As stated in chapter 1, there are usually two teachers in a Reclaiming class and, when someone is being trained as teacher, there are three, including the student teacher. Their teaching style is focused more on techniques and practices than on theology, which is congruent with their ethno-hermeneutics and the elevation of the category of experience. The emphasis on several parallel teachers is also meant to be consistent with nonauthoritarian, anarchist politics. A class is announced through the *Newsletter* and can have between five and fifteen students. It usually runs from 7:00 to 11:00 one night per week for six weeks. The students are given homework, mostly meditations, each week. The classes are arranged in private homes as a continual reminder of the low monetary and noninstitutionalized character of feminist Witchcraft.

The goals of an introductory class such as the "Elements of Magic" are as follows: 1 to make the students familiar with the worldview of Witchcraft through personal and ritual experience; 2 to help them feel at home in Reclaiming's public rituals and gain competence with basic ritual structures; and 3 to teach them to ritualize and conduct simple Reclaiming-styled rituals on their own. The members of Reclaiming's teaching cell believe they reach these goals successfully when teaching within the framework of ritual, work-ing experientially with the four elements, the many symbols of goddesses and gods gathered from around the world, the five ritual tools inherited from the European occult tradition – along with doing trances and spell-work to get people acquainted with some of the magical aspects of ritual.

The class course has a given outline, dating back to when it was first created by Diane Baker and Starhawk in 1979. The first evening is focused on the element *air* and its symbolic and magical associations, the next on *fire*, the third and fourth on *water* and *earth*. On the fifth evening, a complete ritual is performed with the students involved in all the leading parts. The sixth evening the students invite the teachers to a ritual they have created themselves and receive feedback, suggestions and criticism from the teachers afterward. How the elements are introduced and connected to magical exercises will differ with the teachers and their experience and knowledge. Teachings about the goddesses and gods are not singled out to a separate evening but are integrated when working with the elements. It is also expected that the students gain an understanding of the sacred simply by participating in rituals.

When planning the class meetings, it was important for Aradia and Bird to agree on exercises that would introduce the elements both as *substance*, as real nature, and as *metaphors* (or symbols). For example "air" is regarded as equivalent to bodily breath and breathing and oxygen on a real, substantial level. But air also symbolizes the direction east, the east already being a metaphor for social beginnings and mental work. The ritual tool associated with "east" is the *athame*, a handcrafted, black-handled, double-bladed knife. The knife is said to represent air because it makes people pay attention, it cuts the food and separates "good" from "bad" – all of which are believed to symbolize basic human activities. The other elements have different meanings, but each of them is understood to represent a network of correlations between natural worlds, social environments, material culture, esoteric symbolism and the human body. Within ritualized space the body is simply symbolized as a micro version of cosmos.

To convey all these meanings in the first class, the air class, Aradia and Bird agreed to do a trance exercise that combines deep breathing with a mental journey in which the participants play with a five-pointed star – a symbol called pentagram – and the waxing and waning of food, represented by apples. The students were asked to focus upon this symbol, concentrate and use their imagination to turn the pentagram into an apple, to cut it in two, making the pentagram-like seed pattern inside an apple visible. The apple then crumbled and became a seed, which was put in the dark earth "to die", until it again returned as sprouts, growing into a new apple tree, giving imaginary fruits the students could eat.

The texture of the apple itself, with an inner pip and an outer pulp, was also used as an image of the human constitution. The fundamental principles of nature are the pip, situated at the centre core of the human body (Deep Self), while the culturally conditioned person is the pulp, including the emotional body/mind, (Younger Self) and the rational body/mind (Talking Self). The inner micro nature of the human body is thus made identical with macro nature, with life-generating powers.

In the air class, Bird and Aradia also wanted the students to introduce themselves by describing what their internal "weather" was like, if it was cloudy or sunny, rainy, whatever. Homework that week was to do daily breathing exercises in which the students were to try to push their breath deeper and further down inside their bodies by using the skill of "mind over matter." For the next class, the fire class, the students were asked to bring what they considered fire things for the altar.

*   *   *

It is early Monday evening, and the three of us are gathered in Aradia's house to prepare the living room for the second "Elements of Magic" class, the fire class. Furniture is removed to make space for a huge circle of people on the carpet. Wooden boxes covered with table cloths in different colors (white, red, blue, black) are placed in each direction east, south, west and north. These clothed, wooden boxes function as altars. On top of the boxes are set candles and a few things representing the natural elements. On north, representing earth, we place stones and a goddess sculpture. On east, representing air, we arrange some feathers. On south, representing fire, we place incense and some crystals. On west, representing water, we put shells and a water bowl. In the centre, we place an altar for the deities, for the ritual tools and for the sacred objects people might bring to class. The ritual tool and primary symbol for north is the pentagram, for east the athame, for south the wand and for west the cup. Witches use, in addition, a sword to draw an imaginary, magical circle around the physical circle of people holding hands. This is done in order to separate ritual space from nonritual space and declare "the ritual to have begun". The sword, a doumbec drum, and a bowl with saltwater is placed on the floor by the centre altar. The tool for the centre is the cauldron or bonfire, which also may be a symbol of the goddess and her transformative power. In this class we use neither of them. During the ritual, only candles light the room. When the candles are lit, the room looks warm, welcoming and colourful. By the way it is arranged, it is meant to speak to the students' sense of beauty and sensual joy from playing with things.

When the students finally arrive, they wear comfortable clothes and bring pillows to sit on, altar things, food for sharing, pen and paper. The class counts 9 women and 7 men between 18 and thirty-five years old. A group of four young men are gay and dressed up as punks, while the others give no information about sexual identification or sub-cultural belonging through clothes, symbols or oral statements. A woman tells us she has quit her job on the East Coast, left her friends and family and moved to San Francisco. Now she wants to learn more and live according to the path of the goddess.

We open the class by sitting in a big circle on the floor, doing *check-in* (1).[8] Everybody says something briefly about how they feel right now, what kind of energy they bring and how they experienced homework. Then the *working theme* (2) for this evening is introduced. All Reclaiming rituals are intentional: they are focused on something specific which is celebrated or aimed at in terms of making changes. Working with the theme usually comes as an elaborate sequence in the middle of the ritual, after having created sacred space and invoked the powers of the natural and divine worlds. The theme of tonight's ritual is purely didactic, "getting to know the element fire". The theme is normally not introduced and explained outside a ritual context, but since this is a class, the teachers make an exception. Therefore, after check-in, Aradia and Bird start introducing some of their knowledge and ethics about fire and the category of magic.

Aradia opens the lecture, stating that the four elements correspond to deeds required of a magician: to know (air), to will (fire), to dare (water), to keep silent (earth). To work with fire is magical work, which means to work emotionally with energy and then use one's will and imagination to form and direct it as desired. During class, we shall soon experience this energy in an exercise called the "Tree of Life". Aradia explains two forms of magic: The first is *spell-magic*, in which the goal is to affect the divine with one's own will and desires ("my will be done"). This is not an inferior or bad form of magic. Its intention can be healing of illness, bringing rain when there is drought, creating peace in El Salvador, or getting more prosaic but still very important things, like a place to live, a job or a partner. The second form of magic she calls *path-magic,* in which the overall goal is to experience the divine and to give up one's own will in service of the deity ("thy will be done"). Path-magic can also include spell-work, but the desired outcome is never made explicit. Spell-magic is to say, "I want this particular job", while path-magic is to say, "I will take whatever job the Goddess sends forth."

Bird explains (in conformity with Starhawk's definition of ritual just presented) that to be a Witch is to work with energy/power and develop the ability to shape or bend reality. This is something we do all the time anyway, says Bird, because we act intentionally: we extend our own wills into the world and we manipulate the world. To be a Witch is to become conscious of this fact and do it consciously. This in turn is to become more in charge of the course of one's own life and be responsible for the consequences of one's acts. To live as a Witch requires deeply integrated, personal ethics and a sense of what it is to act in balance, he says.

Aradia confesses that she no longer does political spell-magic because her conscience does not allow her to force her will upon the world or to magically "bind" an enemy. This is, to her, unethical. Regarding her own ethical standards, she once failed deeply by doing exactly what everybody warns against, namely, a "love-spell", which is also intended to "bind" somebody and receive their love in return. The essence of a love-spell, according to Aradia, is that it fills the executant with total obsession but that it has no influence upon the desired person. And if it has, the executant is so obsessed that any love affair is doomed to fail. Love-spells are, therefore, exclusively destructive and unethical, and the students are urged to listen to Aradia's advice and stay away from them.

Bird confirms Aradia's experience by referring to his black grandmother. In her Voodoo magic she had no ethics and lived by her-will-be-done only, hexing other people all the time. But, the law in magic is that everything a person creates magically comes back to her three times. His grandmother has denied this and is, therefore, very sick and lonely. The evil spells she intended for others have turned back on her, slowly destroying her. On the other hand, Bird believes that magical techniques are like electricity. They are neither good nor evil in themselves but can be used for either purpose. Bird learned his magical techniques from an evil woman and maintains that he can – like her – do weather-magic (making it sunny or rainy), change traffic lights, delay an airplane so he can reach the airport in time, and so forth. The difference is, he holds, that he does magic for the good of all, while she did it for evil. Bird has no problems with spell-magic and makes it "all the time".

While the two teachers lecture, the students take notes diligently. They do not argue, but some ask clarifying questions. Suddenly one of them wants to know whether I, doing research on Reclaiming and now acting as a student teacher, have any magical experiences myself. The question really is, am I competent to co-teach this class or am I there as a "spy" in disguise? I am hesitant until Aradia rescues me: "Tell them the story about the birth of your daughter, and how you probably stopped the labour with your mind." I do as I am told, and everybody is amazed and relaxed: I am accepted.

After this teaching session, there is a short break. When people return, it is time for ritual. The first step in the process of ritualizing is to transform the living room into ritual space, starting with an exercise called "grounding". It is important to note that there are no scripts read in these proceedings. Everything said and done is spontaneously created in the doing, leaning only on a well-known form. It is the form itself the teachers intend to hand over to the students by the method of imitation and the knowledge of some few basic principles. Except for statements like, "Now we shall ground ourselves; now we shall purify; now we shall call the elements, etc.", nothing further is explained. At this point the students are not expected to ask why, or what things mean, only to "hang on" as well as possible. Neither is it polite to take more notes until the whole ritual is finally closed. Without being told, everybody picks up this attitude.

It's time for the *grounding* (3) exercise. Bird asks everybody to stand up, to shake their limbs loose and relax. We hold hands and breathe deeply and rhythmically, while Bird leads a guided meditation. The imagery used is the world-tree, the Tree of Life, believed to represent cosmos. We imagine that we are a tree with trunk, branches and roots. The roots go through the floor, through the pavement, all the way into the centre of the earth, from which we imagine that we bring up energy in the form of red fire. Entranced by Bird's rhythmical and evocative voice, we use our minds and breath to bring the energy back up, into our bodies, up through legs and arms, following the eastern *chakra* system. When the energy reaches our heads, we also accompany our breath with loud sounds and imagine that our arms are like branches, waving with the sound. The sound accelerates and builds up to a harmony, while we stretch our arms/branches toward the roof. Since the students had breathing exercises as homework, they quickly get involved and raise the sound to its peak. The loud, harmonized hum is called a "power chant", and when done correctly it resonates in the head and in the body. It goes on for about five minutes. Then it ends in a climax when, at a signal, the power chant suddenly stops and there is complete silence. Everybody then lies down on their knees, with the palms of their hands flat and their foreheads touching the floor in order to ground the "left-over" energy by projecting it back into the earth.

This psychophysical grounding exercise is meant to wake up earth energy and to be a first step in reconnecting people with their birth ground, the Goddess. To wake up earthenergy is also believed to balance and renew individual energy, putting people into a light trance. This energy, which is raised, distributed and stored in social bodies as well as in the earth, is always emotionally loaded and, together with the power of will and imagination, regarded as *the* main working tool in Witches' ritual magic.

After grounding, there is *purification* (4). Everybody now sits in circle, looking into a candle flame at the centre altar. With their imaginations, they are asked to give to the candle the energy or feelings which they do not want to bring further into the ritual and to take back from the flame whatever they need or want and store it in the "third eye" at their foreheads. Usually Witches use salt and water as purifiers, but tonight everything is focused on the element "fire". If the ritual were outdoors, we would have stared into the flames of a bonfire.

After purifying, Witches *cast the circle* (5), an act intended to represent cosmos in miniature inside the living room by symbolically separating ritual time and space from ordinary time and space by drawing an imaginary, magical circle around all the celebrants. Everybody rises, and normally Bird would pick up the sword and walk to the north, kiss it and say: "*Holy Mother, in whom we move, live and have our being, bless this circle.*"[9] From there he would begin to walk clockwise, pointing the sword in the four directions while stating, "*By the air that is Her breath, by the fire of Her bright spirit, by the water of Her living womb, by the earth that is Her body, the circle is cast.*" Tonight we do it differently. We cast the circle together by imagining a pale, blue flame coming out of our hands as a sword blade. With our hands stretched out horizontally, we walk around the circle while imagining a circle taking form. In the end, we stretch upward and downward marking the points called "above" and "below", as well as to the "centre", setting *axis mundi*. When we have finished casting the circle, which visually is more like a ball with a pillar in the centre, Bird now proclaims, "*We are between the worlds and beyond the bonds of time, where day and night, birth and death, joy and sorrow meet as one.*" The students are informed that now we have created sacred space and an energy circle that is to be respected. If anybody needs to go to the bathroom, they have "to cut" themselves in and out with their imagination.

It is time to *invoke the elements* (6), the earth, air, fire and water. Within the context of ritual, the elements are also believed to be personal energy forms, guarding "each corner" of the world. They can be addressed as "*Guardians of the Watchtowers of the East . . . etc.,*" as "*Archangels,*" as "*Goddesses,*" as "*Powers of Air*" or simply with sound and body movements imitating the element air,

"*Huuush*", while the arms and the body make wind-like motions. Aradia informs the students that there is no right or wrong way to do this invocation and asks whether there are any volunteers. The woman from Witchcamp offers to call in air, while a totally inexperienced man bravely will call water. Bird will call south, I will call north and Aradia the centre. It is done by each of us walking to the respective altars for each element, turning our palms outward and naming the actual element in our own personal way, for example: "*Eastern Morning/First breath of the soul, Worldview forming/Sacred and whole, Wind of knowledge/simple and wise, bringer of the lightning/that strikes in our minds, Come to us − be here now.*" [10] Everybody then responds, "*Air is here. Blessed be.*"

We are still on our feet forming a circle, and after the elements, Witches *invoke the deities* (7): "God" (sometimes) and "the Goddess" (always). Reclaiming works with many named goddesses and a few gods, and they are mostly called by singing and round dance. The God is called first, then the Goddess. Since this is a fire class and Witches have just celebrated a Sabbat (Bridged's day on February 2nd), Aradia and Bird have decided to call in the Irish goddess Bridged, goddess of fire, poetry and smith craft. The God called is the non personal Horned One, the god of animal power and the principle of compost. We call them separately by different songs, but with the same dance movements: two steps forward, one step backward while holding hands. The songs are more like chants, which are repeated again and again as the energy is raised, peaks and drops. When finally done, we lie down on the floor − exactly the way we did after the Tree of Life meditation. This invocation is equivalent to the ritual element mentioned in chapter 4 called "aspecting " or "drawing down the moon", in which the hidden deity becomes manifest. In a public ritual, the *ecstatic* aspects of calling in and "indexically" becoming deity will be emphasized much more than they are now in a class situation. After a while we sit up, and Aradia states, "*They are here. Blessed be.*" She then turns to the person on her left-hand side, looks into her eyes, kisses her on her cheek, and says, "*Thou art Goddess and God.*" This person kisses the next, and so on around the whole circle.

We have now created a magical circle beyond the limits of ordinary time and space and declared the divine as manifest within ourselves as well as present in the circle. It is time for *magical work* (8) or the *working theme* for the ritual, which today is the element fire. To get more deeply in touch with fire, Bird asks us to stand in circle, close our eyes and hold hands. We use the Tree of Life imagery once more, pushing "roots" into the ground below us. But this time we gather blue light from the centre of the earth instead of red fire. The exercise is to form the invisible blue light into a ball which becomes so real that we experience it as glowing in our hands. We then use our imagination to feel and roll the ball − on Bird's directions − all over our bodies and around the circle. After a while we remodel the ball into a dove. With our imagination we give the bird wings, legs and colour, everything it needs. Bird also asks us to give it a piece of our heart and breath until it becomes an extended part of us. Finally we give this magical bird or thought construction a message concerning something we want, open an invisible window and let it fly into the "other world" to complete what we asked for. Bird reminds us to be prepared for the bird to come back in another form, and if it does, to still give it proper thanks. When finished, we ground the leftover energy by lying down, with foreheads and hands flat on the floor.

The next exercise is led by Aradia and myself. It is a demonstration of energy changes in a person's body field made visible by the aid of a pendulum. Aradia sits on a chair; I stand behind her holding a pendulum in my right hand, just above her head. I ask her, as I have been instructed, to ground herself with roots into the earth and draw new energy into her feet with her imagination (the pendulum now starts to move a little). I ask her to draw the energy up through her legs and body trunk (pendulum moves a little faster) and into the big branches coming out from her head (pendulum makes a sudden shift and moves extremely fast). I tell her that all of a sudden she feels a bowl of cold, mashed potatoes being thrown upon her head (pendulum almost stops immediately), but then somebody comes and removes the potatoes and cleans her head (pendulum now moves a little faster). I finally ask Aradia to release the energy and ground it in the earth (pendulum stops completely).

The exercise seems very convincing, to me as well (I had never seen it done before). People are at this point excited and eager to try it themselves. We divide the group into couples and give each pair one pendulum. Aradia tells them that the person standing is the "reader" and the person sitting is the "medium". The point is not to read objectively, but to experience that both the medium and the reader can influence energy – and therefore the pendulum – with their mind and imagination. The students play for a while, and to many of them this is the first time in their lives that they really have "seen with their own eyes" how concentration and focus of the mind can influence energy and the movements of an object. The excitement is formulated as "Gee! I can move energy! I can learn magic!"

In an ordinary ritual, there would at this point be time to create a *cone of power* (9). Such an energy-cone is made as the participants gather and focus energy by repeated song and dance movements. The goal is to give power to the magical work completed in the ritual, and help it manifest in ordinary reality. Since the magical work this evening is more training than a proper working, the students will have to wait one week before they are introduced to this very important concept. We will return to this ritual element when describing "The Spiral Dance" ritual in chapter 6.

We finish the circle with a *ritual meal* (10). The centre altar is removed, and a big tablecloth is put on the floor. People bring food and drinks to share and place them on the tablecloth. The woman from Witchcamp offers to bless the food. She gives thanks to the gods for things given to us during the evening. After the praises, she breaks off a piece of bread, turns to the person next to her, hands her the bread while saying, "*May you never hunger.*" She does likewise with the cup of juice, saying, "*May you never thirst.*" Then the bread and drink are passed on to the next person, who repeats the procedures. The class is told that ritual eating in Reclaiming is not a sacrificial meal, although we eat substances, the body of the Goddess. It is rather equivalent to feasting – being both celebration and thanksgiving. It replenishes the body after doing magical work and is a way to bring people back into ordinary consciousness.

After we have eaten, the final ritual acts are to *give thanks, dismiss the deities and the elements* (11), and *the circle itself* (12). These are regarded as very important acts since they end a concrete rite, helping the participants to leave the realms of magic and return to ordinary consciousness. It must be done properly so that nobody is left in a semi-tranced, unfocused state. To say "thank you and farewell" to all the powers called into the ritual is also explained as politeness and showing respect. The person who did the invocation also dismisses, "*Thank you, Bridged, for joining this circle and for all the gifts you have brought tonight. Stay if you will, go if you must. As you depart, we bid you farewell.*" Similar phrases are used for the god and each of the elements. At the end, all the participants hold hands in circle while saying, "*By the earth that is Her body, by the air that is Her breath, by the fire of Her bright spirit, by the water of Her living womb, the circle is open, but unbroken. May the peace of the Goddess be in our hearts. Merry meet and merry part and merry meet again. Blessed be.*"

The class is over and people prepare to leave. Their homework is to be aware of energy and fire, to practice the Tree of Life meditation, and to be able to create sacred space. Also, they shall look for water things for the next class.

*   *   *

When everybody has left, Aradia and Bird express great satisfaction with the class. They tell me that the second evening is always a test as to whether a class will take off or not, whether the energy will get to the students and make them mentally able to create and be responsible for a ritual. They believe they already now can say that they will.

And they were right – the class became a success. Nobody dropped out and on the very last evening, four weeks later, the students made a ritual together that was regarded as well working and creative: it was more than a pure imitation of what they had learned in class. When the class was completed the students expressed gratitude and satisfaction, and a majority wanted to learn more. Six women signed up for a "Rites of passage" class for women only, while one of the young men joined a "Pentacle" class. When I completed my studies in 1994, he had been initiated as Witch and had become an active member of the Reclaiming Collective and teaching cell. Although 10 people from this class formed a mix coven, which continued in a smaller version for five years, only this young man found his way into the Reclaiming Collective and community. The others felt more encouraged to bring the Goddess into their already existing communities, and return to Reclaiming only for the large public sabbat rituals.

Interpreting ritual as "what": structure and semantics

We shall now move on from describing the ritual performed in this specific class to the structures and contents of a generic Witchcraft ritual, that is, the general ideas expressed and implied in the act of ritualizing and in the rite itself.[11] I shall also recapitulate some of the qualities of the ritualizing strategy in Reclaiming and add "native" information and exegesis about ritual elements and meanings not already given in class. I shall in particular point out and make explicit aspects of the occult heritage as manifested in the implied worldview of a Witchcraft ritual. I select this information from sources available, amongst them the other Reclaiming classes in which I have participated and Starhawk's books.

Bringing together the different stages of the ritual as described in the previous section, the five major ritualizing strategies to build and end a ritual in Reclaiming are ideally as follows:

I   Preparing to leave *profane* time and space (horizontal magic of everyday life)
    1   Check-in, lecture, discussion
    2   Proclaiming intent and goal of ritual
II   Creating *sacred* time and space (vertical magic of ritual)
    3   Grounding
    4   Purification
    5   Casting the circle
    6   Invoking the elements
III Becoming *sacred* space ("sacred possession")
    7   Invoking the deities
    8   Magical work
    9   Raise a cone of power
IV   Thanksgiving for achieved intent and goal
    10   Ritual meal and praises
V   Returning to *profane* time and space (horizontal magic)
    11   Dismissing deities and elements
    12   Opening the circle

Following the chronological descriptions above, I will now add more information – in particular to the parts I, II and III, which are the most elaborate parts of the ritual.

I   *Preparing to leave profane time and space*

The ritualizing process has a certain rhythm and direction corresponding to the horizontal magic of everyday life versus the vertical magic of ritual, as presented in chapter 4. The celebrants start out horizontally, in profane time. After having spoken their intent and goal, they enter sacred time and space in a vertical move, whereupon they return to the horizontal profane – presumably renewed. As stated above, Witches themselves use the expression "creating sacred space" about ritual. The initial stage in this creation is both formulated by and addressed to Talking Self. In public rituals, there is no check-in. Instead the gathering is begun by somebody in the ritual planning group stating intent and focus for the proposed magical work (8), and explaining the planned ritual acts step-by-step. A ritual is always staged because something is lacking or needs celebration. "Lack" is the most common reason (and theme), and the medicine offered is healing, repair, change or new knowledge. At this point, people might ask questions and, in smaller rituals, also come with other suggestions regarding the proposed magical work. This is a purely intellectual conversation and an important part of the ritual process. It may be repeated in the thanksgiving sequence, and definitely when evaluating a completed ritual.

The ritual proceedings from this point on are consciously intended to awaken Younger Self and Deep Self or, rather, to speak to Deep Self through Younger Self. The interaction between the three selves can be described by this image: Younger Self is the strings of a violin; the sounding board is the semantic structure constituting the universe of Talking Self; and the trance experience or ecstasy of Deep Self is the sound that is produced. The Witches "become" their Younger Self by creating sacred space (II) and they "become" their Deep Self when invoking the gods (III). The entrance to these different states of mind follows the pattern identified as Starhawk's hermeneutics of space in chapter 4: 1 the Witch visualizes a mystical symbol; 2 the Witch enters the symbol by meditatively becoming the power which the symbol points to, and the absent becomes present in the esoteric, indexical symbol; 3 the Witch returns to ordinary consciousness and describes the esoteric experience by a number of metaphors, many of which comply with occult heritage.

But new knowledge and new metaphors to describe ordinary reality are not all that is achieved. Witches also claim to be renewed and strengthened on an energetic level from having ritualized; they also claim that whatever social "problem" they brought to the magical circle has become easier to handle – even when returning to ordinary life. Some even claim to be able to influence and bend social reality directly with their ritual magic – be it the delay of airplanes or the financing of a much needed soup kitchen. By importing the category of magic, Witches suggest that they are in control of their own lives.

Thus, to be in control seems to imply three possibilities: new *knowledge* achieved through immediate revelation or through "a channel already dug" (teachers and initiations); *shaping reality* in conformity with one's will and no longer being a passive object for cultural determination; being able to actually change, grow and *improve one self*. This worldview is genuinely optimistic and a protest against feelings of helplessness, victimization and anger often expressed by ordinary people in western societies who have restricted access to power and influence.

II   *Creating sacred time and space*

When people sign up for class, it is in order to learn how to create sacred space and temporarily separate themselves from the profane. They are taught that the first step in this separating-out process is to delimit a place of power by entering into an imagined centre point, and then greet each of the four directions with their bodies. This event, *casting the circle*, can take place anywhere: indoors, outdoors, in a forest, on the streets. The psychological meaning of casting the circle is, according to Starhawk, to create a safe structure within which people can more easily "change categories" and be able to perform magic:

> The circle is itself a structure; it says to Talking Self, "Look, you who need so much order, within my boundaries you can forget your usual names, you can change categories. You will be faced with many new sensations and experiences, but don't panic. I'm here, standing guard – and only within my bounds do you take your holiday. When I am dissolved, then you can bring back the usual divisions, the ordinary boundaries. Until then, relax."
>
> (Starhawk 1982a:55)

This safe, sacred space in which Talking Self may relax and have her holiday is also called a place *"between the worlds and beyond the bonds of time"*. It is in this extra-ordinary dimension that the relationship between representamen and object is twisted to the extent that anything may shape-shift into another. Witches may now become a tree or a blue flame, journey into the earth (or air, fire, water), or take the earth (or air, fire, water) into their own bodies. Either way, they are expected to experience oneness with the elements as they imagine the circle of bodies being the trunk of a tree instead of human flesh.

The circle as ritual form is also a symbol of nonhierarchical structures and the equal distribution of power and energy, at least as interpreted by Witches. The participants do not stand or sit in rows, facing a most holy altar or sanctuary, but are facing each other. Each single participant is regarded as an altar because the divine is manifest in every being. To enter sacred space, then, is also to seek psychological and spiritual balance by holding a circle within.

The process in which the circle transforms from being a mystical symbol to representing what it refers to is considered an act of magic. By imagination and mediation Witches turn the circle into a mandala, whereas they themselves are *in* the mandala. Trance techniques are the most common mediators, being composed of relaxation, concentration, visualization and projection. Visualization or imagination is the ability to see, hear, feel, touch and taste with the inner senses. Through inner pictures and feelings Witches communicate with Younger Self and, thereby, with Deep Self. Concentration is the ability to focus upon a given image, restricting the field of attention and excluding disturbing elements. Projection is the ability to "send out" energy. This shift in consciousness creates what is experienced as an altered state of consciousness in which solid things and visions become like one. Many celebrants now report that they are able to "move around" in the universe in their "astral bodies." This technique was used in the Tree of Life meditation, in the apple/pentagram exercise, in the ball/dove exercise, as well as when invoking the divine. To help the Younger Self reach this particular altered state, Witches use objects and techniques which they believe will talk to and enchant the child within: sensual altar props, special symbols, compelling words and rhythmical music, nice smells and candlelight.

Grounding

Teachers often make a point that Wicca is eclectic and that their altering techniques are gathered from other religious traditions. It is commonly held that the contents of the Tree of Life meditation, with its imagery, breathing, chakra points and power-chant, are taken from Hatha Yoga. But the concept of a cosmic tree representing *axis mundi* is probably appropriated from the Jewish Kabbalah.[12] The Kabbalistic Tree of Life is a graphic figure with roots in heaven, top on earth and branches to the sides. The figure constitutes a magical ladder between heaven and earth with ten power-spots distributed along the trunk. Each spot or *sephiroth* represents one of ten divine emanations or powers (Scholem 1974). The most High may descend all the way down to Malkuth (the mundane sephiroth), where YHWH is believed to manifest as Shekinah. Likewise may people climb the ladder in the opposite direction, starting their divine ascent by uniting with Shekinah (who represents God's dwelling on earth). Witches turn this mystical figure upside down and insist on a first and primary association between Goddess and Earth, not between God and Heaven. They obviously see a profound difference between working with sky-energy and working with earth-energy.

Purification

The idea of purification in Witchcraft is based upon energetic (not ethical) assumptions taken from sources such as modern esotericism, eastern philosophy and, more recently, humanistic psychology. "Purification" does not mean restitution of fallen nature since no part of the human being is considered "evil". It is rather a cleansing out of negative energies, anxieties and worries that may disturb the concentration and outcome of "magical work". In the candle meditation described above, negative energies were not discharged. They were only projected onto the candle, transformed and taken back. This exercise is in accordance with magical principles stating that nothing in the universe can be thrown away (there is no "outside"). It can only be transformed into something else. Or, as Starhawk puts is, "Magic is the art of turning negatives into positives, of spinning straw into Gold" (Starhawk 1982a:99). The goal of purification is thus to prepare a person's mental, emotional and bodily channels to work energy efficiently.

Casting the circle

In occult, ceremonial magic, the ritual circle is cast and sealed with penta-grams in order to keep out evil spirits. Witches do not believe in evil spirits but draw the circle as a psychic boundary within which everybody may feel emotionally safe and stay focused. They do, however, continue to use the pentagram (★) to symbolize human beings and their mystical dependency upon circles within circles. The esoteric tradition teaches that the five-pointed star represents all of creation, including the four elements and the fifth, which is essence (the centre point of the circle). The star also represents the five stages of life: birth, initiation, mature love, repose, death, as well as the human body with four limbs and a head, five senses, five deeds, etc. The pentagram within a circle is called a pentacle. In the occult tradition, this symbol (✪) represents the human microcosm within the universal macrocosm. Even though the pentagram was not used in the "Elements of Magic" class (except in one meditation), it is commonly drawn in the air at public rituals. This drawing of an invisible figure with an athame is regarded as part of casting the circle or calling the elements.

Invoking the elements

The goal of Wiccan worship is not only to commemorate elemental inter-dependencies or to symbolize a cosmic kinship system. When they gather for ritual, Witches intend to invoke and *make present* all the associated powers of the natural, human and divine worlds by conjuring the four elements. To be able to successfully do this, Witches have adopted the ancient dictum "as above so below", meaning that ritual micro-circles *in fact* may reflect cosmic macro-structures, and that a quartered, *magical circle* in fact may embody the four elements and their affiliated associations. They also believe that each quarter/element is being "watched" by guardian spirits, addressed within ritual space as "Guradians of the Watchtowers of the East."

These figures and names are typical occult heritage, representing a mixture of Greek nature philosophy, stoicism and neo-Platonism, as well as magical spells. In ceremonial magic, the Guardians of the Watchtowers are thought to ward a plurality of neo-Platonic heavens and usually named according to Jewish and Christian archangels: Michael (east), Ariel (south), Raphael (west) and Gabriel (north). The centre of the circle (the fifth element) is associated with YHWH (the four sacred/secret letters representing the godhead in ancient Israel. Each quarter/element is also associated with a ritual tool, as well as with a series of symbolic correlations set between seasons, time, colours, psychological moods, body parts, divine names, celestial planets, etc. This network of proclaimed cosmological correspondences – in which everything existing is regarded as a sign that can be substituted by another sign (within the same sign-family) and eventually decoded by human beings – is in the occult literature called "pillars of correspondence".

Traditionally, these "pillars" are heavily gendered and therefore (according to convention) hierarchically ordered in relation to each other: west is associated with water and feelings, north with earth and body and both with femininity; east is associated with air and intellect, south with fire and spirit and both with masculinity; centre is associated with essence/divinity, transformation and androgyny. This genedered cosmology has more or less been used throughout history of western civilization to legitimize and reinforce ideological and social hierarchies between men and women and to naturalize notions of asymmetrical gender polarity. Thus, traditional occult cosmology is not in harmony with contemporary feminist world-viewing.

Nevertheless, feminist Witch Starhawk listed the occult "pillars of correspondence" in an appendix to the first edition of *The Spiral Dance* (1979a:201–13). She even included the patriarchal Yahve and his archangels, a fact that is rather anacronistic. Even though this has been modified in later editions, Starhawk's readers are still advised to use symbols that are related through occult association to the same elemental pillar when working magic. If, for example, a Witch wants to do magic for prosperity, it is suggested that she chooses candles with the colors black, green or brown, or other symbols representing material reality ("earth"). If her goal instead is to let go or separate herself from something, the proper pillar/element is "air" and the ritual tool the athame. Thus, the athame – which is believed to be a tangible symbol for invisible powers – represents the intellect (air), the wand represents spirit (fire), the cup feelings (water), the pentagram moulded in iron the body (earth), and the Witches' cauldron in the centre represents the fifth element: the divine fire of transformation (essence). When fire burns on alcohol in the cauldron, it is said to represent two different principles merging as one: feminine water gives herself to masculine fire (Cirlot 1962:8). The occult symbol for fire is ▲, and for water ▼. When they are combined to form a hexagram, we end up with the esoteric symbol for the union between macro (masculine) and micro (feminine), the so-called "great rite".

In ceremonial magic, this rite is ideally performed as sexual magic, that is, as actual intercourse between a female representative (micro/human) and a male representative (macro/cosmos) in order to help sustain the powers of life and fertility and make manifest the divine in the couple. In Reclaiming, sex magic is regarded as incompatible with feminist politics and does not take place, at least not within rituals with more than two participants. But the "great rite" is often symbolized in public rituals by holding the athame vertically over the cup as part of the invocation of Goddess and God.

Why have feminist Witches appropriated an erotic worldview and a symbol system that have contributed to essentialize gender and glorify static, authoritarian power relations (such as equating femininity with feeling and inferiority and masculinity with intellect and superiority)? Probably because of their proclaimed urgency to restore – through a powerful holistic symbol – a felt loss of a living cosmos and a magical, spiritual ground to human existence. Being an all-inclusive, holistic symbol that predated Christianity, the quartered circle proposed itself as a beautiful and innocent, pagan way to balance all kinds of binary oppositions, such as those perceived between body and spirit, intellect and feeling, female and male, gods and humans, merger and separation – both in divine and mundane realms.

This dialectic ability ascribed to the "magic circle" has obviously contributed to its unique historical position and made it a favourite strategy in esoteric forms of ritualizing – in particular when attempting to establish a *tangible* web between lived human life and a living natural world. The question is whether the gendered, authoritarian parts of the strategy are integral to the attempt as such, or whether they can be disposed of in times of feminist politics and feminist gender shattering.

According to most Reclaiming Witches, they are dispensable. In their own appropriation of elemental symbolism, the meaning of gender and other uneasy associations from past historical times have been more and more downplayed. They emphasize instead how important elemental symbolism is cross-culturally, and how it can foster human growth and inter-human community. This insight is thus applied to contemporary Witchcraft: the magic circle is a means to integrate an embodied mode of thinking and a deep-felt consciousness of cosmic interconnection in the worshipper:

> The quarters balance each other; experiencing each one I can experience the need for its polar opposite. When I see and think in the East, using my knife to make divisions, I must also be able to feel, to flow, to merge, or I become cut apart. If I burst forth with expression, with passion, in the South, I must also be able to contain fire, to ring it with stones from the North, or I risk burning down the forest. And if I allow myself, in the West, to merge, I need the power of the East to separate again. The earth, without the sun's fire, remains dead, silence without expression.
>
> (Starhawk 1982a:55)

In this quotation, gender is apparently gone, as are the potential hierarchies in the symbolism of the "magic circle". Thus, the enchanted feminism of Starhawk and the Reclaiming Witches entails some problematic compromises, and a few (the relations between human and divine gender) will be discussed further in chapter 7.

But let me already now stress an important point, namely, that the meanings of symbols *from an analytical stance* cannot be regarded as archetypal. Meanings are not inherent *in* the symbol but attributed *to* the symbol through cultural association. It is therefore absolutely possible to appropriate elemental philosophy without adopting it wholesale. As with any other symbolic tradition, occult philosophy can be reformed and twisted in anti-dualist, anti-hierarchical directions. Consequently, in another passage from *The Spiral Dance*, Starhawk states: "The Male and the Female forces represent difference, yet they are not different in essence: they are the same forces flowing in opposite, but not opposed directions" (1979a:27). Although cultural assumptions about the dichotomized and essential nature of "Male" and "Female" have been integral parts of the symbol system of the quartered circle until now, Starhawk takes it for granted that they are dispensable. Yet, she is careful not to erase the notion of gender or sexual difference.

III Becoming sacred space

If ritualizing in Reclaiming is about separating sacred and profane in order to construct a magical person and magical space, its ultimate goal is to awaken, reconnect and work with the spirit inside, the deepest aspect of Self, the Goddess. When introducing Deep Self in a Pentacle class, one of the Reclaiming teachers said,

> As humans we share substances with each other, and yet we are unique. The word "self" refers to that uniqueness. The self sets us apart from anything else, and yet all we need from the universe is really deep inside us. This Deep Self is connected to the cosmos. Deep Self is who you are originally, what you came in the world for, your medicine for the world. It comes before all other selves; it is the best we are, the best we are capable of. We should love that part and bring it through in all we do. It is our spirit-self, and now it is time to awaken it.

On one hand, there are as many goddesses and gods as there are people, animals, plants and other species. On the other, and in spite of this apparent polytheism in which goddesses and gods from many selves and cultures are venerated, Witches are philosophical monists: a named goddess is only regarded as an aspect of divine reality, just as a human being is only a manifest sample of the human species. This monistic thinking, however, does not perceive of reality as a fixed state of being, but rather as a dynamic process of assiduous creation, decay and re-creation. When defining ultimate reality as polar energies symbolized by the "feminine" Goddess and the "masculine" God, Witches are of course deeply affected by the (already) gendered, magical circle.

The Witches' obligation to celebrate the eight solar holidays (sabbats) corresponds to a myth in which the God is imagined as the power of love and desire, the one who continually changes form and face in his forever yearning for the Goddess, who is both lover and birthmother. When they finally meet and merge, the year "turns" and a new season arrives. Furthermore, when people act "like gods", seeking and merging with the Goddess too, they are promised that even the cultural wheel will turn and conjure social balance and harmony.[13]

The Wiccan rituals are both occasions for and narrations of this yearning for the divine. They are also oracles that can tell the tides of waning and waxing in all aspects of life, including *when* certain political actions or creative projects should be started or terminated in order to be successful. To initiate a process that runs counter to general currents in nature or culture is likely to fail. For example, spring with its ritual called *Beltane* is the proper time to initiate or renew love relations and friendships, whereas *Samhain* in late fall is the proper time to start a political action such as the "Prevention Point" needle exchange. At these solar rituals, Witches connect inner and outer cycles, permitting death to feed life and vice versa in a broad sense: "As the cone of power rises, as the seasons changes, we arouse power from within, the power to heal, the power to change our society, the power to renew the earth" (Starhawk 1979a:169). Sabbat rituals thus designate the modes and possibilities in nature, people and society.

Invoking the deities

According to Starhawk, an invocation "channels power through a visualized image of the divine" (1979a:55). In ritual the participants may invoke the goddess by using her anthropomorphic image, whereafter she is experienced as incarnated in the Witches when simultaneously invoked from within. This is an example of how the esoteric indexical symbol becomes a material figure, and how her manifestation is pulled forth by repeated chanting and dancing. When successful, chanting may induce an ecstatic state, which is proclaimed "the heart of Witchcraft – in ritual we turn paradox inside out and become the Goddess, sharing in the primal throbbing joy of union" (Starhawk 1979a:25). When the Witches then declare, "Thou art Goddess," the Goddess-as-deity is believed to be present in a mystical sense in each and every one. She is also represented by an external symbol, such as the "fire of trans-formation" burning in the Witches' cauldron, making her an objectified subject in relation to Younger Self.

The emerging paradox is that Goddess is *simultaneously* internal and external to the human subject. This paradoxical interaction of Goddess and self is not exclusive to Witches. Anthropologist Paul Heelas believes that all possible human conceptions of self and authority may be analysed according to two contrasting systems. One is called "idealist" because the self is regarded as subject and the world her object. The other is called "passiones"[14] because the individual is now the object whereas the world represents agency (Heelas 1981:41). In addition, authority can be conceptualized as internal or external. Heelas argues that the modern, "autonomous" individual represents pure idealism: self is "in control" and authority is internalized in self, making her subject vis-à-vis the world. The "plastic" human being, who has no clear boundaries between herself and cosmos, represents pure passiones: self is "under control" and authority is externalized in relation to the self, making her object vis-à-vis the world.[15]

If we exchange Heelas's concept of "authority" for "Goddess" (the ultimate authority to Witches), we may conceptualize the already outlined dynamic between Goddess and self as follows: when Goddess is understood as immanent life force *in* the individual, authority is internalized and the self is subject (idealist). When the very same life force is understood as an all-embracing, cosmological power, Goddess is not only believed to be *in* the individual, but to *contain* the individual within herself. The self is merely one of many "objects" within divinity, and authority is experienced as externalized (passiones).

What is interesting in Reclaiming is that the fluctuating positions of self and Goddess are *wilfully chosen* and included in their own meta-perspective when explaining their spiritual path to new apprentices. This reality of having a choice is, of course, typical to their identity as modern Americans. But choice is also derived from their hermeneutics, from the belief that ultimate reality *may* speak to them and reveal its knowledge if they dare to interact, merge and be bent. For example, ritual practices are not only regarded as symbolizing and confirming what is already held to be cognitively true by the believer. In and of themselves they have the power – as has all true involvement with people and the natural world according to Witches – to convey new knowledge that otherwise would not be known. Alternatively, if people do not choose or dare to interact, reality (including ritual) will be silent and reveal nothing.[16]

After the invocation of Goddess and God, its time for magical work. I will not analyse this part further since its possible ritual strategies resembles those already introduced. In terms of the time span for the whole rite, this part (including the raising of a cone of power) comes toward the end as an energetic and emotional highlight. When all is completed, the ritual is quickly finished with thanksgiving and "fare wells" to deities and elements. The rhythm of the ritual consists of a long, elaborate beginning with a slow building up of emotional and vital energy, a deep climax towards the end, and a short but firm closure. Witches believe that without a proper closure, what has been accomplished in ritual will not manifest in ordinary reality – only fade away.

Interpreting ritual as "how": strategic interactions between bodies and space

The *ritualization* (in Catherine Bell's sense) taking place in Reclaiming's classes, covens and public gatherings has already been anticipated in the former paragraph and will continue to be discussed in the following chapters. But let me give a brief summary of this process so far: "ritualization" – as it takes place in a Reclaiming class – can be described as a dialectical process of interaction between "magical persons" (ritualized bodies) and "magical space" (a ritualized environment).

Magical space is structured according to esoteric philosophy about living nature and the cosmic pillars of correspondence. It is created by means of symbolic acts homologous to this philosophy in order to delimit and structure an imaginary all-inclusive cosmic circle: everything, also the social world, may be represented in the circle through association. This ritually defined space can be described as an imaginary natural landscape with height and depth, with wind and water, fire and earth, and a deep-rooted world tree with large branches as *axis mundi*.

A magical person is constructed as she physically enters magical space, allows her self to be inscribed with complex layers of (gendered), esoteric meanings, and positions herself vis-à-vis cosmos by imaginatively "becoming" a world tree: a mediator between social worlds, elemental forces and the gods. This ritualized body, however, is not only a mythological tree, balancing at the interstices between the social and the biological, but a cosmic duplicate in miniature which contains, within itself, all possible wisdom, all possible genders and all the elements of being. This is fully expressed when the world tree finally transforms into a manifestation of goddess herself.

A major strategy used in Reclaiming in order to differentiate ritual acts from nonritual acts is a mutual consensus that, in profane time and space, carnal people interact with solid things, whereas in ritual space they also attain imaginary spirit-bodies – as they do when becoming a world tree – and interact with imaginary things. The function of the solidity of ritual props is to enhance this experience and help the subject to "decompose and re-create" her spiritual body. Likewise does the materiality of the ritual tools and symbols give an aura of probability/factuality to the proposition that the elements simultaneously are natural and divine substances, indexical esoteric symbols and correlative aspects of the (gendered) human body, psychology and sociality.

The meanings of all these symbolic associations converge neither in the human body (a living temple) nor in the magical circle (a symbolic temple), but in their systematic interrelatedness. In fact, they constitute a single system of analogies.[17] One consequence of such a circular interdependence is that a (gendered) homocentric worldview continually is balanced by the notion of living nature and cosmological interconnectedness. Thus, we may confirm that the primary function of a monistic, dialectical worldview is not *necessarily* to gender the world nor to determine the human body in terms of sexual essences (although these may turn out to be secondary consequences), but rather to recognize deep kinship between all beings as they participate in the same, pulsating life force (as in Spinoza's philosophy and ethics).

Ritualization in Reclaiming may be a hierarchized social practice in which roles are distributed according to assumed experiences, accumulated knowledge and power, and the primacy of the female sex. Its stated goal is, however, to work toward the transformation of social values, social beings and their social worlds. Visualizations for change and healing performed within magical space and invisible reality are believed to manifest as changes in the mundane world of solidity as well – not only because of magical spells performed in ritual, but because the celebrants are believed to carry a circle within their own bodies even after ritual has been completed and are thus capable of manifesting ritual values in social reality. A prerequisite, however, for changes to occur, is that people completely dissolve the magical circle and re-enter the solid reality of everyday life.

Witches' social strategy of separating solid from imaginary and performing temporary magical rites may be read as an important means to gain a sense of belonging in the world and a feeling of being in charge of one's own life; for the circular movements of bodies between what is regarded as profane–sacred–profane seem to make Reclaiming people and their students spiritually and psychologically stronger and less fatalistic about the way things *really* are in the world.

Notes

1 This is in particular the danger in the individuation process of girls. Object relations theorists hold that the process from primordial unity (with mother) to subsequent separation (from mother) is very different for boys and girls (and, therefore, fundamental when producing sexual identity). Because of a stronger and more undifferentiated same-sex identification between mother and daughter, Nancy Chodorow claims that women often never separate sufficiently from their mothers, making them "eternal preys" for relational issues, ego boundary issues and feelings of lack of separateness and a distinguished identity (Chodorow 1978).

2 Heimbrock (1990:33) writes that magical rituals in all the psychoanalytical traditions are perceived as premature forms of reasoning. Religious rituals are, in general, recognized as "neurotic symptoms, that are unsuitable means to overcome underlying emotional conflicts". The problem is, however, that if ritual in itself is feared to be regressive, in a realistic, psychological sense, then the fundamentally temporary, mimetic and symbolist character of ritual is misunderstood. Erikson is a notable exception who has emphasized the importance of ritualization in identity-development (cf. Ouwehand 1990:134), and so has feminist psychologist Naomi Goldenberg. She claims that, actually, there are basic similarities between object relations theory and Starhawk's discourse: 1 to focus on the past as a central source of meaning; 2 to focus on female images of power and desire and thereby deconstruct central images of patriarchal authority; 3 to describe the individual as formed within the context of community; 4 to recognize fantasy and emotion as a key structure of "rational" thought (Goldenberg 1990:191). Goldenberg underlines that both "schools" "look back in time for the purpose of healing the present" and their common centre is the image of a powerful woman in the past: "Woman" is the stuff out of which all people are made. It is this deep memory of "birth union" (including pre-birth experience and post-birth mothering) that people, according to Goldenberg, turn into philosophical and religious "reflection on the interconnection of human beings with each other and with all the things which make up the body of the world" (1990:202).

3 This observation about contemporary western psychology is taken from M. Rosaldo (1984:142).

4 This was, for example, expressed by Pierre Bourdieu (1991) when reading Arnold van Gennep's and Victor Turner's symbolic phase descriptions of rites of passage (cf. chapter 8). Catherine Bell is deeply influenced by Bourdieu in her sociological concerns.

5 This is what Frits Staal (1975) has suggested.

6 If C. Geertz's "religion is a system of symbols" is combined with Turner/Rappaport's "having *indexical* reference to mystical beings or powers", the result is close to a "what" definition of religion that I utilize.

7 Emotions are often gendered, and occasionally Reclaiming men will identify with the conventional, essentialist western label of being less emotional than women if they don't find access to their own feelings. But the terms "emotions" and "feelings" have different layers of meaning, depending on context. In conformity with the terminology offered by Lutz and White (1986), Reclaiming Witches may

be said to be split between *universalist* and *constructionist* tendencies in terms of how emotions are understood. To the extent that they are *universalists,* emotions are seen as natural, bodily determined and precultural – as psycho-biological facts (cf. Lutz and White 1986:407). Culture does not constitute emotions; it only influences their acceptance/denial and their meanings, and how they are expressed ideally in terms of symbols and behaviour. When identifying with the cultures of prehistoric womanhood, Starhawk takes for granted that she is dealing with a generic human female who *basically* has a psychic (and bodily) constitution similar to her own, and who therefore addresses the same deity: "Goddess is found . . . in mind, body, spirit, and the emotions within each of us" (Starhawk 1979b:263). The immense cultural differences between then and now are mainly seen as questions of social organization, cultural conditioning and technological developments. The human psyche, however, is regarded as a constant. The aim of universalist Witches is thus to expand the register of socially permitted emotions and states of mind in order to prevent "culture" and "cultural psycho-logical discourse" from undermining natural human existence.

To the extent that Witches are *constructionists* emotions are seen as embedded in socially constructed categories, "made up" in order to regulate (or control) human behaviour, morality and identity. The relationship between emotion and the physical body is either more or less ignored or understood metaphorically. Emotions are rather seen as powerful cognitive ideas and judgements that can take possession of an individual, but without really originating from her. An example is the feeling of jealousy. Many informants claim that this "bodily state of mind" is a product of cultural conditioning: It results from and expresses western materialist possessive-ness and competitive mentality. Many Witches, therefore, claim the identity of not being jealous, or of having managed to outgrow "its bore". The political merit of such a cultural relativism is that it reinforces optimistic beliefs about the possibility of changing any cultural institution, also monogamy.

However, the split between universalist and constructionist tendencies in Reclaiming is only an apparent split: they join forces in a deeply cherished romantic worldview in which *natural* emotions are proclaimed as the site of the culturally uncorrupted, pure and "inner self" of *natural* humanity. Thus emotions are, after all, believed by all Witches to be natural, bodily determined and universal, albeit *only those emotions which are considered genuine* (such as love, passion, pride, fear etc.). Jealousy, on the other hand, is considered a conventional emotion, a cultural product of alienation and oppression and, therefore, un-natural.

8 The different stages of the ritual process are numbered from 1 to 12, and some of these stages will later in the chapter be described in more detail.

9 This line is a modification of Paul's speech at Areopagos in Acts 17:28, where he supposedly said: "For 'In him we live and move and have our being'; as even some of your own poets have said." But, according to the commentary in the HarperCollins Study Bible, the quotation may come from the sixth century BCE philosopher-poet Epimenides and therefore be genuinely pagan.

10 These lyrics are from the "Circle Casting Song" by Susan Wolf, taken from Reclaiming's "Second Chants" tape, produced in 1994.

11 Ronald Grimes differentiates terminologically between "rite" and "ritual": rite denotes concrete enactments located in concrete time and space, ritual denotes the general idea of which a rite is a specific instance. Since "ritual" is an empirical notion and Witches themselves are not familiar with this distinction I shall rather differentiate between the generic idea of a type of ritual and the actual ritual taking place.

12 The "Tree of Life" is actually a cross-religious symbol. According to anthropologist James Preston it has often, in the occult tradition, been associated with the feminine life force (Preston 1982:128).

13 The myth goes: "*In love, the Horned God, changing form and changing face, ever seeks the Goddess. In this world, the search and the seeking appear in the Wheel of the Year. She is the Great Mother who gives birth to Him as the Divine Child Sun at the Winter Solstice. In spring, He is sower and seed who grows with the growing light, green as the new shoots. She is the Initiatrix who teaches Him the mysteries. He is the young bull; She the nymph, seductress. In summer, when light is longest, they meet in union, and the strength of their passion sustains the world. But the God's face darkens as the sun grows weaker, until at last, when the grain is cut for harvest, He too sacrifices Himself to Self that all may be nourished. She is the reaper, the grave of the earth to which all must return. Throughout the long nights and darkening days, He sleeps in her womb; in dreams, He is Lord of Death who rules the Land of Youth beyond the gates of night and day. His dark tomb becomes the womb of rebirth, for at Midwinter She again gives birth to Him. The cycle ends and begins again, and the Wheel of the Year turns, on and on*" (Starhawk 1979a: 29). Starhawk claims that the myth is an "oral teaching of the Faery tradition" (1979a:29, 33 note 19), although it is well known in Gardnerian Wicca.

14 The latin word *passio* means "the fact or condition of being acted upon or affected by external agency; subject to external force" (Heelas 1981:41).

15 The mystical level of Tibetan Buddhism, New Age, Humanistic psychology and Protestant individualism are given as examples of pure idealist systems, whereas the psychology of the African Dinka tribe, Shamanism, Exorcism, Fundamentalist Christianity and Behaviourism are passiones systems.

16 My contribution is not to make the distinction between "self as object" versus "self as subject" conscious to the informants – because it already is – but to systematize and rename according to *my* analytical position. I have theologized their world-view and interpreted depths that perhaps were unknown and confirmed how they perceive reality hierarchically.

17 Religious symbolism and self-symbolism do not converge on *any* point, says anthropologist Mary Douglas. Actually, they "sustain the whole moral and physical universe simultaneously in their systematic interrelatedness" (Douglas 1973:140).

6 The Spiral Dance ritual

A celebration of death and rebirth

The most famous ritual performed in Reclaiming is the "Spiral Dance". It is celebrated as a Samhain ritual, preferably on the night between 31 October and 1 November. Samhain is one of the Witches' eight sabbats. According to themselves, this holiday is a pagan, Celtic precursor to the later "All Saints' Day" or "Halloween". In Celtic mythology, 31 October is "New Year's Eve," marking both the entrance to the winter season and to the new year. The Witches' Samhain ritual is thus an effort to revive a pre-Christian new year celebration connected to the changing cycles in the natural and human world.

According to Witches' mythology – dating back to Gardner's and Valiente's constructions in the 1950s – this night in itself represents extra-ordinary time and space. On this night the veil between seen and unseen, dead and living, past and present is believed to be "thin". Now is the time to talk to, grieve for and remember the beloved dead, as well as to remember the limits of human life, the limits of control, and that all must die, will die, when the time comes. The consolation is that death is not a final destination but part of a natural cycle in which new life arises and is reborn. Through the ritual, Witches seek to experience the proclaimed mystery that death feeds new life at many different levels: Every growth is said to be a painful dying, and every end a new beginning, in human life as in nature, just as fall gives birth to winter and winter to spring, just as a seed must die for a plant to come into being, and a plant must perish and "give itself as food" for human life to be sustained.

In the Samhain ritual, Witches use the imagery of the Goddess and the God to symbolize this theme. The Goddess is celebrated as the creative force in nature and in cultural construction, symbolized as the Triple Goddess "Maiden, Mother and Crone". God, symbolized as the Horned One, is celebrated as that which is forever untamed and wild inside, but who forever seeks the Goddess in love. So, while the Goddess is the ground of being, the giver and taker of life, the God is he who is born and dies in an endless cycle. The God is said to die every year on October 31. He passes on to the Kingdom of Death, which in the Faery tradition is called alternatively "The Summer Land", "The Shining Island", "The Land of Youth", "The Shadow Land" or "The Island of Apples", located somewhere in the ocean in the west.

Every soul that dies is said to be received by the earth and grow young again in Summer Land. Then she is reborn among the living as a human child.

This variation of a reincarnation theme is found in a myth called the "Descent of the Goddess" (cf. Starhawk 1979a:29, 159–60). The myth tells that after a while the Goddess descends to the Kingdom of Death to restore the God to a new life. In the meantime he has become the Lord of Death, the Guardian of the Gates to the Shadow Land. The Goddess sleeps with him for three days and three nights and transforms him, through love, into the Divine Child Sun. In the intercourse she consumes him completely, absorbing him in her own body like a seed, bearing him to new life on Winter Solstice, 21 December. In the myth, the descended Goddess addresses her consort like this:

> *Here is the circle of rebirth. Through You all passes out of life, but though Me all may be born again. Everything passes; everything changes. Even death is not eternal. Mine is the mystery of the womb, that is the cauldron of rebirth. Enter into Me and know Me, and You will be free of all fear. For as life is but a journey into death, so death is but a passage back to life, and in Me the circle is ever turning.*
>
> *In love, He entered into Her, and so was reborn into life. Yet is He known as Lord of Shadows, the comforter and consoler, opener of the gates, King of the Land of Youth, the giver of peace and rest. But She is the gracious mother of all life; from Her all things proceed and to Her they return again. In Her are the mysteries of death and birth; in Her is the fulfillment of all love.*[1]

But at Samhain, the God is not yet reborn. It is, therefore, the reality of death and dying and of the pain within life that is the main focus of the ritual.

Halloween in San Francisco

Reclaiming's ritual remembrance of the dead is not acted out in a cultural vacuum. The old Anglo-Saxon celebration of Halloween has become very popular in the US in a secularized version, especially in San Francisco. On 31 October, people carve big pumpkins to make them look like ghosts. In the evening these are placed outside entrance doors with a burning candle inside. This is a signal to the children, who walk the streets in groups – acting and dressed up like ghosts returning from the dead – that they may enter this house to play "trick or treat" with the living. The treats are candies, chocolate and fruit. For the adults, Halloween is a time for masquerade balls and wild parties. Castro, the gay area in San Francisco, has become famous for its lavish celebration of Halloween, with drag shows, masquerades and fireworks.[2]

In the Mission District there is, in addition to Halloween, another tradition for celebrating the dead on 1 November, namely, the Mexican "El dia de los muertos."[3] For the occasion, the stores in Mission have grotesque death decorations in the front windows and sell all kinds of death artifacts; the children construct death imagery and masks in the Mission public schools; the Mission art galleries put up exhibitions like "Rooms for the Dead". This

Latino tradition is not about pumpkins, children and "trick or treat", but about the extended family who feasts and visits with the dead, lightning candles and serving food at the graves of departed family members.

As part of their growing cultural self-esteem, a young generation of Hispanics and other Latin Americans in the Mission took the initiative in the early 1980s to revive a more original form of "El dia de los muertos" and strip away some of its childishness and commercialism. It was a success, and the size of the celebration has been growing every year since. The new part is that, on one evening of the Day of the Dead season, the streets in the old Mission are closed to traffic to give space for a huge, noisy and colourful "Death Parade". The parade includes both children and adults. Its intent is to raise people's political consciousness about the forms of dying that take place among them and rebuild a religious-cultural identity with the magical tradition of walking with and talking to the dead – as if life and death were overlapping realities within one continuum.

The number of people participating in this parade was in 1994 around 2,000, and just as many were spectators. The parade itself included as many whites as people of colour. The individual paraders wore death costumes and carried death associated artifacts. Musical groups and theatre troops participated with huge dolls and masks, acting out death and oppression scenes along the route. One narrow street was formed into a temporary birth channel, through which everybody in the parade had to pass. The new life was celebrated in a park nearby with music, dancing and free food.

Since the Reclaiming Witches consider themselves to be the spiritual descendants of European indigenous people, they participate every year in this parade arranged by their Latin American siblings. The Witches carry huge masks and headdresses that a couple of days later are used in their own rite for the dead. They have also adopted the political outlook of this Latino celebration, with its strong emphasis on deceased ancestors, grotesque skeletons and the special food served for the dead, and integrated it all into their own powerful rites for the season. In return they contribute a spiritual element to this highly ritualized parade: since 1993, Starhawk and the Reclaiming Collective has been asked by the Hispanic arranging committee to set up altars, offer prayers and lead a spiral dance in the park at the closing of the parade.

The telling of an experience

When describing the Reclaiming ritual called the "Spiral Dance" (which is not to be confused with the dancing in the park on El dia de los muertos), I shall – to a certain extent – not use the distant, academic language. I shall, instead, use a more narrative, empathic style and describe selected parts of the ritual from a perspective of involvement. This way I hope to portray how spectacular a ritual can be and to illustrate the ways in which emotions are manipulated and triggered (including by "trance work") in order to make a ritual work successfully. With this emphasis on participatory hermeneutics, I also hope to depict how my own "method of compassion" – in which I become my own informant – may be acted out within the context of ritual.

The actual ritual was about three hours long and had an elaborate structure. My description is not literal but a liberal reconstruction on the basis of several similar, but still different Spiral Dance rituals. One reason for my liberalism is that there already exist several literal manuscripts of the ritual, authored by Starhawk and other Reclaiming people, of which I have two: from 1989 and 1990. They have the copyright to it, but the manuscripts can be acquired, read and used by anybody. Going strictly through the contents of this ritual text does not take us beyond a symbolic and intellectual analysis of semantics, and it gives an incomplete picture of what is really taking place: leaving out the atmosphere, the affections, the sound, the experience of being in the room. Although they are similar, a ritual is not theatre, and manuscript and actual happening are never identical.

However, I shall refer freely to parts of the ritual manuscript and other sources when I find that exact representation of lyrics is important to convey the theological meanings of the ritual. Some elements are taken from other ritual contexts, and the journey to the "Kingdom of Death" is shortened. The litany is close to being authentic and reproduced on the basis of: (1) the above mentioned ritual manuscripts; (2) Starhawk's books; and (3) my own experience from participating in several "Spiral Dance" rituals in the years 1984, 1990 and 1994.

Since the ritual process is dependent on the skilled manipulation of emotions to be successful, the ritual is very vulnerable to people's evaluation. Sometimes a ritual is experienced as boring or as not working. The actual Spiral Dance ritual that I have chosen as the foundation of my description was said to work, and this is an important aspect. It took place at the Women's Building in the Mission District in San Francisco, Friday night, 26 October, 1990. Approximately 300 people participated, and 40 were ritual facilitators. The manuscript to which I mostly refer was written for the Spiral Dance Ritual one year earlier, in 1989. It took place on 28 October, at the Fort Mason Centre at the harbour in San Francisco. Twelve hundred people attended the ritual, and about 120 carried it through. Its size was the reason to write a full manuscript.

Let us now enter the Women's Building, which is *not* a women-only building, 30 minutes before the doors were opened to the public in October 1990, and go from there.

Ritual preparations

The biggest assembly room in the Women's Building is about to be transformed into sacred space (the Witches' temple). The atmosphere is rather noisy and hectic, and about 40 people are now finishing preparing for the ritual. Just inside the entrance door, two men are arranging large leaf branches to make the entrance look more like a threshold or a veiled opening into non ordinary reality. Others have raised huge altars around the walls, while the centre floor is kept free from furniture. At the south altar, a group of eight drummers are rehearsing. Two of them are African and play African conga drums; the others are white and play Middle Eastern doumbec drums. Some young women and men are dancing in the centre of the room, rehearsing their part in the invocations of the elements. A man plays with a slide projector, to test that it works and that the pictures come out right. Two women sit quietly in a corner, trying to memorize their parts. They are both dressed in black, wearing plastic skeletons as a belt around their waists their faces painted black with ashes. One of them has a red cord around her waist, as a sign that she is initiated. In the adjoining rooms, people are about to put on their costumes, gossiping and eating.

The assembly room is beautifully decorated. To the right of the entrance door, there is a table with different accessories for the participants to use: bowls with ashes to paint on the face; old clothes and fabrics to tear when grieving; beautiful flowers to smell; sheets of paper with skulls printed on them. People are supposed to write the names of their beloved dead on the sheets and tag them to the northern altar. This altar is next to the table and is the largest and most important for the ritual to come.

The northern altar is constructed of tables, wooden boxes and black tablecloths, measuring about six by eight feet. The wooden boxes are raised irregularly upon the table, and inside the boxes are placed images of death: pictures of beloved dead, pictures of politically caused death in concentration camps in Germany, in Latin America, in Palestine; pictures of Witches waiting to be burned; pictures of starving children, screaming mothers, drug addicts and street people. In between the various pictures are placed miniature skeletons and skulls, as well as pieces of broken glass and barren branches. Candles are lit all over the altar. At the top of the altar, looking down on all the objects, is the mask of the Crone, goddess of age, wisdom and regeneration. The black tablecloth flows from her head and down to the floor, giving the effect that she holds the whole world and its death and misery in her arms and lap. On the floor, in front of the altar, is placed food for the dead: pomegranates, pumpkins, apples, oranges, coffeebeans, baskets of acorns, Indian corn, candy skulls, cakes, *pan de los muertos* and apple juice. Marigolds in huge vases are placed in between.

The other altars, for west, south and east, are simpler. Large fabrics in colours appropriate for each of the elements are draped from high up the wall, down to the altar table. The west altar is blue with water-associated things on top. The south altar is red, with fire-associated things on top. In front of the south altar, somebody has arranged a dozen Tibetan bells to be played during the ritual. The east altar is white and airy. Headdresses are placed on the altars, and behind the southern altar is a mask of the Horned god. Big goddess figures and skeleton figures are in position around the edges of the room.

The Samhain ritual cycle in Reclaiming this year includes three rituals. In addition to the genuine Samhain ritual, the "Spiral Dance" – also called "A Ritual Remembrance of our Beloved Dead" – about to begin this Friday evening, there is a Saturday night ritual the next evening called "Invoking the Ancestors of Many Cultures" as well as a Sunday night ritual called "Building our Visions of the Future." To the altars already constructed, there will tomorrow in this very same room, be added seven additional altars: altars for the ancestors of "European", "Latin-American", "African", and "Asian" descent, and altars for the "Queer Nation (Gay and Lesbians)", the "Jewish Nation" and the "Arab-Palestinian world". These altars will include a mixture of objects related to cultural or religious heritage and they will be placed in between the directional altars. The ancestral altars are arranged by people who have bloodlines to the different cultures. The shape and content of these altars are not prescribed, but dependent upon the emotions, fantasy and aesthetics of the people who construct them.

Reclaiming's altar practice differs from many Wiccan traditions. While these traditions conventionally use altars as a place for the nonhuman reality, like the elements and the gods, represented by their tools and symbols, to be included/present, Reclaiming tends to use the altars more as a place for staging the conditions of their own human lives, at least in public rituals. So, instead of the altars being a communicational bridge from the nonhuman's point of view, altars in Reclaiming are bridges *from* the living *to* the other world – not the other way around. When the northern altar is overloaded with painful deathsymbols, it is not because death is a major representation of goddess. Instead, death is representative of the human condition and for those humans addressing the Goddess and is, therefore, also a part of the Goddess. This use of altar also differs from the western Christian tradition and is more similar to the old Israelite practice where the altar was the people's place, while Yahweh's place was behind the altar wall. Reminiscence of this practice is found in the Orthodox Church when the basilica is divided into a more profane space in front of the Iconostasia and a most holy space behind it.[4]

The time is close to 8 p.m. About 300 people of all genders are lined up in the street outside the building, waiting for the doors to open. Two-thirds of the people are women. A majority have already bought tickets to the event on a sliding scale of $5 to $10 each through mailorder from Reclaiming. Leftover tickets are sold at the door. The ticketmoney is supposed to cover Reclaiming's expenses arranging the ritual, like rent, costumes, sound equipment, etc. Some of the participants come from other pagan and Witchcraft traditions, and most of the people in line have been to The Spiral Dance before. To the arranging committee they have already sent in names and slides of personal loved ones who have died this year, as well as names of the newborn. Yet, many of them bring additional photos for the northern altar in their pockets.

In the assembly room Rose asks everybody to finish their preparations and gather in a circle. She asks how many *graces* and *dragons* there will be at tonight's ritual, graces being the white-dressed who take care of newcomers and disabled people, guiding them to the different altars and answering questions – while dragons are the ones guarding the entrance door, having responsibility for not letting anything disturb the ritual proceedings and keeping potential trouble out. The 40 people in the circle inform each other briefly about their particular responsibility during the evening's ritual, like "I have arranged and shall attend the south altar", "I shall call the Mighty Dead", "I shall manifest the Goddess in the invocation", "I shall drum", "I shall do child care", etc. Then everybody holds hands while Rose offers a prayer for good energy and a good ritual, asking the goddess to give her blessings, to fulfill their intentions and give them strong visions. When the prayers are finished, she says: "*This circle has never been here before, and shall never be here again. But remember, there is no end to the circle, no end. Are we ready to let people in?*" Everybody nods and the doors are opened.

Creating sacred space

The drummers play freeform; the lights are dim; the incense smells sweet; and the celebrants[5] start to enter sacred space through the veiled opening. As they pass through the branches, or through what some Reclaiming Witches like to interpret as an inverted birth-channel into the divine womb,[6] they are purified with the sprinkling of salt water and feathersmudging by children. The graces move around quietly, like spirits, and ask people to write the names of their beloved dead on the sheets for the northern altar. People place their personal items on the altar and then walk slowly and informally around the room. They greet friends, listen to the music, adore the other altars, breathe in the atmosphere. Some are dressed in black costumes and are face-painted; others wear ordinary clothes. When everybody has entered the "divine womb", a single blast of a conch shell announces that the ritual is about to begin.

People gather in a circle, and priest Raven casts a circle around the space, using Gwydion's sword (Gwydion is a well-known Faeryinitiate, an elder and a departed beloved dead). Raven starts in the centre in solemn silence, pointing the sword to the north, kissing it and saying: "*Holy Mother, in whom we move, live and have our being. From you all things proceed, and unto you all things return. Bless this circle.*" He turns to the north, and from there he walks the edges of the whole circle while proclaiming: "*By the Earth that is Her body, by the Air that is Her breath, etc.*"

As soon as Raven is done, a small chorus of six start to sing an old English ballad for the season, "*This ae night*". The refrain is a prayer, "*May Earth receive thy soul*", that whoever gave hose and shoes, silver and gold, meat and drink for sharing shall be received by the Earth, and not be burned to "the bare bane" by the purging fire.

Then priestess Macha, one of the black-dressed with miniature skeletons and a red cord around her waist, enters the centre of the circle. She greets

everybody, explaining briefly the ritual's participatory nature, what the ritual theme is about and the symbolic meanings of "Goddess" and "God".

*   *   *

Priestess Deborah brings us "back" to the assembly room and to the ritual we are about to create by asking everybody to prepare to enter an altered state of consciousness by imaginarily "grounding themselves in the Earth, which is the Mother" and together becoming a blossoming tree. She raises her voice and talks in a slow, evocative manner while walking a big circle in the centre. A single drummer is tapping with the rhythm of her voice,

> *Join with us now and breathe deeply, and be ready to enter darkness.*[7]
> *Close your eyes, breathe deep, feel the Spirits gathering.*
> *Breathe like a seed awakening in the soil, breathe power from the Earth and from the Air.*
> *Reach deep inside, to the centre and source within . . .*

Except for Deborah's voice and the sound of light breathing, there is complete silence. We stand next to each other in circle, still a little shy, but crowded and warm, with eyes closed. Graces place themselves in the crowd to help Deborah raise and move the energy and mould our shyness into a free breathing. Our chests move up and down, slowly. Some bodies are starting to wave slightly, from one side to the other. This grounding is a most sensual exercise, taking us directly from Macha's intellectual explanations to a childlike sensation of being a tree, tasting and smelling the earth and her energy, trying to create a feeling of a centre within: a plaza maybe, with flowers and palm trees and a water fountain.

> *Reach down with your breath; reach down with your heart; reach down with your needs and desires. Reach down, the way roots reach down to the raw heat of the Mother. To the source, beyond need and desire, beyond knowing . . .*
> *Reach down to touch that power and pull it up . . .*
> *up through your toes and legs, up into the cradle of your sex,*
> *filling your belly, your lungs, your head . . .*

The breathing becomes heavy, and the crowd noisy but relaxed. All the bodies are now moving back and forth. There is a tingling of something in the body when breathing in and up. Feet are stamped, efforts made to make the breathing smooth.

> *Filling your self and beyond your self . . .*
> *And reach up all the way trees reach with branches, up until you stretch from Earth to Sky.*
> *And open your heart to that power moving through you.*

Let it grow. Let it blossom, weaving through each of us.
Let it build on itself on your breath. Let it rise . . .

At this point, Deborah almost shouts, but her voice is hardly heard. The crowd
has built up the sound to a loud and noisy O-o-m, while holding on to their
internal imagery made according to Deborah's instructions. A few add energy
with animal-like screams or the sounds of birds. Arms are stretched up, higher,
higher; voices are loud. Deborah is in the centre of the circle, leading and
raising the intensity of the energy, higher and higher. Then, all of a sudden,
when the sound has reached its peak, she gives the signal to stop by stopping
herself and lowering her arms.

Let it fall, gently, like petals, like rain, washing over us, connecting us all.
And down to the Earth, and down to each other, and down to our Deepest selves.
And know and drink in this blessing.

The energy has dropped to calmness. We kneel down on the floor, quiet and
breathless, warm and exalted. When we sit up, there is a peaceful atmosphere
in the room. Nobody says a word for a while. We just look at each other,
smiling, while tasting and relishing a feeling of bonding. A couple of women
next to me whisper to each other, "She is really good, Deborah, really good.
Its like she got a new power after her initiation."

After grounding, it is time for invoking the elements. They are called as the
chorus, musicians and dancers perform "The Guardian Song".[8] When done,
the elements are blessed by priestess Deadly,

Blessed be the elements of life, Earth and Air, Fire and Water. They are sacred to us
because they sustain all life. And the circle of life is what we are committed to serve:
the cycle of birth, growth, death and regeneration, happening again and again, in
Moon and Sun and season, in fruit and seed and blossom, in the powers we name
Goddesses and Gods, in the lives of animals, and in our lives as women and men.

Change of self: becoming divine

In every Spiral Dance ritual goddess and god are called by a special song
composed by Starhawk. It is structured as a call and response between the
women, manifesting the Triple Goddess (Maiden–Mother–Crone), the men,
manifesting the Horned One, and the chorus, accompanied by drums. The
people manifesting the deities wear headdresses or carry masks,

3 goddesses	*For you can see me in your eyes*
	When they are mirrored by a friend
Chorus	There is no end to the circle no end
	There is no end to life there is no end

Maiden	*For I am the power to begin*
	I dream and bring to birth what's never been
	There is no end to freedom, no end
Chorus	There is no end to the circle no end . . .
3 goddesses	*For you can hear me in your voice*
	And feel me in each breath that you breathe in
Chorus	There is no end to the circle no end . . .
Mother	*For I am the power to sustain*
	I am the ripened fruit and growing grain
	There is no end to my abundance, no end
Chorus	There is no end to the circle no end . . .
3 goddesses	*And you can feel me in your heart*
	When it beats with the heart of a friend
Chorus	There is no end to the circle no end . . .
Crone	*And I am the power to end*
	I am the Crone who cuts the cord that I spin
	Though all things that are born must die again
Chorus	There is no end to the circle no end . . .
3 goddesses	*For all proceeds from me and all returns*
	All that returns from me comes forth again
Chorus	There is no end to the circle no end
God	*I'm the word that you can't define*
	I'm the color that runs outside the line
	I'm the shiver running up your spine
	Break the pattern, I'll make a new design
Chorus	There is no end to the circle no end . . .
God	*I am the wild bird that won't be tamed*
	The desires that you don't need to name
	I'm the branch that becomes the flame
	When the fire's done burning, I remain
Chorus	There is no end to the circle . . .
Goddess and	*For all proceeds from me and all return.*
God together	*All that returns from me comes forth again*
	The sun arises and descends
	The seasons turn and turn again
Chorus	There is no end to the circle no end . . .
Goddess and	*I am the honey taste of passion's heat*
God together	*the fear running through your heartbeat,*
	I am dancing through your lightened feet,
	desire so fierce and love so sweet.
Chorus	There is no end to the circle no end
	There is no end to life there is no end

Goddess and	*And you can touch me with your hands*
God together	*Reach out and take the hand of a friend*
	There is no end to the circle no end
	There is no end to life there is no end.

The first and the last verses contain the most important statements for the ritual theme and for ritualizing as such: "*And you can see me in your eyes/When they are mirrored by a friend . . . . And you can touch me with your hands/Reach out and take the hand of a friend*". The goal of the invocation is to make the divine manifest in the participants and to make us conscious of the sacredness of our own being and of another being. Divinity is not merely conceived as narrative at the level of myth and parable, but understood as manifest, as one who can actually be felt by touching and seeing "the other".

We do as we are told "by the gods"; we reach out and take the hand of a friend. We join in the chorus's singing as we look into each other's eyes, blinking and perhaps feeling timid as we try to *see* the other as sacred. We change partners, we look into new eyes, seeing something different but still of the same. The song is slowly urging us to begin to dance, to free-form chant and to drum. When the energy has peaked, the dancing ends and we ground, as usual, by lying down.

The litany: Ancestors, Beloved Dead and Mighty Dead

The priestesses Macha, Arachne and Pandora enter the centre of the circle, turning toward the northern altar. Macha holds a pomegranate in front of her, intended for the Mighty Dead. Arachne holds the bread, intended for the Ancestors. She also walks with a three-feet-long Ancestor Stick, hung with bells and colourful cloths. Pandora holds the chalice with apple juice, intended for the Beloved Dead. Macha is the first who starts speaking:

> *This is the time when the veil is thin that divides the worlds, the seen from the unseen, the day-to-day from the mysteries. This is the time when our Beloved Dead return to us, to visit us. What is remembered lives!*
>
> *Mighty Dead of the Craft, wise ones, you who have gone before. We have made a feast for you, please come and be part of our feast. Teach us your wisdom, celebrate with us and share with us our food and gifts.*

Macha walks to the northern altar and places the pomegranate there, the food that symbolizes our gift or offering to the Mighty Dead. Then Arachne takes over. She pounds the Ancestor Stick three times, and says:

> *We remember the Ancestors. We have come to this land from many places, many bloodlines, many cultures. Many races meet here. Our ancestors were poor and rich, oppressors and oppressed, slave-owners and slaves. But in every heritage there is a*

history of those who fought for freedom in every language spoken. In every blood stream is a current, and these are the spirits we call:

We call on you, the healers, the namers, the risk-takers, those who dared to love, those who dared to see, and those whose mistakes can teach us now. Here is our feast for you. Our altar is filled with food and light, with acorns, pomegranates, pan de los muertos, with flowers and fruit and the colors of all the quarters of the world. May our songs, our poems, our voices and our moving feet make you welcome. Come! May you feel at home among us! What is remembered lives!

Arachne walks to the northern altar with the bread as she invites the Ancestors to join us. Pandora takes over, addressing the more personal, Beloved Dead. She asks them to come and celebrate and drink the apple juice with us. She too states that "what is remembered lives", and places the chalice upon the altar.

Then it is time for the scripted part of the litany, in which our personal Beloved Dead are named very specifically. Pandora reads the list of names of people who have died this last year, names that the celebrants have sent in, while John shows us their pictures with the slide projector. We lie on the floor on our backs, listening and watching the pictures, which are projected onto the ceiling. Graces send fabrics around to tear if needed when grieving and crying, and bowls of ashes to rub on the face. A man plays the Tibetan bowls very softly as Pandora reads:

We remember you who have died this year, our mothers and fathers, our family, spouses, friends, children and lovers, companeros and companeras. We name you and honor you, your lives, your sorrows, your gifts, your deaths. And we release you to make your journey.
   What is remembered lives!
   We remember Sara Hendrix, who died of cancer in September;
   We remember William Robertson, who died as a newborn;
   We remember Peter Frank, dying from AIDS;
   etc., etc.

Pandora's list is very long. Many people are crying; fabrics are being torn. Some are sobbing loudly and are comforted by friends. Pandora is done, and it is time for us, the celebrants, to raise our voices and remember our beloved dead – whenever they died. Some speak out loudly; others whisper:

I remember my aunt, a closeted lesbian who loved me as her own child;
I remember my mother, who died when I was too young to know her;
I remember Wally; he was my lover;
I remember Wally; he was my lover too . . .[9]

Some are laughing in the midst of crying, while the sound of fabrics being torn cuts through the room. Every time a beloved dead is named with a sentence or two, a whole story is told. When people weave together the threads of the different stories about foremothers and forefathers, they strengthen the bonds of community between themselves. By publicly naming and honouring the dead, each one of us gives to "the other" value, remembering who we are and where we come from.

Priestess Rose takes over the litany, naming the nameless and forgotten by the way they died, a custom Witches have learned from the Nigerian Yoruba tradition, which is strong in certain communities of Black people in Oakland, a city close to San Francisco. Rose is accompanied by a drumbeat, while we repeat with her the basic mantra "what is remembered lives":

> *This has been a hard year. Many that we love are gone,*
> *AND MANY THAT WE NEVER KNEW!*
> *We remember*
> *you who died of hunger,*
> *and you who died of torture,*
> *and you who died without shelter,*
> *and you who died of the poisons in the air and the earth and the water,*
> *and you who died in the streets,*
> *you who died in wars – Jalapa, Belfast, Beirut, Soweto, San Salvador . . .*
> *What is remembered lives – to change!*
>
> *Remembering*
> *all those who died from AIDS.*
> *You who died in the arms of a lover,*
> *and you who died unloved . . .*
> *What is remembered lives – to teach us how precious life is!*
> *Remembering*
> *the women who have been sold,*
> *the women who have been raped,*
> *the women who were used until worn out and left alone to die . . .*
> *What is remembered lives – to change us!*
>
> *Remembering*[10]
> *all those who have been burned.*
> *The women burned for being strong and obstinate;*
> *burned for a small profit;*
> *burned for being sexual, for loving other women,*
> *the men burned for loving men;*
> *the heretics burned for unpopular opinions;*
> *the scientists burned for revealing new truths;*
> *the thinkers burned for their visions;*
> *and the Witches . . .*

Rose's voice is strong and hoarse; she almost pushes out the words, while the celebrants wail and cry – louder and louder when hearing the word "witch":

We remember the Witches who danced in the dark,
and were burned for remembering that this life, this Earth, this world of
day and night,
is the true body of the sacred.
And She is in us, and needs us to care for Her.
We remember the flames rising,
the scorched smell of our own flesh, the pain and the ecstasy of rising.
What is remembered lives – to rise from ashes,
to be our beacon,
to change,
to be changed,
to change us.
So there is never again the burning, the bomb, the bullet.
What is remembered lives – so that we may live,
in the turning wheel,
in the endless spiral dance of life, renewing itself, endlessly.
Live to serve life.
Live so that all of life may thrive!

Trance journey to the "Island of the Dead"

The atmosphere in the Women's Building is now dense and warm, and many people are giving signs that they are deeply moved emotionally. It is time to get up on our feet and set sail for "The Shining Island", which means to turn "this island and all its inhabitants" into an indexical symbol, whereafter the celebrants may visit the island in trance. As noted in earlier chapters, to trance means to be able to meet, talk to and dance with the beloved dead on this island beyond the limits of the physical body.[11]

*   *   *

A shift in theological meaning is taking place. Our mourning and grieving of the dead shall in a short while yield to our celebration with the dead. Our despair and rage over the reality of political death, the killing and oppression of people, shall give way to an experience of turning ends into beginnings. In this theological universe, the dead are not really dead, but alive in another world, a spirit world. From there they can teach us, give us healing powers and visions to take care of worldly business. And also, one day, the dead will have grown young and will be reborn among the living.

In the first symbolic universe, Witches express an attitude toward death that is in accordance with the Jewish and Christian tradition and a modern worldview: death is an enemy, a total destruction from which nobody returns, a condition which causes complete and eternal separation from the living, although the dead may live on as memory ("what is remembered lives"). Therefore, death gives rise to mourning and rage amongst the next of kin; and to express the grief is, by modern culture, regarded as healthy and healing. Even though Christianity offers belief in resurrection and in a life beyond death, the attitude toward death as a state of being equal to annihilation is common in western culture. Inclusion of celebratory aspects alongside the mourning is often avoided because this, by most people, would be regarded as a reduction of the worth of individual life – of its uniqueness and singularity. Celebration of an *assumed* spiritual state of being beyond death would be a degradation of the *reality* of life in a body. Belief in immortality and re-incarnation threatens the status of death as the ultimate evil.

The second symbolic universe is premodern and pagan. Here we are invited to accept a concept of reality in which a sharp division between the living and the dead is regarded as superficial and illusionary. This outlook is the privilege of the initiated, but in this particular ritual every lover of the Goddess is persuaded to listen to its truth and to join the Reclaiming priesthood on their journey to the Island of the Dead. Here they can also meet the Goddess, who says, "*Enter into Me and know Me, and you will be free of all fear. For as life is but a journey into death, so death is but a passage back to life, and in Me the circle is ever turning.*"[12] At the Island of the Dead the celebrants can experience immortality and the promise of reincarnation with their inner senses and Deep Self.

∗ ∗ ∗

In the centre of the ritual circle, dancers are now about to create images of a ship. The lights are misty and the trance drumming begins. Starhawk leads the trance, which is unscripted. She moves around in the centre, tapping her doumbec drum, while the rest of us walk slowly clockwise, with eyes closed. Sometimes we bump into each other, but it's all right.

> *Breathe deep, and let your breath take you down,*
> *down to the place of magic where death and life are not separate,*
> *and though a dark ocean divides us from the Ancestors,*
> *this circle becomes the boat to ferry us across.*
> *Listen – hear the lapping of the waves on the shore.*
> *Smell the ocean breeze. See the water.*
> *And prepare to set sail for the island where birth and death meet.*
> *We are going to look for help from the Ancestors; help for our lives,*
> *and the threatened life on the Earth.*
> *We are going to the great cauldron womb of rebirth, were all possibilities are formed,*
> *and the dead walk with the unborn.*
> *Breathe deep. At the bottom of your breath is the way to the island.*
> *You are at the sunless shore where the sun and the moon and the stars never shine,*
> *A ferryman is waiting for you. Who is he? What does he ask of you to*
> *take you over?*
> *Are you willing to give it? . . .*

Now, you take a step on board his ship, and you feel it rock beneath you
with the waves.
Together we set sail . . .

Priest Robin breaks into the trance, reading miscellaneous stanzas from Celtic
poems:

Far beyond those waves, there is an Island,
around which glisten the horses of the sea . . .
There it is always like May, the month of strawberries,
of fair weather, of wild garlic, of delicate roses, of prosperity.
There, there is neither "mine" nor "thine"; [13]
every cheek there is the color of the foxglove.
There is a tree there; from roots to crown one half is aflame
and the other green with leaves. Its flowers,
its crest and its showers on every side spread over the fields and plains . . .

Starhawk continues the trance work, taking us to this Island described by
Robin:

Smell the breeze. Hear the scraping of the ship as it reaches the shore,
and see how the land is shining.
Here is all that ever was – the Ancestors, Goddesses, Gods, Spirits,
all the crowd around to greet us. Hold out your arms. They will help you ashore.
The air is fragrant here, and you begin to hear music. Your feet want to
move, to dance.
For this is the place everything is always dancing. Come and join the dance!

The drums play up, and the chorus start singing a song taken from the
repertoire of the popular, female soul group "Sweet Honey in the Rock". [14]
People sing and dance, getting high and light-footed from being in trance. [15]
After a while the energy drops and Starhawk continues:

As you dance, somebody is coming to greet you, one of your Beloved Dead . . .
Hold out your hand; feel the clasp of a spirit hand, and look . . .
Take your time, and speak with your Beloved Dead.
Walk together in the apple orchards of the Goddess . . .
Now, let your Beloved Dead lead you to the rim, to the edge of the Island . . .
And when you reach the rim, look out, back to the world of night and day.
And feel how the earth calls to us, and what the world needs from us.
And let the dead give you power, to heal and to create.
Hold out your hands. Take in the power . . .
Now, let your Beloved Dead take you to the centre of the Island.
Take hands to bring our power together . . .
Make the circle. Hold it strong in your hands.

The cauldron of the Goddess is placed in the centre. Look into its flames,
let yourself see the vision that can be born, the vision we can create together.
See it take shape for you, that world we want to create . . .
What step can you take toward this vision, small or large, in this new year? . . .
The time has come, now, to say good-bye to this island and to the spirits
we've met here . . .
Look, is someone hanging around you? . . .
If you want a child, open your womb, your seed and call.
If you don't, tell the spirits firmly to look somewhere else . . .
Feel the ship scrape on the shore of the living world.
Say good-bye. Step ashore.
Smell the night air of this city. Feel the solid floor under your feet,
and let the ship, the sea and the island fade back into the night.

* * *

A few days later, Priestess Aradia tells me that she strongly dislikes utopian paradises. She finds the "Shining Island" or the "Island-of-Apples-and-Always-Summer-and-Good-Weather" to be extremely boring. She, therefore, closes her ears to Starhawk's trance work very quickly. Instead she immediately goes to the rim of the island and finds herself a library. There she enjoys reading until everybody is finished and ready to return to ordinary life. "I believe that this life holds paradise, this life of change and movement. To follow the path of the Goddess is to live in paradise. It's not an easy path, but it's a true path", Aradia says.

Witches also have different opinions about the Mighty Dead, and some do not even know who they really are. In a break during the rehearsal, before the ritual started, I asked a group of experienced Witches (whom I know well) to tell me the difference between the Ancestors, the Beloved Dead and the Mighty Dead. They all agreed that the Beloved Dead are ordinary people whom they have known personally. They were not sure about the Mighty Dead, but one of them believed they were identical with the Guardians of the Watchtowers, being addressed earlier in the ritual when the elements were invoked. During this discussion, Starhawk passed by. The Witches asked her opinion. Starhawk answered,

> The Ancestors are our bloodline or cultural heritage. The Beloved Dead are the people we know and remember. The Mighty Dead are powerful Witches that do not have to reincarnate, who live on the astral plane as sources of power and protection, almost like semi-gods.

While this group was satisfied with Starhawk's answer, Aradia was not. She agreed that the Mighty Dead are departed Witches with special powers, but not that they are beyond reincarnation. In her opinion, such an expression connotes a value system in which this life on the planet earth is a place not worth returning to. Instead, she believes that everything exists simultaneously in common time and space. This means that when we call the dead, we also call an aspect of ourselves. Aradia believes that she herself has lived before and that a certain aspect of her will always be part of the reality called "Kingdom of Death". But, she states firmly that only initiated Witches know how to call the Mighty Dead properly and actually make them appear. This is not because the initiated have learned a formula, but because they have met and been presented to the Mighty Dead during their initiation ritual. To have met somebody qualifies one to know how to call somebody and ask them to be present.

Aradia also tells me that some Witches are concerned with whether they have the right to call on the dead, wake them up and disturb them. She thinks this is a naive way of looking at reality. First, the dead will not listen and come if they do not want to. Second, the dead are both dead and alive simultaneously. As she has already explained, Witches only call an aspect of a being when calling the dead.

When I ask her why she believes that the dead know something we don't, why they have something to teach us, her answer is that they have experienced death in their present state of being and that they love us. She believes that the Christian Church warns against calling the dead because not all spirits are benevolent,

> But frankly, I think the reason why the Church and its priests dislike our spiritual practice is that they in general are negative to any form of energy work, of doing magic or addressing spirits. The one godhead takes care of everything, while we are his passive children, alienated from the rest of creation. This gives a powerful clergy and a dependent and submissive laity, but it certainly is not my worldview. Each of us are priestesses and priests, and we are free to cooperate with all of creation, the living and the dead, the seen and the unseen, when we take responsibility to create a better world.

Dislike of ritual elements can be expressed as sharp comments while the ritual is taking place, especially if somebody, who is about to call in the elements, uses cultural or ideological imagery that is not regarded as "politically correct" by anarchist, feminist pagans. This is in particular the case if, for example, women call in the Goddess by dressing up as imitations of Isadora Duncan, or if men call the God by imitating the moves and cries of an illusory Wild Man, which is not uncommon. Comments are also made if the ritual seems static or the energy is not raised. In both cases, people may get bored. Intellectually flat or non dynamic rituals are considered "boring", and anything boring is a deadly sin among many Reclaiming people. If and when such rituals are performed, there are always people ready to call the Reclaiming Collective "high church", "Catholic", "middle-class" or "mainstream" – which is the worst insulting language thinkable in this particular community.

Dancing the Spiral – raising a cone of power

The vision taking form as we were looking into the cauldron of the Goddess at the "Island of the Dead" shall now be given a magical form (or turned into a spell) and, then, be sent out into the world to manifest. In order to do this we need a power-song and a power-dance, a Spiral Dance (cf. chapter 3). This focused dancing and singing, building up energy around a concrete image, is called "raising a cone of power". People always wait for it to happen; and, when done in the form of a Spiral Dance, it is experienced as the real highlight of the ritual. Some of the reasons given are the affinity and connection that are said to be felt with the other celebrants and the mystical experiences that many claim to have when spiralling.

* * *

Raising a cone of power is regarded as *the* magical work of Witchcraft. It is said to be exclusive for this spiritual path, meaning that it is not taken from the western occult tradition but that Gardner/Valiente took the idea from somewhere else. The energy form of a cone of power is literally imagined as a cone. The circle of dancing Witches forms the bottom base of the cone, while the top of the cone points toward the roof. When the energy peaks, the cone – believed to hold the image/spell that the participants desire to manifest – is suddenly "released". This releasing is said to be a mental act in which the leading priestesses imaginarily let go of the visual image of the cone holding their spell, sending it out into the universe. When the dancing ends, the "leftover" energy is finally grounded permanently.

Particular to Reclaiming is that they have developed this Gardnerian practice to a level where they create room for ecstatic experiences by the aid of shamanic trance and possession techniques borrowed from non-western religious traditions. Such techniques are alien to, and regarded as primitive by, western occultism. The cone-of-power work in Gardnerian-like covens is often formalized, stiff and short. People may be exhausted because they are in bad physical condition, but their state of mind, and the group's state of mind, does not necessarily have anything to do with ecstasy. The fact that this energy work is done differently in Reclaiming is one of the reasons for its success and why so many different people choose to be connected with Reclaiming. As priestess Macha says, "My experience is that Reclaiming people know how to work and raise energy like nobody else in the pagan communities." Those who don't like their emphasis on ecstasy disparagingly call Reclaiming the "Pentecostal Witches".

* * *

The Spiral Dancing in the evening's ritual begins when the chorus sings our prayers for the new year while we hold hands in a circle.

A year of beauty/Let it begin now
A year of plenty/Let it begin now
etc.
May all who hunger now be fed,
May we heal the soil that grows our bread . . .
May all the forms of love be blessed
and all the colors of our skin be praised
Like sisters, like brothers
May we take care of each other
etc.

The celebrants answer repeatedly, all through the dancing:

And let it begin with each step we take
And let it begin with each change we make
And let it begin with each chain we break
And let it begin every time we wake.

The difference between an ordinary circle dance and the spiral dance is that in the latter the circle is cut to make a head and a tail. Starhawk is the snake's head and the rest of us its body. We continue to sing, but we also start to move slowly with her to the left, the direction of death: two steps to the left, one step to the right. We dance toward the centre until the body of the snake is completely coiled. Then Starhawk starts to coil the body in the other direction, to the right, the direction of rebirth and life. As we dance out from the centre, we form two rows facing each other. Every single participant passes everybody else's face and eyes and breath very, very closely. This "seeing the other" is by most celebrants explained as the mystery of the ritual. They describe it with the words "complete happiness", "love", "peace", "ecstasy", "immersion", "communion". The dancing and singing go on and on, into the centre and out again, for maybe half an hour or more. In the beginning, people quickly get inspired and happy, but also tired and out of breath. But we continue, and continue, and it is first when we reach beyond the point of tiredness and the feeling of having lost control of legs and steps that the energy flows smoothly and starts to rise in a cone. The singing builds up in rhythm and loudness, in the same manner as in the other exercises described. The difference is the length of the energy work because the goal is not only an altered but also an ecstatic state of mind.

It then happens again. When we are coiled together, the song ends in a loud, synchronized o-o-m. We raise our arms, let go of the energy, and drop down on the floor. We lie in silence for a long time – until our heartbeats and breath are more normal. Priestess Ann tells me later that ecstasy to her is a physical sensation:

> Basically I let go of all resistance – to anything – and just trust. To trust is easier in a coven, but to let go is easier in a larger ritual. The physical sensation I feel is like tingling. I can feel the energy rushing, and then I

know that we are starting really to raise energy. Feeling my mind step into a trance, so I can sort of watch myself from the outside, that I am really trancing, really connected to the words that I am saying, to the energy that I am feeling. At the end there is complete exhaustion, and a true amelioration of whatever psychic condition I had before we started.

As we lie and sit down, exhausted and peaceful, the names of the newborn this year, in the community and among family and friends, are sung out loud by priest Kelly.

* * *

The ritual is closed in the ordinary fashion: the blessing of the food and drinks that sustain our lives in the form of a symbolic ritual meal; the thanksgiving to the Elements, the Gods, the Mighty Dead, the Ancestors and the Beloved Dead for their gracious participation.

Personal transformation?

In chapter 5, I anticipated a definition of ritualization as the intentional interaction between social bodies and a ritually defined and structured space in order to induce change or confirmation in the ritualists. In the case of Witchcraft, ritualization involves the creation of a magical person and a magical space for whom and in which death may shape-shift and be experienced as the inner truth and seed of life. This fluidity of life and death as if they were circles within circles may also be recognized in the symbolic structure of the Spiral Dance ritual.

The celebrants continually move in a centrifugal fashion inward, always inward. They do it when they go from ordinary consciousness to extraordinary and when they leave one worldview behind, in which death apparently is the last enemy, and enter another, deeper worldview, in which death is just a passage back to life. They also do it when they enter the womb of ritual space, from which they move on to the womb named the Island of the Dead, in which they may have their powers and selves transformed in the cauldron of visions, said to be the womb of the Goddess.

Many Witches, for whom the ritual works, use the word "immersion" when they later make an attempt to describe this inward-spiralling process. They tell me how important the anthropomorphic symbols of Goddess (associated with femaleness) and God (associated with maleness) are to understand this process, because no other symbolic representation can, in their opinion, convey a complete immersion as well as the sacredness of erotic love between woman and man. Some celebrants even claim that their own experience of a good ritual can be compared with "making love" with their partners, except that, in ritual, "it's all in the heart and on a psychic level. But it's that same feeling of being taken over a little bit when surrendering; its that same feel of complete happiness and fullness".

In fact, many informants feel that the sexual embrace of the lovers as a path to the sacred has been veiled in the Jewish and Christian religions of their formative years. This path to mystical union, and its accompanying sanctification of human sexuality and of the enveloped, gendered character of human life, may be hard to imagine without some form of bitheistic conceptualization of the divine. The monotheistic God of Judaism and Christianity, who is believed to be radically transcendent but also radically present and active in all aspects of human life and history, may easily be imagined to sanctify ecological interconnections between all natural beings, as well as activities such as befriending, peacemaking, forgiving, loving, creating, ordering, mothering, fathering, even conceiving the fetus in the womb (the power to bring forth new life). But as long as this godhead is lacking a female side, human sexuality cannot be sanctified as divine mimesis. For although God conceives the Son, and the Trinity is perceived to be related also through inner dance (trinitarian perichoresis), it is rather unusual to imagine or symbolize God as present in the embrace and lust *between* human lovers, in the lovemaking, in the orgasms. Even Jesus, who is said to have lived a full human life (and to have experienced friendship, hunger, temptation, pain, etc.), has not been commemorated with narratives of his knowledge of the embrace of a beloved, at least not in the official teaching. The only caresses his body apparently experienced were those of his mother (and father) and of the anointing hands of a woman.

Starhawk repeatedly points out that without symbolizing the divine as both Goddess and God, the human embrace will become peripheral to religious discourse, as will the positive reality of sexual difference, love and attraction. It will also rule out erotic imagery as appropriate means to convey the experience of "immersion" in ritual without being accused of profanizing the divine. The shadow side, however, to a bitheistic concept of divinity is the temptation to rank female and male powers and to transfer their hierarchies into social paradigms. Also, most lesbian and gay Witches do not feel compelled by the imagery of a god-man who embraces a goddess-woman or vice versa. Some are therefore deeply involved with developing a concept of a divine queer spirit instead, beyond the heterosexual symbolic matrix they feel is too dominant at Reclaiming's public rituals.[16]

But priestess Ann, who does not venerate queer spirits, has no emotional resistance to internalizing the teachings embedded in the divine embrace of Goddess and God. She is convinced that the gift of ritual is

> personal empowerment and a real love of differences between people. I love meeting in ritual and giving everybody space, whoever they are. Ritual basically helps me affirm life; it takes me right down to the deepest reasons why I live. It gets me in touch with my centre, my inner-core being. It is indeed very centreing and very grounding; it tends to open my heart. And I think that's the most basic definition of an affirming action. From there I think you act in a new and positive way.

As Goddess descended to the "Kingdom of Death" and restored the God back to life through merging, most Witches claim to merge their hearts when trancing and dancing in the Samhain ritual. They say they leave the ritual with a feeling of having reaffirmed their friendships, community and their own existential reasons for living. Despair and meaninglessness are declared as being transformed into hopes for a good life. This is their frame of reference when proclaiming ritual and ritualizing as a "method" to renew and regenerate contemporary culture: it is a potential tool for relinking with the divine and bonding with human fellows and the larger natural world.

However, all confirming judgements about specific rituals depend upon a first and primary agreement: that the actual ritual worked. So-called boring rituals renew and regenerate nothing. Witches' measurements for whether a ritual worked include experiential, emotional and intellectual standards. But the overall transformative aspects of ritual seem to be judged by what M. Rosaldo terms "embodied thought": that the subject can report having experienced the affectionate and internal movements described above on the basis of having been fully involved and of having "moved energy". This transformation from feeling separate to feeling temporarily joined, and returning to daily life with a feeling of meaning, purpose and vitality, is, of course, open to further interpretations. Is it caused by the Goddess (her gift/grace)? Is it caused by ritual itself (intrinsic to the indexicality of ritual and to the magical techniques used)? Or, is it triggered as a pure therapeutical effect from manipulating emotions and having a good time? Such possible interpretations are seldom discussed since the Goddess is regarded as final cause in any case, acting on the self either as internal being (other-than-deity) or as external relation (deity).[17]

*   *   *

In the above narrative I have attempted to show that ritualizing in Reclaiming is constituted by bodily acts such as breathing, moving, reading, chanting, dancing and imaginative journeying within the context of a worldview that weaves together Witchcraft mythology, esoteric philosophy and contemporary cultural thought. It is the totality of this process, not isolated elements, that has the ability to construct embodied experiences of merger and separation. Trance techniques borrowed from other cultures do not alone induce them. It is only when bodily movements and mental journeys are performed within the context of western, poetical language and imagery that age-old, shamanic techniques seem to "gain" their powers to deeply alter the consciousness and embodied thinking of western people. Whether these alterations are permanent, and for the good, can in reality only be decided by the people involved and their significant others.

Notes

1 Starhawk 1979a: 160. This is the Faery/Starhawk version of a myth that is used by all traditions of Witchcraft. The myth is not read in the Spiral Dance ritual but partly acted out "in trance" as a symbolic journey to the Kingdom of Death. Except for the womb imagery and the meeting with goddess and god, the categories sex/intercourse and the incestuous 'lover and son' relationship, central to the myth, are passed over in silence. The myth is also used in connection with the initiation ritual.

2 To some American Christians, and in particular to the Fundamentalists, Halloween is an improper, heathen tradition. At Halloween 1990, this resulted in a big confrontation in downtown San Francisco. TV evangelist Larry Lee arranged a crusade from his headquarters in Texas to San Francisco with 3,000 of his followers. They rented the gigantic Conference Hall by the Civic Centre, from which they spoke the last judgement over San Francisco, comparing it with Sodom and Gomorra. Larry Lee condemned the city of San Francisco as a devil's place, possessed by the evil demons of Homosexuality, Feminism, Divorce, Murder, New Age, Witchcraft, Anarchism, Social Welfare, Children's Rights, Sexual Freedom, Free Choice (of abortion), Liberation Theology, etc. He requested that his followers proclaim Holy War against this place of sin and degeneration and, if necessary, shed their blood, as their Lord Jesus once had done. Outside the Hall, armed police forces were protecting Larry Lee from attacks from about 500 furious citizens, of whom many were gay, alternativists and pagans, who had gathered in a spontaneous demonstration in the afternoon of 1 November. As the hours passed, the crowd got more and more angry, reckless and ironic. They confirmed Larry Lee's self-appointed self-importance when apparently identifying with the imagery of the prototype heathens of degenerate Rome, screaming: "*Give us the lions; kill the Christians*".

3 This tradition is a mixture of indigenous (pre-Christian) religiousness and a Mexican version of Catholicism.

4 This is information given in conversations with Professor Martin Ravndal Hauge at the Faculty of Theology in Oslo about the Israelite practice. According to Demetrios Delaveris in the Greek Orthodox Church in Oslo, orthodox believers can express the realities of their lives in the profane area, whereas the altar is placed in the holy area, where only priests can approach it. The altar table itself is a meeting place between male humans and God.

5 The notion "celebrants" is indigenous. It is Reclaiming's own name for the people who attend their rituals, used when they are writing manuscripts or speaking publicly.

6 The idea of the whole ritual being a womb, in which people are transformed, is quite common among Witches. The image of the womb is also used in the "Descent of the Goddess" referred to above. The mythical Island of the Dead, which we shall encounter further on, is also perceived as a womb, as is the cauldron of the Goddess, standing in its centre. A paradise in itself is like a womb: every condition is unchanging; everything is automatically being taken care of; the relationship between subject/acting and object/outcome is one of inseparability.

7 A grounding is never scripted. This one is taken from the 1989–manuscript, in which it is written to suggest for the reader how it can be done and what kind of imagery and words can actually be used. We can know for sure that Deborah never said exactly these words.

8 I do not describe this part of the ritual but refer the reader back to the detailed description of an ordinary Reclaiming ritual in chapter 5. "The Guardian Song" calls in the four elements.

9 Words taken from Starhawk 1987: 308.

10 This historical part of the litany is always the same, while the first, more updated part changes for every year.

11 We are now about halfway through the three-hour-long ritual.

12 From the myth where the Goddess descends to the Kingdom of Death, cited in full in chapter 5, n. 13.

13 This imagery is similar to that used in ancient and medieval utopian literature (cf. chapter 3).

14 A song called "Breaths" with lyrics by the Senegalese poet Birago Diop. The lyrics, important for the context, go: "*Listen more often to things than to beings . . . / 'Tis the ancestor's breath when the fire's voice is heard / 'Tis the ancestor's breath in the voice of the waters / Those who have died have never, never left / The dead are not under the earth / They are in the rustling trees . . . / They are in the wailing child . . .*"

15 Priest Timothy tells me later that the dancing at the Island of Apples is a dance-possession. The dead has no bodies, but this way they can dance and feast. He describes to me a worldview very similar to contemporary Zanzibari's (East Africa) as outlined by Kjersti Larsen in her PhD dissertation, "Where Humans and Spirits Meet. Incorporating Difference and Experiencing Otherness in Zanzibar Town" (Oslo 1995).

16 Since the mid-1990s, lesbian and gay Reclaiming Witches have organized a separate Witchcamp in the US that is open to all genders and people of queer spirit.

17 The Samhain ritual may also be read as a narrative that articulates Reclaiming Witches' worldview and discernments of the self and the sacred as such, independent of individual proofs of its truth. According to this interpretation, increased sensitivity in regard to imagination and emotionality is just an indication of increased ritual and narrative competence.

7 Women's mysteries

Creating a female symbolic order

The Reclaiming community is open to both women and men. Classes are taught to anybody who seriously wants to learn the path of the Goddess. Public rituals are planned and conducted by both genders. But, as described in previous chapters, Reclaiming also identifies explicitly with feminist assumptions that western culture is profoundly patriarchal and with feminist political strategies for the liberation of women and other oppressed people. As part of the process of creating an alternative social contract, they invent new symbolic universes and ritual acts that in particular aim at representing women's sociality, religiosity and sense of being in what they regard as new and liberating ways. But they also experiment with new lifestyles and sexual identities and challenge conventional gender roles on a deeply felt personal level:

> The feminist movement has prompted the culture as a whole to re-examine questions of maleness and femaleness. For the definitions are no longer working. They are oppressive to women and confining to men . . . . When we ask the questions "What is femaleness? What is maleness?" we are stating our willingness to change in ways that may seem frightening, for our conditioning to experience our gender in culturally determined ways runs very deep and in a primary way determines how we experience ourselves.
>
> (Starhawk 1989a:8)

In this citation, Starhawk argues in her nominalist fashion, as if male and female are solely human definitions that eventually have turned out to be oppressive and possessive metaphors (cf. chapter 4). To experience ourselves in new, liberating ways, we obviously need to break free from culturally determined gender roles and redefine sexual difference. The problem, however, is that Reclaiming is not only a feminist but a spiritual community as well, advocating goddess religion and magic as *the* new option for women (and men). When Starhawk explains why this tradition has opened a new possibility of "female identity" for women, her language and categories change. Now she emphasizes more than anything her experience of being allowed to see her own body as sacred, "in all its femaleness, its breasts, vulva, womb, and menstrual flow". She also feels permitted to see the wild power of nature as well as the intense pleasure of sexual intimacy as central paths to the sacred, "instead of being denied, denigrated or seen as peripheral". Furthermore, because the goddesses and gods are perceived not only as symbols but also as real channels of real power, Starhawk believes they can "open doorways for us into new dimensions of our possibilities" in the ongoing cultural transformation with which she is involved (Starhawk 1989a:2–8).

Even though Starhawk never loses sight of the fact that our experiences of gender are culturally determined, she hesitates to say that "sexual difference" is a social construction. In fact, she takes the position that "sex is the most basic of differences; we cannot become whole by pretending differences do not exist, or by denying either male or female" (Starhawk 1979a:27). For her feminism is, to a certain extent, determined by her magical worldview. As witnessed in the citations above, this worldview demands of her, so to speak, that she deduce sexual difference from the category of nature and correlate its conceptualizations to the category of the divine, which are both linked to a dialogical, androgynous Deep Self and experiences of essence: life-generating powers, energy as vital principle, divine substance. Furthermore, vital energy is said to be constituted as erotic and polar opposition between the two forces or principles "female" and "male".

The problem is that these principles, which flow in opposite but not opposed directions, and which *both* women and men are said to contain – otherwise they would not exist, are represented in her religious paradigm by two gendered symbols: Goddess and God.[1] Yet Starhawk underlines that Goddess and woman are not identical. Goddess does not symbolize women's qualities but the power to create, regardless of sex. God does not symbolize men's qualities but the "compost principle" in all life. In their different aspects, Goddess and God are apparently equally important and determinant in "the cycles of birth, growth, death, decay, and regeneration revealed in every aspect of a dynamic, conscious universe" (Starhawk 1989a:228).

But, although Starhawk is clear that the female and male principles should not be taken as a general pattern for individual female and male human beings, many Witches are not. And why should they be? Is not one of the reasons for reclaiming *Goddess,* the female genus for divinity, that to worship her is believed to empower women, strengthen their sense of Self, and redefine the values associated with femininity? We only need to look to the Reclaiming rituals to learn that gendered divine reality is a cosmic mimesis of gendered human reality, or the other way around: I have not yet experienced a case in which a man/male priest has entered the position of the priestess and personified the Goddess by "drawing down the moon" (although people tell me it may happen), and neither has a male Witch ever called himself Aphrodite.

To many Witches, Goddess and God are even perceived hierarchically: Goddess is taken to be primary because she is seen as giver of life; God is taken to be secondary because he represents that which is born. Their hierarchical relation is not restricted to the level of symbolic language, but regarded as a literal facts: Goddess is more than a symbol and has, in fact, revealed herself as primary, as creator and nurturer, being identical with the inherent vital principle of the human body, with spirit or Deep Self, to the extent that the inner self is "sexed". Women are therefore closer to the Goddess than are men. If these Witches also call themselves feminist, we must ask: why is this gyno-centric divine gender hierarchy ethically more advanced and liberating than Jewish and Christian androcentrism?

There is a constant tension in Reclaiming between the radical extremes of these viewpoints: Goddess as mystical symbol, equally important to women and men, versus Goddess as birthing, female lifeforce; gender as structuring and meaning-making metaphor versus sexual difference as ontological reality. In order to situate the Witches within a broader feminist landscape and better understand their *cosmic* version of feminism, I shall, for the purpose of this chapter, reduce and divide current feminism into three main schools: sexual equality (1), sexual polarity (2), and sexual difference (3) feminism. These schools agree that the very reason women as a social group are oppressed is that they differ from men. But they strongly disagree on what the difference consists of and how far it extends.

The sexual equality school agrees with (a certain reading of) Simone Beauvoir that "one is not born a woman, one becomes one". Both "woman" and "man" are socially constructed, as are the hierarchical binary oppositions associated with them in order to define "gender". In the Marxist dichotomy between biological and sociological, they choose the latter. The female body is not perceived as an existential situation or as entailing a deeper mystery; it represents merely the sign and site of oppression. In order to explain the representations and the images attached to the corporeal reality of the female, sexual equality feminists exclusively call upon history, social conditioning, and the binary structure of thinking (Braidotti 1989:96).[2]

The sexual polarity school, on the other hand, has chosen the opposite pole: the biological. It assumes that femaleness and maleness are congenital predispositions in the individual. Women's femininity is either set in singular opposition to masculinity, or perceived as constituted by a certain, reified mixing of female and male principles, energies, or even metaphysical substances, manifest in both women and men.[3] The more radical essentialists do not perceive of these principles as complementary at all, but, rather, as antagonistic. They attach ethics to biology and claim that femaleness is superior to maleness. There are a variety of branches of the sexual polarity school, but all of them are preoccupied with women's experiences as being radically different from those of men and as reservoirs of new, feminist politics.

The sexual difference school, mainly influenced by French philosophy and psychoanalysis, argues that sexual difference is an empirical fact universally but refuses to choose between simple, causal explanations, whether biological or sociological. Rather, the sexed body as the seat of difference is seen as the threshold of subjectivity: it is neither a fixed biological essence nor a historical entity, but an embodied situation and the point of intersection between the biological and the social. Thus, sexual difference is perceived as ontological, not as accidental, peripheral, or contingent upon socio-economic conditions (Braidotti 1989:101). This school agrees with the "equalists" that "woman" as defined in western culture is a confined social construction. In fact, we know nothing about her except as a complementary mirror-image of "man". But, instead of eliminating the meaning of sexual difference, these feminists claim the necessity of invoking she-who-is-not-yet-known (as well as "the he") by constructing a new sociality, a new cultural space in which otherness can come into being and unfold a real sexual difference.[4]

While the political aim of sexual equality feminists is to realize equal rights between women and men at all levels in (reformed) society, sexual polarity feminists aim at retrieving original complementarity through a strategy of reaffirmation of the feminine side, unmaking hierarchical notions of sexual polarity created by patriarchal culture. When it comes to fighting for equality in the cultural and economic order, sexual difference feminists agree with both schools. Luce Irigaray, who is a leading figure of the sexual difference school, argues that feminist politics must obtain a mimetic essentialist strategy in regard to "what exists" and return to women's community as a source for alternative politics, affirmation and invention of "that which exists not". She believes the tactical question in feminism today is how to strengthen the feminine side of the male–female dichotomy and the practical one is how to construct a horizontal ethical relationship between women (cf. Irigaray 1993a). To find answers, feminists must dare to get involved with the "hermeneutics of paradox." For example, "motherhood" is foundational to the patriarchal domination of women, while at the same time being one of the strongholds for female identity (Braidotti 1989:96). Irigaray suggests that women enter this paradoxical stance in order to reattend to and resymbolize the foundations and ethics of "love": the maternal body as the site of origin, the relationship between mother and daughter, as well as motherhood itself.

Irigaray holds the mother–daughter dyad to be *the* prototype of female relations. It is therefore pertinent that women attend to and symbolize this vertical relationship in "externally located and durable representations" if they shall succeed in their attempts to create horizontal relationships as "sisters". She argues that the mother–daughter prototype is non-symbolized in any profound and positive sense in western culture – except in the "Demeter and Persephone"[5] myth – and that this is an urgent problem if woman is ever to separate from "mother" and achieve an ontological status as a *real* other in western society (Whitford 1989:120). Irigaray's feminist programme implies nothing less than the creation of a female sociality, a female genealogy, a female symbolic and a female contract in which women may *represent* their difference (also between themselves), whether in language or in another social form, such as a religion.

Although individual Reclaiming Witches may adhere to any of these feminist schools and even mix positions in complete confusion, I find that Irigaray's visionary, elemental feminism gives the best framework to understand the sexual politics underpinning "cosmic" feminism and the path of the Goddess: it recognizes the primacy of the bodily, material roots of subjectivity and of the enveloped, embodied character of the spiritual self. In chapter 4, I discussed the importance of applying a sign theory to Witches' ethno-hermeneutics that could include, instead of reduce, the acclaimed indexicality of magical religion: that it is not purely a system of meaning, but also a technology to interact with the elemental world. This nonreductive argument is also valid in regard to Witches' acclaimed indexicality of the magical person: as twice born, with a sacred body and divine self. When listening to inner, Deep Self, one may hear the voice of a culturally conditioned person. But, as Witches insist, one may also hear the voice of the Goddess. When perceiving the human body, one may see a culturally gendered and determined person. But one may also see the body of the Goddess, manifesting as one of the two ontological principles (female and male), or as an interesting combination of the two (queer or inter-sex).

A main objective of this chapter is thus to describe how Reclaiming Witches define "woman" and the differences between "woman" and "man", thereby making relevant among themselves a search for women's spirituality as something different from men's. For although men and women work jointly together in all community tasks and on most ritual occasions, both parties recognize that the other – through birth and constitution – is part of women and men's "mysteries". "Mysteries" refer primarily to bodily life cycles and are usually celebrated in various rites of passage connected to childbirth, puberty, menopause, etc. Gender-segregated circles, and in particular those of women, are very important in Reclaiming Witches' communal and spiritual life, although they do not necessarily appear so from the outside, from Reclaiming's more public scene. When I asked Catherine, one of my informants, what constitutes sexual difference, and what makes it so urgent to Reclaiming women to regularly move in and out of a "room of their own", she gave an answer that is quite representative:

> Obviously, it is the experience of pregnancy and birth. This is not culturally relative; it is absolute. How is this relevant to "women's spirituality" as differentiated from "men's spirituality"? I think it is this: we are all, both men and women, born "alone," and we die "alone." These are the most basic, fundamental phenomena of the human experience. What they teach us is our aloneness in the universe. Yet, women, and only women, also give birth, and that experience is the next most primal event of the human experience that a person can have. And that experience teaches us, profoundly and preconsciously, about our connectedness. The moment and aftermath of delivery is, in spite of the pain and suffering, also an event of overwhelming joy, even ecstasy. It is a body/mind/spirit event that intertwines self/other/pain/joy. Yet at the same time, the woman giving birth is face to face with death, or at least with "not-life" because she is, at that time, in the gateway between the worlds. In my

coven we say that Goddess is this gateway. So there is a direct experience of the sacredness of life which only otherwise comes when a person, man or woman, actually faces his or her own death.

When women create religious paradigms, seeking the deepest, or highest, truth, we somehow conceive of the most holy, the most sacred images as ones of connection and interdependence. Conception *is* connection; for a woman to conceive means that another human being grows from within her body. Thus "women's religion" is inevitably and essentially about connection and interdependence. I think this has deep psychological roots. I think women and men experience and therefore understand reality, i.e., everything from the human experience to the nature of the universe, in profoundly different ways. It also informs our search for spiritual fulfillment differently. How and whether women's spirituality is apparent in a particular culture, that is, how it manifests, is another matter.

According to Catherine, the whole idea of religion and of religious ritual as a resymbolization of the existential dilemma between separation and connection, independence and interdependence, and its emphasis on the importance of repeated experiences of merger, is really a description of women's spirituality. We may also note that she does not thematize merger *with* "the most holy", but points out that experiences of connection and interdependence in ordinary human life are most sacred images of divine reality.

Since I only have access to women's circles, I shall concentrate on the attempts in Reclaiming to define and give form to a women's spirituality, or in Irigaray's terminology, to a female symbolic order. This implies how they depict and experience the *mysteries* of women's bodies, female friendship, mother–daugther genealogies, and divine guidance in daily life affairs, and how they construct horizontal relationships among themselves. To a certain extent I will also discuss how essentialism and other feminisms are manifested and contested and question the women's apparent success: have they managed to create a cultural space in which "real" sexual differences are brought forth, or do they merely repeat a sexualized cultural discourse on the binarity of being?

The ethnographic description, which is the empirical basis for the discussions, will cover how a group of women explored "women's mysteries" in a Reclaiming class called "Women's Magic", the coven Gossip that grew out of this class, and how the coveners have bonded since then – including their performance of the puberty rite called "first blood" for a young girl (already partially described in chapter 1). In the final part of this chapter, I shall discuss some implications for Reclaiming's sexual politics and for men's position in the community.

I have chosen the Gossip women and their social network mainly for practical reasons: since I also happened to be in the "Women's Magic" class, I was a member of Gossip from the very beginning (1984). I also choose them because they are representative of the community and of people associating with it. The Gossip women are highly educated, participate in several lifestyles and often confess to different opinions. Some of them are very active, either in the Reclaiming Collective or in the community, and hold a lot of personal power and influence. Others are nonactive and express a strong dislike for Reclaiming as community, although they have embraced its teachings and ritual practices as their personal worldview. Another striking trait of the group, at least in its initial phase, was the mixture of sexual identities (heterosexuals, bisexuals and lesbians), the practice of nonmonogamy and intense political activism.[6] During the course of time some of these traits have changed or have become less dominant. They have, however, always added to the complexity of viewpoints in the group.

Women's bodies as sacred space

When I was introduced to Reclaiming in the fall of 1984, it was through the "Women's Magic" class, taught by Dora and Deadly. Their goals for the class were stated in the *Reclaiming Newsletter* as "bringing magical change into our daily lives using ritual, group work and our magical tools. Invoking the Triple Moon Goddess and the Earth Goddess, asking Her inspiration for empowerment as we explore Women's Mysteries." When designing the class, Dora and Deadly had been inspired by Z. Budapest, who represents a Dianic, lesbian-separatist brand of Witchcraft. Dora had recently attended a Dianic ritual and liked Budapest's focus on the female body and its link to divine, lunar cycles. She felt that it represented a powerful aspect of feminism, undercommunicated in the Reclaiming community out of fear of offending the men and the anarchist equalist ideology.

Another source for Dora and Deadly's associative connection between the Goddess, moon and female body cycles is Esther Harding's *Women's Mysteries – Ancient and Modern*. This book was first published in English in 1955 and had a major influence on feminist Witchcraft and goddess spirituality in the 1970s. Harding's essentialist thesis is that patriarchy is recognizable by a shift from feminine moon-worship to a masculine sun-cult: "In the days of moon worship, religion was concerned with . . . the worship of the creative and fecund powers of nature and of wisdom that lies inherent in instinct and in the at-one-ness with natural law. But the worship of the sun is the worship of that which overcomes nature" (Harding 1971(1955):31). Her medicine for modern women is to return to ancient myths, symbols and rituals in which she believes people celebrated the feminine principle and worshipped the "moon goddesses".

The "Women's Magic" class met every Monday night for six weeks at Dora and Deadly's collective household in the Mission district and included nine women (with me). Susan (30), Artemis (35) and Ruth (38) (introduced in chapter 3) already belonged to the Reclaiming community and had taken several classes. They were anarchists and active in the Direct Action community. Susan and Artemis lived in the same anarchist household and were the mothers to two small children. Ruth lived in a collective and had two teenage sons. Their intention in joining the class was to learn from Dora – whom they admired for her magical skills – and to meet other women with whom they hoped they could form a coven. Anna (38), the mother of two girls, had recently been introduced to Witchcraft through a weekend workshop with Starhawk at Esalen. At the time she was working her way into Reclaiming socially through a love affair with one of the long-term teachers. Therefore, she already knew Dora, who was a friend of her lover. Susan, Artemis, Ruth and Anna were bisexual and lived in nonmonogamous relationships – Anna within the framework of a nuclear family. Ruth and Anna had finished their Masters in Social Science and had prestigious, well-paid jobs. Susan and Artemis were craftswomen, working to establish the earlier described Compost Ranch in Sonoma County.

Nell (20), Megan (31), Lisa (26), Judith (29) and I (28) had no previous connection to anybody in the class, and when we undertook the transition from class to coven, Megan, Lisa and Judith decided not to join. Megan was a lesbian plumber and experienced with Dianic Witchcraft, which was being taught in the East Bay area by Z. Budapest. Nell, Lisa and Judith were heterosexual. Judith was a full-time political activist with affiliations with the Democrats, while Lisa was a nonpolitical Zen Buddhist. Nell was raised as a feminist by her liberal, agnostic parents and had recently discovered religious feminism, such as Witchcraft, through reading. Her plan for Graduate school was a PhD in Social Anthropology.

*   *   *

We are gathered at Dora and Deadly's collective household for our first class. We sit, drinking tea, in a circle in a cosy living room, lit by candles. The atmosphere is relaxed and informal, and Dora invites us to do check-in. Since Ruth, Susan and Artemis are friends with Dora, they go first and mark a level of sharing that is quite intimate, later copied by the others following her. In contrast to what was expected in the "Elements" class (cf. chapter 5), we not only inform each other briefly about our energy level right now but tell life stories, as if we are a regular "consciousness-raising" group in the women's movement. We hear about domestic partners, kids, lovers, jobs, struggles with jealousy, demanding mothers, neglect, self-image and fear. Check-in lasts for about an hour and a half and becomes a ritual in itself. For every new gathering we add bits and pieces to our individual life stories, and deepen the level of intimacy in the group. Parallel to this deepening of psychic and emotional sharing, some of the women also strip off their clothes and reveal more and more of their physical bodies. This is done without any comment, or "because it is so hot in here". The sweater goes at the first Monday meeting; the trousers at the second; bra, watch and glasses at the third – until most of them are completely naked, showing an attitude of pride about thick thighs, scars and signs from having given birth, sagging breasts and bulging bellies. A few of the more shy women are inspired by these "exhibitionists" to let go of *some of* their clothes, while a couple of us don't even loosen up a belt – until it is explicitly asked for as part of the blood ritual (see below).

Just like in the "Elements" class, the teaching takes place within the framework of ritual. After check-in, these undressed, half-dressed and fully dressed women perform all the formal proceedings of a Reclaiming ritual. We cast the circle, breathe as a Tree of Life, purify with salt and water, call the elements and the Goddess. Dora and Deadly have chosen goddesses from around the world whom they think fit the purpose of their teaching. Male deities are not invoked; neither is the esoteric gender polarity associated with the elements used.

As part of teaching the first evening, Dora and Deadly want us to tell what we associate with the notion "women's mysteries". After some discussion, a list is made. All the associations are characterized by an effort to distinguish women from men by means of certain qualities believed to be essential and innate to female beings. The women's essentialist strategy is simply to invert maleness as cultural norm and claim women's specialness and superiority instead – first of all within the field of basic life-and-death processes. Some of the meanings associated with "women's mysteries" are:

> *Women are closer to death than men since they often care for dying people and talk to the dead*
> (men induce death through killing but are distant in the process of natural death).[7]

> *Women give birth to new life, experience pregnancy and are deeply linked to future generations*
> (exclusive for women; men cannot give birth).

> *Women's bodies are related to natural, changing cycles such as the phases of the moon*
> (exclusive for women; men's bodies do not mirror natural cycles).

> *Women's menstruation and blood are related to the elements of water (emotion) and earth (body)*
> (exclusive for women; men represent more air (mind) and fire (spirit)).

> *Women's menopause represents a new change in the body and in her emotional state of mind*
> (exclusive for women; male bodies have no menopause).

> *Women have a capacity for transformation and channelling, in the birth process and through work*
> (similarity between channelling and birth-giving capacity).

> *Women are shape-shifters and creators and have the skills to let go of their "creations"*
> (similarity between letting-go and birth-giving capacity).

Women's sexuality is floating and their orgasms slow and long lasting
(men's sexuality is penetrating, reaches its climax fast).

Women have intimate communities where they love and support each other and join their "powers"
(men's community and power are more oriented toward status than intimacy).

Women's wisdom is gained through embodied experiences of change and transformation
(men value the wisdom of the mind (secondary), not the wisdom of the body (primary)).

*   *   *

At this point, I am deeply disturbed and disappointed about the course and content of this class. When I decided to study Reclaiming Witchcraft for my academic research and applied for grants to travel all the way to San Francisco, it came from a fascination with Starhawk's visionary writings (and Luce Irigaray's philosophy). Although Starhawk can also stumble in static, essentialist notions, I had never read anything so mindless as these women's statements about the so-called female nature. Did they really believe this, that women according to "their nature" were emotional and nurturing while men were brainy? Had they never experienced evil and abuse from non empathic, fiery women? Didn't they think women were co-responsible for, and not only victims of, the misery of the world? When I carefully tried to argue that their notions about essential womanhood were nothing but romantic, idealized constructions, nobody really cared to listen. They just stared at me, until Ruth (one of the social scientists 10 years older than me) said in a friendly tone: "We know, it's just that it's not relevant right now."

This was probably my first lesson in what Irigaray could have meant when suggesting that women, for tactical reasons, would benefit from strengthening the feminine side of the culturally defined male–female dichotomy. But it took some years for me to apprehend.[8] I continued to have similar reactions, not least when participating in rituals in which the Goddess was invoked by young women imitating ballerinas or pin-ups from men's magazines. When I asked the Reclaiming elders how they could let this happen, I did not really get a "good" answer until Aradia took me aside:

Yes, you are right, these images of Goddess are politically incorrect and very silly. And if we wanted our rituals to be nice and clean and theologically consistent, we would of course dismiss these young women right away, and perform all ritual acts ourselves. Instead we choose to involve as many as possible in the public rituals, no matter how far they have come in regard to personal development or theoretical insight, and just use occasions like these to practice the very difficult art of tolerating those not yet illumined by the latest fad in feminist theory, which really means to accept people for who they are and where they are.

Her irony helped me finally get the point: people need affirmation and acceptance for "what is" before they can change toward "what is not yet".

*   *   *

Dora and Deadly obviously share Aradia's attitude and do not comment, correct or add to the associations listed above. Instead they explain that the purpose of the class is to join in a common journey wherein we will learn to appreciate ourselves as women, to honour our bodies as sacred and our procreativity as divine ("woman" is the stuff out of which all people are made) and to stop shaming ourselves for bleeding and being "restricted" by natural cycles. They want us to exchange shame for pride, the feeling of restriction for privilege, and to see a link between the western, cultural degradation of women's bodily constitution and the history of ecological exploitation and misogyny. They believe the above is all based on a moral hierarchy made between culture and nature, between men and women. According to Dora and Deadly, natural human conditions, like bodily constitution, are neither moral nor immoral; they are simply facts of creation, of coming-into-being from the original birth union, and therefore sacred. Consequently, they are pleased to see how the women in the class already feel free to be naked and "unveiled". They hope that when the course is over, we will feel empowered as women and walk our lives with a new pride – having learned that we all are living manifestations of the Goddess. Later in this class we shall learn how to return to the "cave of the mothers" and bring about embodied memories of ourselves as newly born, as foetuses, as unborn. We shall remember first experiences of masturbation and find out how old we were when becoming aware of "having a gender". We shall also celebrate female ancestors and political heroines, dress up in red and tell our experiences of first menstruation.

After Dora's lecture, we are asked to partake in an exercise in which we lie down in a circle and look into a mirror in the centre. The mirror's reflection represents the Goddess, and when we see ourselves, we supposedly see her. A drum beat takes us into a light trance. In this state of mind, we are asked to turn the mirror into divine water. When we look into our own/her eyes in the water we connect what we just named "women's mysteries" with their source: the Goddess.

As part of the meditation we may ask the Goddess/Deep Self for specific gifts. The women ask for self-love, self-acceptance and self-pride, for strength and determination in their jobs, for strength to be honest, for creativity and self-discipline. Their requests are offered as prayers but often lack the initial communication to another person typical in the formula "Dear God, please give me . . ." The prayers may instead be phrased as: "I need strength, and I open myself for strength right now."

A delayed blood-rite for adult women

In the fourth class with Deadly and Dora, we tell first menstruation stories, and in the fifth we perform a delayed "first blood" ritual for ourselves. We are told that the ritual will take place in a "red atmosphere" in terms of decorations, food and drinks, and it is expected that we are nude during its performance. Two women find this to be "too much" and decide not to come. Their absence is acknowledged by the other women, but not commented upon. Since nudity is a key symbol this evening, it needs introduction.

Ritual nudity is of Gardnerian heritage. Symbolically, it is related to the utopian goals of intimacy and peace that Gardner suggested for the life and work of a coven, labelled "perfect love and perfect trust". This statement is also a password used in the secret initiation ritual, denoting the dual character of this social act: "love" refers to the level of friendship and mutual affection that is required from initiators and initiates in order to successfully perform the ritual; "trust" refers to the attitude of being willing to give up one's will and submit oneself to the will of another person (the initiator's) and undergo whatever this secret ritual process demands. This submissive act requires deep trust that the other's will is a good will. Love and trust are key notions to describe the existential level of being promised to those who dare to enter a magical circle. Ideally, these notions also express the Witches' devotional attitude toward the Goddess. Nudity is, consequently, the material, bodily, ritualized symbol of this attitude, which, in a ritual context, is associated with pride, vulnerability, sensuality, honesty, and equality, as well as with the remembrance of how human life is brought into the world: as a naked body, through a naked body. Ritual nudity symbolizes that the participants, at a deep level, are one body, one being, one member, as it symbolizes the innocence of beginnings, of conversions, of being born again.

We must go back to medieval Europe to find accepted expressions of religious, ritualized nudity in western culture. According to Caroline W. Bynum, nudity was then a typical expression of symbolic reversal. It was the property of holy or pious men (not women) and was, on a symbolic level, linked with imagery of poverty, weakness and femaleness.[9] Witchcraft contests this tradition by equating femaleness with strength and nudity with pride, making associative links to nudity that are experienced to be continuous with the "natural" and the "ordinary". And, in the context of Witches' naturalism, a naked *man's* body doesn't symbolize femaleness, but masculine pride, vulnerability, etc., as listed above. Nevertheless, ritual nudity is, for many obvious reasons, not common in Reclaiming's mixed covens and classes, and certainly not in public rituals. The effect it has when actually being used in the "Women's Magic" class is adding "depth and daring".

After casting the circle and calling the directions, we form a circle while standing with our arms around each other. Deadly tells a story about the first paradise – or the story about a girl growing up – going roughly like this:[10]

> *Once upon a time all women lived together on one island, and all the men on another island. The women were like sisters and lived together in peace and love. Mother Moon herself taught them all they needed to know. One day a man arrived at the island in his boat. They had never seen men before, but invited him to live with them and shared with him all that they knew. He liked it and was happy with the women for a long time. After a while he started to miss his brothers and asked the women to come with him and join a community with both women and men. The women asked why, and what the men had to offer them. For the first time there were disagreements between the women. Somebody wanted to go, while others found the suggestion odd. Then the Moon Goddess showed her face, and said: "I have always known that this would happen, that a time would come when you who are sisters would be separated. But to help you remember your origins and common roots, you shall bleed once a month. Even though you choose different lives, you shall always know and remember that you are sisters. And you shall celebrate the differences between you." The women then celebrated the first blood-ritual ever, and never before had the moon been shining so white and silvery.*

Deadly gives no interpretation of "the myth", and we respond by calling in the Moon Goddess, "*Holy maiden huntress/Artemis, Artemis/New Moon, come to us.*" The chant goes on for a while, and then we declare her presence. We kiss the woman next to us and tell her, "*Thou art Goddess.*" It is time for magical work, the proper celebration of our blood. We start to sing as we walk in a long procession to the bathroom,

Power of blood, rain from the Dark Moon
Power of life and death, flow from our wombs.

We continue to sing, while each one of us is put into the bathtub and watered with a red, warm liquid that Dora pours all over our naked bodies. The liquid is made of three different herbs, including hibiscus, and symbolizes blood. The bathtub is beautifully decorated with flowers, herbs and incense. Before being "baptized" we stand in the bathtub and declare out loud a wish for ourselves, witnessed by the others.

After the bath ceremony, we return to the living room. We form a circle, and Dora brings out a jar with red ochre. She kneels down in front of Susan and paints red ochre on the area between her navel and her pubic hair while saying, "*This is the blood that brings renewal. This is the blood that brings sustenance. This is the blood that brings life.*" Then Susan receives the jar to anoint "the womb" of the woman next to her. The procedure goes on until everybody has had her womb, including her genitals, symbolically sanctified with red ochre.

Now is the time to tell stories or read poems, anything connected with menstruation. We tell each other about menstrual cramps and emotional turbulence when bleeding, we give advice and Nell, who has brought white fabrics, shows us how to make our own sanitary pads. The round is ended with Dora telling the story about Nicole and her "first blood" ritual. Nicole, whom we met in chapter 1, was the first girl in the community to have a menstruation ritual *for real* and, in 1984, the only one. Dora tells us how they did it. This is a very moving story which in particular interests Anna, who will be the first among the women present to have teenage daughters.

In spite of different sexual identities, lifestyles and values, and regardless of whether we have experienced childbirth, we have bonded as a common, naked body and, for now, defined "woman": she is a being who bleeds monthly.

Coven life: perfect love and perfect trust

Judith, Megan and Lisa felt overwhelmed with nudity, the demand for intimacy and the untraditional lifestyles represented by a majority of the women in the class, and decided not to partake in the transition from class to coven. But the other women, Anna, Susan, Artemis, Ruth and Nell, were enthusiastic – both with the class and each other – and decided to form a coven. With Artemis's friend Tanya, who joined at this point, and myself, the group counted seven women. The coven constituted itself in November 1984 and has met regularly every month since. Seventeen years later (in 2001) it includes exactly the same women, even though some have been gone for periods of time due to travelling and "temporary" residence outside the San Francisco area. Susan and Artemis have continued to come to coven meetings even after moving to the Compost Ranch in Sonoma. I am on a life-long leave of absence, but was included again in Gossip when I returned from Norway to do regular fieldwork, starting in November 1988.

Every coven has its individual characteristics. What marks Gossip is: (1) stability: no change of people; (2) multigenerationalism: differences in age ranged between 20 and 38 years in 1984; (3) nondogmatism: strong anarchist bent; (4) nonelaborate rituals: simple magic focused on supporting daily life activities and turmoil; (5) emotional intimacy and support: check-in as an independent, ongoing ritual element; (6) emphasis on sexual identity: affirming interest in nonmonogamy and bisexuality; (7) sensuality: emphasis on body celebration, nakedness, food, gossip, joking relations, and "having a good time"; (8) a certain moral relativism: strong impact from the social sciences and an academic way of thinking; and finally (9) low profile on marking opinions: avoidance of intellectual arguing, standpoint-taking and confrontation of differences and disagreements.

Some of these characteristics were already initiated in class and continued to have an impact as the coven developed its own style. The heritage from class is obvious in the areas that I have called (5) emotional intimacy and support, (6) emphasis on sexual identity and (7) sensuality. The gossip element was not introduced in class but was added by Ruth, Anna and Nell, who have picked up the supposedly positive social importance of gossip from their comparative cultural studies in the social sciences. Ruth, especially, firmly believes that gossip is the social glue in small-scale societies, including both a caring for other people, sharing of information across group membership and social control of potential rule-breakers. One of her friends wrote an article about the topic in the *Reclaiming Newsletter*, stating that

> Gossip serves as an opportunity to mirror the events in our lives by the reactions of others . . . . Gossip helps to establish "norms" of behaviours. By circulating certain positive or negative information about individuals or situations, communities sanction or condemn these behaviours . . . . Don't cease feasting and gossiping, just be more conscious of its power.[11]

The gossip-and-food element has become a strong identity for the coven, and from early on the women for fun chose it as their slogan, "*Gossip now, gossip later, never cease feasting*".

Stability is another important feature of the coven. Stability is the result of a highly developed sensitivity to *not* confronting differences and disagreements, *not* "breaking" into the interior person but instead encouraging the skills of active listening. A focus on discussions and disagreements, or a demand for "complete honesty", or for "political correctness", will tend to split a group. The elders of the coven, Ruth and Anna, have especially represented this attitude with active support from Susan and Artemis.

Backing off from too much social interaction is also a strategy to keep the coven intact. This avoidance is, of course, relative as long as Anna, Ruth, Susan and Artemis are active in the broader Reclaiming community and thus meet regularly on various social occasions, from political meetings and actions to community rituals. Nell and Tanya only attend public rituals. They do not identify themselves as belonging to the Reclaiming community, although they are members of a Reclaiming coven. In any event, the goal for Witches' coven life stated above, is to experience "perfect love and perfect trust". This goal seems almost unobtainable in real life. Its modified version in Gossip can be summarized as "respect for your sister's identity and selfhood". Learning and practising respect within the frameworks of ritualized sisterhood obviously involve abstinence from too much social interaction outside coven life, as well as abstinence from opinionated discussions and moral judgement, and from the urge to fix or correct other people's lives. It involves, in other words, a refusal to reenact the vertical and moralistic mother–daughter prototype in our culture and its unclear distinctions between self and other. This, however, applies only to the sociality of ordinary consciousness: in ritual space, Gossip women merge as one unified "self", again and again.

Another reason that Gossip and other Reclaiming covens are of a relatively long-lasting character is that the focus for coven rituals is always the joys and sorrows of ordinary, daily life. The coveners work together on behalf of themselves and not on behalf of abstract ideological/political goals or out of an obligation to ritualize mythical narratives. The weakness of ideological rituals in creating stability in small groups is that political climates and the "good cause" always change. The weakness of only ritualizing foundational myths is the implicit demand to believe in the basic narrative of the myth. But, faith in myth is always in danger of turning into a loss of faith in myth, and if such happens, it may split a small circle. To ritualize ordinary life, however, is to interpret the here-and-now within the context of a simple spiritual framework. This ritualizing strategy is relatively more stable because it is experienced as more adventurous and more true. It is nonrepetitive and nonpredictable, and its actuality and closeness to individual fate deeply engage the people involved.[12]

A last important feature that has contributed to Gossip's success, is the women's growing distaste for elaborate rituals and occult paraphernalia. During the first years of coven life, a coven ritual was always well prepared by one or two of its members. They would prepare the room, including ritual equipment, in proper colours, propose a ritual theme, and have a planned outline for how the ritual should proceed to work the theme. As the years have passed, the ritual structure has become more and more relaxed. Today, they do not agree upon the ritual theme or its procedure until after check-in. Then is chosen a theme that is related to what is actually going on in one of the women's lives. Maybe she needs physical or emotional healing, strength, clarity, etc. When a theme is chosen, the women in Gossip perform their magic without any ritual tools and artifacts at all, except maybe candles if it is dark and flowers to make the room pretty. They only bring to circle their bodies and their voices, sometimes also a drum. Chanting, energy work, trances, laying on of hands, spontaneous words, sounds and movements – these are their modes of doing magic. But, even though they no longer use the Witches' tools or symbolic pillars of correspondence, they still use the structure and symbolism of the basic ritual outline, as well as the mythological imagery of the tradition when doing trances. And though there are no altars in the room and no altar objects, they still cast the circle, call the elements and the Goddess.

The coven Gossip has also changed vocabulary over time to designate its internal changes regarding rituals. When they did ritual the "proper way" as learned in class and observed in public rituals (well planned, with tools, etc.), the women talked about "having circle". Today, when they ritualize solely to cope with existential matters in individual women's lives, they call their gatherings "doing magic." The Gossip women are conscious and proud of this change. One of the first things Anna told me about when I returned to San Francisco in 1988 was the changes I would see when joining the coven again:

> The circle has matured since you left. Now we move energy intuitively, with no words at all. And when check-in is done, we just know what to

do and how. Probably because we are more sure about ourselves, and really know the kernel in what we are doing. As you know, nobody likes structure – except me. Can you believe it, I am the most conservative in the group! The good thing, though, is that we experiment with the form constantly, and do not feel restricted to the "right way". You will soon see it for yourself.

The other side to this change is that none of these anarchist, "rebellious" women has asked for formal initiation or actively pursued this particular path of the goddess, except two (one being me; see the Introduction). To some of the older, initiated Witches in the community, this is Gossip's weakness, keeping it away from real magical growth. But this is a dubious opinion, since no other covens in the community (to my knowledge) have managed to stay together in love and trust for 17 years.

Half a year later I interviewed my circle sisters individually and asked them what the coven meant to them. Susan had no doubts, declaring:

> The circle probably rates as the most important thing in my life – it really does. It is almost as if Frank [her partner] could leave, and Minerva [her lover] could leave, and if I still have the circle then I'll be OK. I get so much healing out of coming together with these particular women. The magic that happened between us in the beginning has lasted throughout, and the transformation of my problems with jealousy would not have happened without the coven.

Anna, who at the time had been betrayed by her lover, was grieving. She took some days off work, called me, and together we went to visit Susan and Artemis in Sonoma. We circled together, listened to her, held her when she cried – and within hours she expressed that "her spirit was returning". Later that evening she explained to some other women what a coven was like:

> We can do magic for anything, personal or political stuff. But most of all, we love each other and are always there for each other. Men and women lovers come and go, children come and go, but we never leave. We practice the magic of love. You know, the whole issue of perfect love and perfect trust in Witchcraft. There is something totally unobtainable about it, and also there is something to it.

Nell is the youngest in the coven, eighteen years younger than Ruth and Anna. She emphasized her process from being a kind of outsider to becoming a full member:

> For a very long time I felt I didn't know the other women that well. At some point I was not sure what I was doing there. But something still kept me going and I think it was really enjoying hearing about other

women's lives – women who were very different from me, and much older. I have learned a lot from this, and in important situations Ruth and Anna have been my role models. Now I feel that the primary focus is not the magic we do or don't, but my close relationship with and love for the women in circle. My magic has also changed. I don't do spells anymore. Instead of asking "my will be done" I ask to be on "the right path". My experience is that I don't always know what is best for me. To put a lot of energy into something that may turn out "wrong" is not very meaningful.

To Tanya and Artemis, the coven was important because they felt accepted and included as who they are. Over time, they had been given challenges from the other women that helped each of them to grow. Ruth had, since day one, been more intrigued by check-ins and emotional bonding than by trances and spells:

> For years we have shared a spiritual path and confessed our lives without being judged. That in itself creates bonding and love. If I am sick, depressed or broke, the first thing I'll do is to call my circle-sisters, and not my other friends. And I know they'll be there, and that they can help me.

All the women in Gossip were sure they could never have developed this kind of love and trust for each other in a mixed group of both women and men. This is a common experience among Reclaiming women, often explained with reference to the sexual tensions/attractions that always seem to show up in mixed groups and that, over time, tend to split them. However, this is not an argument to explain the social relations within Gossip since a minority in this coven are heterosexuals, whereas the others are bisexuals and lesbians. The potential for sexual tension/attraction has therefore not been ruled out. One probability is that the group is merely manifesting a general ethical potential present within any community of women, almost as if love and trust are the "real secrecy" of womanhood when undistorted by socialization, male dominance and patriarchal society. Another (and more likely) probability is that Anna and Ruth's cultural strategy ("active listening, no arguing") represents the true magic of the group.

Interesting, so far, is the fact that change of sexual *identity* from bisexual to heterosexual or lesbian has not been celebrated or ritualized – neither in Gossip nor in the larger Reclaiming community – although it usually involves a major change in a woman's life, not least if she has children. Choice of sexual *partner*, on the other hand, qualifies for extensive ritual celebrations. Is the fact that transformations of sexual identity are not celebrated or made occasions for ritual reflection a sign that the Goddess, after all, is not connected to the sensuality of human sexual activity, only to sexuality as a general *idea*? Or is it simply that sexual identity is seen as an ideological preference, as a disembodied, rational, free choice, which can be done over and over again, limited only by the ideal options of modernity and not by any innate bodily dispositions or desires?

Such questions are seldom raised in Reclaiming community, and never in Gossip. Thus, the emphasis on blood as the basic commonality of womanhood, rather than on women's sexuality or procreative abilities – which might otherwise be expected from people confessing an erotic worldview and a Goddess who is continually birthing – may be regarded partly as an emic statement that genderedness, after all, is more important than sexual identity, partly as a strategy to avoid complicated reasoning. From an analytical stance, however, women's blood is nothing but a metonymic representative for the totality of women's bodies, including what is seen as its anatomical, libidinal, procreational, mental, psychological and emotional features.

Women's "first blood" and feminism

When Gossip had existed for four years, Anna's daughter Sonia turned thirteen. She soon started to bleed and a circle of women performed a "first blood" ritual for her and with her. One purpose of such a modernist rite of passage is to reverse the mainly negative connotations of women's menstrual flux in western culture. Furthermore, to revalue menstruation is an attempt to revalue the female body, the female being, and female sociality, as well as the female genealogies of mothers and daughters. Before discussing Sonia's "first blood" ritual, let us briefly look at the ideological reasoning legitimizing both this ritual and the adult imitative counterpart performed in Dora and Deadly's class.

When constructing Sonia's ritual, the women were inspired by menstruation narratives of tribal cultures. Buckley and Gottlieb (1988) argue that in tribal societies menstrual blood is usually regarded as a primal substance infused with plural and ambiguous meanings. Depending on the context, it is seen both as a polluting, malignant force and as a purifying life-force. A menstruating woman is thus powerful and can affect nature positively as well as negatively. As life-force, menstrual blood is viewed as a manifestation of creative power, particularly in the sense of fertility. The use of menstrual blood both in fertility rituals and in love charms is widespread.

In other contexts, a menstruating woman is regarded as polluted. She cannot cook or approach holy ground, crops, cattle or men. Neither can she participate in religious ceremonies. Otherwise she will pollute the surroundings. A woman may also be defined as unclean for a certain period after childbirth, in which case she has to be purified by a priest before reentering the community.[13] In the Ancient Israelite religion, such a pollution theory was codified as normative, and the tradition was adopted both in Christianity and Islam.[14] To what degree prescribed rules of clean and unclean were actually practised in daily life, in a rigorous way, is another question. But regardless of the answer, western Jewish and Christian traditions have, on a *symbolic* level, conferred upon women's blood a negative value.

When Reclaiming women invent a ritual to celebrate "first blood" for their daughters, they want to challenge any assumptions still alive in western culture and in the girl that a bleeding woman is unclean. As witnessed in the "Women's Magic" class, they believe that such a notion is oppressive. To be raised with menstruation as a shameful condition, a taboo or even as a non-subject is said to mark girls' and women's apprehension of their female bodies and selves negatively.

Menstruation in modernity is not so much associated with shame as with a physical handicap that negatively differentiates women from men. A woman is culturally encouraged to eradicate this "handicap" as much as possible, and she is offered different means to help her in this effort. She can make her blood invisible and without odour by using tampons and thereby appear as a man's equal. If she has menstrual cramps, a doctor can prescribe analgesic medication. This way her "handicap" will not affect her labour and she can work on equal terms with a man. In various ways she can try to "forget" the fact that her body is part of a natural, reproductive cycle with intervals similar to the lunar phase, and which repeats itself 10 to 13 times a year for maybe 40 years.

There has, to a certain extent, been a joint attempt of the corporate world and "sexual equality" feminism to make women's periods socially invisible or unimportant. The purpose of this "alliance" is to help eliminate gender roles and the notion that women's biology is women's fate. According to these feminists, women have an equally efficient working capacity as men. The fact that a woman bleeds and gives birth is not an indication of her natural predisposition for housework and intellectual inferiority, nor of her lacking talent for statesmanship. Psychological differences between women and men are viewed as determined by socialization and imitation (culture) alone, not by bodily constitution or bodily drives (nature). The body is rather seen as an uninteresting biological constant and the circumstances around women's bodily reproductive capacities are perceived as purely "technical". An un-intended implication of this position is that western hierarchies between culture and nature easily are repeated. Nature becomes raw material, a technical object, to those cultivating, social forces that really creates human beings and infuses meaning.

Defenders of "sexual polarity" are of a different opinion. They argue that the modernist effort to make a woman's bodily distinctions, such as menstrual flux, invisible and unimportant is to ask her to suppress her femininity and give away her female power. This suppression also implies the reinforcement of "culture over nature", which already – in western societies – is associated with male over female. However, the danger of just turning hierarchies on their heads in favour of women is always striking in essentialist feminism. This may happen when menstrual blood is seen as a metonymic representative of both womanhood and Goddess (divine life force). In the mythic narrative about the origin of blood ritual told in the "Women's Magic" class, negative analogies were made between women's paradisiacal sisterhood on a remote island and the community of men. In fact, sexual difference was represented as a loss, and the very presence of a man caused disharmony and quarrelling between women, destroying their peaceful community. Their dispute could only be healed by the Goddess, and only among those who listened to her and celebrated her mandatory blood ritual. This theme is repeated by Anna when describing coven life to some friends: perfect and divine love can only be attained within a community of goddess-worshipping women. The Goddess has now assumed a monistic, static character and stands in apparent contradiction to the erotic polarity usually ascribed to the universe; for as formulated by Starhawk, "Desire is the primal energy [of the universe], and that energy is erotic: the attraction of lover to beloved, of planet to star, the lust of electron for proton" (Starhawk 1979a:25).

The social effects of performing "first blood" rituals may, however, be very positive on the community at large; and the symbolic meanings structuring this ritual process are of course more complex than the metonymic blood component indicates. Let us, therefore, return to Sonia's blood ritual to observe how a young girl is taught to value her body, her sexuality, her "femininity", as well as her community, within the context of feminist Witchcraft.

Sonia's blood ritual: learning from women and community

Reclaiming women, and in particular those in Gossip, were excited when Sonia started menstruating. The celebration of Nicole's first blood, which Dora told us about in the "Women's Magic" class, had been an important event, and people waited for the second young Reclaiming girl to enter puberty in order to establish this celebration as an option in the "Reclaiming tradition".

Sonia was raised as a pagan and agreed early to have a blood ritual performed for her. When turning 13 she also attended her first Reclaiming class for teenagers. Otherwise, she is mostly interested in heavy metal music and classical ballet. She has danced since she was 5 years old and her goal is to become a professional dancer. Sonia's parents, Anna and Richard, who both work as social scientists, joined Reclaiming when their daughter was 7. Anna's religious background is otherwise Methodism and Unitarianism, while Richard is an ex-Catholic. In the late fall of 1988, Anna started to prepare for Sonia's blood ritual by making a long, hooded ritual robe in dark green wool with black silk lining as a gift for her daughter. She also asked Sonia to think of a new name for herself.

In early February 1989, the blood finally came, and everybody was happy. Anna took the day off and Sonia skipped school. Mother and daughter had lunch in a nice restaurant. Here the two of them made plans for the blood ritual. They agreed upon which women should be invited to the "women's mysteries" part – and thereby to the planning group – and who was to be invited for the community ritual and the party afterward.

Firmly guided by her mother, Sonia chose 11 women for the "women's mysteries". They included all the women in her mother's coven, as well as

Dora, Nicole, Hera, Starhawk, Terry (a friend of the family) and her Unitarian grandmother (mother's mother). I was lucky to be part of the event since it happened during one of my fieldwork periods, and within the context of my coven.[15]

The leading figure at the planning meeting for Sonia's first blood ritual, was Hera, Nicole's mother. She agreed that Sonia's ritual should be personal and different from Nicole's. But she was eager to make sure that we included certain elements from that first ritual in order to create continuity and tradition. She wanted these elements to cover a ritual tying of mother and child, as well as the basic structure of the ritual process established with Nicole's ritual. This structure was, according to Hera, tripartite. It should comprise ritual time for Sonia's separation from childhood, a time for her transition to puberty and a time for her reintegration back into community as a new person. Hera had learned this ritual structure (separation, transition, reintegration) from reading Arnold van Gennep and Victor Turner's "what" theory on the essentials of coming of age rituals globally.

Sonia did not take part in the actual planning of her ritual and was completely ignorant of the ritual structure and of what would happen to her in the blood rite. She was only asked to find a new name for herself and to prepare a personal gift to the community. Everything else was a secret.

In chapter 1, I described the first part of Sonia's blood rite, how she was separated from the larger community and taken by a group of women – including her mother and grandmother – to Lincoln Park. Here she was tied to her mother with a cord and later cut loose, accompanied with the words: "*When you were born, you came to the world tied to your mother's body. As the umbilical cord had to be cut at that time for you to live, so the cord between the two of you has to be cut now. But the bond between you shall never be cut, because that is a bond by heart.*" Let me continue the narrative from this point on.

Transition and reintegration vis-à-vis women

The time has come for Sonia to confront her aloneness and be the subject of a transitional journey. From Lincoln Park, there is a beautiful view to other parks, paths and roads. In the remote distance we can barely see the head of a statue depicting the Roman goddess Diana. Starhawk points to the statue and asks Sonia to run over there alone. Sonia hesitates and argues that she might get lost. Starhawk answers that now she has to run, alone, through the forest. "*The cord is cut, and this you must do on your own. And you will make it; don't be afraid. When you reach the statue, go close to her and meditate on the virgin goddess Diana, and your own coming into maidenhood.*"

Sonia does as she is told, and the rest of us follow at a slow pace. We carry with us plenty of flowers, and when we finally reach the statue, Sonia is there. We do not ask what she has experienced on her little journey or if she was "taught" anything when meditating on the meaning of this ancient female deity. We just form a circle in complete silence a few feet away. Nicole, the 18 year old among us, gathers the flowers still in our arms into a big basket, walks over to Sonia, and hands them to her. Then she takes Sonia by the hand and leads her into the centre of the circle of adult women. Sonia's grandmother is seated under a pine tree, watching the ritual from there.

We stand close together with our arms around each other. Starhawk starts drumming as we teach Sonia who the Goddess actually is by repeatedly singing, "*Listen, listen, listen to my heart's song; I will never forget you, I will never forsake you. I will always love you, I will always be with you.*" Some people, walking by, stop to listen and watch. Sonia, still in the centre, is shy and blushes all over her face. For a long time she only stares down at her feet. But we continue to sing, and after a while she raises her head, as if the spirit moves her to a place of strength. She then looks calmly into our eyes, one by one, as she slowly turns clockwise in the circle. To watch this shift from shyness to calm and conscious eye contact is a moving experience, and some of the women, including her mother, start to weep (while still singing) over this apparent sign of an emerging adult who dares to be acknowledged by a community "of equals". All kinds of feelings and memories are aroused in the women present – their own menstruation histories, the way they were introduced to the adult world, the privilege of being part of creating Sonia's blood ritual, dreams and hopes for their own daughters and their futures. For not only are we participating in shaping Sonia's gender identity and sense of a spirit within, but we are also remodelling our own.

The second part of the ritual takes place in Anna's living room, where all share of their adult "women's mysteries" experiences with her daughter (Sonia's grandmother does not come with us for this part of the ritual). We are seated on the floor, with Sonia included in the circle, although not yet integrated into the women's community. She still experiences transition, while we represent the elders – those who have gone before her. Now we prepare to tell her the female heroines' stories. Within the context of ritual space, our speech may also be heard as the speech of Goddess.

This rite of puberty does not cut ties between mother and daughter by physically (or permanently) separating the daughter from her mother, for example, as in patrilocal marriage. But the old relationship between Sonia and Anna is changed and takes on a new symbolic status: they are becoming "sisters". A taboo in the traditional mother–daughter relationship in the US is broken, for Sonia shall not only hear about blood but also about sexuality and the women's experiences with men – the kind of men who, in Sonia's eyes, are "fathers".

We have brought food for a potluck lunch, and as we eat, seated in a circle, we tell Sonia our personal stories about blood. A majority of the women have no good memories of their first menstruation. Ruth had no idea what it was before the blood came pouring out of her. She was scared, and her mother was shameful when telling her what it was. Susan's Jewish mother was hit in the face by Susan's Jewish grandmother when she started bleeding. Nell, on the other hand, says that she looked forward to her first blood and that her mother was always open about menstruation as well as sexuality. Starhawk says that we tell these stories in order to remember all women's stories, so the painful experiences do not have to be repeated. Instead we share with the intention of creating something new.

The women then tell stories about how their partners react when they "have their moon". Terry's husband cannot stand to see her sanitary pads nor to caress her body when she menstruates. Terry herself feels strong and open during this period, but her husband thinks that she represents the rawest in nature and that her blood is disgusting. Hera's husband regards her blood as the most natural thing in the world. He always wants to make love to her when she is "on her moon," and afterward they make fun of his red penis. Artemis wants to be alone when bleeding. She meditates a lot and looks at her blood period as a renewal of body and mind.

Nicole gives advice about body flux and warns against certain contraceptives. Tanya informs Sonia about how the body temperature drops during ovulation and how day-to-day knowledge of body temperature can be used as a natural contraceptive. Dora says that she uses her blood for working magic and that there are different forms of magic corresponding to the cycles of the body and the moon. The waxing moon almost pours out, in a literal sense, the energy of extension and initiation of new projects. It is the time for magic focused on exterior action and results. Full moon is a time for celebrations. The waning moon contains the energy of contraction and inwardness. It is a time for meditation and for the magic that truly helps to let go of what has been.

Anna tells Sonia that she does not choose whether she wants to bleed or not. She shares this experience with all women throughout the world, irrespective of race and culture, whether she likes it or not. When celebrating blood ritual, women remember that all females are sisters, even though the differences between them are as many as the stars. The blood is a sign that the woman's body is sacred, because the cycles of the blood have their archetype in the universe. The same force moving the ocean between the tides is moving the egg in a woman's womb, and this force is lunar. That's why women say, "I am on my moon" when they bleed. A menstruating woman is similar to the moon; she is powerful and energetic.

Sonia listens to these stories, advice and teachings in complete silence, with a shy smile on her face. She is given the opportunity to ask us questions, but has none. Then we dress her up in a new silk outfit and wrap her in Anna's gift: the ritual cloak of green wool. Anna says that the cloak is magical and can be used for dual purposes: one side is ordinary, to keep warm; the other side is magical, to enchant frogs into princes! Then Sonia reveals to us her new magical name, *Aurora*, designating her new status. Mother and daughter enter the centre of the circle and we sing to them, "*It's the blood of the Ancients that runs through our veins/and the forms pass, but the circle of life remains.*" We raise a cone of power as we sing, which in the end is "grounded" in Sonia.

This new Sonia/Aurora, who is now reintegrated into social life as part of women's community, is finally honoured with gifts: silk underwear, necklaces, goddess figures, a belt, condoms, a basket full of magical remedies (fabrics, buttons, shells, etc.) to make spells, as well as the ritual knife, the athame, used earlier to cut the cord between mother and daughter in Lincoln park. Starhawk's coven has made her a special necklace of black and red beads, feathers and cowrie shells. A cowrie shell is said to have the form of the female sexual organs. Sonia is told that when she wears the necklace with the biggest cowrie shell turning inward, she is blessed by the Goddess. When the shell turns outward, it symbolizes fertility. Sonia must wear it this way only when she explicitly wants to become pregnant.

Re-integration vis-à-vis the community

The third and final part of the ritual takes place in the Women's Building in the Mission. We arrive in the early evening and are greeted by almost 60 guests, including Sonia's little sister. Richard has arranged the room and prepared the party together with his male coveners. They have made four beautiful altars, one for each element, and a huge potluck dinner table in the north. Many dishes on the menu are red, like salmon and strawberry mousse. A big cake with *Aurora* written on top is the dessert.

The gathering begins with ritual. Richard bids his daughter welcome as the young woman Sonia, who is now initiated to the women's community, and as the magical person Aurora, who has now decided to walk the path of the Goddess and to learn to bend, and to be bent by, the world. It is time for the Reclaiming community to honour and celebrate this person. The ritual includes the traditional steps, and I shall describe only the magical work designed in particular for this occasion:

1. After creating sacred space and calling the Goddess, women pick a red bead and men a white one from a little jar that is passed around. They "charge" the beads by blowing into them good wishes and blessings for Sonia. Afterward the beads are given to Sonia, who is instructed to make a necklace of them as a sign of this community's love for her.

2. Sonia gives us her gift. While a singer performs "*There is no end to the circle, no end*" – well known to the celebrants from the annual Samhain ritual (cf. chapter 6) – Sonia dances classical ballet in a white robe in the middle of the circle.

3. We all dance the Spiral Dance in a new choreography. Women and men are divided by gender and age groups. Starhawk walks first with her drum, then Sonia, then the row of women from the eldest to the youngest child, and finally the row of men from youngest to eldest. When the energy reaches its peak in a cone of power, the women suddenly move to the centre of the circle, pick Sonia up and set her on the top of the cone; they throw her in the air and rock her. After grounding, there is another gift-giving ceremony with Sonia seated in the centre of the circle. When the ritual ends, there is finally rock music, dancing and a potluck dinner.

*   *   *

Whether this ritualized process helped Sonia to establish an identity as a sexually mature young woman and to appreciate herself for who she is, was too early to tell in 1989. Just after performing Sonia's blood ritual, Nicole told me that she was mainly embarrassed during her ritual five years before. She recalls that her main reason for letting it happen was to satisfy her mother and her expectations. But today she is happy she did it and feels that the event was a special gift that marked her value as a female person. Even though Nicole is not active in the Reclaiming community, it was important for her to participate in Sonia's rite of passage. She relived her own ritual and was an equal member of an adult group of women – all of whom she highly respects.

To the adult participants, Sonia's rite of passage was a major event and commented upon for a long time afterward. One of the male elders told me that pagan rituals performed for the younger generation give him a feeling of being part of a profound process of cultural change. Another person made a point of how such rituals strengthen the bonds within the community and confer new meaning upon everybody's experience of continually growing and changing. A third one said that, to her, the ritual was a most beautiful expression of kinship and lived life, and picked out Sonia's dance in the centre of the community ritual as the most moving point:

> You know, in our rites of passage, a girl is celebrated because she starts bleeding and enters a new phase. But the maid also shows the community who this little puppet who is about to blossom eventually will become. She tells us of her being and of her way, and this is what happened when Sonia danced for us.

Some months after her initiation Sonia wrote a letter to the *Reclaiming Newsletter*. She acknowledged the ritual and the gifts and told that she now – after the ritual – was permitted to go to the late-night movies. She expressed pride, but also confessed that the worst part had been to run up to the Diana statue, ". . . because I was out in the public in my ritual robe . . . by the road, with people watching!!" The best part of ritual was when the women lifted her up in the middle of the Spiral Dance: "It was great! I felt secure, warm and full of powerful positive energy." She ended the letter by encouraging other young girls in the community to also have a blood ritual performed, because it is "special, powerful, memorable and something to cherish".[16]

Later, I asked Sonia if anything now distinguished her from her friends since they did not have a blood ritual performed and she did. She said, "Not really. Maybe that I always look at the sky and am conscious about the formation of clouds. I don't think they do." One and a half years later she confided to me that she was tired of Reclaiming people and all their talk about love, but never practising it. Similarly to Nicole, she insisted that she only did the blood ritual because her mother wanted it. "I did the ritual for my mom. I was not really part of it. It was more important for the women than for me. But I liked the community ritual a lot." At this point, Sonia did not identify with the "inner circle" who defined her "women's mysteries" but with her father's circle: the larger non-esoteric community.

Sonia went through some turbulent and rebellious years during her puberty, but eventually turned out to be a mature young woman. She went to college to study dance and has indeed realized her dream: she has become a professional dancer and body worker. Like Nicole, she now appreciates her blood ritual and identifies with its intimate "women-only" structure. She also identifies as a pagan and participates in blood rites for other young girls in the community as often as she is invited. When her sister finally came of age, she played Nicole's role in the "women's mysteries" part, leading her into the sacred circle with flowers in her arms.

Rites of puberty for girls and boys

When planning Sonia's blood ritual, the women primarily wanted to give Sonia an experience of women's community as sacred space, to give her a good feeling about her female body, and to encourage her to break away from the bonds of childhood and take a new step. They also wanted to find an acceptable way to include men in the ritual process. Nevertheless, the ritual symbolism and acts also expressed a certain codified knowledge about what it means to be a woman in contrast to being a man. Let us now look at the different meanings conveyed through this ritual.

Reclaiming's celebration of female puberty is, first of all, an extended part of their critical discourse on nature and culture in general. The formalized interactions between ritualized space and ritualized bodies were, therefore, not meant as a tribute to conventional definitions of the categories "nature" and "culture", "woman" and "man" – a convention in which "female is to male as nature is to culture."[17] A young woman is ideally celebrated for her earthiness and connection with the lunar cycles, for blood and ovary and her potential to give birth, for breasts and growth of hair, for the body growing in strength and beauty, for sexuality, for separation from mother and father, and for her abilities to create with head, heart and hands. A young boy is similarly celebrated for his connection to the wheel of the year, for his sexuality and his seed that carries the potential for new life, for cracking voice and growth of hair, for the body growing in strength and beauty, for sexuality, for separation from mother and father, and for his abilities to create with head, heart and hands. The two young people are, in this ecological perspective, not celebrated for cultural gender or gendered moral characteristics but for physiology, for life itself.

Nevertheless, by its very happening, this celebration also integrates a young girl in a symbolic discourse named "women's mysteries", just as a boy is by the "men's mysteries." As already pointed out: from an emic point of view, "mysteries" refer to those functions and cycles in women's and men's bodies connecting them to the universe, to nature, to the sacred. A female is said to pass through three monthly cycles (or mysteries) and three transitional stages in linear time, all corresponding to three aspects of the "Moon Goddess": *Maiden* (new moon), *Mother* (full moon), and *Crone* (dark moon). During the course of her life, a woman Witch will first be initiated to *Maidenhood*, that is, to knowledge of her own body, its abilities and its relation to the larger world. Second, she will be initiated to *Motherhood*, that is, to a sexually mature, creative and powerful woman. Third, she is initiated as an elder, as an experienced wise woman, a *Crone*, after her menopause.[18]

The picture is, however, more complicated. Sonia was not only celebrated for physiology and as partaker in a cosmic drama mirrored in her body, but she was also included in a social community of women. This community is culturally determined, with its own narrative and interpretation of what it means to be a woman. As explicitly accounted for when describing Dora and Deadly's class, "mysteries" also refers to this narrative. In this room, which has the sexed body as criterion for membership, Sonia's cultural gender identity is created by reference to cultural definitions of sexual differences and by pointing out similarities in women's experiences as opposed to men's. The fact that women menstruate is, within this framework, transformed into a valuable quality to the female gender as such. It links her to the universe in an exclusive manner; it gives her a special capability for practising magic. As soon as they enter this world of gender-segregated essentialism, Reclaiming women do symbolically rank themselves above men.

Are there any similarities between Sonia's blood rite and girl's puberty rites cross-culturally? According to Bruce Lincoln's observations, the custom of placing a novice on a symbolic pedestal in her menstruation ritual, even speaking of her as "goddess", is common in traditional cultures. But he regards this as a purely illusionist strategy to teach the girl to accept social inferiority since she, in most cases, is not expected to gain access to political power (Lincoln 1981:106). The nature and significance of female initiations are therefore more cosmic than social: "Rather than changing women's status, initiation changes their fundamental being, addressing ontological concerns rather than hierarchical ones" (Lincoln 1981:103). If we, however, compare the rites of puberty for girls and boys in Reclaiming, we find that both are "feminine" as defined by Lincoln: also a boy's puberty rite addresses onto-logical concerns rather than hierarchical and social ones. This gender harmony among young people in Reclaiming is the result of a conscious "sexual equality" strategy in a late modern pagan community in San Francisco. It does not stem from a desire to teach either girls or boys social inferiority.

The difficult politics of women's mysteries

The "glorification" of femaleness and women's community yielded in the above is not necessarily in accordance with all Reclaiming Witches' daily life experiences or intellectual integrity. But most women seem to grant exception to their intellectual struggle with these questions every time they participate in gender-segregated rituals. Thus, these social occasions take on the quality of liminal communitas in which it is fully accepted, again and again, to equate femaleness with the powers of ultimate reality, to mirror the Goddess's cosmic movements in their own womanly bodies, and to confirm themselves as beautiful, powerful beings, worthy of love and respect. When the ritual is over, they return to their families, communities and society at large, apparently with much confidence, ready to reenter social discourses that may or may not pertain to deeper nuance and complexity in regard to sexual difference.

But some refuse, or lack the ability, or are not helped properly, to reenter the consciousness and categories of mixed-gender society. Their discourse on the Goddess and her supposed relation to sexual difference is disassociated from its original context and formulated in terms resembling lesbian-separatist Dianic Witchcraft. These Witches treat the Craft solely as a "woman's religion", and in ritual they only call the Goddess. When I participated in Z. Budapest's class in Oakland in February 1989, I was taught a reversed Catholicism that stated that the Goddess moves through women rather than through men because only women represent her true image. Consequently, she can only be served by women priestesses. High priestess Budapest explained that

> Goddess always comes to us first because the female species is closer to her – although she can, if she wants to, move through men. In fact, men and women are not different, men are just another kind of woman. The female X-chromosome is basic to both sexes, and not the male Y-chromosome. Men have a little larger sex-organ, and they are not as pretty as we are. But Mama made a variation for some reason.

In the 1980s, this degradation of men could also be heard in the Reclaiming community, although mostly as jokes at women's gatherings. Songs and singing, and the accompanying twisting of lyrics, were a popular medium through which it was accepted to ridicule men.

How did Reclaiming men respond to essentialist Witches, to those who never left the liminal space of women's spirituality groups but ended up internalizing derogative notions of men as a normative, social paradigm, or to the fact that they could be ridiculed at gender-segregated gatherings, a practice obviously inappropriate for men to imitate? In the 1984 fall edition of *Reclaiming Newsletter*, the same in which Dora and Deadly announced their "Women's Magic" class, another member of the Reclaiming Collective, David Kubrin, addressed this topic with reference to his 11-year-old son. The boy, who often accompanied his mother to women-only circles, was frequently heard singing, "We don't need the men/we don't need to have them 'round, except for now and then." Both the content of the song and the fact that his son had picked it up worried David. He wanted to challenge the confusing sexual debates in the community and address the role of the God in goddess-centreed spirituality, "How are we to understand male sexuality? . . . Certainly talk of the 'male mysteries' in whatever men's magical group I've been in were almost always dominated by nervous jokes".

David's concerns initiated a *Newsletter* discussion that lasted for several years, engaging Witches far beyond the Reclaiming community.[19] The male essentialists referred to the occult thesis "as above so below", and argued that just as women had goddesses, men needed gods restricted for "male use only". Some gay men (Donald and Sparky) could tell of revelations in which a queer god named "Singing Bear" had revealed himself: "He was all queer. And he was for queers alone. He could come only when queer voices called to him." They introduced a concept of segregated divinity linked up to people's sexual differentiation, giving us one god for each orientation: Diana for lesbian women; Singing Bear for gay men, etc.

Also a female Witch, Rowan, could witness that she had met a male god who was exclusively for men, his name being "Night Singer": "The sense was so strong that this was a male mystery, that his knowledge was not for me . . . . Where are the men? Will no one search him out?" The point of her argument was to attract more men to Witchcraft and to make women rethink their critical attitudes, "Instead of encouraging them to get on with the important work of reclaiming the Gods and redefining the idea of male and men, we greet them with suspicious diatribes on male character, and in most traditions insist that they acknowledge the Goddess as supreme deity." Rowan's essentialism is outstanding since she explicitly refers to the occult thesis that mundane life mirrors, or should mirror, divine reality: "I want my sons to grow up in beautiful strength with their special Gods to identify with. . . . And for this to happen there must be a place for the Gods. In men, in paganism, in women. As above, so below".

Rick Dragonstongue, who also is a member of the Reclaiming Collective, is a woman-identified man, but not gay. He argued against Rowan that, since women have been oppressed for thousands of years and just recently have started to claim their power, it is not yet time to balance the Goddess and God: "Our society as a whole as well as most individuals need the Goddess more than they need the God right now . . . the only way to approach a balance of spiritual power between the sexes is for women to assume a greater ritual importance." Rick argued in a "sexual equality" fashion in favour of idealized women against the male essentialist claim of a separate god, but also against the non idealized, empirical woman, Rowan. Rick was credited by many Reclaiming women for his bravery and for the politically correct attitude they felt was expressed by his "courtesy feminism".

In the years to follow, more and more Reclaiming people expressed being uncomfortable with vulgar or radical forms of essentialism and with the tendencies in the community to link morals with biology. And in 1989, Starhawk finally questioned the traditional identification of Goddess as role model and of femaleness as a specific quality. When reviewing the 1979 edition of *The Spiral Dance* in 1989, she wrote:

> Today I don't use the terms female energy and male energy. I don't identify femaleness or maleness with specific sets of qualities or predis-

positions. While I have found images of the Goddess empowering to me as a woman, I no longer look to Goddess and God to define for me what woman or man should be. For any quality that has been assigned to one divine gender can elsewhere be found in its opposite. If we say, for example, "Male energy is aggressive," I can easily find five aggressive goddesses without even thinking hard. If we say "Female energy is nurturing," we can also find male gods that nurture . . . . The Goddesses and Gods are not figures for us to copy – they are more like broomsticks: grab hold, and they will take us away somewhere beyond the boundaries of our ordinary lives.

(Starhawk 1989a:8)

But, even though Starhawk disassociates herself from the idea of female and male as "reified qualities, like liquids that could fill us" (1989a:8), she only rejects a psychological reification theory and its implicit tendency to define female and male in restricting moral categories, for example, that females are loving and males are aggressive. But she still clings to "female" and "male" as linked to life-generating divine forces, even though she hesitates to fill them with content. As long as "female" is linked both to "woman" and "life-force", empirical women will inevitably be said to share an essential similarity with Goddess that men do not: they give birth, although "this fact" only applies to her aspect as immanent other-than-deity, literally being the body of the world. The question is, is this consciously chosen value a fruitful strategy in terms of creating a more humane society, or is it not? [20]

My studies of Reclaiming's subcultural women's circles, organized within the larger gender-inclusive (although predominantly female) community, have demonstrated that essentialism is used as a strategic device to establish women-only covens and conduct gender-segregated rituals. In Reclaiming's case, these activities have contributed significantly to produce a ritualized body/magical person with a strong sense of self and of her capacities to love and bond without submission – an obvious fruit of ritualizing according to a female symbolic order. The ritualized devotion to Goddess in women-only circles seems also to have opened a new sensual path to the sacred – in addition to the powers of nature and the embrace of the lovers: the experience of "perfect love and perfect trust" in the life and work of a same-sex coven. These ritualized social strategies probably represent a qualitatively new trait in the history of western women.

The shadow side, however, to gender-segregated communitas is the temptation to rank female and male powers and transfer their hierarchies into social paradigm, although this is the stumbling stone in all religious discourse. The fact that such exercises still take place in Reclaiming is a sign that a major goal of feminist Witchcraft, namely, to revalue and reinterpret the categories of "nature" and "body" beyond cultural programming and without discrimination of one sex against the other, has not yet been reached. Many Witches will, however, respond that this goal cannot be reached successfully as long as they live in a patriarchal society. For the time being, their challenge is more to remain open to continuous reflection and refinement of any working concept in the "house" they have "come home" to and stay true to their experiences of multiple realities and choice of strategy: sexual difference is the existential foundation from which they act and operate, sexual polarity is their affirming, strengthening and tactical position, while the struggle for equality of the sexes is their final goal both in their own community and in the global social and economic order.

Notes

1 This way of thinking is expressed in the Faery tradition's creation myth. According to this myth, the Stargoddess, who represents undivided wholeness before creation, created the universe by making love to herself. She saw her own reflection in the curved mirror of black space and fell in love with it. She drew herself out as "the other", and called her "*Miria, the wonderful*". Their ecstasy burst forth "*in the single song of all there is*" and the Goddess became filled with love. "*She gave birth to a rain of bright spirits that filled the worlds and became all beings.*" But in that great movement, Miria is swept away, and the further away she moves, the more masculine she becomes, until she is the Blue God. "*But always desire draws Him back toward the Goddess, so that He circles Her eternally, seeking to return in love*" (Starhawk 1979a:17). The ultimate being in this myth is a purely feminine omni-creatrix. She creates "the other" as an extension of herself, another female, a mirror image of her Self. After merging in ecstasy this other slowly becomes a male god, the Blue God. It is the Blue God who includes both poles, female and male, and who is truly androgynous, not the Stargoddess. When the Goddess gives birth, the birth is proto-genetic. She is omnipotent and becomes pregnant through pure ecstasy and joy, not through intercourse with a male god. All earthly and cosmic beings are offspring of her body, created by her love affair with her Self. In addition, all beings have, deep inside themselves, an androgynous Divine Self: the Blue God. This is so, whether they are male or female.

2 The advantage of this position is a tremendous political optimism regarding the social possibilities for full sexual equality: for men to learn and take over traditional female tasks such as childrearing and housework, and for women to learn and take over traditional male tasks such as political agency and warfare.

3 In the latter case, all empirical women and men "contain" female and male principles, the male side being a woman's animus in Jungian terminology. Jungian essentialism is therefore labeled "*double* dichotomy" by feminist scholar Petra Junus (1995:260).

4 Some of these feminists insist that modern, western culture in reality is homosexual: it allegedly consists of one sex (the man) interacting with himself, i.e., with his binary mirror image and complementary opposite called "woman". Their goal is thus to create a real hetero-sexual society, i.e., a society that *de facto* accepts sexual difference, including sexual identities and practices. By twisting linguistic semantics they have confused many contemporary feminists of a different opinion.

5 It was the sacred mysteries of Eleusis that in antiquity celebrated the finding again of a daughter goddess (Persephone/Kore) by her divine mother (Demeter), although Demeter had to compromise with Hades (Mylonas 1961). Gerald Gardner claims that modern Witchcraft is spiritually kindred to the Eleusinian mysteries (Gardner 1954:82).

6 Plural sexual identities were also the marks of the group's first teachers: Dora was heterosexual and Deadly lesbian.

7 The contrasting definitions of men that I add in parentheses were in most cases not stated explicitly, but indirectly assumed. I choose to state these definitions to give the reader a more complete picture of the gendered dichotomies that were operative in class.

8 In the summer of 1985, I enthusiastically put forth the preliminary results of my research for a group of Reclaiming people. I spelled out the tacit patriarchal notions of the pillars of correspondence in western occultism that I had found in their symbol system and stated that Reclaiming Witches were not as radical as they claimed to be. In fact, to a large extent they were only replacing one patriarchal tradition (Jewish and Christian religions) with another (western occultism). But nobody shared my enthusiasm over these findings. Finally, one male member started to talk. He said my analysis sounded great, logical and convincing, except that it made him completely depressed. A woman agreed with him and said: how could it be that feminist Witchcraft was only a reproduction of esoteric, patriarchal tradition when in fact this religious path had changed her life and given a completely new meaning to what it meant to be religious, and what it meant to be a woman and have "a life"? I was struck by her comment. What was the revitalizing power of feminist Witchcraft that I was not able to catch with my symbolic analysis? It had something to do with the transformative potentials of ritual and the way in which the self was ritualized, respected and integrated into the community. To focus my study entirely upon the reinvention of feminine and magical symbols was missing the point, although "goddess" and "magic" were the headlines through which feminist Witchcraft came across to new people. This was an important incident when I, for my PhD, decided to enter this study from a somewhat different angle, and with the methodological tools of anthropology: now I wanted to study Witchcraft as a lived religion and ritualized practice, not merely texts and textual symbols.

9 Bynum 1987:34. We have also encountered nudity as a ritual practice in the heretical heritage line going back to the Free Spirits (cf. chapter 3).

10 I wrote my notes after the event and cannot claim to quote exactly the words said. I heard the same story told at a women's solstice camp in Nevada, called *Her Voice, Our Voices*, in June 1985.

11 *Reclaiming Newsletter* No. 38, spring 1990.

12 Some Witches juxtapose magical ritual with religious ceremony to emphasize the difference between ritualizing narrative for conservative goals and ritualizing lived life for transformative goals. The distinction is taken from Max Gluckman (1962: 22).

13 Buckley and Gottlieb 1988:30–40. The authors address the shortcomings of mainly using pollution theories in the analysis of menstrual meanings and call for more positive and more complex approaches. They believe that one of the reasons that pollution theories have been predominant in anthropological studies cross-culturally is the fact that both informants and ethnographers have mainly been men.

14 Mary Douglas 1988:57. Douglas proposes that holiness, for example in Ancient Israelite society, was given a concrete physical expression by explicit rules of avoidance of the polluted and unclean. Rosemary R. Ruether points out how Moses instructed Israel – according to Exodus 19:15 – not to go near a woman in order to be purified and ready to receive the commandments (Ruether 1987:143).

15 Anna was responsible for the "women's mysteries" and the big community ritual, while Richard took care of the party. In a boy's initiation rite, these roles are switched.

16 *Reclaiming Newsletter* No. 35, summer 1989.

17 This famous parallel was formulated by anthropologist Sherry Ortner in 1974.

18 Similar life-cycles associated with the Witches' pantheon of male deities, like the waxing and waning of the Green God have not – to my knowledge – been developed for boys. The model for boys' initiation rites in Reclaiming has been inspired more by ethnographic accounts from tribal cultures than by traditional Witchcraft lore.

19 The gender discussion in Reclaiming was launched simultaneously with an escalating interest in *men's politics* on the alternative scene in general, in particular the so-called Men's Mythopoetic movement initiated by Robert Bly (1992). This movement wants to restore men to a new male power-from-within which allegedly is grounded in Earth spirituality, and not conceived as oppressive to women. It has attracted a lot of men who feel overrun by feminist women, even men in Reclaiming. Those interested in spirituality want to reclaim a male earth-God and not a female Goddess. Yet, the Mythopoetic movement has offended many women and triggered fear that a new war between the sexes is returning. Starhawk has also contributed to these discussions (Starhawk 1992), although not in the *Reclaiming Newsletter*. Here she kept a low profile for a long time.

20 The strong position of essentialist feminism within goddess spirituality has also been noted by Eller 1993, Greenwood 1994 and Junus 1995. According to Greenwood, feminist Witches in Britain also view the body "in essentialist terms" and in order to connect with true self "they have to strip away layers of patriarchal conditioning" (1994:6). In fear of essentialism, many scholars, among them Caroline W. Bynum, are critical of Witches' and goddess-worshippers' attempts to "restore" a female face of God.

8   Initiation

Transforming self

Traditional Witchcraft differentiates between two aspects of religion and two levels of knowledge: *exoteric* and *esoteric*. Exoteric aspects of religion are said to deal with the "religious needs of society", providing, for example, meaningful rites of passage to mark natural and social rhythms, while esotericism concerns mystical knowledge and personal change.[1] Exoteric Witchcraft refers to rituals and knowledge that are public and accessible to anyone, not least through books and manuals. Esoteric Witchcraft, on the other hand, refers to exclusive knowledge about the tools and meanings of inner, personal transformation. This knowledge is claimed to be mystical, ancient and universal. It is passed on as ritualized, special language and only to candidates seeking the Witches' initiation. Although such terminology is not used in Reclaiming, its esoteric heritage is apparent in the initiation ritual.

The mere fact of practising initiation tends to split Reclaiming Witches into disputing camps. The camps range from "real anarchists" who condemn initiation as elitist because of its esoteric modalities and, therefore, take a moral standpoint against it; those who couldn't care less and really are uninterested in the whole subject; those who are intrigued by it and maybe would want it for themselves, but "really don't feel that witchy"; to those who identify 100 per cent as Witches by dedication through initiation. All these viewpoints can coexist, for example, within one and the same coven. But underneath the pluralism we find a current working in favour of initiation. For every Witch deciding to be initiated, at least two others are influenced by her decision. Having witnessed the initiation process of a significant other, they feel pushed to reexamine their own attitudes and role models. If the influence is marked, questions might be: "When I see how much Catherine has changed since she was initiated – maybe there is something to it?" And, "If Catherine could decide to be initiated, maybe I should consider it as well?"

Reclaiming initiation is a reformed version of Faery initiation. Faery is a highly secretive, ceremonial tradition that offers two levels of initiation (Gardnerians have three degrees). Reclaiming has taken certain ritual elements from Faery: the basic outline of the initiation, the most secret and sacred inner-circle part, and the idea of (eventually) invoking the Goddess and God by their secret, proper names. However, when Starhawk created a new version of Witchcraft, as published in *The Spiral Dance*, she and her female friends also changed important parts of Victor Anderson's Faery initiation. They ordained one initiation instead of two and prolonged the whole ritual process considerably. This applies, in particular, to the pre-initiation process: the Reclaiming apprentice is given practical challenges that are intended to promote personal growth and change. The women have added an extensive "meeting the elements" to the secret ritual, arranged individually for every new candidate. These are exclusive Reclaiming traditions, not common among other Witches, which have resulted in a totally different focus and, therefore, also a different meaning to the entire initiation process. The values of secrecy, esoteric knowledge and exclusive membership, often associated with men's secret societies, are moderated, whereas initiation as a path to personal growth, in order to cope with the challenges of daily life, is emphasized. To a certain extent this fact corresponds with Caroline W. Bynum's thesis (cf. Introduction) that women's religiosity manifests itself as an extension of everyday life, while men's religious practice often tends to stand in contrast with or to reverse the social order of things. In Reclaiming's case, however, the thesis needs modification since it pertains to feminists of both genders, not only to women, although the ritual initially was created by women. Also typical for Reclaiming is the fact that it is not a requirement to go through the initiation ritual in order to become a member of a coven, the Collective or the community.

Initiation is an individual choice, and on this level it can be motivated by a desire for a variety of "objects", such as personal growth, wisdom, religious experience, magical power, social position, adventure, feeling special, love, protection, priesthood, ultimate meaning, meeting the Goddess, establishing friendships. As an exoteric, social act, its meaning is more specific. First-degree initiation is, generally, regarded as a personal commitment to the Goddess and to the Craft of a particular tradition. But the ritual is also a celebration of a transformed person who has demonstrated, by taking on all given challenges, that she is "willing to suffer to learn". By 1990, there were about 23 first degree initiates in this sense in Reclaiming. Reclaiming as a tradition does not offer further initiation degrees. However, the Faery initiates *in* Reclaiming may offer them. The second Faery degree is primarily a sexual rite, in which the secret names of the deities are said to be revealed, preferably at the peak of orgasm in the arms of one's beloved. As far as I knew in 1990, six Reclaiming people had undergone this rite. Considering that the Reclaiming community in SF at this point included approximately 50 people in its inner circles, with a larger community numbering around 130, the number of initiates was modest. A majority of the initiates of both categories were women. In this chapter I shall discuss initiation exclusively as practised in Reclaiming.

Apprentice seeking initiators

In order to be initiated, the person must herself take an active step and ask for it. One is typically not offered initiation or given the suggestion by anybody that she is worthy of it. The wish to be initiated may be put forth after having completed the three basic six-evening classes in Reclaiming, which equals one week at Witchcamp, and after having been in the Craft for "one year and a day". Since the whole concept of initiation is alien to most modern, western people, they usually need a lot more time just to become adjusted to the idea. Anyone already initiated can be asked, and for this ritual there is no gender segregation. Women may ask men, men may ask women, and quite often a mixed gender group will facilitate the initiation ritual. The only rule is that the apprentice must ask more than one person for initiation. She might get a yes, she might get a no. The uncertainty of the answer is explained with reference to *karma, friendship* and *challenges*.

To be an initiator is to build a "karmic bond" with the one being initiated; that is a bond of mutual influence and destiny in this life and in the lives to come. A relationship grounded in meta-physical bonding is serious, and both parties have to consider carefully with whom they get involved. The requirement for personal knowledge through some kind of friendship has developed as a minimum of protection. If an initiator is hesitant about whether she really wants to build such a bond with the one asking, or if she finds that the apprentice is not yet ready for initiation, she will probably say "no". Personal knowledge is also necessary so that each initiator can give the apprentice suitable, or good, challenges. "Good" in this context does not mean "nice", but rather "pricking weak spots and shadows". To be trustworthy when starting somebody else's change, personal knowledge is a presupposition. Very often, this friendship grows deeper during the initiation process.

The challenges given are mostly aimed at people's addictions. A man who was drinking beer daily, but not considered an alcoholic, was challenged to quit drinking completely for a year and a day. An overweight woman was challenged to exercise three times a week for an hour. A woman with little knowledge of, and strong prejudice against, non pagan religions was challenged to study another religious tradition seriously. A challenge shall not be moralistic but is meant to come from the Goddess via the initiator. If the initiator does not receive a challenge to pass on, she can tell the apprentice that the Goddess will challenge her directly, and that she will know when it happens. A challenge is meant to be met; "trying my best" is not sufficient. The beer-drinking man did not accept his challenge but was angry and wanted to negotiate it. This is rarely possible, and he was not initiated. Usually it takes a year before the initiators agree that the challenges are completed. Only then can the initiation process be set with the esoteric initiation ritual.

When Witches try to explain to me the essence of initiation, they call it *an intentional act to give up one's will in order to surrender to the Goddess, who is perfect love and perfect trust and perfect care*. To some extent an initiation process resembles religious conversion often associated with sect membership: it reenacts an idealized imitation of the parent–child relation, a relation in which the apprentice ultimately seeks to merge with the perfect love object.[2] When asking for initiation, the apprentice temporarily puts somebody in the position of authority, of Mother and Father. And because of challenges and the implicit demand for obedience (equivalent to childrearing), she will probably regress back to childish behaviour. In the process of giving and receiving challenges she asks the other to see and name her "shadow" sides. From this "seeing" the initiator shall extract a challenge which, on one side, shall promote self-illumination by stating something essential about the apprentice today and, on the other, give her a direction for change. To refuse the challenge is to pretend that you did not ask for it of your own free will in the first place. It is to act as if somebody is trying to control you by uninvited meddling in your daily business and way of being.

But initiation is also radically different from conversion to a sect, first of all in terms of pedagogics. In initiations, the authority structure is a conscious and time-limited one, set up for the purpose of personal refinement to help the individual develop inner authority. In sectarian conversion stories this may or may not be the case, but an often-heard version is that the convert is set in a continuous hierarchical relationship with an omnipotent, male authority figure (Ullman 1989). The goal of Witches' initiation is not to stay within a human parent–child relation, but exactly the opposite: to grow out of it forever by being "reborn" as a new and wiser being, as a child of the Goddess.

Modernists and traditionalists

If the goals of initiation are so idealistic, why is the phenomenon such a delicate theme in Reclaiming? This is because dedication, obedience and the supposed swearing of oaths are regarded as attitudes in conflict with anarchist politics. Anarchism is a modernist ideology, basically rejecting any kind of hierarchical truth holding and the making of esoteric, secret knowledge. This modernist argument against initiation holds that all knowledge is exoteric and that everybody already has access to power, to a power-from-within. Furthermore, all available knowledge is potentially inside every person, and an exterior human teacher is really not necessary for an apprentice to learn. This view was integrated into Witchcraft in the early 1970s by Z. Budapest. Inspired by the women's movement and a blend of sexual equality feminism with essentialism, Budapest claimed that all women are already priestesses and initiates to the Goddess by virtue of being women. This egalitarianism, which in Reclaiming is made gender neutral, is official language in all branches of feminist Witchcraft today.

Arguments explicitly favouring initiation I will call *traditional*. They state that there is hidden wisdom in what is old, in what people have done before, and maintain the value of esoteric knowledge, which is only accessible to initiates. This kind of knowledge is, by the non-initiates, often believed to be instrumental (like mathematical formulas), for example, knowledge about advanced forms of magic to attain power, knowledge about the mystical invocations to call spiritual beings, and knowledge about the true naming of deities. Whatever this knowledge in fact might turn out to be, it is believed to be handed down secretly from "the ancients" through the esoteric traditions. The elders of contemporary Witchcraft have reobtained possession of this tradition, which can open up the universe to a select few, to those who are called as priestesses or priests. Being on this path, Reclaiming's initiation is among the most secretive of all the Craft traditions.[3]

At first glance, these two viewpoints do not easily harmonize. In Reclaiming's teaching policy the problem is solved by undercommunicating traditionalism. The Collective does not act as elders, offering advanced teach-ing to a selected few, but urges people to learn on their own or through common efforts in the coven. They argue, in a democratic and egalitarian fashion, that the power and the knowledge are already inside, available to everybody. This applies to ritual acts as well, for example, the one in which Starhawk anointed Sonia at her "first blood" ritual (chapter 1 (and 7)) while declaring, "*nobody can give you power; you already have the power within*". If the subject of initiation comes up when Starhawk teaches in non-Reclaiming contexts, she is likely to talk about it as devotion and commitment to the Goddess, and not as a tradition, and to insist that anybody is free to initiate themselves. Mostly the theme is passed over in silence, and neither Starhawk nor other Reclaiming teachers often talk about initiation outside their own circles.

But people who are eager to learn more, who disagree with the concept that "any knowledge is already inside" because they do not experience its truth, will find that initiation really is the next "class" they need to take. They will also be confirmed in this viewpoint by those who have already been initiated and told that if they want to develop spiritually and personally, they should ask for initiation. None of the initiated Witches I interviewed ever regretted their choice; nor were they disappointed with the long initiation process or the final ritual. On the contrary, they emphasized that initiation was the most powerful, special event in their life. But what exactly did the initiation offer them? Did they perform an act of piety, dedicating themselves to the Goddess, or did they enter a sister–brotherhood of magicians, obtaining secret, but instrumental, magical formulas? Initiated Witches are often reluctant to answer these questions directly; instead they will repeat the specialness of the event and insist that it caused profound changes. Over the last years, several typical anarchist Witches have asked to be initiated. This is a sign that initiation is observed to have a positive effect on those undergoing the rite. With time it has resulted in more affirmative attitudes toward initiation in the community at large.

By virtue of being an initiatory religion, Witchcraft is destined to operate in terms of teachers and apprentices, initiates and non-initiates, differentiating between those who have and those who have not. But as documented, this unmodern heritage does not prevent anarchists from feeling at home in Reclaiming. Those who join this diverse community seem to be drawn by a basic desire: there is something the Reclaiming people have that they also want to have. This "something" can be hard to name, but they clearly have "it". I will argue that this desire is not very different from the desire pushing people to ask for initiation, an act that transfers them from one camp to another, but within one and the same community.

The desire separating insiders from outsiders

According to sociologist Pierre Bourdieu, the separation of insiders from outsiders is an essential feature of all rites of passage. He therefore suggests that we rename such rituals as rites of institutions. Bourdieu is therefore critical of the theory developed by Victor Turner (and Arnold van Gennep), although he agrees that Turner's notion of a four-staged "social drama" underlying ritual (understood as "what") gives an adequate systematic description of its phases. But the theory does not raise questions of the social function of the ritual or of the social significance of its selection and boundary making:

> This theory does not conceal one of the essential effects of rites, namely that of separating those who have undergone it, not from those who have not yet undergone it, but from those who will not undergo it in any sense, and thereby instituting a lasting difference between those to whom the rite pertains and those to whom it does not pertain.
>
> (Bourdieu 1991:117)

One may ask whether there is a lasting difference between initiates and non-initiates in Reclaiming. The two parties do not seem to be separated by an absolute limiting quality as, for example, in the case of gender or royalty, examples given by Bourdieu, in which one social group is defined through initiation in opposition to another; for in Reclaiming, all individuals are potentially initiates, even those opposing initiation. The qualities separating insiders from outsiders are not external to the individual with respect to group belonging, but rather internal. They become manifest as differences regarding worldview, emotionality and social skills within a social group. The characteristics of people choosing to undergo an initiation ritual seem to be (1) profession of a traditional worldview that values knowledge that is "handed down" from the ancients, and (2) an emotional desire for the unknown "it", believed to be in the hands of the already initiated, combined with an emotional conditioning permitting the individual to perform the wilful act of giving up her own will – for a certain period of time – in order to attain the "it". In this context there seems to be a strong interdependence between worldview and emotionality, a condition also documented by Chana Ullman in her study of religious conversion. She concludes that in the development and function of beliefs within the self, "world views are adopted or rejected not as isolated systems which may or may not have internal coherence, but as congruent with the lives of persons, intertwined with their dispositions, emotions, and desires" (Ullman 1989:193).

The third and final characteristic is (3) a strong social position, including friendship with people already having been initiated. As stated earlier, without this friendship, there is nobody whom the individual can ask to facilitate the initiation, nobody to be given challenges by or to perform the rite. Being a loner, you may still ask, but you are likely to get a "no", as was the case with Fallon in chapter 1. In other words, a person must be dedicated and willing to take emotional risks, socially ambitious and/or successful, but not too anarchistic to be initiated into the Reclaiming tradition. According to the ethos of Reclaiming Witches, such social and personal attributes are potentially available to everybody in the community and are, therefore, unable to create absolute and lasting differences between groups in Bourdieu's sense. One may, of course, question this supposition further. However, that is not the subject now.

Since in previous chapters, I have already accounted for worldview and social relationships, I shall in the following be content to focus on the desired "it" of initiation, that is, on the specific "object desire" that seems to circulate in the initiation process. The narrative framework of initiation is set by the existential dilemma of separation versus unity, within which the subject is struggling to find and to name the precious object, the "it", which is expected to bring forth spiritual and personal fulfilment. However, the ritual process gains its dynamics from the candidate's belief that "it" is possessed, somehow, by other initiates. Symbolic interaction between ritualized space and ritualized bodies not only reenacts the dilemmas of this drama. It is also believed to magically partake in their solution. The initiation ritual may thus be said to process a basic human existential that is structured as an emotional triad:

$$Y$$
$$X \qquad (a)$$

which shall be read, the person X believes that the person Y has the precious object (a); *X therefore desires Y to get (a)*. The precious (a) is not necessarily defined in any specific sense and, according to a psychoanalytic interpretation, its existence is entirely created by the power of X's more or less conscious belief. X believes that the mystical (a) *is* ultimate truth, a truth so "potent" that it may suspend the pain of separation and fulfil all desire.[4] However, in order to connect with (a), the *real* object of desire, X creates a displacement in which Y becomes the object of desire instead, so that *Y becomes (a) for X*. The triad (X–Y–(a)) is now reduced to a dyad (X–Y), in which Y=(a) for X. Y changes position from a person holding the key to the desired object to becoming a final desirable object herself. X now believes that Y embodies (a).

This triadic/dyadic structure can be found in all aspects of human life, including religious belief systems as well as love and sexual desires. A typical example is the X who longs for the desired object "love". When X falls in love with Y, he does not want "love" any longer, but the beloved Y, who is believed to be a personification of love (a). I shall not discuss the general claims of psychoanalytic theory. I shall merely use the formula as an entrance to discuss what I will call *initiatory desire*. This particular desire can be formulated as an apprentice's (X) desire for a helper (Y) to be incorporated into an estimated space (a), which of itself is believed to hold truth, power or love (a). In the context of initiation, the objects of desire (a) can be plural, but still interrelated in terms of their spatiality. The primary desire is to be part of an unknown circle, a spatial continuum attributed with high expectations regarding its content, which eventually will be disclosed.

In this context initiation is to enter a "room" that cannot be known otherwise. This implies that the room is of such a character, or is made into such a character, that it is not intelligible in language alone. The quester must embody it and be embodied by it. Until then, it will continue to represent the unknown but highly desirable "it". Furthermore, the door to this room can only be opened by someone (Y) who has already "been" there, who is believed to already have "it" (a). If the psychoanalytical observations about displacement and transference are valid for the initiatory desire, we may then expect the helper (Y) to slowly be projected as identical with the desirable object (a), believed to embody the expectations of the unknown circle in her persona, so that Y becomes (a) for X.

In a certain phase of the initiation process, we shall see that X displaces the object of desire (a) with Y. But the displacement is temporary for when the ritual is completed, the candidate is expected to have learned that Y has nothing that she didn't already have herself: Y is not (a); Goddess is. And the Goddess is already inside X, as well as in Y. The ritual verifies for X that (a) is in fact desirable, but not as a property of Y, and with a different content than expected. Thus, the initiation process resembles a setting for personal growth in which the basic human object desire is challenged to evolve and be transformed onto a more mature level. A mature X can let go of objectifications and instead relate to Y as equal *subject*, a unique creation/manifestation of Goddess, and nothing else. When this happens, the initiation process really brings to light that the emotional structure X–Y–(a) is in fact immature; it belongs to and describes the eternal child, the non-initiated.

Finally, we shall address the nature of initiation as an experiential rite. Initiation is a ritualized process, and all its strategies are rooted in the body, or rather, in the interaction of the social body within an environment constituted by esoteric symbolism. To go through an initiation is to be willing to go through certain performances and emotional processes which, by virtue of being orchestrated, are believed to reveal new insights and to transform the actual subject. Since these new insights are expected to be personal and nonanalytical, initiations tend to be connected with secrecy and silence. Religious initiations are sensory experiences focused on the active and direct tasting of "the body of god" – in contrast, for example, to a traditional sermon where the individual is more passive. If ritual as "what" can be defined as prescribed patterns of symbolic enactment that express and move us into our shared values,[5] the definition of religious initiation rituals must elongate "the symbolic" to include "the index" in order to take in the "mystical real". For initiation not only moves us into our shared values as represented symbolically, but claims to offer an experience of real and direct encounter with divine reality. It is more than a symbolic representation *of* religious beliefs/shared values, since the meaning of the ritual and the transformations it brings forth are believed to be immanent in and effected by the ritual itself.

Case: Catherine's initiation process

We shall now examine the ritual process of a first-degree initiation ritual in Reclaiming through an initiation story generously given to me by a woman named Catherine. To get "it", Catherine had come to Reclaiming in 1983. She asked for initiation in 1987 and was initiated in 1989. When she joined Reclaiming, Catherine was 36 years old, mother of a boy, married to Orion, and just entering a career path as an Assistant Professor in Spanish. She has been a political activist since the student revolt at UC Berkeley in the late 1960s.

Catherine is a typical intellectual feminist, critical and outspoken, but also with a reputation for having a strong desire for control. She was brought up in a liberal, Protestant home, and in her adult life she joined the congregations of both Quakers and Unitarians. When she finally left the Christian church it was because she could no longer bear up against its patriarchal language and imagery. Catherine and I met in one of the Reclaiming classes and, because of similar backgrounds and an aptitude for critical opinions, we very soon established a friendship.

Catherine is bisexual, having an "open marriage" with her husband. This means a mutual agreement permitting other sexual partners. Soon after joining the community she found a lover among the leading women in Reclaiming. This relationship made her move very fast into the inner social circles. In the spring of 1985 she was already involved with a coven and had become a member of the editorial board in the Reclaiming Newsletter. Six months later she was asked to be a member of the Collective. Catherine's lover had been an initiated Witch for many years. Catherine was, therefore, from the beginning exposed to the code of those who have "it" and those who haven't.

I will present Catherine's initiation process through the stories she gave during three different interviews. The first was recorded in June 1985, long before she even considered initiation. It was rather structured, with prepared questions. The second interview was conducted 10 days before her initiation in the early spring of 1989, and the third we did five days after this event. These interviews were more like conversations, but they qualify as interviews – both to her and to me – for two reasons: they were recorded, and the intent of our conversation was to answer my questions. The duration of the three interviews was respectively 2, 1.5 and 3 hours. Together they portray how Catherine changed her mind, from being against initiation in 1985 to favour it in 1989, as well as her growing insight into what it means to become initiated. In addition, Catherine and I socialize a lot and have discussed the topic of initiation on several occasions. In the process she made it clear several times that she only gave me her story because I was her trusted friend and because I said I needed it for my study.

As the process developed, it was difficult for Catherine to keep her commitment to me, although she did. Especially the post-initiation interview, which we did very soon after the actual event, was hard. It was hard for her to talk about an experience that felt deeply sacred within the context of a recorded interview. It was also hard for me to ask questions for the purpose of academic research that would not, somehow, be intrusive or profaning to her experience. Although Catherine's attitude was to keep silent about anything secret, she did not want to mystify the experience by not sharing it; so she shared it. And she did it generously, honestly, knowing that she somehow laid herself bare.[6]

I shall describe Catherine's initiation process, which purposely is surrounded with secrecy, without exposing "secrets" other than those available to anybody. I will, rather, try to deepen all my informants' understanding of what initiation is all about and acknowledge their pride at having undergone such a demanding process. My concerns in this endeavour are two. First, I want to document how the actual preparation for initiation and the ritual itself have the power to transform – being a performative and emotional act of commitment and devotion, rather than being a question of dogmatically joining prearranged belief systems. Second, I want to demonstrate how Catherine's attitude toward the act of initiation is changed from modernist to traditional – and back again – as she gets more involved with Witchcraft, the Reclaiming community and with her lover.

The initial event: the crisis[7]

Catherine asked for initiation into the Reclaiming tradition in January 1987. She asked because she wanted to become a healer. At the time she had been part of the community for three years. She decided to ask for initiation because she felt that she somehow needed the particular healing techniques and esoteric knowledge of the Craft to become a *real* healer. At that point she had also started to coteach a class in Reclaiming called "Magical Healing Arts". She found that, besides being a successful scholar, she was able to learn to help people heal.

The actual incident that made her consider initiation happened at Witchcamp in the summer of 1986; and in my retelling of it, I shall use Catherine's own formulations. One day when Catherine was halfway through Witchcamp, she needed a break from what she describes as "psychic experiences and intense, hard work". She therefore went to a laundromat to wash clothes. While waiting outside for her laundry to be done, she suddenly heard somebody screaming, as if being beaten, from inside the laundry room. She went in to see if her help was needed and found a teenage girl, Miel, lying on the floor in great pain. Miel's friend asked people to help. She explained that Miel would get these attacks on and off and that she didn't have any medication with her today. But everybody present in the room was backing away. Somebody called the local chiropractor, but when he came, there was nothing he could do either.

> I realized that no one was gonna help her and that I had to help her because she was not breathing – she was screaming and crying, and she was not taking in oxygen and her color was changing. So when the chiropractor came and I could see that he was completely useless, I just decided to take over. And I did . . . . I instinctively used healing techniques. I held her like a midwife; I helped her to breathe. And then I called in the elements from the ocean. I was speaking to her. I ribbed a window in her third eye, and then I brought in the water from the ocean. In the meantime someone had called the fire rescue people, and all these guys came to give her oxygen. But by the time they came I already had her breathing. When they left the chiropractor turned around and looked at me and said: "She was lucky you were here . . . . Are you some kind of a social worker or something?"[laughter] And I said: "No, actually I am a Witch. It was Witchcraft." He acted very calm, and later in the conversation he said: "By the way, that Witchcraft, that is a pretty strong word." And I said: "Yes I know, and I do not usually use it with people I don't know." And then I looked him straight into the eyes and said: "But you saw it in action [laughter]."

Catherine told me this story three times in the same interview, revealing new details every time. The way she helped the girl was to sit down on the floor with the girl's head in her own lap, asking permission to help her, telling her that she would help her to breathe, and then breathing with her as a midwife, breathing in, and breathing out, for a long, long time. When the girl finally relaxed and was breathing by herself, Catherine started to work on the pain in her head. She put her into light trance by saying, "The cement [you lie on] is cold because it is on the damp earth here on the coast by the ocean. And the ground here is very cold because it is next to the ocean, and the water and the breezes bring in the coolness." Then she made circular movements on her forehead to open a "gate" in the third eye for the coolness to enter the girl's head and release her pain. Catherine's healing technique was to activate the vital energies in her own body as well as in Miel's through breathing, "forming" this energy into a mental image of cold water and, then, imagining additional, healing water being poured into Miel's forehead. She worked with all the elements but fire in the trance induction.

Doing this work, Catherine had a basic experience: the way she was able to help the young girl was to connect with her, and not to separate from her:

> My instinct was to connect with her. It is very strange, but I felt that the way to help her was to be connected with her rather than to be separated from her. And that that somehow was a key to healing.

By acting on her instincts she found the power to heal, but she also experienced her power in a context with other people in the room:

> I controlled everybody with my eyes. It was incredible, because all of these men [the chiropractor and the fire rescue people] with their equipment also came in and asked her [Miel] questions! [laughter] And then I would like go on and answer some questions, and then I would just look at them and sort of—I cannot describe it—make them do what I wanted them to do. And they would do it; it was unbelievable.

When she finally left the laundromat with her clean clothes and went back to Witchcamp, Catherine was amazed with herself and what had happened. There she told the story to Starhawk, who said she had done the psychic equivalent of a mother's lifting a truck off a child, something you can't normally do. Starhawk suggested that she go and lie down in the garden and "ground herself". To ground in this context means to give the vital energy that was at work in the healing process back to the earth. It would also help Catherine cleanse herself from the illness of the girl's energy. While lying on the ground, she had another significant experience:

> It is very hard to describe, but in words [this is] the way it would be: I was lying on the ground, under a tree, kind of in an unconscious state of mind. And then I kind of opened my eyes, or else in trance, I saw the trees and the bushes and everything around me bend, leaning in towards me. And the Goddess or something, some power said to me: "If you will do this work, if you will do healing work, I will take care of you."

Until then, Catherine was not considered by anyone in the community to be in the possession of healing powers. She was usually categorized among the antimystical sceptics, advocating the Goddess mostly for ideological reasons. When I asked her if she had ever experienced anything like this before, she replied, "No, of course not, are you kidding?" Her story was, therefore, regarded as amazing by everybody. Because of this, and because it had an element of objectivity to it (it was witnessed by many people), Catherine was urged to tell her story in front of everybody at Witchcamp. The key message to her fellow campers when telling the story was: "If I can do it, we all have the power to do it."

From this experience, Catherine says she learned that "the skills we are talking about are real. It is not a metaphor; we can heal." And she honours Witchcraft for having provided the tools she used in the healing:

> Much of what I did with this girl has to do with my own life experience and my own wisdom. But the techniques, the ability to draw out from myself what is there, that I learned from the Craft. So, that is why I am interested in the Craft in particular. I mean, it wasn't Buddhism, it wasn't

Christianity; it was the knowledge of the elements, the knowledge of the way to work psychically, which is connecting instead of separating.

When back in San Francisco, she started to coteach the healing class. After doing that for a long time, she suddenly realized that, yes, teaching the magic of self-healing *was* the healing work she was supposed to do. When Catherine asked for initiation it was to confirm and respond to her revelations and chosen path and to learn more skills.

The challenges[8]

Lying in the garden at Witchcamp in the summer of 1986, Catherine had a revelation: she experienced being called directly by the Goddess to do her work, namely, to become a healer. In return for surrender she was promised divine caretaking, that is, love and protection. However, in order to *really* become a daughter and a priestess of Goddess, Catherine had to find midwives who could ordain her into this new position. Initiation is such an ordination, confirming her call, marking a new identity; and the initiators are the midwives, who for a limited time period take on the deputizing role of the Goddess. The question of their willingness to bond karmically with the apprentice *forever* is a sign of their extra-ordinary and representative function.

In the early winter of 1987, Catherine asked five women, including her lover, to initiate her – and at first they all said yes. None of her coven sisters were asked because none of them were initiated. Later, one of these five women withdrew her commitment, and for a time Catherine felt hurt and abandoned. She never considered asking a man to help initiate her. She explains that she does not trust men deeply enough on a spiritual level to have them come so close. Catherine trusted her husband, who also identifies as a Witch, but she believed he did not have the necessary knowledge.

In the process of choosing initiators and meeting their challenges, Catherine's emotional framework was dramatically changed from devotional self-obliteration to self-righteous struggle, from obediently accepting the grace of the Goddess to aggressively pushing her initiators to give her what she was obliged to have. She was taken over by the structure of the initiatory desire as described earlier, duplicating a parent–child relation as well as displacing the object of desire into human relationships. This change in behaviour might seem surprising and risky. What if the initiators had turned their backs on her? But according to Starhawk, the initiation process always "stirs up a lot of shit, both in the one being initiated, and in the initiators". This "stirring up of shit" is welcomed because it is believed to be the first – and often necessary – step in personal growth (cf. the afterplay to the processing ritual in chapter 3).

When I asked Catherine why she chose the particular women for her initiation, she gave three different answers during our conversation, but in this order:

I chose women that I felt would be important for my path in the Craft and for me as a person.

X takes initiation very seriously. She will see that I get the whole experience; she won't cut any corners. I respect her. But I think I mostly chose her out from what I think she can give me, without me knowing what that is.

I understand absolutely that I can initiate myself . . . and I don't think these four women really know anything that I don't. It is because they are initiated in a particular tradition; it is that knowledge. Because I am wanting the tools and techniques of the particular knowledge of this particular kind of training that it matters to me, and that I do it in that way. I don't know how, but it will turn out that I need it . . . . I just instinctively trust that it will turn out that I need whatever it is that I am gonna learn, you know [laughter]. So, maybe I am wrong.

In this phase Catherine seemed to be confused about what she really wanted and why. In the first answer she admits that she chose the women positively, for who they are qua persons. In her second answer Catherine objectifies and introduces the mysterious "it", saying, "I mostly chose her out from what I think she can give me, without me knowing what that is." But in her third answer Catherine is very clear that the women do not have anything in themselves; neither does initiation provide a mysterious "it." The women are reduced to a necessary link, almost in a technical sense, between herself and the desired tools to become a healer. Catherine's desire to be initiated was, at this stage, not motivated by religious sentiments, but by pragmatism and ambition: she needed initiation to become a healer and to gain the social position of an initiated Witch, exercising the power to say "yes" and "no". Initiation had become instrumental, resembling an entrance ticket to a workshop where tools are crafted, and had, for the moment, lost its initial aspect of devotional act.

Catherine also expressed strong discontent with the time span of the initiation process. An apprentice will usually be initiated within a year from the time the question is put forth. In her case it took two years and three months from the day she asked for initiation until it happened. This is a very long time to wait, compared to the situation of others in the community, and it made Catherine extremely upset. She tried to push the women to decide for a date, but nothing happened. Once, when she had an argument with one of the initiators about why she had to wait so long, she lost her temper and yelled at her initiator. When she later tried to deal with this incident and apologize, she was only told to meditate upon her anger.

Having chosen four initiators, Catherine was supposed to receive four challenges from four surrogate mothers. The first challenge came shortly after she asked for initiation in 1987. The last challenge she did not get until a few weeks before her actual initiation in 1989. This also made her upset. Catherine's first challenge was to participate in six Wicca rituals outside the Reclaiming tradition. The second was to be "sky clad" (nude) whenever possible in ritual and not to wear either contact lenses or a watch for one year and a day. The third was to develop rituals and ritual material for children. And the fourth – which she received just before the initiation – was to do four rituals, one for each element, and in this way explore her shadow. "Exploration" in this context means trance work, the attempt in Witchcraft to connect with Deep Self and attain true knowledge about her deepest motivations and feelings. Catherine was asked to write down her experiences when performing these rituals in a Book of Shadow, which is a personal record book about the work done in ritual. She was somewhat disappointed with all these challenges and felt they were not challenging enough. In my interview with her 10 days before her initiation she told me that, "the challenges have been interesting, but so far nothing more than that. I have lived with my shadow a lot. You can't be a nonmonogamous and bisexual person and not have confronted your shadow . . . . I constantly live with a lot of negative stuff."

Catherine felt that the women perhaps, after all, did not know her so well, or maybe did not care enough. To make the picture more complete she therefore gave herself a challenge, a challenge to be *honest* and not give in to her vanity, which was to please and impress.

> My challenge to myself is to be as completely within myself as I can possibly be during the initiation. And by that I mean to be absolutely true to my core. Not to respond any time to any other purpose other than to be true to myself. That may be hard, given who my initiators are. I think that I would want to please them, want to impress them. I would want to prove myself to them. And the challenge to myself is to keep the mirror in front of myself all the time. I am very clear that I am proving myself to myself only.

The basic initiatory desire determining this discourse is as follows: Catherine (X) believed that initiated women (Y) had healing powers (a). Catherine, therefore, desired a special relationship with these women in terms of an initiation ritual to get healing powers herself, spelled out as Catherine (X) desired initiation (Y) from initiated women to gain healing tools (a). The positions of "women" and "initiation" are ambiguous; they can both attain the status of (Y) and be objectified for another purpose. But we shall see how Catherine, in order to gain healing powers (a), slowly undertook a time-limited displacement in which the two possible Y's (women and initiation) became the object of desire instead, so that initiated women (Y) became *the* source of healing powers (a) for Catherine (X), just as the initiation ritual (Y) became *the* source of healing powers (a) for Catherine (X).

Magical preparations

When Catherine asked for initiation, the four women never asked her why she wanted it. Neither was she ever told what an initiation actually involved, nor what would happen during the ritual. She was only told to wear black (which in this context symbolizes a shroud, normally used to wrap a dead body, to write a "magical will", and to give her "magical tools" to her initiators the day before the initiation ritual. The women never told her what a magical will is, or explained how to get or make magical tools; and she knew they would not answer if she asked. She, therefore, "just did it".

Magical tools had never been an intimate part of Catherine's pagan practice. According to her it is because of her Protestant background, having been taught a strong dislike for attachment to religious objects. Consequently, she did not find time to buy tools until two days before initiation, and for the first time in her five years with Reclaiming she entered an occult shop. The wand, the tool for fire and south, she made herself. In the evening she purified all the tools by salt and water and passed them over fire. The next day she took them to her initiators.

As described earlier, the tools are four and correspond to the four elements and the four directions. The fifth element, the centre, is thought of as pure essence and most commonly symbolized with a cauldron. Catherine's favourite symbol for the centre is the mirror, which to her symbolizes that the Goddess is inside and "that she does not have to prove herself to any other than herself". We recognize Catherine's own challenge in this expression, which really meant that she, Catherine, who has the Goddess inside, must stop doubting her value as a person. She carries ultimate value inside and is worthy of unconditional love. Whether Catherine shares all the symbolic meanings normally attached to the elements and the tools was never a question in our conversation. Her attitude was to do as she was told and to see what happened when she let go of opinions and, as we shall see, eventually let go of control.

Catherine interpreted both the magical will and the black dress as signs of a death and rebirth theme that she would confront in the ritual. She also expected to be tested in the final ritual (especially for courage and survival skills), to be abandoned for a certain amount of time, to be purified, and then to be accepted in some way into the circle of initiates. This knowledge she had from being in the Craft so long and from impressions of what is done in other cultures. Catherine claims that she deliberately had not yet read any books on Witchcraft or about initiation. In her will she indicated that she wanted to be remembered and to be called upon by her beloved ones after her death.

The initiation ritual[9]

Catherine's initiation took place on a Saturday night. She was told to spend the whole day in solemn silence, leave the house at 6:30 p.m., and wear warm, black clothes. She was told to walk to Lincoln Park half a mile from her home, and sit down by the statue of the Thinker and meditate on "thinking and non-thinking, and the un-thinking of non-thoughts". She did everything as she was told. She left home with nothing but her magical will, her Book of Shadow and small gifts for her initiators in her backpack. She brought no ID card, no watch and no money. From the *Mother Peace* tarot deck she brought the "Charge of the Goddess", and memorized the lyrics on her way to the park. She was silent and dressed as if going to a funeral.

After she sat about two hours alone in the park, meditating and watching the sun set, her initiators came. They were suddenly around her, and before she could see them she was blindfolded. In this act, Catherine crossed over and started "dying". Not a word was said. The women led her to a car. They took her to a place by the ocean and told her that she would be challenged and tested by the elements directly. The process proceeded in complete silence.

Catherine was first taken to the Gates of Earth to pass its test. They removed the blindfold, gave her a tray of many different kinds and colours of beads, a string and a flashlight and said she should make a necklace expressing her relationship to the earth and the material world. When finished, she lubricated it with dirt from the ground, consecrating it to the earth. Later she is supposed to carry the necklace around her neck as a sign of her rebirth.

The blindfold was then put back on and she was taken to the Gates of Air to pass its test. She was given a skull to hold in her hands. She guessed it was a bird's skull. She was then told to make a song for her ancestors. This was a difficult task for Catherine. In the lyrics she called on her ancestors to come and dance in her heart, "*You who danced in the woods and sang with the animals/you who once looked death in the face and smiled without fear.*"

As part of the test for fire, the four women lit candles very close around Catherine's body. If she moved she would be burnt. This she knew, so she stood very still. She trusted the women fully. She knew that, ultimately, it was her own distrust and fear of being burned, potentially causing her to move her body, that was being tested here.

After passing the test of earth, air and fire she was taken back into the car and driven to another place by the ocean. All her clothes, except the blindfold, were taken off, and she was sent into the cold waters of the Pacific. Two women went with her. It was freezing cold to the other women, but Catherine enjoyed it a lot and felt warm. She did not want to leave the water, and was finally asked by one of her initiators to let them know when she had passed the test of water. Catherine describes this experience as "ecstatic", even if she says she can't describe what happened. She maintains that she was in trance during most of the initiation and that it had already started in the Park.

During the initiation, Catherine cried a lot. Her crying in the water she felt to be connected to Yemaya, the Yoruba water goddess whom she met in trance when working on the challenge to explore her shadow. She felt that her whole initiation became water dominated.

I met her [Yemaya] there as Aphrodite, who rises on the shell and, down from the deep water, can read people's desires. My whole initiation became water oriented. In the water I felt that I really liked this initiation. It was fun and silly and just beautiful. I completely gave my self over, I gave my will over to these people. If they said stop I stopped, if they said turn left I did. I had given it all to them, I did not decide anything . . . . We held hands [in the water] and I felt a strong tie. I felt the stupidity in going into the water in such cold, dark and rainy weather. It was just like being a child, and playing in the waves with your friend . . . . Under the whole initiation I did not feel left. I had that feeling of being cared for, and in a way all this attention, being bathed in attention from these wonderful women.

Being in the water was the beginning of Catherine's transformative process, which also included a symbolic change from adult to child, although she actually played with the Guardians of the threshold of death. The autonomy and individual freedom associated with the adult is exchanged for the purity and inner freedom of the child. She is, temporarily, removed from defiled adulthood and returned to the liminality of innocent childhood. Catherine used the word "ecstatic" about her experience of "being just like a child", while repeatedly telling me that what happened is almost impossible to talk about: "It is beyond words." Somehow it was about giving herself over to the women and feeling total trust. It was about giving herself over to the elements and being merged with them. It was about dedicating herself to the goddess and feeling the waters of Yemaya flowing down her cheeks as tears. When I asked how all this could happen when they were not even talking together and she was blindfolded most the time, she just stated, "Revelations and understanding would come all the time, thousands every second." When I pointed out that it was interesting that she merged with the elements, that they were not treated as metaphors or symbols but as real, she answered, "Yes, and that is, of course, what the Craft is about."

Having passed the test of all the elements, Catherine was put in the car again and driven to one of the initiators' houses. One room in the house had been made into a temple. They sat her down in a chair nearby that room and asked her to tell them about her challenges, why she wanted to be initiated and why she picked each of them to initiate her. They also asked for her magical will. Catherine was still blindfolded when giving her account.[10]

Catherine told them that she wanted to be initiated to become a healer and that Witchcraft was the spiritual tradition she wanted to learn from. She felt connected to her ancestors and believed that they danced in the green fields with the animals and knew how not to be afraid of death. She told them that she had meditated on her anger and that she had also been confronted with her anger when doing trance work on her shadow. She had learned from this work that hurt and pain and fear are the underside of anger: "I realized then that what I was afraid of, was that they [the women] did not care about me, that they would forget about me. Ultimately it [anger] is a fear of death, of annihilation."

After this confession to "the Knights of Death" (the four women), marking her symbolic death, Catherine was taken to the bathroom for a ritual purification and rebirthing bath. The room was decorated with flowers and burning candles. Into the bathtub were put all kinds of herbs and flowers, and the room smelled of incense. She was helped into the water and lightly washed. Still blindfolded, she was left alone to search for a new name for herself. This was given to her by several goddesses, among them Yemaya. It is a secret name, connected to the elements of water and earth.

Half an hour later, her sponsor came into the room and asked if she had been given a name and if she was ready to enter the sacred circle. She also let Catherine understand that it was not too late to change her mind. Catherine was told the questions she would be asked when entering the circle and the right answers to them. She was then led by hand by her sponsor to the temple entrance. After being tested of her worthiness to enter the sacred circle of Witches, her blindfold was finally removed. From this point on she was part of a secret ceremony, with permission to see secret things and to hear secret words.

Catherine's initiators have instructed her not to tell anybody what happened in this very circle. She keeps this promise, not least by stating that she hardly remembers anything because of her trance state, although everything that happened was "beautiful and right". She was asked questions; she made promises, but not to anything that did not feel right. While talking in one of our conversations about her feelings connected to the secret ritual, she suddenly said,

> All the oral things are exactly what you would think. It is all the forms and the substances that we already know. And it is the closest to anything I would call high magic, or ceremonial magic . . . . It was more solemn, more scripted in a way, more formal, less individual, probably more conforming . . . . But besides that it felt so intimate, so religious. It feels sacrilegious to talk about it; it feels like a violation of that holy ceremony to even talk about it.

The pledge she had made for herself to be fully her core self during the initiation was not experienced as difficult at all. Nothing happened that did not feel part of her, even though some parts came totally as a surprise:

> I feel I did something in that part of the initiation, I feel as if I dedicated myself to the Goddess in a formal way. I didn't know I was going to do that. I did not know that would happen. That's a way in which I feel different. You know, all the women in my coven would say they don't join anything. I have never had that. On the contrary . . . for me it is very powerful in saying, of course, I have reservations; everybody always has

reservations; of course, nothing is perfect. But there comes a time when you have to do it, I mean you either are or you aren't. I really feel that way about being a Witch. I like to say "Yes, I am a Witch." I am not just studying Witchcraft; not, I am interested in feminist spirituality; not, I am a goddess worshipper; not, I am a pagan. I am a Witch. I understand what that means. It is an act of the Crone . . . . There is this Christian hymn used in Protestant circles *"Once to every man and nation comes the moment to decide, in the fight between good and evil for the good or evil side"* . . . . Just changing the words from "Once" to "Often," that is how I feel about a choice like this.

After completing the secret part of the ritual, Catherine's initiators gave her presents, and she gave them some small gifts as well. Then they revealed for her their secret names and closed the circle by feasting and having a good time. The ritual was done at 3:30 a.m. Sunday. At that time it was nine hours since the initiation ritual had started.

The secret ritual part – according to literature

Even though Catherine was not permitted to reveal anything from the secret part of the ritual, Starhawk has written at length about the initiation ritual in *The Spiral Dance* (1979a:159–64). We also have an important source for what actually happens in Witchcraft initiations in Stewart Farrar's book *What Witches Do*, first published in 1971. Farrar is an Alexandrian, British Witch, a tradition close to the Gardnerians (cf. the Introduction). Although the Faery tradition claims to be different from the Gardnerian, even in some respect to initiation, one of my non-Reclaiming informants who is initiated in both Faery and Gardnerian Witchcraft told me in 1990 that all Craft traditions, including Faery, are influenced by Farrar's very important revelations about Wiccan rituals and beliefs. This informant also told me that *The Grimoire of Lady Sheba* (1972) has the complete initiation text, if I really wanted to know the exact details.

Since then I have experienced the initiation ritual myself (1994). Like Catherine, I found the secret part to be very ceremonial and surprisingly scripted, but, unlike Catherine, this part did not move my religious sentiments onto any emotional level of really feeling transformed. To the extent I was spiritually moved, it happened in the first part of the ritual, which is a Reclaiming innovation that is not concealed behind the veil of secrecy. The secret part, to me, was a little disappointing because it was just as occult and stilted as I had thought it would be. In a way I already knew it. Its function for me was more to finish the whole initiation process and to welcome me ceremonially to a closed sister/brotherhood, among the living as well as the dead. But in the end, I had the same feeling of gratitude toward my initiators as Catherine had, finally recognizing how much work and time they had invested just for me.

When entering the secret circle, I was – like Catherine – in a light trance state. I was in this condition thanks to deprivation of food and drink, a very long and extremely hot ritual bath and hours of blindfolding. My memory of spoken words and symbolic details in the secret ritual is vague. What I especially remember is the order and the sequence of the performative acts,[11] and my memory is supported by a recognition of what I had already studied. This means that when, for example, I remember the blessing that was said over my body, it is because I have read it, or heard about it, so many times, that when it happened, I experienced it as, "okay, so this is where the blessing comes in". It also means that the details that I did not expect to be part of the ritual, are probably forgotten, or I remember them because they surprised me. I will not be able to truly retell the ritual unless I eventually perform it myself, being somebody else's initiator and thereby in the position of having "legal" access to the script (although this will not happen, since my work is not to be a sponsor for Reclaiming Witchcraft). The only important thing to note here is that the secret part of the ritual in 1994 was very close to the version printed in *The Spiral Dance* in 1979, and that this version again is very similar to other Craft traditions. It is, therefore, unlikely that the sources of the Faery initiation ritual were different from those available to Gardner. And as mentioned, one of these sources is a variety of Masonic rites. This is obvious to anybody briefly acquainted with the tradition of Freemasonry and its offspring.[12]

My purpose is not to reconstruct or analyse the exact content of Reclaiming's initiation ritual by finally revealing their secrets, but to document a story of personal growth taking place in Catherine during her initiation process. Since I claim that the total ritual process – including choice of initiators, challenges given, ritual preparations, time span, etc. – is the medium of this "transformation narrative", I need to include a probable version of the secret ritual part in my narrative to complete the picture. The secret part is, or may be, a significant experience to the initiated and it also testifies to Reclaiming's occult heritage. I shall, therefore, very shortly suggest what might have happened to Catherine in the secret ritual, using Starhawk's text from 1979 as a main source. I wrote this description before I was initiated myself and gave it to one of my initiators. I did this to prevent any suspicion toward me for revealing secrets that were not possible for the noninitiated to collect through literary or oral sources.

*   *   *

While Catherine was in the bathtub, her initiators and priestesses put on their ceremonial garments (black and brown ritual robes) and prepared a proper ceremonial space for the ritual in the temple room. The circle was cast in a traditional way, and the elemental guardians, the elements, the gods and the Mighty Dead were properly called in with scripted, fixed lyrics. The initiators purified themselves and raised energy from the earth into their bodies. The room was declared a magical place "between the worlds, beyond time and space, where birth and death meet as one", in order to make of Catherine a priestess and a *real* Witch. These acts are believed to convert the circle into a power vortex, a space where Catherine could merge with and embody her longed-for magical healing tools. As we shall see, the circle also represents the "Kingdom of Death" or the "Womb of the Goddess", and the ritual form corresponds to the Descent of the Goddess, the Witches' myth in which the Goddess enters the Kingdom of Death, stays for three days and makes love with death, thus experiencing the circle of rebirth (cf. chapter 6). Catherine's ordination as priestess is, in other words, valid forever, even in future reincarnations, and in all states of being, alive or dead, since it was staged in a room believed to contain all possibilities simultaneously. We remember that Catherine's ritual intent was to move beyond anger and the fear of death in order to experience an aliveness that is able to see through the word "annihilation", that it has no true reference in reality. She was prepared to take in the message of the Craft myth, to leave the ritual bath as somebody not-yet-born to human life, and to enter a room between the worlds of definite form.

1 Before entering the sacred circle between the worlds, Catherine's sponsor tied a thin cotton cord loosely around her wrist, saying:

And she was bound as all living must be who would enter the Kingdom of Death.

Then another cord was tied around one ankle, and the Sponsor said:

Feet neither bound nor free.

The cords, according to Starhawk, symbolize that entrance into Witchcraft is a free choice but that, once Catherine stepped onto this path, she set in motion currents that would impel her forward.

2 Catherine was naked and blindfolded when presented to the circle. In this state she was led to the Gate of the East in the circle, representing the beginning. One initiator acted as challenger and asked:

Who comes to the gate?
Catherine answered:
It is I, . . . [her new name], child of earth and starry heaven.
Challenger:
Who speaks for you?
Sponsor:
It is I, . . . [her secret name].
Challenger pointed the athame toward Catherine's heart and said:

You are about to enter a vortex of power, a place beyond imagining, where birth and death, dark and light, joy and pain, meet and make one. You are about to step between the worlds, beyond time, outside the realm of your human life. You who stand on the threshold of the dread Mighty Ones, have you the courage to make the essay? For know that it is better to fall on my blade and perish than to make the attempt with fear in thy heart.

Catherine:
I enter the circle with perfect love and perfect trust.

Challenger pointed the athame to the earth, kissed Catherine, and pulled her forward into the circle, as a midwife pulls forth a baby from her mother, saying:

Thus are all first brought into the circle.

In Farrar's version the challenger would go behind the apprentice, embrace her and push her into the circle with the force of her own body to mark the new birth.

3 The blindfold was now removed, and the new-born Catherine was given the mirror to see "her Self", that is, the divine within. Then she was led by hand and presented with her new name to the Guardians of the Watchtowers of the four directions, or better, to each of the elements, as one who would be made Priestess and Witch. Next she was led to the altar in the north, where the priestess-initiator, by an act of social reversal, knelt in front of Catherine. She was given the fivefold kiss on the parts of the body here named, while the initiator "adored" her and proclaimed:

Blessed are your feet, that have walked the sacred path/Blessed are your knees, that kneel at the sacred alter/Blessed are your sex, without which we would not be/Blessed are your breasts, formed in strength and beauty/Blessed are your lips, which shall speak the sacred names.

4 Catherine was measured with thin cord, from head to toe, around the head and chest. Knots were tied to mark the measurements. Then she was pricked in the finger with a needle, and the drops of blood were smeared on the cord. With this cord in her hand, the priestess asked:

Are you willing to swear the oath?
Catherine:
Yes I am.
Priestess:
Are you willing to suffer to learn?
Catherine:
Yes I am.

Then Catherine swore to always be silent and keep secret what needs to be kept secret. After that she knelt, placing one hand on her head and the other beneath her heel, saying:

All between my two hands belongs to the Goddess.

This is probably the part Catherine is referring to in the interview when telling that she dedicated herself to the Goddess and that it came as a surprise to her.

5 Catherine was lifted up by all her initiators and carried three times around the circle. Then she was laid face down before the altar and pressed into the ground. Gradually the pressing changed to stroking. They chanted her new name and raised a cone of power over her, giving her power to open her awareness, to heal and work magic. She was told:

Know that the hands that have touched you are the hands of love.

After this Catherine was supposedly told some of the Craft myths and "mysteries and secrets [were] revealed", as Starhawk writes in *The Spiral Dance* (1979a:164). This might also have been true in 1989.

6 Catherine was consecrated on her forehead and on her breasts with oil. And finally, the tools Catherine bought the previous day were handed to her. They were also consecrated and their uses explained. After this part, the feasting began. Catherine was honoured as a newborn and a wise one, as one who knows the mystery: that all life is interconnected and that death is not an end. She had died from her old consciousness in which life is equal to separation and death, and experienced rebirth to a new consciousness in which life is equal to bonding and living through "dying". She had attained a new identity, now being an ordained priestess and a dedicated Witch.

*   *   *

As stated, this suggested description is not to be taken too literally. Many rituals in Reclaiming have been changed since *The Spiral Dance* was published, and, to some extent, this is true for the initiation. But the basic structure of the secret part in Catherine's initiation ritual (in 1989) was probably as described above.

Post-initiation[13]

After the initiation, late Saturday night, Catherine went home with her lover. She explains to me that their relationship has now moved to "a whole new level". The whole ritual left her in a semi-trance state, which lasted for three days. In her summary of what she learned from being initiated, Catherine says:

Most of it I have already said in the telling of the story. Some of it is only insights into life, how it works and what religion is. Not in an abstract way, but basic, like the lesson with my anger. I learned ways to use the Craft; I got spiritual knowledge from the work I did. A lot of little things that only are present in context. Not something you can write an essay about [!]. It is certainly a bonding with the women that initiated me . . . . And the secrets are not the kind that gives me power over anybody else; it is not the formula of a neutron bomb. The only secret is that it is so intimate; that's what cannot be shared. It is just that it is so personal. It's for me.

On Sunday, the day after the initiation, Catherine went with her family to a birthday party in the community. A few people congratulated her on the initiation. She realized some days later that those were all initiates themselves. The conclusion she draws from this is that somehow her relationship with the initiated people has changed, not her relationship with others. The bond between them is that "they share the willingness to do it", to be initiated.

Catherine's movements from scepticism to surrender

I have made a point of Catherine's changing attitudes toward initiation and the essential meaning of becoming an initiate several times. The process of change can be observed from 1983, when she first became part of the community, to spring 1989, after being initiated. The process took several years, and in that respect she is a typical Reclaiming initiate. But to what extent was she aware of these changes herself? To my understanding, only retrospectively, and only partially. The changes she went through derived from social and ritual processes and were not deliberately chosen by Catherine. And her initial desire, when first asking for initiation, was neither to change nor grow but rather to achieve something instrumental. As we know, she very soon moved from being in need of healing tools to being in need of women. This was a crucial turning point. The beginning of her transformation started when she dared to surrender her will and well-being to the admired women, trusting that her role models did not represent an initiatory tradition alien to her values and integrity. But it was first when Catherine was able to let go completely of her object of desire, be it for tools, for secrets or for the initiated women, that we may say she was changing. To let go of desire was, for Catherine, identical to letting go of control and being satisfied to meet herself as a child and as a goddess.

The process of her movements from scepticism to surrender becomes obvious when we consult the interviews. In an interview conducted as early as June 1985, I asked Catherine whether Witchcraft is a religion for the few with a special vocation, and whether initiation was necessary to become a Witch. In 1985 Catherine did not yet call herself a Witch: she felt that the word did not communicate anything. Therefore, she found my proposition to be rather silly because everything is already available to everybody:

> I think that is silly. The religion is based on the elements everyone participates in and is of reality. It is a recognition of the connectedness of

everything that is. I don't say that everyone practices the religion, whether they know it or not. But certainly it is available and accessible and valuable for everyone. I think that there are more esoteric aspects of Witchcraft which are interesting and attractive to me, like trance work and psychic stuff, but I don't know that much about them, and I don't know how essential they are really to being a Witch.[14]

At that time, Catherine did not want to be nostalgic about the past or make herself believe that the spiritual practices of the Witches of earlier centuries were more advanced than what she and her community had at the time:

My guess is that we have everything available to us that everyone has ever had because we get our teachings from nature and the earth. For me the basis of the religion is in the physical world. So we have exactly the same teachers as the women did anciently. What we may have lost is an accumulated knowledge about it, and maybe a tradition of stories. But fundamentally we haven't lost anything because the wind still blows and the sun still burns and the water still flows. I really do believe that is where we get our lessons. I am not saying that symbolistically; I mean it in a very profound way . . . . One of the most wonderful things about it [Witchcraft] is that you don't have to believe in anything stupid like transubstantiation to be a Witch. All you have to believe in is that we need air, fire, water and earth to live. Who can argue with that? It is so clearly true that it is wonderful. We start from there so that we draw all our lessons from that and our recognition of our connectedness with each other and all living forms . . . . We are all part of the same thing, in a very real sense, not as a metaphor, but real . . . . This recognition is not a revelation; it is an experience.[15]

When I asked her what the point of initiation really is in feminist Witchcraft, considering that the body of knowledge she talked about is something you can get from inside yourself, she answered that to her the whole thing about initiation was a little mysterious. She felt that initiation for the most part had to do with defining oneself as community, that the secrets might be useful for community purposes, for bonding, for creating a strong group.

When I met Catherine again three years later (November 1988), she had asked for initiation and waited for it to happen. I was surprised and asked why she had changed her mind. Catherine's answered that she wanted "to know it all and to have it all", and that she was too curious to not want to see what they had to share with her. She also wanted to be part of the group of initiates because she had experienced the reality of its existence.

When going through Catherine's statements from June 1985, November 1988 and spring 1989, before and after initiation, it is quite visible that she moves from:

1 placing initiation in the realm of group psychology and sociology: initiation as a group-defining act and key to entering the space of shared values. She does acknowledge its positive function but also finds it a little mysterious. This is a typical attitude toward initiation in Reclaiming, not too rejecting, not too affirming. Having a love affair with an initiated woman, who is active both in Reclaiming and in the pagan community, gives Catherine small glimpses into the world of initiates. She has learned to respect it. She holds the analytical view of an outsider, of one who does not yet call herself a Witch (June 1985).

2 to placing initiation in the realm of education and social status. Catherine has now become part of the discourse of initiation; she has stopped observing it from outside. Initiation is not any longer an interesting phenomenon but something she has to take a stand for or against, either in terms of its educational value or in terms of the position it can give her. Her decision to be initiated is motivated by what she needs, almost in a practical sense, to become a healer and develop herself in the Craft, as well as by the fact that initiation is a key to becoming a member of a new, although vaguely perceived, social group (November 1988).

3 to placing initiation totally in the realm of vocation and education, but still in a somewhat technical sense. She does not any longer talk about initiation as a key that will open sociologically defined doors. Catherine is now very close to the actual initiation and has completed all her challenges. At this point she is committed to being initiated because she wants fully to become a Witch. She believes she needs the tools and the knowledge a Craft initiation can give her. Not only does she want to be initiated, she is obliged to because the Goddess has called her to do it. She does not choose a "reformed" version, as, for example, being initiated by her coven in a ritual that is completely made up for that occasion. She chooses the old, traditional way. And because she knows that her coven sisters are not in favour of her choice, she hardly talks about it. Anyway, she is concerned that the people who know her have respect for her decision and don't consider it superficial. She compares her initiation to the discipline of doing art: it is when the aspiring ballet dancer has first undergone the discipline of learning ballet that she is free to make up her own dances. So also with the Witchcraft initiation. Catherine definitely looks upon the act as something that will give her instrumental knowledge in the artform of healing (spring 1989, before initiation).

4 to finally placing initiation in the realm of existential and personal trans-formation. Going through initiation, Catherine gives birth to a "new baby" whom she dedicates to the Goddess. The unknown "it" is finally revealed as "a new Catherine, the true Catherine". She moves on in her educational path by finding her way "back home", to the religion of her

ancestors. She learns the path of the "give away", meaning that in order to become a healer and a bender in the world one has to "give oneself" to the Goddess. She gains wisdom and learns that the trial of initiation is fundamentally ethical: it is to take a stand "for the good" and accept the full consequence of her experience that everything is interconnected. Healing is based on the principle of interconnection, not on separation. Her dedication, then, is a pledge to manifest Goddess in the world through healing work, through connecting and bonding. Other people's opinions about her initiation do not interest her. She claims that initiation is a very personal, spiritual experience: "It is not an image; it is not an investment. If so, it would then be a place where other people's opinions would get in the way." She now tells me that she never previously considered, who was initiated and who was not, and argues eagerly that initiation, in fact, has nothing to do with elitism or with the making of a group within a group. Instead it has to do with risking trust and love, says Catherine, who now likes to say, "Yes, I am a Witch" (spring 1989, after initiation).

During these four stages, Catherine moved from a traditional outsider's point of view, in which initiation is interpreted in terms of group psychology and the making of social identity, to an insider's point of view based on a profound existential experience "beyond words". The wheel that turned and turned to bring forth this process was not the reading of books or appropriation of passed-on esoteric knowledge. In Catherine's account, the turning of the wheel was her willingness to bond and merge with the elements and with other people, a willingness to be touched and changed. Through this act Catherine relocated her spiritual focus from speculations on the social and symbolic *exegetical meaning* of initiation, and its various occult subtexts, to a more existential and *experiential meaning*. This new meaning is not a repetition or internalization of a "correct" or "official" meaning, but the creation of a new, individualized text.[16] This text is recognizable as my retelling of Catherine's story as given to me.

When this is said, it is also true that Catherine, in addition to her core experience of surrender, love and connection, did achieve all the social and elitist qualifications listed under 1, 2 and 3 as well. She did gain higher social prestige; she did attain membership in the group within the group. She was also educated and given new social and symbolic power: social in the sense that from now on she can initiate others, and hers is the power to say "yes" or "no"; symbolic in the sense that she is believed to possess direct access to the power source and that she is able to communicate successfully with the Mighty Dead. As stated earlier (in chapter 6), the Dead are powerful Witches of many life spans who have stopped reincarnating. They live eternally on the astral plane as spirits and may be contacted and asked for advice, protection and help by contemporary Witches – granted that they were properly introduced in the initiation ritual. In other words, to be initiated is to enter a new kinship structure. It is not based on biological bloodlines, but on spiritual affinity. It extends beyond life and death, including Catherine, her initiators and the Mighty Dead within the same family group – who now can meet across time and space and gather, whenever they need to, inside a magical circle.

The elements of Catherine's growth process

In Reclaiming's initiation ritual, religion is reclaimed as meaning *relinking:* making whole what was broken apart, relinking humans with their source of being, with their fellow humans, with the natural elements, with their Deep Self, relinking body and spirit. As discussed in chapter 5, one intention with this definition is to be able to put psychological therapy back into what is regarded as its original context: magical ritual. From this angle, it is not difficult to see Catherine's initiation process as a long therapeutic drama, in which her whole life was acted out in front of her and through her, over and over again. The ritual did in fact have a strong effect upon her, equipping her with the unexpected tools of wisdom and higher consciousness, tools that presumably will help her to live a deeper and more honest life.

The pedagogic underlying Catherine's initiation process is closely linked to Witches' holy hermeneutics: it presupposes an alienating dichotomy between body and mind that can only be healed by surrender and merger, also found in the classical scheme for bringing up children. This scheme emphasizes the category of experience and takes for granted that sensory experience is primary in the learning process, whereas cognitive knowledge is secondary. Children understand acts before they understand words. They express themselves through body language before they speak. They have a bodily experience of the world before they learn to name and interpret it. A pedagogical tradition derived from this childrearing philosophy must necessarily assume that the most transformative tool to change a human being is the breaking down of words and external, adult identities until she is like an innocent, trusting, speechless and naked newborn, who thereafter is "forced" to learn a new interpretation of life the way small children do: through bodily experiences, symbolic language, emotional turmoil, mimetic games, intuitive communication and performative arts – rather than through intellectual analysis or appropriation of dogmatic beliefs.

Catherine's most liminal experience was when she entered the darkness of losing control because she was not yet able to see her blocks and blind spots: she did not understand that her experience of control over the people at the laundromat, and her unveiled excitement about it, was challenged by her initiators' prolongation of her initiation. She was also challenged to be nude in ritual but did not see that this act symbolizes emotional nakedness and honesty. And when challenged to meet her shadow, she did not manage to go in deeply. She deluded herself into believing that she had always been in contact with her shadow since she has a nonmonogamous lifestyle. But her chosen women "made her suffer in order to learn", for without meeting her shadow and "the stirring up of shit", Catherine would not have experienced growth or transformation.

To give priority to embodied, emotional experiences represents a rather old educational tradition regarding human growth. We find it in initiation rituals cross culturally and in the archetypal structure analysed forth by Victor Turner: separation, liminality, communitas, reintegration. We also find it in the subcultural teachings and ritualized traditions of western esotericism. The modern "talking cure" to heal and make a person grow represents a somewhat different tradition. Psychotherapy is commonly regarded as a derivation and secularization of the Catholic confession, which values intellectual reflection above bodily experience. But the process of transference, turning the therapist into a temporary object of desire, is also crucial in this tradition in order to heal successfully.[17]

The most important hermeneutical principle circulating in Catherine's story is the authority given to experience and to intuitive, embodied thinking. In her preinitiation remarks, she repeatedly says that she does not know what she will gain from being initiated, but, whatever it is, she knows she will need it. She knows from her instinct, she says; she knows from inner experience. This kind of knowing is experienced by Catherine as nonlinguistic. She is acting from an inner source of knowledge, and its value as final authority to the Witches is reinforced by the structure of the initiation process: Catherine is not asked why she wants initiation until minutes before it happens. She is given no information about ritual proceedings and never told what initiation really is about – thereby making sure she knows what she asks for. When instructed to write her magical will, Catherine says she knows instinctively that she is not supposed to ask what that is; she is supposed to know. And, in fact, she does know. She trusts that her intuition knows. In other words, the initiation ritual in Reclaiming is built upon a structure demanding from the apprentice a certainty about being initiated to such a degree that she is willing to go through whatever it is, without the safety of being told in advance what will come. The nature of this kind of nonlinguistic knowing is symbolized both by the lack of conversation between Catherine and her initiators and by the complete silence of the first several hours of the initiation ritual. Also, when Catherine was angry because the initiation date continued to be postponed and she never received her final challenges, she was not given adequate answers, just told to meditate upon her anger.

By the end of Catherine's initiation her confusion about the real object of desire was finally resolved: not into a conclusion, but into a new perception. She experienced that her object of desire was not in accordance with the reality of things. Her new perception was born from the revelation that neither the women nor the tools of initiation carried the truth, but rather that she already possessed the object of desire inside herself. When leaving home on the day of initiation, Catherine brought with her the "Charge of the Goddess" text as printed on Vicky Noble's tarot deck. In her post-initiation reflections, Catherine interpreted this as a sign that she already knew in-tuitively what her initiation was about, although she was not yet conscious of it. In the "Charge of the Goddess", the Goddess is believed to speak to her children, and her speech ends like this:

> *And you who seek to know me, know that your seeking and yearning will avail you not unless you know the Mystery: for if that which you seek you find not within yourself, you will never find it without. For behold, I have been with you from the beginning, and I am that which is attained at the end of desire.*[18]

Catherine's revelatory experiences of growing into a new level of conscious-ness were brought forth by the final initiation ritual, which reenacted the whole initiation process and, obviously, brought together for her that which earlier had been only fragments.

However, if the final meaning of the initiation ritual is human growth, and not to hand over instrumental knowledge, why the secrecy? Because it triggers the initiatory desire for the unknown "it". The whole initiation process implies that without experiencing the pain of the never ending desire, *X desires Y to get (a)* and the process of displacement, *Y becomes (a) for X,* within a consciously staged setting, it is difficult to come to terms with this emotional structure and move on. The motivation for Catherine's wish to be initiated is quite representative. She desired "something" badly, and its names were mutually replaceable: healing tools, initiated women, to be part of a special group, trust, care, love. The initiation process was not set before Catherine's desire was turned on its head and evolved into a new one: not to get but to *give.* By asking for initiation, Catherine initially asked for the object "love, care and acceptance". Instead she learned that she already had love and that her work was to manifest it, give it out. The ritual unveils the desired "it", the holy secret, in declaring that there are no secrets, except the secrecy of *silence*: knowledge from inside, and the secrecy of *growth*: to be willing to suffer to learn. Having undergone the initiation ritual, Catherine could finally end the circle by, ironically, once again being reconciled with the egalitarian slogans in Reclaiming, those stating that "all is inside", that anybody has access to all the powers and all the knowledge within themselves, and that self-initiation is just as legitimate as the initiation she has undergone. But today she knows its truth from an experience of humility and trust, not from ideological postulates. The difference between ideologically and experientially knowing the same is crucial. Ideological knowledge is regarded as superficial, and its truth can be overruled and lost in power-over games in which the individual loses sight of life as interconnected. Experiential knowledge, though, is believed to be of a profound character, hopefully preventing Catherine from ever misusing power-over or putting herself in separation from the web of life.

*   *   *

In accordance with the view that initiation is an education for managing daily life, as well as an ordination, it is regarded as a never-ending process. Catherine's initiation is believed to have set in motion currents that will irrevocably impel her forward for many years to come. Especially the first year after the initiation is said to be hard. Catherine's emotional shadow sides were expected to become really burdening, pushing her to make necessary changes in her lifestyle. And in fact, for Catherine, the next few years were all extremely turbulent. She changed identity from bisexual to lesbian, divorced her husband, moved to another city and became a single mother of her teenage son. The new sexual identity was a major change in Catherine's life and, in particular, to her son.

Catherine is still active in Reclaiming and her profile has continued to be that of an outspoken and critical feminist. She strongly opposes exclusiveness, although she advocates the necessity for women-only space and rituals, offering teaching to women-only groups. With time she has also become a respected elder, one who is often asked for initiation. Although she once learned that the ancients did not have any access to knowledge different from hers, she honours western esotericism for handing down a method for personal growth which, according to Witches, was about to be lost in our culture. Catherine values initiation as a powerful, transformative process and is quite clear that there is a big difference between a Witch and a *committed* Witch. The first one worships the Goddess; the second one you can, in addition, count on.

Irrespective of whether Catherine's felt transformation of herself can be proved or not, Reclaiming Witches have contributed profoundly to the gendered field of religion by reclaiming and reforming a traditional rite of initiation and incorporating it into an otherwise elaborate expression of a newly invented female/feminist symbolic order. Resistance against secretive ritual acts and dislikes of hierarchical structures separating the learned from the ignorant, is normally (and for good reasons) very strong among feminist theologians and religionists. But blind resistance also risks throwing out the gold with the garbage – the gold in this case being a certain form of pedagogic, namely the mystery rite. The mark of a mystery rite is to convey knowledge and insight through bodily thinking, feeling and acting that otherwise cannot be known, and to actively stage a process of psychological displacement and transference in order to induce personal and spiritual growth in the candidate.

This esoteric method has been as controversial in the field of religion as has Freudian analysis been in the field of psychotherapy. However, just as feminists have appropriated psychoanalysis and reformed its theory and practice to suit their own liberation schedule, time is ripe for twisting methodological knowledge about the mystery rite from the hands of western esoteric societies and other androcentric brother/sisterhoods, and use it in the service of feminist theological reflection, women's spiritual growth and maturity and deepened experiences of autonomy and attachment (cf. Conn 1993: 254).

Reclaiming's merit is to have managed to develop a form to the mystery rite that is both traditional and accommodated to individual needs, and that unanimously has been experienced as deeply meaningful by those who have decided to enter this time-consuming and challenging quest.

Notes

1 Cf. Vivianne Crowley (1996:81). Such a differentiation among aspects of religion was originally introduced by the perennial philosopher Frithjof Schuon (cf. Knitter 1985:47)

2 Chana Ullman (1989) writes that religious conversion to sects is probably motivated by a wish to merge with the perfect love object (p. 145) or, from a psychoanalytic perspective, to install a perfect authority, replacing the biological parent with another (p. 193).

3 To a certain extent we may say that religious feminism also proclaims the belief that truth is hidden in the "Old Ways." But for something to be *old enough* in the goddess-worshipping spirituality movements it has to be at least 10,000 years old. Paleolithic and neolithic cultures, of which we know very little, are acceptable; European occultism, on the other hand, is embarrassingly close.

4 My reading of this triadic structure is inspired by the Lacanian psychoanalytical school (cf. Lauridsen 1982; Mitchell and Rose 1982; Gallop 1988). I am aware that feminists discuss in what ways the libidinal structure of "feminine desire" is different from the "phallic sexual economy" and womens relation to *jouissance*. This discussion is too complex and internal to psychoanalytical theorizing to be considered by me in the present context (cf. also Lacan 1982).

5 This definition is almost identical with Caroline W. Bynum's suggestion in 1991:29, a reformed version of Victor Turner's famous definition.

6 When Catherine read the first draft of this chapter (1989), she felt uncomfortable when seeing herself exposed for analysis. But she continued to keep her commitment, not withdrawing her permission, restraining her criticism, in order to help me have my object of desire: good ethnography. She has, however, given me helpful comments to factual points in the narrative.

7 Source: interview conducted before initiation in spring 1989.

8 Source: interview conducted before initiation spring 1989.

9 Source: interview conducted after initiation in spring 1989, and literature on Witchcraft.

10 In my own initiation ritual (in 1994) the aspect of ritual dying was made more explicit: still being blindfolded, I was taken through a huge stone labyrinth and laid down in its centre. I was wrapped in my shroud and left alone on the cold ground for a long, long time. When they finally returned the women encircled the symbolic graveyard, which also symbolized the circle of death and rebirth, while singing, "When we are gone, they will remain/Wind and rock, fire and rain/They will remain, when we return/The wind will blow and the fire will burn." Afterward they read out loud my handwritten will. Finally they "woke me up," led me out of the labyrinth and put me, who now was an "unborn fetus," in a hot tub, the comforting and purifying waters of "the womb."

11 My memory corresponds to a semantic theory claiming that performative acting is primary, whereas spoken words are secondary when constituting meaning in the individual (cf. Greimas 1974).

12 The heritage from nineteenth-century Freemasonry and its diverted lodges, such as the Golden Dawn, is so well kept in Witches' initiation rituals that we can even find parallels, both in some structural elements and in certain formulations,

between the Reclaiming tradition and that of the Christian Masonic brotherhood in Scandinavia. Their rituals have been published by the Norwegian theologian Sverre Dag Mogstad (1995). The revelations of secret texts and ritual forms are not complete, but, still, the act of publication has been strongly annoying to the brothers involved. Public knowledge of the rituals undermines their pedagogical effect on the apprentice. This criticism is, to a certain extent, also valid in regard to my writings about Reclaiming (cf. the Introduction).

13 Source: interview conducted after initiation spring 1989.

14 Source: interview June 1985.

15 Source: June 1985.

16 This viewpoint differs from Victor Turner's theory on ritual symbolism. He suggests that the scholar, for interpretive reasons, adds the indigenous ritualist's *exegetical* meanings onto the *structural, immanent* meaning in order to encompass the total meaning of the ritual and of the ritual symbolism. Catherine's sudden insights suggest, however, that indigenous interpretations of ritual experience not only are additions: they can twist the whole meaning of the ritual. Just as Witches slowly are changing the symbol "witch" from meaning "wicked" to meaning "healer" by living as if that were inevitable, they might have the power to change the symbolic meaning of "occult initiation" by acting as if that had already happened.

17 It was Freud who discovered the process of displacement and transference as crucial in psychological healing. It is also important to stress that psychotherapy and psychoanalysis are not the same. Analysis is *not* primarily an intellectual talking cure, reflecting on personal issues, but a technique to remember what is repressed and to become more conscious of unconscious hidden drives and desires. The psychoanalyst works with body memory, silence between words, the unsaid, associations or intuitions connected to particular words, imagery and dreams, but takes no interest in conferring a predefined symbolic meaning upon the patient's memory. His/her main healing tool is transference, that is, gaining so much trust that the patient can project earlier experiences upon him/her and possibly solve them by reliving them consciously and unconsciously (Freud 1980 [1917]). As we see, there are many similarities between this healing tradition and the process of initiation.

18 Starhawk (1979a:77). The "Charge of the Goddess" is also quoted in chapter 4.

Conclusion

Reclaiming Witchcraft and theology

The aim of this book has been to demonstrate how Reclaiming people build religious identity and agency from the position of a Witch: a person living at the intersection of nature and culture, the ordinary and the extraordinary, and constantly dialoguing with ancient European paganism, contemporary western religiosity and personal experiences. I have shown how Witches perceive of themselves as having left the Father's House (Jewish and Christian religion) and returned "home" to the Self (Goddess religion) with a call to heal western women's (and men's) alienation from community and spirituality and to become benders of human and societal developments. I have also sought to describe the ritual processes and practices through which this complex identity is embodied and how ritualization is used to create a sacred space where divine merger and human growth may take place and where visions of a new culture and new forms of spirituality can be born.

I have chosen these themes from my understanding of Witches' discourse as predominantly *diagnostic*. Witches interpret the existential scenario, which makes necessary a transition from "my Father's house" to "my Self", in terms of a western culture that suffers from spiritual incompetence: it does not know how to "grow people"; it has no sacred women (priestesses) "at home"; it has forgotten that the givenness of the envelopes that hold us (body and eco-system) cannot thrive within oppressive theological and clerical structures and that an empowered sense of self and female agency grows from nourishing homes, circles and dwelling places and from respectful remembrance that life is something granted. Their ensuing diagnosticism implies distinctions between cultural disease and personal integrity, theological lies and mystical truth, social alienation and spiritual belonging or, more basically, the dialectics of regeneration: *separation* and *merger*.

I have sought to approach these themes from many different angles, as if I were moving around the circuit, throwing different colours of light on a nonsynthetic, common theological centre. My goal, however, has not been to analyse and criticize Witches' contributions by the standards of systematic Protestant theology, which is my field, nor to position myself in relation to their beliefs. My goal has been to write a book that can serve as an example of having listened to and participated and merged with "the other", on premises set by "the other", in order to understand and represent their reality constructs as honestly as possible. Assessing this participation in terms of further "positioning" would be nothing but obliterating and arrogant. Moreover, a full discussion of Witchcraft in comparison with selected representatives of academic theology is a subject of its own, beyond the scope of this book.

Let me nevertheless, very briefly, reiterate some of the findings and conclusions from this predominantly empirical investigation in terms generated by the discipline of theology. We shall start with the ideal narrative, the one Reclaiming Witches happily embrace, and finish with a slightly more critical story. The ideal narrative may be compared to generalized theological discourses, the not-so-ideal narrative to revisions made in accordance with updated historical knowledge, including individual experiences and beliefs, which to a certain extent contest Reclaiming Witches' ideal self-representations. But before turning to these particular narratives, let me situate this project in its broader theological context.

As stated in the Introduction, I have studied Reclaiming Witchcraft as a qualified religious and theological expression, developed by contemporary feminist lay women (and men) in response to spiritual and cultural experiences of being exiled from biblical religion. From the perspective of social anthropology, Witches' alternative expression may sound just as deviant as mainstream theology. From the perspective of feminist theology, however, Witches may be said to formulate answers to some of its own concerns, for example, to the conviction that universalist theological representations of "woman" and "man", and their shared human nature, are androcentric colonialist notions and highly insufficient to express "first-world" or "third-world" people's sense of self and relationship with an ultimate ground of being. Furthermore, favoured western theological images of the divine are charged with representing a *male* symbolic order and thus inadequate to express feminist women's (and men's) faith. If an ideal in feminist theology is to include voices and perspectives from all genders and queer spirits, and represent the realities of the world in which we live more meaningfully – at least as it appears to feminists, witches, people of colour, third-world tribes, and other "queer" persons – how may the discipline of theology be revised?

Some of the Reclaiming Witches' contributions have been to rework female agency and sacred space, including the idea of growing and revitalizing the subject and her surroundings by means of religious ritual. By starting with a working model of the universe that includes interconnected realms of matter and spirit, they claim to have inherited/created a religious alternative that is pagan and pre-Christian in essence. I believe this thesis needs modification and have therefore attempted to show that Witches, explicitly and implicitly, argue with western theology over issues regarding "the nature of reality" and that their constructions are probably linked to a counter-cultural heritage line in the Christian tradition itself, even though borrowings from ancient European and indigenous cultures worldwide have obviously also been incorporated. In fact, the contents and possible limits to their argument seem to be determined by an accumulated pool of historical discourse in western culture, which includes both hegemonic and deviant theological positions and ritualizing strategies.

For example, Reclaiming Witches assume that the western hemisphere is sick and ailing because it denies the *immanentist* nature of Reality: that the universe is alive and interconnected at all levels; that the elemental power giving birth and life is female and sacred; that humans are a mode of the divine and that infants are "twice born" – of divinity first, of humanity second; that community entails the mystery of being joined and being separate; that the self is relational and gendered and that communion and initiation is its goal; that ethical imperatives are derived from a universal power-within, manifesting as inculturated human conscience. In Starhawk's language, these immanentist dimensions of the nature of reality are summed up as "interdependence, community and immanence".

However, to perceive of the world in immanentist categories is not totally foreign to westerners, at least not to esotericists and mystics; neither is the Witches' subsequent, magical model of the universe. In historical theology, we may confront immanentist arguments in disputes – for example, in those between Luther and Erasmus – over whether God, in relation to humans as *imago dei,* should be thought of in terms of categories of "being" or "relation", whether the connection between divine and human reality is one of continuity or discontinuity. But the tendency to rank values associated with transcendence above immanence and praise the rational, disembodied and solitary self above the passionate, embodied and communal self, is more a trait of modernism than it is of Christian theology, at least in a historical perspective.

Nevertheless, Witches address this *spatial order* between transcendence and immanence critically, both its philosophical and theological implications, and, inevitably, call into question taken-for-granted notions about human and divine nature – for both notions are intrinsically related to spatiality. For example, images of God as a being who immanently indwells cosmos as an enclosing, birthing and sustaining power both presuppose and give rise to "mothering" and "femaleness" as root metaphors, whereas God's extraterrestrial seclusion from creation, God as transcendent and wholly "other", although related, invites both female/mothering and male/fathering metaphors. Theological disputes about the "location" of divinity, which can be interpreted as transcendence versus immanence, may thus be regarded as implicit arguments over the "genderedness" of the divine (cf. McFague 1993; Salomonsen 1994, 1999).

Therefore, when representing Reclaiming Witchcraft for a theological account, I shall simply approach it as a distinct (sub)branch of western theology. In addition to its immanentist, spatial orientation, feminist Witchcraft is distinguished by being nonchristological, nonacademic, transcultural and womanish. When presenting Witches' alternative from this perspective, I will, however, adapt to their terminology and idealized self-representation.

Reclaiming Witchcraft as an idealized theological discourse

Reclaiming Witches' suggestion regarding the relationship between humanity and divinity is to perceive of their connection in terms analogical to birthing and creation as *process*: never-ending, complex processes of formation and growth, of separation and interdependence, in a lineage from procreation to birthing to maturity to decay, with many and paradoxical levels of being *and* relating. The nature of human beings is, according to Witches, not fully determined in the act of physical birth; it is, rather, a slow coming into being through parenting, communing and ecological enveloping in which "the other", understood in a broad sense, sets fundamental premises for becoming and for how innate, natural potentialities for growth may be developed. Humans may be "grown" in love and respect or in debasement and cruelty. Thus, "growing", not principles, determines human nature.

Physical birth is not the point of no return in which Goddess is revealed to be either present or absent in regard to human nature. Neither are initiations or baptism seen as authoritative, mediating acts in which "the missing part" is finally invoked into place. By virtue of being ritual acts, they both symbolize – for example, commitment, faith, growth, conversion and covenanting – and make such experiences happen. But they do not represent miraculous events altering human nature, infusing human beings with a divine grace that was previously absent. They merely enlarge, sanctify and rechannel what already is. Yet the initiation ritual is an option for rebirth and becoming once again.

Witches regard humans as embodied, passionate, gendered selves, inserted in nature and culture and irrevocably left to create life in organic harmony with this dependence. They are not constituted pointedly but along a continuum, in which divine origin is found at one end and inculturation at the other. The "indwelling Goddess" or "Deep Self" represents all potentialities, the very best in every being. Human parenting represents limiting form, that which nourishes or prevents growth. In this sense are humans said to be twice born: of the Goddess first and primarily (their Deep Self or spirit-within) and from a human female secondarily (their body/mind/soul). The human female mother is, however, also a manifestation of the Goddess, as is the process of growth itself. Accordingly, to be a human being, male or female, is *to be another mode of the Goddess.* The building of spiritual connections with the extended family (including people, plants, trees, sun, moon) is regarded as an integral part of the job of growing up and as measurement of emotional maturity. Neglect in this process causes not only ecological imbalance, but also personal immaturity. Rebuilding these connections is part of healing and finally becoming an adult, that is, responsible and at home in the universe.

The spatial universe invoked by Reclaiming Witches is multidimensional, with depths and heights and inner and outer, hidden and manifest levels of being and appearing. Immaturity and imbalance are, therefore, partly seen as resulting from a dualistic model of the world in which the human subject is

forced to make choices according to "either–or": either transcendence or immanence, sin or grace, evil or good, female or male. Immaturity is also seen as emanating from androcentric theology and the exclusive elevation of "male experience" and worldviewing, preventing, in fact, both women and men from gaining their powers-from-within.

A main error in the spatial orientation of contemporary, mainstream western culture is said to be that of confusing "power-over" with "power-from-within". The first kind of power refers to *external* social positions based on claims of authority, implying control and feelings of superiority in regard to others. The ethics of power-over may also be conceptualized as an ethics of transcendence, referring to a vertical axis tending to value that which is transcendent, disconnected and above. This, in turn, may reinforce human inequality and hierarchical decision making. The second kind of power refers ideally to *inner* strength and integrity. The ethics of power-from-within is, therefore, equal to the ethics of immanence, to consensus decision making and the feminist-anarchist politics of small-scale communities like Reclaiming. The hegemonic cultural patterns of corporate American society are believed to support and reinforce power-over, thus impeding people from finding their powers-from-within. The consequence is that people are prevented from really growing up, which means cultivating their power-from-within toward the realization of a third ethical principle: "power-with". This form of power represents the sensibility and ability to make choices for action, separating morally right from wrong, distinguishing between the social forces sustaining life and those promoting death.

Witches also criticize western religious traditions for having abolished fertile rites of passage that can promote a child's initiation to puberty, or an adolescent's initiation to adult maturity. Such rituals are believed to denote more than a formal passage from one social group to another. They are seen as instrumental in themselves, in a magical sense, for the development of inner authority and integrity, primarily through their capacity for sublimating the dilemmas of separation versus regeneration and for transforming emotional separation into temporary unity. Growth is believed to take place exactly within these dialectical movements. Ritualizing is also understood to have the peculiar ability of combining two levels of human life: it forms and transforms people; it forms and transforms community and culture. Religious rituals create bonds between humans and gods, between humans and nature, and create interhuman fellowship. But ritualizing also educates, mediating knowledge and values through symbolic communication. Witches equate their own rituals with appropriating the ethics of immanence and learning the path of the Goddess.

"Goddess" is conceptualized as partly inhabiting the subject already (Goddess as other-than-deity), partly as only *related* (Goddess as hidden deity), and as ritually invoked in order to temporarily possess the subject as *being* (Goddess as manifest deity). In order to heal, Witches say they connect with Goddess as "energy", that is, as material divine forces, through so-called channelling or aspecting. While magically connected, they may move divine energy spatially by manipulating their own emotions and mental imagery with the (uncorrupted) power of the will.

The Witches' rituals are, however, regarded as *the* medicine in promoting human growth and change, and the initiation-to-Witch ritual is attributed with the greatest of magical options. One reason for this attribution is the therapeutic challenges given to the candidate; another is the amount of rebirthing magic that they claim is being performed. Magic, as used in Reclaiming, is both a cognitive and performative category: it represents a different means of knowing and a special medium to effect and transform reality. Witchcraft rituals are, in general, intended to re-symbolize divine origin, recontextualize the bodily sexed self within the universe and process human relationships.

Divinity is believed to manifest in and sanctify the world as it is: natural cycles and seasons, mind, body, spirit and emotions. Spiritual union is sought in mundane life, in passion, sensuality, and relationship – through being fully human. Religion is simply said to mean relinking with the indwelling power of being and with all her outer manifestations and is regarded as a constant in human culture. However, Witches do not believe that their religious path is the only true one.

The path of the Goddess is manifold. To find the path at all it is necessary to acquire new knowledge. This knowledge is conveyed via two routes: as teachings directly from the Goddess when "captured" by her (mystical experience, intuition, revelation, visionary insight) and as teachings handed over by humans trying "to capture" her (doxa, ritual symbols, magical techniques, classes and books). Knowledge is measured as true and false on the basis of feminist interpretations of our daily life experiences as bodily, sexed selves, and by the overall norm of promoting women's emancipation and true humanity. A common denominator for all Witches is that they regard sexual love and childbirth as most sacred events and the birthing power itself as female and divine.

A person who enters the path of the Goddess as a "Priestess and Witch" may become a healer and bender of the world. Like Ruth at Barbara's BQ, she may perceive of Witchcraft as "centreing to her existence" and as a way to live her daily life. Or she may, like Michael, attempt to balance her various selves, "learning to love and love deeper". Either way, Witchcraft rituals will teach her the path of emotional honesty and help her mature according to the potentialities of her individual nature. This balanced life is regarded as imperative to psychological and spiritual health. To run counter to the givenness of life will in time create alienation and spiritual illness. In and of herself a healthy person, as understood by this terminology, is believed to be ethically and emotionally integrated, acting from the principle of power from within. Ultimately, the path of the Goddess unifies spirituality with politics and is regarded as *the* key to visions of a new, revitalized society.

Reclaiming Witchcraft as a not-so-ideal research narrative

In previous chapters, I have described feminist Witchcraft as part of a larger new religious movement attempting to overwrite Jewish and Christian religion and culture with (neo)pagan inventions. For many feminist Witches it is important to assure others that their alternative is not *fully* invented but somehow spiritually anchored in the peaceful cultures of prehistory, those faithful to the Goddess and the sacredness of all life. In order to retrieve foremothers, Starhawk has written at length about presumably prepatriarchal neolithic cultures and, for example, attempted to analyse the passage in Sumer from a supposedly "egalitarian and goddess-centred society" to a "stratified and god-centred" one. In her constructions of Witchcraft, the past is obviously a primary resource on which feminist identity is built. But her text does not represent academic, historical research and should only be valued as inspiration for reformist creativity here and now.

In this book I have attempted to point out how a large portion of the contents of Reclaiming Witches' spiritual practices and worldviewing stem neither from "women's experiences" nor the pagan past but from a subcultural European heritage line. The *initial* knowledge of the Goddess is not gained from "relinking with the divine within"; it is gained from relinking with this heritage line and its inclination to continually re-interpret founding mythologies to western civilization. The trunk of Witches' deification theology has an ideological lineage back to the counter-cultural Church in early modern Europe. Esoteric symbolism and ritual structure are of occult western heritage, first formulated as "Witchcraft" by the Briton Gerald Gardner, whereas notions such as "energy" and "Deep Self" are derived from eastern influence, Theosophy, transpersonal and Jungian psychology. Reclaiming women's contributions have mainly been to reinterpret this heritage line, launching syncretistic experimentation, ritualizing and mystical experience as basic methods, and women's emancipation and dignity as ethical stances. Worshipping a female deity, reanimating the universe and perceiving the sexed body in ecological terms may, however, be regarded as new and original within recent western history.

Yet the phenomenon named "feminist Witchcraft" is a result of conscious cultural choices and not of divine visitation or a brand new comprehension of the reality of human life in western society. The people studied have been raised with different religious traditions in the contemporary US, mainly Jewish, Catholic and Protestant. In the book, Starhawk represents the Jewish approach and the voice of the "founding mothers", while Catherine stands for the Protestant approach and Aradia the Catholic. Their joint agenda and creativity may in and of themselves be regarded as interreligious dialoguing, carried out in curious exchange with many non-western traditions as well. Although dialoguing consistently takes place at the edges of western religiosity, it never happens completely outside of it.

My aim in pointing out unacknowledged contextual frameworks and unadmitted origins is not to devalue Reclaiming Witches' path or work but, rather, to avow the interconnections, complexities, contradictions and dialogues that are part and parcel of human sociality and, therefore, of religious community building. I have also attempted to describe how Reclaiming people construct individual stories of "coming home" from very individual pasts to balance their reliance on "historical" roots. In order to systematize, I have named one hermeneutic strategy "utopian Witchcraft" and another "generic Witchcraft". The most obvious differences between these two approaches appear in definitions of human nature and in hopes invested in the idea that Witchcraft and (neo)paganism might change society in a more radical and democratic direction. While utopian Witches tend to localize the origin of human misery to the external environment, almost turning cultural conditioning into a reified power of its own, generic Witches operate with a split human subject closer to Protestant theology and psychotherapy.

As I have documented, Reclaiming community is also the ground for gender conflicts, power games and hierarchies between insiders and outsiders, a reality that clearly opposes the proclaimed intention of valuing power-from-within more than power-over. This is a disappointing reality to many utopian Witches who have identified oppression with patriarchal religion, assuming that a "re-linking with the divine within" will disclose a more noble nature of the human *inner* self. This conflictual reality is not so disappointing to those Reclaiming people who regard human beings as noncoherent subjects, always continuous with the sacred reality of the elemental powers of life (goddess as other-than-deity), often discontinuous with divine will (goddess as deity), but successively growing and developing. Both groups agree that the competence to differentiate between good and evil is innate; the question is rather *how much* the will and its capability to manifest are corrupted.

However, all Witches strongly oppose the view that "original sin" adequately describes the human condition. This was explicitly expressed in the interviews conducted after reentering Catholic Mass and in the processing ritual at Witchcamp (described in chapter 3). "Sin" is only *part* of reality, a disruptive and destructive element, but not constitutive of it and never stronger than those forces constantly renewing, healing and sustaining life. To actually accept the notion "sin" as constitutive of human reality, Witches equate with worshipping "death, crucifixion and suffering", a spiritual trait they project onto the "Fatherly house" they claim to have left.

This does not mean that they are ignorant of human shortcomings and evil, but that a main theological platform is this: people need acceptance, affirmation and sanctification of "what is" before they dare to encounter their own "shadows", not least to open up for the crafting work of the spirit and change into "what is not yet". This thesis – which stands in reversed ratio to the Fathers of the European Reformation – structures the whole entering process into the Craft, including the outline and progress of ritualization.

When a person approaches Witchcraft for the first time, she is invited to affirm and celebrate a strong sense of self. In particular, women are mirrored over and over in all the beautiful, powerful traits projected onto the Goddess. Not until strong enough in their "ego" sense of self are they considered ready to submit to the path of initiation. Walking this path, they are expected to be ready to confront "their own shit", turn around, move on, and change. But not everybody asks for initiation, which in any case does not lead to any form of entitlement in the Reclaiming tradition.

If we bracket the growth processes instigated in an initiation process, Witches seem to have untwisted the Protestant succession of "justification" and "sanctification" in their own ritual cycles: the self undone by justification is not thereafter remade and sanctified according to the law of love, but the other way around. What is at stake in Witches' "liturgical theology" can thus be compared to Serene Jones' recent observations regarding the chief Protestant article in relation to processes of "sanctification" and "whole-making" in the mothering lap of Church or community. She argues that if people, who have experienced nothing but fragmentation and disintegration – which is often women's felt situation, are met with a request for repentance and a call to change, their undone self will just continue to fall apart. Instead of recapitulating the abuses and losses of lived life, the history should be turned around: first a centring of the subject, then a call to repent; for only in sanctification, not in justification, is agency implied: growth, regeneration, change and new becoming (Jones 2000).

Ritualizing is Witches' primary social strategy for this centring and new becoming. Rituals are thought of as prime loci for the invested optimism regarding human growth and change and considered main avenues to insight and renewed agency. Ritual space in Reclaiming is structured according to a cluster of important symbols: the quartered circle and the esoteric pillars of correspondence; the sensual visibility of the human body and its symbolic function as *axis mundi* between human social reality and cosmos. Within ritual space, Witches tend to symbolize *natural* life as a dwelling in cosmos and as representing a state of being prior to sociality and the domain of *culture*. Ritualization, therefore, is deeply paradoxical, since the natural can only be reached through cultural symbols and by communing with socially and ethically "other" human fellows.

Aided by notions like "magical work" and "emotional honesty", Reclaiming Witches have attempted to restage theological beliefs about original bliss and the mysteries of love, community and creativity. They have also strived to process the realities of human separation, isolation and hurt, particularly in the initiation ritual. But, as described in this book, vain hyper-activism and hyper-ritualism and elitist attitudes toward those who just live ordinary lives and have no outstanding "deeds" to boast about (as was the case with Fallon), are just as possible outcomes as personal growth and change.

Finally, the book describes an attempt to create a female symbolic order. By this I mean the efforts to face up to sexual differences as ontological positions, formulated from an awareness of being a bodily sexed self in authority of language, history and theology. I have documented that such creativity tries to respond to the following concerns, noted in the Introduction: the envelopes that hold us (body and ecology) and the elementals constituting gender, the nature of sisterhood, maternal origins and female genealogies from mother to daughter. In regard to the religious aspects of this female symbolic, Reclaiming women interpret human existence, and reflect on the nature of *being* female, by means of goddess symbolism and sexualized cosmologies. A basic feature of Reclaiming women's religious expressions may be regarded "scandalous" in terms of its contextual particularity and self-centredness: within the sacred space of covens, they link experiences of bodily elementals, such as breath, feelings, menstruation, sexuality, procreation, birth, abortion, eating, digestion, sensuality, aging, etc., with their basic life experiences, such as belonging, love, hate, separation, reconciliation, mothering, letting go of children, leaving mother, friendship, growth, work, repose, etc. Only secondarily are they concerned with establishing doxa or considering the universal and nonself-centred implications of their faith and ethicality, as is the norm in academic theology.

My studies bear, to a certain extent, similarities to Caroline W. Bynum's historical observations on medieval women mystics: she found that these women used religious symbols that were in continuity with their sense of social and biological self, being deepenings and appreciations of what "woman" was perceived to be, rather than being negations. On the other hand, enhancement of daily life experiences is not specific to Reclaiming women but to all Reclaiming people. While Bynum found that these features were characteristic of women's religiosity, they apply, in Reclaiming's case, to both women and men. The explanation is probably that Reclaiming Witchcraft is not only formed by women but by feminist mystics, and that their tradition resembles a subcultural heritage line in European culture which, in medieval times, was associated with women (and heretics). My work, therefore, seems to confirm contemporary findings that spiritual experiences reported by Witches from various Craft traditions tend to emphasize both merger with nature and religious transfigurations of the ordinary, irrespective of gender (cf. Carpenter 1994).

Reclaiming Witchcraft in relation to feminist theology and theory

What is Reclaiming's contribution to contemporary theology? The European Reformation was marked by a new interest in the phenomenon of personal faith and believing, which in time replaced adherence to unchanging dogma. As formulated by Calvin, "Our constant endeavor, day and night, is not just to transmit the tradition faithfully, but also to put it in the form we think will prove best" (Gerrish 1993). The urge to assess dogmatics with ethics and ontology with epistemology and to critique every finite form of religious expression claiming to conform with the authority of the infinite is commonly called the "Protestant principle" (Driver 1987:215). Although Reclaiming's modernist endeavours are obviously determined by such a relativist, hermeneutic position – for example, when they judge any form of religion, including pagan religions, as oppressive and idolatrous if they reinforce patriarchal social structures – they also go beyond the ethos of Protestant epistemology, which is to *symbolize* meaningfully finite God/ess *in front of* infinite God/ess. By retrieving conceptual frameworks from ancient and indigenous cultures, they refocus questions of ontology and the givenness of life, and add religious worldviewing as imperative to the moral agenda of modernity. This priority shows up, for example, in their emphasis on magical ritual. Magic is seen as the transformative, healing aspects of ritual, explained as operative on the assumptions that the universe is interconnected *for real* – not as a metaphor or image, but as an ontological truth about the nature of reality. The way in which feminist Witches ritualize is therefore an important contribution to Protestant academic theology: It describes a method to cope with paradoxical levels of human reality and to integrate epistemological as well as ontological notions of reality. Furthermore, its unifying aim is not only to articulate concepts but also to stir the spirit and regenerate sexed, bodily beings.

What, then, does Reclaiming have in common with feminist theology? When assessing potential sexism and idolatry in religious language and institutions, feminist theology – whether Protestant or Catholic – works in alignment with the historical-critical methods of the Protestant principle: it works from radical ethical norms prevailing in the women's movement, such as justice, equality and liberation, not from immutable traditional dogmas. The dynamic and hierarchical relationship between applied ethics and inherited dogmatics is summarized in the following question put forward by a Catholic feminist theologian: "If something consistently results in the denigration of human beings, in what sense can it be religiously true?" (Johnson 1994:30). So, when feminist theologians expand the ethicality of the Protestant principle to include the agenda of women and queer spirited people's emancipation, they converge on an interpretive criterion stating that *whatever denies, diminishes, or distorts the full humanity of women is not redemptive* and is, therefore, without theological authority (Johnson 1994:30, who here refers to Ruether). Positively, this criterion implies that what promotes the full humanity of women is of the Holy, a criterion we are already familiar with from Reclaiming.

Furthermore, Christian feminism criticizes biblical revelations as being "male revelations" (Ruether 1987:146). The burning bush did not address women; the Word was delivered to representatives of a male world. Even Jesus' prophetic criticism of religion included, according to Ruether, the sexism of religion only indirectly. It was *male suffering,* in the hands of male religious and political authority, that was exclusively lifted up as salvific paradigm in the stories about Jesus. Why haven't female suffering and subjectivity been taken seriously as a locus of divine revelation in this religious tradition? A common answer, which Ruether also embraces, is that historical circumstances and sexist, cultural gender assumptions prevented this from happening. It has been conceptually *unthinkable* to experience Christ as a crucified woman or, say, to make God/ess present in the torment of a woman who has been raped, in any historical period of the Jewish or Christian tradition. Thus, since the feminist challenge to Christianity cannot find sufficient response in previous historical practices, or in the Bible, the tradition must be transcended. Ruether believes it is time for women to speak their own experiences, of hurt and victimization, survival, empowerment, and new life, as places of divine presence and, out of these revelatory stories, to write new stories:

> Feminists must create a new midrash on scripture or a "Third Testament" that can tell stories of God's presence in experiences where God's presence was never allowed or imagined before in a religious culture controlled by men and defined by male experience. This Third Testament is not simply a religion for women. Just as women have been able to experience themselves in the crucified rabbi from Nazareth, men must be able to experience Christ in the raped woman and thereby come to experience the question mark this directs at a male culture in which the tortured female body is regarded pornographic, rather than the expression of the sufferings of God.
>
> (Ruether 1987:147)

Ruether believes that this new womanly or feminist midrash will not only have to dialogue with patriarchal religion, but also with feminists of many other religious traditions: Jewish, Muslim and Buddhist, as well as those who break away from historical religions and seek to revive visions from repressed memories of ancient goddesses and burned witches. Ruether thus includes feminist Witches in her dialogue about new possibilities for envisioning "God's presence", anticipating a joining of forces in order to transform androcentric culture and religion.

Reclaiming's contribution to Ruether's call is not a new midrash on the Hebrew scriptures but an elementary outline of a new "third testament" under the guidance of an indwelling spirit, favourite literature and their own communal and individual experiences. Neither is their desire to make "the suffering female" a paradigm of "God's presence" but rather to instigate a cultural turn from sacrifice and suffering to fertility and birthing power as the genuine foundation of human life and sociality.[1]

Furthermore, the feminist theological tradition to which Ruether belongs seems to lack an explicit theory of the genderedness of being. Ontological claims about sexual difference as a primary position of the subject are discarded for epistemologically based gender studies (semiotic studies of textual, theological and cultural *meanings*). As a "sexual equality" feminist, Ruether's aim is to restore women to full humanity, as if human beings have temporarily been attributed with a primary and universal *human part* and a secondary, particular and transmutable *gendered part*. But this refusal to consider sexual difference as something other than cultural decoration or essential complementarity is probably an important reason that female suffering is *not* lifted up as the locus of divine revelation in the Jewish and Christian traditions: the anthropology of western theological thinking knows only one human subject. It is therefore unlikely that theological sexism will abate until subjectivity itself is understood as gendered, making it impossible to speak of the ontology of being as anything less than the being *of* women and *of* men. Thus, by their recognition of gendered subjectivity and of its rootedness in the thresholds of the body, Reclaiming represents a challenge to the hegemonic position of "sexual equality" in feminist theology.

In order to *establish* her subjectivity and achieve a goal of her own, Luce Irigaray has encouraged women to symbolize the female roots of their genealogy (mother–daughter) and the female image of origin (divinity). How can we dwell on earth without goddesses? asks Irigaray. She traces the Indo-European root meaning of Heidegger's term "Being" to also signifying "Dwelling", concluding that both stem from the Greek goddess Hestia, who was seen as guarding the flame of the domestic hearth. This divine space was watched over by women in the home; and when a daughter married, her mother would light a torch at the altar "of her own hearth". According to Irigaray, this transmission of "sacred flame" signifies the woman's fidelity to her divinity and female genealogy, which again attests to the sacred character of the dwelling place called hearth/home (Irigaray 1993b:19).

Feminists from many places in the world, in particular those who belong to the so-called Baby-boom generation and who were formed by the second wave of feminism, are – as suggested by Irigaray – about to reclaim female agency, genealogy and divinity and thus about to achieve *ontological status* for women in their hemisphere. This whole project, which requires that female subjectivity and the experiences of the bodily, sexed self be taken seriously, demands an essentialist strategy: a willingness to listen to and enter into dialogue with empirical women, that is, with beings who are socially constructed within the cultural binary opposition woman/man, *as though* they were expressing the otherness of a subject position *really* other than a non-man.

In this dialogue we may surprise ourselves, as is true in the case of Reclaiming, to find that female divinity and genealogy are appreciated by women as well as men. For both parties in the Reclaiming community say they turn to "the Goddess" and her emancipatory rituals because she enables them to sustain their joint path toward "sanctification of the earth", "spiritual transfiguration of the ordinary" and "regeneration of Selves" as fundamental symbols and magico-religious practices in contemporary religiosity and society. The study of this path has just begun. As it grows in complexity and differentiation, my findings will probably need to be modified and context-ualized further, not least with respect to the forever unfinished questions regarding gender similarity versus gender difference in a given culture, in a given community, as well as those regarding "gender" as such: Will it continue to be a meaningful category?

The research that needs to be done next is a focused study of the Reclaiming men and a follow-up study of Reclaiming's own recent changes to make room for the next generation, the so-called Generation X (cf. Berger 1999). How does this new generation, steeped in both postmodernism and feminism and radically involved in gender shattering as well as bodily experimentation, envision their spiritual path? They seem to be caught between deconstructive and constructive impulses at the same time that they are playfully breaking down gender categories in a way previously unknown at such a broad level. How will this generation respond to Reclaiming's notion of gendered subjectivity? Will it continue to be relevant or will it be perceived as hopelessly nostalgic? Is it merely one strategy among others (as compared to those, for example, of the queer Witches), or will it turn out that thinking in terms of gendered subjectivities will become a welcome relief for the "ailments" of Generation X?

Irrespective of whether the Reclaiming tradition will prove to be inherently adaptable to gender shattering or not, and irrespective of whether this modernist playfulness is a short-lived fad or not, feminists in the Reclaiming tradition have made a significant contribution to the gendered field of religion. In a time when most ideological movements are afraid of truth-claims and tend to narrow their field of action to epistemology and semiotics, Starhawk advocates "a working model of the universe that includes interconnected realms of matter and spirit" and adds, "most of us prefer the term 'Goddess' for the weaver of this web".[2] In addition to being a metaphorical utterance, conveying the outline of a simple cosmological model, it also represents her understanding of the Real. For without certain ontological claims, it is difficult to believe that magic is possible and that rituals may affect the world. Furthermore, up against prevailing feminist attitudes, Reclaiming Witches have dared to retrieve esoteric and pagan heritage lines within western spirituality and to combine them with a radically new emphasis on ritual as a means to personal and social transformation. Particularly interesting is their reformation of a traditional rite of initiation and its intrinsic process of psychological transference into a device for growth and transformation of feminist persons – thus challenging conventional feminist critique of secretive clubs and rituals. As documented in this book, inducing change is basic to all magical forms of ritualizing; and some feminists of the twenty-first century obviously find such activity deeply meaningful and life enhancing – at least as experienced in the Reclaiming version of the Witches' Craft and in other feminist circles (cf. Procter-Smith and Walton 1993; Caron 1993; Northup 1997). Finally, the ways in which Reclaiming Witches review the importance of rituals other than the liturgy, the importance of symbols other than the theistic "God", and the importance of cosmologies other than scientific or semiotic creeds are, of course, challenging to any theological discourse.

Continuing the reformation?

In late modernity, human beings in the western world have been able to develop their self-reflexive, analytical rationality to a high degree of sophistication. Correlatively they have gained full options for individual freedom and autonomy. But, as many critics have argued, parallell to these advances, they have lost kinship with cosmos and a sense of belonging to a larger, spiritual web of life: they seem confused about their origin and goal, about their dependence upon natural and communal life, about the fact that their bodies and souls are engendered and not their own creations. The question posed by new religious visionaries has therefore been: how may we epistemologically put ourselves back "into" cosmos and restore a more "capacious" spiritual ground of being – without losing freedom or rationality and without resurrecting superstitious and deadly cosmologies?

This question is not very different from how modern theology may read its own contemporary challenge as a harmonizing between those who regard the connection between cosmic/divine and social/human realms in terms of discontinuity and those who perceive of the same connection in terms of continuity and mutual "embrace". In chapter 4, I discussed Robert P. Scharleman's contribution, how he seeks to overcome this dividing line by differentiating conceptually between God as "deity" (god as *related* to the world) and God as "other-than-deity" (god as *being* incarnated in the world), claiming that this all-inclusive image of God is genuinely Christian. Such reconciling attempts, as demonstrated by Scharleman, are also attempts at continuing the Reformation and may be called a *third path* in theological inquiry. This path is not restricted to the western world. It may be encountered in third-world Christian churches trying to explore new spiritual directions and gain new theological insights through, for example, closer contact with the (abandoned) pagan religiosity of their ancestors, and in first-world indigenous traditions, like those of the Native Americans and the Sami people of Scandinavia, striving to incorporate the spirituality "of the land" into a position of an inherited "Old Testament" (cf. Charleston 1996). It may also be encountered outside academic theology in "white man's" religious America, for example, when "queer" spirits – such as the Witches – seek to revitalize western spiritualities by retrieving forgotten sources of ancestral wisdom from an acclaimed pagan past.

Reclaiming's response to the ventures of late modernity represents a major challenge to contemporary third path theology, whether feminist or not: they have returned to a highly literal description of the human condition as deeply embedded in a living cosmos, a cosmos constituted by the four elements and enveloped by the heartbeat and will of "the Goddess". The aim of returning to pre-Socratic pagan ideas is to ground the body and free the spirit and make devotion, love and responsible action possible. But, since similar movements and motivations may be found within the horizon of (Jewish and) Christian theology globally, we must also ask: are Reclaiming Witches really post-Christians or are they merely post-church and post-synagogue?

Although Reclaiming's spiritual alternative has been described in this book *as if* it represents a new religion and the practitioners have been partly portrayed as converts, I have also argued that historically it is probably more correct to contextualize Reclaiming Witchcraft as a subcultural branch of Jewish and Christian traditions. This also makes sense in light of the many Reclaiming members with dual religious identities, especially the Jews and the Catholics. Moreover, in 1997, the community made an important move, confirming my reservations about naming their religious practices and beliefs a new *religion*: in opposition to many other Witchcraft traditions, not least the Gardnerians who explicitly define Wicca as a new religion, Reclaiming people agreed to confine the definition of their tradition − as stated in their Principles of Unity − to include only common values and worldviews and exclude theological propositions of belief, even though such propositions are usually shared by Witches.

Reclaiming Witchcraft is, in other words, *not* defined as a religion but as a spiritual path springing from values that non-Witches are obviously also welcome to agree with and eventually join. When the goal was to define their tradition as open, affirming and still evolving, a shared − but simple − philosophy of religion and ontology of being were regarded as more important than to reaching consensus on which theological tenets appropriately express Reclaiming Witches' faith. The question is whether this explicitly non-dogmatic attitude will isolate Reclaiming from other Witchcraft traditions or, rather, result in new alliances far beyond (neo)paganism and thus promote the growth of this unfinished spiritual tradition in directions that will actively contribute to a much-needed continued Reformation under a much larger ecumenical horizon.

Notes

1 The cultural theory of "sacrifice" as foundational to human life and society was refined in 1987 by René Girard, Walter Burkert and Jonathan Z. Smith (cf. Hamerton-Kelly 1987; see also Girard 1977).
2 From the article "A Working Definition of Reclaiming" (http://www.reclaiming.org)

Appendix A

Question guide interviews,
1989–1990

A. Choosing Witchcraft

1 Do you call yourself a Witch?
2 Why did you become a Witch and not only a pagan or a goddess-worshipper?
3 What does it mean for you to be a Witch?
4 Did you choose this spiritual path from any important personal experiences?
5 Have you been involved in other religious communities or spiritual groups before Witchcraft?
6 Have you told your parents that you are a Witch; are you public about it?
7 How/when did you find out about Witchcraft? What brought you to the path? Books, people, etc.?
8 Is Witchcraft open to everybody? Why choose a religion with such a loaded reputation?

B. Religious belief

9 Have you ever had what you consider spiritual experiences?
10 Can you tell me the essence (core beliefs/fundamental theology) of Witchcraft?
11 What or who is Goddess/God to you?
12 Are the gods real entities outside of you, or metaphors for powers in you?
13 Do you believe in one goddess or several goddesses?
14 How is the relationship between you as woman/man and Goddess/God?
15 Why do Reclaiming men reclaim the Earth God?
16 What is the difference between women's spirituality and men's?
17 What did you learn about God from parents, church or school when you grew up?
18 Which symbols in the Craft are most important to you?
19 What do you think is the historical origin of the symbolism?
20 What do you mean by the notion "symbol"?
21 Are the Craft myths important to you?
22 Do you work with ritual tools?
23 What do you consider to be the historical roots of the ritual tools?
24 Is there anything in the Craft tradition that disturbs you?

C. **Rituals**

25 What is the purpose of Witchcraft rituals? What is the meaning of ritual?
26 What do you like most about doing ritual?
27 How do rituals affect you?
28 Do you experience Goddess in ritual?
29 What is the focus of the rituals you perform? What is the occasion for performing them?
30 Why do you think Witchcraft has initiation rituals?
31 Are you initiated? Do you want to be? Why/why not?
32 Why do you think people have such different opinions about initiation?
33 Can you tell me about your initiation? Who did it? What kind of challenges did you receive?
34 Why are there so many secrets associated with initiation?
35 Who do you think created the Faery/Reclaiming initiation ritual(s)?
36 Have you had a second initiation? In what sense did it add to the first initiation?
37 How did the experience of being initiated affect your life?
38 Did initiation open doors to new knowledge and new groups?
39 Is initiation compatible with anarchism and grassroots politics?
40 Does initiation create elitism or a group within a group?

D. **Coven work and magic**

41 Are you in a coven or are you a solitary Witch? Women/men/mixed coven? Why? How often do you meet? Since when?
42 What do you do when you gather for circle/coven?
43 Does coven work influence your daily life?
44 What have you learned from being a Witch? Have you experienced any changes?
45 Can you heal? How do you do it?
46 Do you work magic? How do you define magic? Do you use any divination systems?
47 What do you regard as the purpose of magic? Can you give examples?
48 Why do you work magic? Does it make you happier? Do you see any fake magicians around you? Why call a ritual performance magical?
49 How do you feel when you read the news about people who use magic for evil?
50 Can the use of a pentacle for evil purposes influence the power of pentacles as such?
51 Are you sure that what you send out comes back three times (cf. Book of Job)? Is the universe structured according to human morality?
52 Have you ever been hexed or involved in magical wars?
53 Is there nothing good in secularization? If 10 million Americans learn how to work magic, will that improve this culture? Have you any fears that superstitions will tangle with magic?
54 How can you guarantee that you are not teaching magic to the wrong person?

55 Do you see differences between ceremonial magic and the magic practised in Witchcraft? Ethics? Laws?

E. Roots of Witchcraft

56 Where does your knowledge of Witchcraft come from?
57 Who taught it to you and from what sources? Important people, books and classes?
58 Have you read Starhawk's books? Is Witchcraft an old or a new religion?
59 What are the historical roots of Witchcraft? A particular "Old Religion"?
60 There are many different Craft traditions; why did you choose Reclaiming/Faery?
61 In what ways is Witchcraft related to the Goddess Movement, to New Age, Neo-Shamanism, Voodoo and the Occult?
62 How important has the women's movement been for the creation of Witchcraft?
63 What are the roots of the Faery tradition? Is it an inherited living tradition? Kahuna/Voodoo?
64 What are the main differences between Faery and Reclaiming?
65 Do you believe in a common source for all initiation rituals (such as *The Grimoire of Lady Sheba*)?
66 Why are all Craft rituals so similar in form if they are not coming from the same source?
67 Can you be a Christian and a Witch, or a Jew and a Witch, simultaneously?
68 Do you participate in the broader pagan community?

F. Community

69 Is Reclaiming your community? Why/why not? What other communities are important for you?
70 Was it easy/difficult to become part of Reclaiming?
71 How many classes have you taken? Who were the teachers? Did they check out your ethics?
72 Why are you a member of the Reclaiming Collective/the *Newsletter* cell?
73 What is decisive in regard to people's opportunities for power and influence in the Collective/community?
74 What are the procedures for selecting new members for the Reclaiming Collective?
75 Is your household part of the community? Can you describe your community networks?
76. Why do you live collectively (or as single, or in a nuclear family)?

Appendix B

Reclaiming principles of unity

"My law is love unto all beings . . ."
The Charge of the Goddess

The values of the Reclaiming tradition stem from our understanding that the earth is alive and all of life is sacred and interconnected. We see the Goddess as immanent in the earth's cycles of birth, growth, death, decay and regeneration. Our practice arises from a deep, spiritual commitment to the earth, to healing and to the linking of magic with political action.

Each of us embodies the divine. Our ultimate spiritual authority is within, and we need no other person to interpret the sacred to us. We foster the questioning attitude, and honour intellectual, spiritual and creative freedom.

We are an evolving, dynamic tradition and proudly call ourselves Witches. Honouring both Goddess and God, we work with female and male images of divinity, always remembering that their essence is a mystery which goes beyond form. Our community rituals are participatory and ecstatic, celebrating the cycles of the seasons and our lives, and raising energy for personal, collective and earth healing.

We know that everyone can do the life-changing, world-renewing work of magic, the art of changing consciousness at will. We strive to teach and practice in ways that foster personal and collective empowerment, to model shared power and to open leadership roles to all. We make decisions by consensus, and balance individual autonomy with social responsibility.

Our tradition honours the wild, and calls for service to the earth and the community. We value peace and practice non-violence, in keeping with the Rede, "Harm none, and do what you will." We work for all forms of justice: environmental, social, political, racial, gender and economic. Our feminism includes a radical analysis of power, seeing all systems of oppression as inter-related, rooted in structures of domination and control.

We welcome all genders, all races, all ages and sexual orientations and all those differences of life situation, background, and ability that increase our diversity. We strive to make our public rituals and events accessible and safe. We try to balance the need to be justly compensated for our labour with our commitment to make our work available to people of all economic levels.

All living beings are worthy of respect. All are supported by the sacred elements of air, fire, water and earth. We work to create and sustain communities and cultures that embody our values, that can help to heal the wounds of the earth and her peoples, and that can sustain us and nurture future generations.

http://www.reclaiming.org/cauldron/welcome.html

Bibliography

Abrams, M.H. (1973) *Natural Supernaturalism*. New York: Norton.

Adler, Margot (1986 [1979]). *Drawing Down the Moon. Witches, Druids, Goddess-worshippers, and Other Pagans in America Today*. Boston: Beacon Press.

Albanese, C. (1990) *Nature Religion in America*. From the Algonkian Indians to the New Age. Chicago: Chicago University Press.

Aune, Michael B. (1994) *"To Move the Heart"*. *Rhetoric and Ritual in the Theology of Philip Melanchthon*. San Francisco: Christian Universities Press.

Bachofen, J.J. (1861) *Das Mutterrecht*. Basel: Schwabe.

Bakker, H.T. (1990) "An Indian Image of Man: An Inquiry into a Change of Perspective in the Hindu World-view". In *Concepts of Person in Religion and Thought* (eds) Hans G. Kippenberg, Yme B. Kuiper and Andy F. Sanders. Berlin: Mouton de Gruyter.

Beauvoir, Simone de (1974) *The Second Sex*. New York: Vintage Books.

Bell, Catherine (1992) *Ritual Theory, Ritual Practice*. New York: Oxford University Press.

Berger, Helen A. (1999) *A Community of Witches. Contemporary Neopaganism and Witch-craft in the United States*. Columbia, SC: University of South Carolina Press.

Berger, Peter L. (1970) *A Rumor of Angels*. New York: Doubleday.

—— (1980) *The Heretical Imperative*. New York: Anchor Books.

Blonsky, Marshall (1985) *On Signs*. Baltimore: John Hopkins University Press.

Bloom, Harold (1975) *Kabbalah and Criticism*. New York: Continuum.

Bly, Robert (1992) *Iron John. A Book about Men*. Shaftesbury: Element.

Bonewits, Philip Emmons Isaac (1989) [1971] *Real Magic*. York Beach, Maine: Samuel Weiser.

Børresen, Kari E. (1995) *Image of God*. Minneapolis: Fortress Press.

Bourdieu, Pierre (1991) *Language and Symbolic Power*. Cambridge: Polity Press.

Bowie, Fiona (1990) *Beguine Spirituality*. New York: Crossroad Publishing.

Braidotti, Rosi (1989) "The Politics of Ontological Difference". In *Between Feminism and Psychoanalysis* (ed.) Teresa Brennan. London: Routledge.

Brown, Karen McCarthy (1991) *Mama Lola: A Vodou Priestess in Brooklyn*. Berkeley: University of California Press.

Buckley, Thomas and Alma Gottlieb (eds) (1988) *Blood Magic. The Anthropology of Menstruation*. Berkeley: University of California Press.

Budapest, Z. (1976) *The Feminist Book of Lights and Shadows*. Venice, CA: Luna Publications.

Building United Judgement: A Handbook for Consensus Decision Making (1988) A Centre for Conflict Resolution. Madison, WI: Nes Society Publisher.

Butler, Judith (1990) *Gender Trouble: Feminism and the Subversion of Identity.* New York: Routledge.

Bynum, Caroline W. (1986) "Introduction: The Complexity of Symbols". In *Gender and Religion. On the Complexity of Symbols* (eds) Caroline W. Bynum, Stevan Harrell and Paula Richman. Boston: Beacon Press.

—— (1987) *Holy Feast and Holy Fast.* Berkeley: University of California Press.

—— (1991) "Women's Stories, Women's Symbols: A Critique of Victor Turners Theory of Liminality". In *Fragmentation and Redemption. Essays on Gender and the Human Body in Medieval Religion* (ed) C. Bynum. New York: Zone Books.

Caron, Charlotte (1993) *To Make and Make Again. Feminist Ritual Theory.* New York: Crossroad Publishing.

Carpenter, Dennis D. (1994) "Spiritual Experiences, Life Changes, and Ecological Viewpoints of Contemporary Pagans". Unpubl. PhD dissertation, Saybrook Institute.

Castells, Manuel (1983) *The City and the Grassroots.* Berkeley: University of California Press.

Charleston, Steven (1996) "The Old Testament of Native America". In *Native and Christian. Indigenous Voices on Religious Identity in the United States and Canada* (ed.) James Treat. New York: Routledge.

Chodorow, Nancy (1978) *The Reproduction of Mothering.* Berkeley: The University of California Press.

Christ, Carol P. (1982) [1978] "Why Women Need the Goddess: Phenomenological, Psychological and Political Reflections". In *Womanspirit Rising* (eds) C. Christ and Judith Plaskow. San Francisco: Harper & Row. All citations are from the 1982 edition, in *The Politics of Women's Spirituality* (ed.) C. Spretnak. New York: Anchor Books.

—— (1987) *Laughter of Aphrodite. Reflections on a Journey to the Goddess.* San Francisco: Harper & Row.

—— (1997) *Rebirth of the Goddess: Finding Meaning in Feminist Spirituality.* Reading, MA: Addison-Wesley Publishing Company.

Cirlot, J.E. (1962) *A Dictionary of Symbols.* New York: Philosophical Library

Clifford, James and George E. Marcus (eds) (1986) *Writing Culture.* Berkeley: University of California Press.

Cohn, Norman (1975) *Europe's Inner Demons.* New York: Basic Books.

—— (1981 [1957]) *The Pursuit of the Millennium.* New York: Oxford University Press.

Conn, Joann Wolski (1993) "Toward Spiritual Maturity". In *Freeing Theology. The Essentials of Theology in Feminist Perspective* (ed.) Catherine Mowry LaCugna. San Francisco: Harper.

Crapanzano V. and V. Garrison (eds) (1977) *Case Studies in Spirit Possession.* New York: John Wiley & Sons.

Crowley, Aleister (1987 [1929]) *Magick in Theory and Practice.* New York: Dover Publications.

Crowley, Vivianne (1989) *Wicca: The Old Religion in the New Age.* London: The Aquarian Press.

—— (1996) "Wicca as a Modern-Day Mystery Religion". In *Paganism Today* (eds) G. Harvey and C. Hardman. London: Thorsons.

Csordas T.J. (1994) *Embodiment and Experience: The Existential Ground of Culture and Self.* Cambridge: Cambridge University Press.

Daly, Mary (1973) *Beyond God the Father.* Boston: Beacon Press.

—— (1981 [1978]) *Gyn/Ecology: The Metaethics of Radical Feminism.* London: The Women's Press.

Daniel, E. Valiente (1984) *Fluid Signs: Being a Person the Tamil Way*. Berkeley: University of California Press.

Daniel, Stephen L. (1986) "The Patient as Text. A Model of Clinical Hermeneutics". In *Theoretical Medicine*, no. 7.

Douglas, Mary (1973) "Critique and Commentary". In *The Idea of Purity in Ancient Judaism* (ed.) Jacob Neusner. Leiden: Brill.

—— (1988) *Purity and Danger: An Analysis of Concepts of Pollution and Taboo*. London: Ark Paperbacks.

Driver, Tom F. (1987) "The Case for Pluralism". In *The Myth of Christian Uniqeness* (eds) John Hick and Paul F. Knitter. Maryknoll, NY: Orbis Books.

—— (1991) *The Magic of Ritual: Our Need for Liberating Rites that Transform Our Lives and Our Communities*. San Francisco: Harper & Row.

Duerr, Hans Peter (1982) *Drömtid. Om gränsen mellan det vilda och det civiliserade*. Lund: Symposion Förlag.

Dyrendal, Asbjørn (1993) "Hekseri og økologi. En tekstbasert analyse av naturopp-fatningen hos Starhawk". Unpubl. MA thesis. University of Oslo, Department of the History of Religion.

Eilberg-Schwartz, Howard (1989) "Witches of the West: Neopaganism and Goddess Worship as Enlightenment Religions". In *Journal of Feminist Studies in Religion* 5 (1).

Eliade, Mircea (1964) *Shamanism*. Princeton: Princeton University Press.

Ellen, R. F. (ed.) (1984) *Ethnographic Research. A Guide to General Conduct*. London: Academic Press.

Eller, Cynthia (1993) *Living in the Lap of the Goddess. The Feminist Spirituality Movement in America*. Boston: Beacon Press.

—— (2000) *The Myth of Matriarchal Prehistory. Why an Invented Past Won't Give Women a Future*. Boston: Beacon Press.

Engdahl, Horace (ed.) (1977) *Hermeneutik*. Stockholm: Raben & Sjögren.

Ewing, Katherine P. (1994) "Dreams From a Saint: Anthropological Atheism and the Temptation to Believe". In *American Anthropologist* 96 (3).

Faber, M.D. (1993) *Modern Witchcraft and Psychoanalysis*. Rutherford: Fairleigh Dickinson University Press.

Faivre, Antoine (1992) "Introduction I". In *Modern Esoteric Spirituality* (eds) Antoine Faivre and Jacob Needleman. London: SCM Press.

Farrar, Stewart (1983 [1971]) *What Witches Do*. Custer, Washington: Phoenix Publications.

Favret-Saada, J. (1980) *Deadly Words. Witchcraft in the Bocage*. Cambridge: Cambridge University Press.

Fortune, D. (1935) *The Mystical Qabalah*. London: Ernest Benn.

Fox, Selena and Dennis D. Carpenter (eds) (1996) *Circle Guide to Pagan Groups*. Mt Horeb, Wis.: Circle Publications.

Frazer, Sir James G. (1922) *The Golden Bough*. London: Macmillan.

Freud, Sigmund (1980 [1917]) *Psykoanalyse*. Oslo: Gyldendal Norsk Forlag.

Frymer-Kensky, Tikva (1992) *In the Wake of the Goddesses: Woman, Culture, and the Biblical Transformation of Pagan Myth*. New York: Free Press.

Gallop, Jane (1988) *Thinking Through the Body*. New York: Columbia University Press.

Gardner, Gerald (1949) *High Magic's Aid*. London: Michael Houghton.

—— (1982a [1954]) *Witchcraft Today*. New York: Magical Childe.

—— (1982b [1959]) *The Meaning of Witchcraft*. New York: Magical Childe.

Geertz, Armin W. (1990) "Religiøsitet som menneskelig grundbestemmelse." In *Menneskesynet*. (ed.) Sigfred Pedersen. København: Gad Forlag.

Geertz, Clifford (1979) "Religion as a Cultural System". In *Reader in Comparative Religion* (eds) W. Lessa and E.Z.Vogt. San Francisco: Harper & Row.

Gennep, Arnold van (1960 [1909]) *The Rites of Passage*. Chicago: University of Chicago Press.

Gerrish, B.A. (1993) *Continuing the Reformation. Essays on Modern Religious Thought*. Chicago: The University of Chicago Press.

Gibbons, Jenny (1998) "Recent Developments in the Study of The Great European Witch Hunt". In *The Pomegranate. A New Journal of Neopagan Thought* 5.

Gimbutas, Marija (1982) *The Goddesses and Gods of Old Europe*. Berkeley: University of California Press.

—— (1989) *The Language of the Goddess*. San Francisco: Harper & Row.

Girard, René (1977) *Violence and the Sacred*. Baltimore: John Hopkins University Press.

Gluckman, Max (1962) "Les Rites de Passage". In *The Ritual of Social Relations* (eds) Daryll Forde, Meyer Fortes, Max Gluckman and Victor Turner. Manchester: Manchester University Press.

Godfrey, Brian J. (1988) *Neighborhoods in Transition: The Making of San Francisco's Ethnic and Nonconformist Communities*. Berkeley: University of California Press.

Goldenberg, Naomi R. (1979) *Changing of the Gods*. Boston: Beacon Press.

—— (1990) *Resurrecting the Body. Feminism, Religion and Psychotheraphy*. New York: Crossroad.

Goodman, Felicitas D. (1988) *Ecstasy, Ritual and Alternate Reality: Religion in a Pluralistic World*. Bloomington: Indiana University Press.

Graves, Robert (1966 [1948]) *The White Goddess*. New York: Farrar, Strauss and Giroux.

Greenwood, Susan (1994) "Tapping into the Sacred: Power and Charisma in Contemporary British Magical Practices". Unpubl. paper read at the EASA conference, Oslo.

Greimas, A.J. (1974) *Strukturel Semantik*. Odense: Borgen Forlag.

Grimes, Ronald L. (1990) *Ritual Criticism. Case Studies in its Practice, Essays on its Theory*. Columbia: University of South Carolina Press.

Gross, Rita M. (1996) *Feminism and Religion: An Introduction*. Boston: Beacon Press.

Hackett, Jo Ann (1989) "Can A Sexist Model Liberate Us? Ancient Near Eastern 'Fertility' Goddesses". In *Journal of Feminist Studies in Religion* 5 (1).

Hamerton-Kelly, Robert G. (ed) (1987) *Violent Origins: Walter Burkert, René Girard, and Jonathan Z. Smith on Ritual Killing and Cultural Formation*. Stanford, CA: Stanford University Press.

Harding, Esther M. (1971 [1955]) *Women's Mysteries – Ancient and Modern*. New York: Harper & Row.

Hardman, Charlotte (1996) "Introduction". In *Paganism Today* (eds) G. Harvey and C. Hardman. London: Thorsons.

Harner, Michael (1980) *The Way of the Shaman*. New York: Bantam Books.

Harrison, Jane (1955 [1903]) *Prolegomena to the Study of Greek Religion*. New York: Meridian Books.

Harvey, Graham and Charlotte Hardman (eds) (1996) *Paganism Today*. London: Thorsons.

Hayden, Brian (1998) "An Archeological Evaluation of the Gimbutas Paradigm". In *The Pomegranate. A New Journal of Neopagan Thought* 6.

Heelas, Paul (1981) "The Model Applied: Anthropology and Indigenous Psychology". In *Indigenous Psychologies: The Anthropology of the Self* (eds) Paul Heelas and Andrew Lock. London: Academic Press.

—— (1996) *The New Age Movement*. Oxford: Blackwell.

Heimbrock, Hans-Günter (1990) "Ritual and Transformation: A Psychoanalytic Perspective". In *Current Studies on Rituals. Perspectives for the Psychology of Religion* (eds) H.-G. Heimbrock and H.B. Boudewijnse. Amsterdam: Rodopi.

Heinämaa, Sara (1997) "What is a Woman? Butler and Beauvoir on the Foundations of the Sexual Difference". In *Hypatia* 12(1).

Howell, Signe and Marit Melhuus (1993) "The Study of Kinship; the Study of Person; a Study of Gender?" In *Gendered Anthropology* (ed.) Teresa del Valle. London: Routledge.

Humphrey, Caroline and James Laidlaw (1994) *The Archetypal Actions of Ritual.* Oxford: Clarendon Press.

Hutton, Ronald (1996) "The Roots of Modern Paganism". In *Paganism Today* (eds) G. Harvey and C. Hardman. London: Thorsons.

—— (2000) *The Triumph of the Moon. A History of Modern Pagan Witchcraft.* Oxford: Oxford University Press.

Irigaray, Luce (1993a) *An Ethics of Sexual Difference.* Ithaca, NY: Cornell University Press.

—— (1993b) *je, tu, nous. Toward a Culture of Difference.* New York: Routledge.

Jackson, Michael (1989) *Paths Toward a Clearing.* Bloomington: Indiana University Press.

Jacobs, Janet Liebman (1989) *Divine Disenchantment. Deconverting from New Religions.* Bloomington: Indiana University Press.

Jacobsen, Thorkild (1976) *The Treasures of Darkness.* New Haven, CT: Yale University Press.

Johnson, Elizabeth A. (1994) *SHE WHO IS. The Mystery of God in Feminist Theological Discourse.* New York: Crossroad.

Jones, Prudence and Nigel Pennick (1995) *A History of Pagan Europe.* London: Routledge.

Jones, Serene (2000) *Feminist Theory and Christian Theology: Cartographics of Grace.* Minneapolis: Fortress Press.

Junus, Petra (1995) *Den levande Gudinnan. Kvinnoidentitet och religiositet som förändrings-process.* PhD dissertation, University of Uppsala. Nora: Bokförlaget Nya Doxa.

Keller, Catherine (1986) *From a Broken Web. Separation, Sexism and Self.* Boston: Beacon Press.

Kelly, Aidan A. (1984) "Inventing Witchcraft". In *Iron Mountain - A Journal of Magical Religion* 1.

—— (1991) *Crafting the Art of Magic, Book 1. A History of Modern Witchcraft, 1939–1964.* St Paul: Llewellyn Publications.

—— (1992) "An Update on Neopagan Witchcraft in America". In *Perspectives on the New Age* (eds) J. R. Lewis and J. G. Melton. Albany: State University of New York Press.

Kertzer, David I. (1988) *Ritual, Politics, and Power.* New Haven: Yale University Press.

King, Francis (1970) *Ritual Magic in England.* London: Neville Spearman.

King, Ursula (1993) *Women and Spirituality. Voices of Protest and Promise.* London: Macmillan.

—— (ed) (1995) *Religion and Gender.* Oxford: Blackwell.

—— (ed) (1998) *Faith and Praxis in a Postmodern World.* London: Cassell.

Knitter, Paul F. (1985) *No Other Name? A Critical Survey of Christian Attitudes Toward the World Religions.* Maryknoll, NY: Orbis Books.

Kramer, Samuel N. (1963) *The Sumerians: Their History, Culture, and Character.* Chicago: University of Chicago Press.

Kristeva, Julia (1981) "Women Can Never Be Defined". In *New French Feminism* (eds) E. Marko and I. de Courtivreon. Bregthon: Harvester Press.

Kubrin, David (1981) "Newton's Inside Out: Magic, Class Struggle, and the Rise of Mechanism in the West". In *The Analythic Spirit* (ed.) Harry Woolf. Ithaca: Cornell University Press.

—— (1987) "Burning Times', Isaac Newton, and the War Against the Earth". Unpubl. paper.

Lacan, Jacques (1982) "God and the Jouissance". In *Feminine Sexuality: Jacques Lacan and the Ecole Freudienne* (eds) J. Mitchell and J. Rose. London: Macmillan.

Larsen, Kjersti (1995) "Where Humans and Spirits Meet: Incorporating Difference and Experiencing Otherness in Zanzibar Town". Unpubl. PhD dissertation, Institute and Museum for Anthropology, University of Oslo.

Lauridsen, Palle Schantz (1982) "Normalt er jeg ellers cool". In *Litteratur & Samfund* 35.

La Vey, Anton (1969) *Satanic Bible*. New York: Avon Books.

Leland, Charles Godfrey (1974 [1897]) *Aradia: Gospel of the Witches*. New York: Samuel Weiser.

Lerner, Gerda (1986) *The Creation of Patriarchy*. Oxford: Oxford University Press.

Lerner, Robert E. (1972) *The Heresy of the Free Spirit in the Later Middle Ages*. Berkeley: University of California Press.

Lévi-Strauss, Claude (1979) *The Raw and the Cooked*. New York: Octagon Books.

Lewis, Gilbert (1980) *Day of Shining Red*. Cambridge: Cambridge University Press.

Lewis, James R. (ed) (1996) *Magical Religion and Modern Witchcraft*. Albany: State University of New York Press.

—— and J. Gordon Melton (eds) (1992) *Perspectives on the New Age*. Albany: State University of New York Press.

Lincoln, Bruce (1981) *Emerging from the Chrysalis: Studies in Rituals of Women's Initiation*. Cambridge, MA: Harvard University Press.

Logan, Jody and Patti Martin (2000) "Reclaiming: History, Structure, and the Future". *http://www.reclaiming.org*

Lugh (1984) *Old George Pickingill and the Roots of Modern Witchcraft*. London: Taray Publication.

Luhrmann, T.H. (1989) *Persuasions of the Witch's Craft: Ritual Magic in Contemporary England*. Cambridge, MA: Harvard University Press.

Lutz, Catherine A. and Geoffrey M. White (1986) "The Anthropology of Emotions". In *Annual Review of Anthropology* 15.

McCance, Dawne (1990) "Understandings of 'the Goddess' in Contemporary Feminist Scholarship". In *Goddesses in Religion and Modern Debate* (ed.) Larry W. Hurtado. Atlanta: Scholars Press.

McFague, Sallie (1993) *The Body of God*. Minneapolis: Fortress Press.

Magliocco, Sabina (1996) "Ritual is my Chosen Art Form: The Creation of Ritual as Folk Art among Contemporary Pagans". In *Magical Religion and Modern Witchcraft* (ed.) James R. Lewis. Albany: State University of New York Press.

Mahler, Margaret, F. Pine and A. Bergman (1975) *The Psychological Birth of the Human Infant*. New York: Basic Books.

Matthews, Carol (1995) "Neo-Paganism and Witchcraft". In *America's Alternative Religions* (ed.) Timothy Miller. Albany: State University of New York Press.

Mauss, Marcel (1985) "A Category of the Human Mind: the Notion of Person; the Notion of Self". In *The Category of the Person. Anthropology, Philosophy and History* (eds) Michael Carrithers, Steven Collins and Steven Lukes. Cambridge: Cambridge University Press.

Mellaart, James (1967) *Catal Hüyük, a Neolithic Town in Anatolia*. New York: McGraw-Hill.

Melton, J. Gordon (1987) "How New is New? The Flowering of the 'New' Religious Consciousness Since 1965". In *The Future of the New Religious Movements* (eds) David G. Bromley and Philip E. Hammond. Macon: Mercer University Press.

—— (1991) "Modern Alternative Religions in the West". In *A Handbook of Living Religions* (ed.) John R. Hinnells. London: Penguin Books.

Merchant, Carolyn (1983) *The Death of Nature: Women, Ecology and the Scientific Revolution*. San Francisco: Harper & Row.

Merriam-Webster's Collegiate Dictionary (1995) 10th ed. Springfield, MA: Merream-Webster.

Miller, Timothy (ed) (1995) *America's Alternative Religions*. Albany: State University of New York Press.

Miller, William D. (1982) *Dorothy Day: A Biography*. San Francisco: Harper & Row.

Mitchell, J. and J. Rose (eds) (1982) *Feminine Sexuality: Jaques Lacan and the Ecole Freudienne*. London: Macmillan.

Mogstad, Sverre Dag (1995) *Frimureri: Mysterier, fellesskap, personlighetsdannelse*. Oslo: Universitetsforlaget.

Moi, Toril (ed) (1987) *French Feminist Thought. A Reader*. Oxford: Basil Blackwell.

Murray, Margaret A. (1921) *The Witch Cult in Western Europe*. Oxford: Oxford University Press.

—— (1931) *The God of the Witches*. London: Sampson Low.

Myerhoff, Barbara (1984) "Rites and Signs of Ripening". In *Age and Anthropological Theory* (eds) D. I. Kertzer and J. Keiths. Ithaca, NY: Cornell University Press.

Mylonas, George E. (1961) *Euleusis and the Eleusinian Mysteries*. Princeton: Princeton University Press.

Neel, Carol (1989) "The Origins of the Beguines". In *Signs: Journal of Women in Culture and Society 14* (2).

NightMare, M. Macha (2000) "Reclaiming Tradition Witchcraft". http://www. reclaiming.org.

Northup, Lesley A. (1997) *Ritualizing Women: Patterns of Spirituality*. Cleveland, Ohio: The Pilgrim Press.

O'Keefe, Daniel Laurence (1982) *Stolen Lightening. The Social Theory of Magic*. New York: Vintage Books.

Orion, Loretta (1995) *Never Again the Burning Times. Paganism Revived*. Prospect Heights, IL: Waveland Press.

Ortner, Sherry (1974) "Is Female to Male as Nature is to Culture?" In *Woman, Culture and Society* (eds) M.Z. Rosaldo and I. Lamphere. Stanford: Stanford University Press.

Ouwehand, Eva (1990) "Women's Rituals: Reflections on Developmental Theory". In *Current Studies on Rituals* (eds) H.-G. Heimbrock and H. B. Boudewijnse. Amsterdam: Rodopi.

Petersen, Anders Klostergaard (1995) "Den protestantiske traditions ritualforståelse". In *Fønix* 19 (1).

—— (1996) "Ritologien - et forsømt teologisk område". In *Dansk Teologisk Tidsskrift*, 59 årg.

Pike, Sara M. (1996) "Rationalizing the Margins: A Review of Legitimization and Ethnographic Practice in Scholarly Research on Neo-Paganism". In *Magical*

Religion and Modern Witchcraft (ed.) James R. Lewis. Albany: State University of New York Press.

—— (2000) *Earthly Bodies, Magical Selves.* Berkeley: California University Press.

Preston, James J. (ed) (1982) *Mother Worship.* Chapel Hill: University of North Carolina Press.

Pritchard, James B. (1958) *The Ancient Near East. Vol. 1: An Anthology of Texts and Pictures.* Princeton: Princeton University Press.

Procter-Smith, Majorie and Janet R. Walton (eds) (1993) *Women at Worship: Interpretations of North American Diversity.* Louisville, KY: Westminster John Knox.

Procter-Smith, Majorie (1995) *Praying with our eyes open.* Nashville, TN: Abingdon Press.

Ranke-Heinemann, Uta (1990) *Eunuchs for the Kingdom of Heaven.* Harmondsworth: Penguin Books.

—— (1994) *Putting Away Childish Things.* San Francisco: Harper San Francisco.

Raphael, Melissa (1999) *Introducing Thealogy: Discourse on the Goddess.* Sheffield: Sheffield Academic Press.

Rappaport, Roy (1979) "The Obvious Aspects of Ritual". In *Ecology, Meaning and Religion* (ed.) R. Rappaport. Richmond, CA: North Atlantic Books.

Reclaiming Newsletter 1, Winter 1980.

Reclaiming Newsletter 19, Fall 1984.

Reclaiming Newsletter 35, Summer 1989.

Reclaiming Newsletter 38, Spring 1990.

Renfrew, Colin (1992) *Den indo-europeiske gåte: arkeologi og språk.* Oslo: Pax Forlag.

Ricoeur, Paul (1988) *Från text till handling.* Stockholm: Symposion Bokförlag.

Roberts, Wendy Hunter (1998) *Celebrating Her: Feminist Ritualizing Comes of Age.* Cleveland, Ohio: The Pilgrim Press.

Roberts, William O., Jr (1982) *Initiation into Adulthood: An Ancient Rite of Passage in Contemporary Form.* New York: The Pilgrim Press.

Rohrlich, Ruby (1980) "State Formation in Sumer and the Subjugation of Women". In *Feminist Studies* 6, Spring.

Rosaldo, Michelle Z. (1974) "Woman, Culture and Society: A Theoretical Overview". In *Women, Culture and Society* (eds) M. Rosaldo and L. Lamphere. Stanford, CA: Stanford University Press.

—— (1980) *Knowledge and Passion.* Cambridge: Cambridge University Press.

—— (1984) "Toward an Anthropology of Self and Feeling". In *Culture Theory: Essays on Mind, Self and Emotion* (eds) Richard A. Shweder and Robert A. LeVine. Cambridge: Cambridge University Press.

Roszak, Theodore (1969) *The Making of a Counter Culture.* New York: Anchor Books.

Rubin, Gayle (1975) "The Traffic in Women: Notes on the 'Political Economy' of Sex". In *Toward an Anthropology of Women* (ed.) Rayna R. Reiter. New York: Monthly Review Press.

Ruether, Rosemary R. (1983) *Sexism and God-talk.* London: SCM Press.

—— (1986) *Women-Church.* San Francisco: Harper & Row.

—— (1987) "Feminism and Jewish–Christian Dialogue". In *The Myth of Christian Uniqueness* (eds) John Hick and Paul F. Knitter. Maryknoll, NY: Orbis Books.

—— (1992) *Gaia & God.* San Francisco: HarperCollins.

—— (1998) *Women and Redemption.* Minneapolis: Fortress Press.

Russell, Jeffrey B.R. (1985 [1972]) *Witchcraft in the Middle Ages.* Ithaca: Cornell University Press.

Salomonsen, Jone (1991) *Når gud blir kvinne. Blant hekser, villmenn og sjamaner i USA.* Oslo: Pax Forlag.

—— (1994) "Er 'Gud vår Mor' avgud eller sann gud?" In *Norsk Teologisk Tidsskrift*, 495.

—— (1996) " 'I am a Witch—A Healer and a Bender.' An Expression of Women's Religiosity in Contemporary USA". Unpubl. diss., University of Oslo.

—— (1999) *Riter. Religiøse overgangsritualer i vår tid*. Oslo: Pax Forlag.

Sanday, Peggy Reeves (1981) *Female Power and Male Dominance: On the Origins of Sexual Inequality.* Cambridge: Cambridge University Press.

Sandars, N.K. (ed) (1960) *The Epic of Gilgamesh*. Harmondsworth: Penguin Books.

Sanders, Andrew (1995) *A Deed without a Name: The Witch in Society and History.* Oxford: Berg Publications.

Sayers, Janet (1986) *Sexual Contradictions. Psychology, Psychoanalysis, and Feminism.* London: Tavistock Publications.

Scharleman, Robert P. (1982) "The Being of God When God Is Not Being God: Decontsructing the History of Theism". In *Deconstruction and Theology* (ed.) T. Altizer. New York: Crossroad.

Scholem, Gershom G. (1946) *Major Trends in Jewish Mysticism*. New York: Schocken Books.

—— (1974) *Kabbalah*. New York: New American Library.

Searle, Mark (1992) "Ritual". In *The Study of Liturgy* (eds) Cheslyn Jones *et al*. New York: Oxford University Press.

Sered, Susan Starr (1992) *Women as Ritual Experts: The Religious Lives of Elderly Jewish Women in Jerusalem*. New York: Oxford University Press.

Shallcrass, Philip (1996) "Druidry Today". In *Paganism Today* (eds) G. Harvey and C. Hardman. London: Thorsons.

Slater, Herman (ed) (1978) *A Book of Pagan Rituals.* New York: Samuel Weiser.

Smith, John E. (1981) "The Tension between Direct Experience and Argument in Religion". In *Religious Studies* 17.

Staal, Fritz (1975) *Exploring Mysticism.* Berkeley: University of California Press.

Starhawk (1979a and 1989a) *The Spiral Dance. A Rebirth of the Ancient Religion of the Great Goddess.* San Francisco: Harper & Row.

—— (1979b) "Witchcraft and Woman's Culture". In *Womanspirit Rising: A Feminist Reader in Religion* (eds) Carol P. Christ and Judith Plaskow. San Franscisco: Harper & Row.

—— (1979c). "The Goddess of Witchcraft". In *Anima* 5.

—— (1980) "Ethics and Justice in Goddess Religion". In *Anima* 7.

—— (1982a) *Dreaming the Dark: Magic, Sex and Politics.* Boston: Beacon Press.

—— (1982b) "Witchcraft as Goddess Religion". In *The Politics of Women's Spirituality* (ed) Charlene Spretnak. Garden City, NY: Anchor Press.

—— (1987) *Truth or Dare: Encounters with Power, Authority and Mystery.* San Francisco: Harper & Row.

—— (1989b) "Ritual as Bonding". In *Weaving the Visions: New Patterns in Feminist Spirituality* (eds) Judith Plaskow and Carol P. Christ. San Francisco: Harper & Row.

—— (1990a) "Power, Authority, and Mystery: Ecofeminism and Earth-based Spirituality". In *Reweaving the World: The Emergence of Ecofeminism* (eds) Irene Diamond and Gloria Feman Orenstein. San Francisco: Sierra Club Books.

—— (1990b) "Declaration of Four Sacred Things". *Reclaiming Newsletter* 38.

—— (1992) "A Men's Movement I Can Trust". In *Women Respond to the Men's Movement* (ed.) Kay Leigh Hagan. San Francisco: Harper & Row.

—— (1993) *The Fifth Sacred Thing.* New York: Bantam Books.

—— (1997) *Walking to Mercury.* New York: Bantam Books.

—— (2000) "A Working Definition of Reclaiming". http://www.reclaiming.org.

—— M. Macha NightMare and the Reclaiming Collective (1997) *A Pagan Book of Living and Dying. Practical Rituals, Prayers, Blessings and Meditations on Crossing Over.* San Francisco: Harper.

—— Anne Hill and Diane Baker (1999) *Circle Round: Raising Children in Goddess Traditions.* New York: Bantam Books.

—— and Hilary Valiente (2000) *The Twelve Wild Swans: A Journey into Magic, Healing and Action.* San Francisco: Harper.

Tambiah, Stanley J. (1979) "A Performative Approach to Ritual". In *Proceedings of the British Academy* 65.

Thomas, Keith (1971) *Religion and the Decline of Magic.* New York: Scribner's.

Torrens, R.G. (1973) *The Secret Rituals of the Golden Dawn.* London: The Aquarian Press.

Trevor-Roper, H.R. (1970) "The European Witch-craze and Social Change". In *Witchcraft and Sorcery* (ed.) M. Marwich. Harmondsworth: Penguin Books.

Turner, Victor (1967) "Betwixt and Between: The Liminal Period in Rites of Passage". In *The Forest of Symbols* (ed.) V. Turner. Ithaca: Cornell University Press.

—— (1969) *The Ritual Process.* Chicago: Aldine.

—— and Edith Turner (1978) *Image and Pilgrimage in Christian Culture. Anthropological Perspectives.* New York: Columbia University Press.

Tyler, Stephen A. (1986) "Post-Modern Ethnography. From Document of the Occult to Occult Document". In *Writing Culture* (eds) James Clifford and George E. Marcus. Berkeley: University of California Press.

Ullman, Chana (1989) *The Transformed Self: The Psychology of Religious Conversion.* New York: Plenum Press.

Valiente, Doreen (1989) *The Rebirth of Witchcraft.* London: Robert Hale.

Weaver, Mary Jo (1989) "Who is the Goddess and Where Does She Get Us?" In *Journal of Feminist Studies in Religion* 5 (1).

White, Hayden (1987) "The Absurdist Movement in Literary Criticism". In *Tropics of Discourse.* Baltimore: John Hopkins University Press.

—— (1988) "New Historicism: A Comment". In *The New Historicism* (ed.) H. Aram Veeser. New York: Routledge.

Whitford, Margaret (1989) "Rereadig Irigaray". In *Between Feminism and Psychoanalysis* (ed.) Teresa Brennan. London: Routledge.

Widmann, Peter (1989) "Teologi som antropologi". In *Menneskesynet* (ed.) Sigfred Pedersen. København: Gad Forlag.

Willow, Vibra (2000) "A Brief History of Reclaiming". http://www.reclaiming.org

Winnicott, D.W. (1974) *Playing and Reality.* London: Penguin.

Wolf, Deborah G. (1979) *The Lesbian Community.* Berkeley: University of California Press.

Wolkstein, Diane and Samuel N. Kramer (1983) *Inanna, Queen of Heaven and Earth: Her Stories and Hymns from Sumer.* San Francisco: Harper & Row.

Woodhead, Linda (1996) "Untangling the Historical Roots of Alternative Spirituality". Paper presented to the international conference on Nature Religion Today, Ambleside (England), April 1996.

York, Michael (1995) *The Emerging Network: A Sociology of the New Age and the Neo-Pagan Movements.* London: Rowman & Littlefield.

Young, Iris Marion (1997) *Intersecting Voices. Dilemmas of Gender, Political Philosophy, and Policy.* Princeton, NJ: Princeton University Press.

Index